IMMIGRATION: TRENDS, CONSEQUENCES AND PROSPECTS FOR THE UNITED STATES

RESEARCH IN LABOR ECONOMICS

Series Editor: Solomon W. Polachek

IZA Co-Editor: Konstantinos Tatsiramos

Volume 23: Accounting for Worker Well-Being – Edited by Solomon W. Polachek

Volume 24: The Economics of Immigration and Social Diversity – Edited by Solomon W. Polachek, Carmel Chiswick and Hillel Rapoport

Volume 25: Micro-Simulation in Action – Edited by Olivier Bargain

Volume 26: Aspects of Worker Well-Being – Edited by Solomon W. Polachek and Olivier Bargain

RESEARCH IN LABOR ECONOMICS   VOLUME 27

IMMIGRATION: TRENDS, CONSEQUENCES AND PROSPECTS FOR THE UNITED STATES

EDITED BY

BARRY R. CHISWICK

University of Illinois at Chicago, USA

and

IZA – Institute for the Study of Labor, Bonn, Germany

IZA

ELSEVIER
JAI

Amsterdam – Boston – Heidelberg – London – New York – Oxford
Paris – San Diego – San Francisco – Singapore – Sydney – Tokyo

JAI Press is an imprint of Elsevier

JAI Press is an imprint of Elsevier
Linacre House, Jordan Hill, Oxford OX2 8DP, UK
Radarweg 29, PO Box 211, 1000 AE Amsterdam, The Netherlands
525 B Street, Suite 1900, San Diego, CA 92101-4495, USA

First edition 2008

British Library Cataloguing in Publication Data
A catalogue record for this book is available from the British Library

ISBN: 978-0-7623-1391-4
ISSN: 0147-9121 (Series)

For information on all JAI Press publications
visit our website at books.elsevier.com

Printed and bound in the United Kingdom

08 09 10 11 12 10 9 8 7 6 5 4 3 2 1

Working together to grow
libraries in developing countries
www.elsevier.com | www.bookaid.org | www.sabre.org

ELSEVIER   BOOK AID
International   Sabre Foundation

CONTENTS

LIST OF CONTRIBUTORS   *vii*

INTRODUCTION
   Barry R. Chiswick   *1*

SECTION I: IMMIGRANT FLOWS AND ADJUSTMENT

MIGRANTS TO AMERICA SINCE 1986
   David M. Reimers   9

IMMIGRANT SKILL TRANSFERABILITY AND THE
PROPENSITY TO INVEST IN HUMAN CAPITAL
   Harriet O. Duleep   43

MODELING IMMIGRANTS' LANGUAGE SKILLS
   Barry R. Chiswick and Paul W. Miller   75

SECTION II: IMMIGRANT LIFE

GREEN CARDS AND THE LOCATION CHOICES OF
IMMIGRANTS IN THE UNITED STATES, 1971-2000
   David A. Jaeger   *131*

IMMIGRANT AND NATIVE ASSET ACCUMULATION
IN HOUSING
   Sherrie A. Kossoudji   *185*

FIRST- AND SECOND-GENERATION IMMIGRANT
EDUCATIONAL ATTAINMENT AND LABOR
MARKET OUTCOMES: A COMPARISON OF THE
UNITED STATES AND CANADA
   Abdurrahman Aydemir and Arthur Sweetman   *215*

SECTION III: IMMIGRATION POLICY

IMMIGRATION AMNESTY AND IMMIGRANT'S
EARNINGS
   Ira N. Gang and Myeong-Su Yun   *273*

WELFARE REFORM AND IMMIGRANTS: DOES THE
FIVE-YEAR BAN MATTER?
   Robert Kaestner and Neeraj Kaushal   *311*

IMPACTS OF THE POINT SYSTEM AND
IMMIGRATION POLICY LEVERS ON SKILL
CHARACTERISTICS OF CANADIAN IMMIGRANTS
   Charles M. Beach, Alan G. Green and   *349*
   Christopher Worswick

LIST OF CONTRIBUTORS

Abdurrahman Aydemir	Family and Labour Studies Division, Statistics Canada, Ottawa, ON, Canada
Charles M. Beach	Department of Economics, Queen's University, Kingston, ON, Canada
Barry R. Chiswick	Department of Economics, University of Illinois at Chicago, Chicago, IL, USA; IZA-Institute for the Study of Labor, Bonn, Germany
Harriet O. Duleep	Thomas Jefferson Program in Public Policy, College of William and Mary, Williamsburg, VA, USA
Ira N. Gang	Department of Economics, Rutgers University, New Brunswick, NJ, USA
Alan G. Green	Department of Economics, Queens University, Kingston, ON, Canada
David A. Jaeger	Department of Economics, College of William and Mary, Williamsburg, VA, USA
Robert Kaestner	Department of Economics, University of Illinois at Chicago, Chicago, IL, USA
Neeraj Kaushal	School of Social Work, Columbia University, New York, NY, USA
Sherrie A. Kossoudji	Department of Economics, Institute for Labor and Industrial Relations, University of Michigan, Ann Arbor, MI, USA

Paul W. Miller	Department of Economics, University of Western Australia, Western Australia, Australia
David M. Reimers	Department of History, New York University, New York, NY, USA
Arthur Sweetman	School of Policy Studies, Queen's University, Kingston, ON, Canada
Myeong-Su Yun	Department of Economics, Tulane University, New Orleans, LA, USA
Christopher Worswick	Department of Economics, Carleton University, ON, Canada

INTRODUCTION

Barry R. Chiswick

1. HISTORICAL BACKGROUND

Immigration to what is now the United States has been a contentious issue from the earliest days of the European settlement. Perhaps the earliest recorded incident of contention occurred over 350 years ago in 1654, when 23 Jewish refugees sought refuge into New Amsterdam, fleeing what they rightly believed would be the extension of the Portuguese Inquisition to Recife in Brazil. Peter Stuyvasant's objection to their settlement was rejected by the Dutch West Indies Company. The tension between those opposing further immigration on either social or economic grounds and those favoring it has continued over these three and a half centuries to this very day.

The intensity of the debate waxes and wanes in a seemingly cyclical pattern. To a great extent the relative strength of the pro- and anti-immigration forces reflects events in the economy. During periods of economic expansion and seemingly unlimited employment opportunities, the pro-immigration forces are in ascendancy, while during periods of economic contraction and rising unemployment the anti-immigration forces tend to prevail. The structure of the U.S. economy also matters, with land owners, especially in the past, and owners of capital, especially in the past 140 years, tending to favor easier immigration, while those whose primary incomes have come from their labor services have often favored restrictions.

Immigration: Trends, Consequences and Prospects for the United States
Research in Labor Economics, Volume 27, 1–6
Copyright © 2008 by Elsevier Ltd.
ISSN: 0147-9121/doi:10.1016/S0147-9121(07)00011-8

Since the late 19th century the Federal government has played a significant role in regulating who may legally enter the United States, under what circumstances and for how long. Race and ethnicity have mattered. Immigrants who are "different" by race, religion and ethnicity are often the victims of prejudice that results in efforts at exclusion. At different times the "other" differs, but anti-Catholic, anti-Semitic and anti-Asian sentiments have shaped immigration policies in the past. As a result, the prohibition of Asian immigrant laborers, literacy tests (introduced in 1917), the national origin quota systems, and, since 1965, a complex array of visa categories coupled with formal and informal amnesties have all been the features at one time or another of U.S. immigration law.

The complexity of the immigration debate has intensified over the past few decades because of changes in the role of the United States in the international arena, changes in the way Americans view themselves, and changes in the U.S. economy.

Since the end of World War II, we live in a global economy with the United States taking a leading role in world affairs. The post-war period saw the emergence in Asia and Africa of independent nations from their colonial-dependent relations. The obviously racist national origins quota systems, which started with the bar to Asians and was extended with the national origin quota acts (1921 and 1924 legislation), was an anachronism. A new regime for rationing immigration visas was needed. This view was reinforced by the U.S. Civil Rights movement which emphasized focusing on people as individuals, rather than evaluating them on the bases of their race or ethnicity. The question was how to implement a seemingly non-racist immigration policy. In this spirit, the primary mechanism for rationing visas became the family ("To whom are you closely related?") instead of the country of origin ("What is your race or ancestry?"). The humanitarian spirit was extended from families to include explicit provisions for refugees, although international political factors often determined what constituted an eligible refugee. There has always been some interest in the skills of immigrants. The migration of artisans was often subsidized in the colonial period. The post-war revisions included specific provisions for the immigration of high-skilled workers, whether under permanent visas or temporary visas.

The immigration policy debate has been shaped by other changes as well. The growth of the role of government in providing medical, educational and income transfer benefits (in kind and in cash), especially to low-income families has implications for the impacts on the U.S. economy of low-skilled immigrants. The change in the structure of the economy, from a growing demand for production workers in factories and mines to an economy with a declining demand in these sectors but a high demand for workers with high levels of technical and managerial skill, also has implications for immigration policy.

2. OUTLINE OF THIS VOLUME

In this complex environment, immigration policy has again risen to the forefront. What has been recent immigration history and what have been the consequences of these inflows of people? The purpose of this volume is to address these contemporary issues.

The nine research papers were presented at a conference with the same name as the title of this volume, held at the University of Illinois at Chicago in September 2005. The papers were revised on the basis of the comments from the formal discussants, the questions and discussion from the other conference participants, and referees.

Part I is Immigration Flows and Adjustment. To set the stage for the discussion, in the first essay, "Migrants to America Since 1986", David Reimers, a historian of immigration and ethnic minorities, presents background material on migration flows to the U.S. since the passage of the 1986 Immigration Reform and Control Act (IRCA). In the decade of the 1990s and since then, legal immigration averaged about one million per year, with about 70 percent entering under one of the family-based categories. In absolute members this is on a par with the average annual number in the peak decade (1905–1915), but relative to the size of the U.S. population it is one-fourth of the immigration in that decade. It is estimated that in recent years approximately 400,000 undocumented aliens entered the U.S. annually, disproportionately from Mexico, but the net increase is much smaller because of the high propensity for Mexican undocumented aliens to return.

Harriet Orcutt Duleep then addresses "Immigrant Skill Transferability and the Propensity to Invest in Human Capital". Using data from the U.S. decennial censuses, she finds substantial convergence in the earnings of immigrants at arrival to that of their native born counterparts. Indeed, the speed of improvement is inversely related to the immigrant's initial earnings position, other variables being the same. She concludes that "immigrants who initially lack transferable skills provide the host country an under-valued, highly malleable resource that may promote a vibrant economy in the long run."

4 BARRY R. CHISWICK

Barry R. Chiswick and Paul W. Miller focus on "Modelling Immigrant's Language Skills", an important skill that is specific to a destination. Using data on adult male and female immigrants from the U.S. census, they demonstrate that immigrants' English language proficiency is greater the higher the level of their schooling, the younger their age at migration, the longer they have been in the U.S., the "closer" is their origin language to English, and if they live in an area where relatively few other people speak their origin language. The findings are robust with respect to statistical estimation techniques, across genders, and across censuses (1980, 1990, 2000).

Part II, Immigrant Life, focuses on where immigrants live, their housing ownership patterns and their investment in their own and their children's education. David A. Jaeger studies "Green Cards and the Location Choices of Immigrants in the United States, 1971–2000". Using administrative data from the Immigration and Naturalization Service (1971–2000) and data from the decennial census, he examines the places of residence of new immigrants. He finds that new immigrants, especially relatives of permanent resident aliens, tend to settle where others from their home country already live. Local labor market conditions also matter for all categories of immigrants, but more so for male employment-based visa recipients and refugees. Both groups have a greater propensity to go to where the jobs are more plentiful and offer higher wages.

"Immigrant and Native Asset Accumulation in Housing" is the theme of Sherrie Kossoudji's contribution. She examines the home ownership "gap" between immigrants and natives, measured by home ownership per se, the value of purchased homes, and the equity the owner has in the home. The foreign born who have become naturalized citizens have ownership characteristics similar to or superior to comparable native-born Americans. Immigrants who are not U.S. citizens, because they are recent arrivals, expect to return or for some other reason, are less likely than the native born and naturalized citizens to own the dwelling in which they live. It is unclear the extent to which this is due to aliens have greater difficulty in access to financial capital (home mortgages) or to unmeasured reasons as to why they are not citizens.

Abdurrahman Aydemir and Arthur Sweetman study "First and Second Generation Immigrant Educational Attainment and Labor Market Outcomes: A Comparison of the United States and Canada." The authors note the divergent patterns in the source countries and the criteria for rationing visas used by the U.S. and Canada over the past 40 years, with Canada placing much greater emphasis on the immigrant's own skills. They show, using comparable census data, that immigrants to the U.S. have a lower level of education than Canadian immigrants. The children of immigrants in Canada have an educational advantage over third (and higher order) generation Canadians. The implications for earnings of these educational differences across generations are explored in both the U.S. and Canada.

The final section in this volume, Part III, is on Immigration Policy. Three recent policy concerns are considered: formal or blanket amnesties for illegal aliens, welfare reform for low-skilled immigrants, and whether the adoption of a Canadian-style immigration policy would enhance the skill level of immigrants to the United States. Ira Gang and Myeong-Su Yun in "Immigration Amnesty and Immigrant's Earnings" compare U.S. amnesty policy to that of other countries. Amnesties appear to be part of a package of policies, or a political bargain, that includes stricter enforcement of immigration law (border controls, internal or interior enforcement and penalties on employers). Using data from the Mexican Migration Project they analyze the effects on earnings of the amnesties granted to Mexican illegal aliens in the United States and find a positive effect of legalization on their earnings.

"Welfare Reform and Immigrants: Does the Five-Year Ban Matter?" is the theme of the study by Robert Kaestner and Neeraj Kaushal. Among other changes in welfare provisions, the 1996 welfare reform generally banned future immigrants to the U.S. from receiving Federally funded benefits for their first five years. Keastner and Kaushal analyze the effect of the change in welfare provisions, including the 5-year ban, on the employment, hours of work and wages of low-income women, the group most likely to be effected by the welfare reform. They find that overall the welfare reform increased employment and hours of work, and in the short-run decreased the wages of low-income women who are not U.S. citizens. They found little direct evidence of the impact of the 5-year ban per se. This may have been due, in part, to state policies that thwarted the intent of the Federal ban.

Given the similarity in many respects of the United States and Canada, an analysis of the Canadian "point system" for rationing visas is worthy of consideration as an alternative to current U.S. practice. This is done in the paper by Charles Beach, Alan Green, and Christopher Worswick "Impacts of the Point System and Immigrant Policy Levers on Skill Characteristics of Canadian Immigrants." The issue is studied using the unique Canadian Landings Database from 1980 to 2001. They studied several "skills": education, prime age and fluency in either English or French. The immigration policies were successful. The skill level of immigrants decreases in a recession because of a decline in the proportion in the immigration flow who are skill tested. If greater weight was given to a particular skill, the average level of this skill increased. Because those admitted under skill categories had higher levels of skill than other immigrants, the average skill level increased when a greater proportion of immigrants were admitted under skill categories. And, the larger the total inflow of immigrants, the lower was its average skill level. By implication the U.S. could increase the skill level of its immigrants by increasing the number and proportion admitted on the basis of their own skills, as distinct from their kinship ties or other criteria not directly related to high levels of skill.

ACKNOWLEDGMENTS

The conference and this conference volume would not have been possible if not for the support of the Smith-Richardson Foundation. Mark Steinmeyer of the foundation was very helpful throughout the course of this project. Supplemental support for the project came from the Department of Economics, University of Illinois at Chicago and the Institute of Government and Public Affairs, University of Illinois. Administrative services for the conference and the preparation of the conference volume were provided by Carol Martell and Jennifer Nero of the Department of Economics, University of Illinois at Chicago, as well as the Institute of Government and Public Affairs, University of Illinois.

A special thank you is due to the authors and the other conference participants, in particular the discussants: Carmel U. Chiswick, University of Illinois at Chicago; Deborah Cobb-Clark, The Australian National University; Joseph Ferrie, Northwestern University; John Iceland, University of Maryland; Paul W. Miller, The University of Western Australia; Cordelia Reimers, Hunter College; David Ribar, George Washington University; Seth Sanders, University of Maryland; and Stephen J. Trejo, University of Texas at Austin.

Finally, we are indebted to Olivier Bargain and Solomon Polachek, co-editors of Research in Labor Economics, and Elsevier Publishers and IZA – Institute for the Study of Labor for making possible the publication of the conference papers.

SECTION I:
IMMIGRANT FLOWS AND ADJUSTMENT

MIGRANTS TO AMERICA SINCE 1986

David M. Reimers

ABSTRACT

Since 1986, when the immigration Reform and Control Act was passed, migration to the United States has grown steadily. This includes immigrants, nonimmigrants, undocumented immigrants, and border crossers. Immigration averaged nearly one million annually from 1990 to 2002, with family unification accounting for over 70 percent of the new immigrants. The number of nonimmigrants topped 30 million by 2002, most of whom were tourists. Estimates for undocumented aliens topped 400,000 by the turn of the 21st century, in spite of large increases in funding from the Immigration and Naturalization Service and substantial new positions along the Mexican-United States border. The exact number of border crossers is not known, but the federal government has noted that well over 200 million crossings (mostly along the Mexican border) are recorded each year. In response to tighter controls on migrants after 9/11 the numbers coming to the United States dropped in 2003. However, they increased again in 2004. It appears that the figures will increase in the future.

Immigration: Trends, Consequences and Prospects for the United States
Research in Labor Economics, Volume 27, 9–42
ISSN: 0147-9121/doi:10.1016/S0147-9121(07)00001-5

REGULAR IMMIGRATION

Current Immigration Policy

While Congress has enacted a number of immigration laws since the end of World War II, current policy is based on the Immigration Act of 1990. As specified by that law, the current policy provides preferences for family unification, employment, and diversity. The four family preferences are flexible and allow between 416,000 and 675,000 immigrants. The largest family preference (114,000) is for spouses and unmarried children of resident aliens. The other family preferences consist of visas for unmarried sons and daughters of U.S. citizens and their children (23,400); for married sons and daughters of U.S. citizens (23,400); and lastly, for brothers and sisters of U.S. citizens, including their spouses and children (65,000). Outside these family preferences is another immigrant category aimed at family unification: for spouses, minor children, and parents of U.S. citizens. This category has no numerical limits.

The employment preferences consist of a number of categories and total 140,000. This figure includes their immediate family members. Employment categories are for skilled workers, investors, professionals, or others with special occupations. In the 1990 Act the diversity visa (DV) category was set at 40,000, but numbered 50,000 after 1999. No nation receiving diversity visas can have more than 3,850. Refugees are admitted under the Refugee Act of 1980, which provided for the President to consult with Congress; in recent years this level has been set at 70,000.

Current policy gives all nations the same allotments, with each country limited to seven percent of the total and dependent areas to two percent. In 2004 the ceiling for nations was 30,130; for dependent areas it was 8,608.[1] Overall, immigration has increased substantially and averaged approximately one million annually from 1990 to 2002.

IRCA Amnesties

In the era since 1985, the first major change occurred only after prolonged debate which started in the 1970s when undocumented immigration began a rapid ascent. Congress finally enacted the Immigration Reform and Control Act (IRCA) in 1986.[2] The discussions centered on three areas: how to restrict undocumented immigration, an amnesty, and a temporary worker program. In the end IRCA permitted 2.7 million unauthorized aliens to become legal immigrants. Nearly 1.5 million persons were granted an amnesty if they had entered the United States illegally before 1982 and had maintained residency since that time. Others qualified under the Special Agricultural Workers (SAW) section that allowed unauthorized persons to apply for immigrant status if they had worked in agriculture at least four months between 1985 and 1986. More than half of those covered by these amnesties were Mexican, but beneficiaries came from all parts of the globe. The Congressional committee recommending SAW believed that only a few hundred thousand persons would qualify under its provisions, but 1.3 million eventually received the amnesty.[3]

IRCA did not increase permanent immigration quotas; the amnesties provided for one time admissions, which showed up within the few years allotted for applications. However, as the newly authorized immigrants received their green cards (resident alien status), they in turn were able to sponsor family members to join them. Indeed, a few years later Congress expedited family unification when it permitted family members of those receiving an amnesty to become resident aliens if they arrived after January 1982. Down the line, if the IRCA recipients chose to become U.S. citizens, they could sponsor their brothers and sisters under the fifth preference, or even immediate family members outside of the quota for each nation.

Diversity Visas

A little-noticed provision of IRCA provided 10,000 green cards to be determined by lottery. When Congress abolished national origins quotas in 1965, Ireland was sending few persons to the United States, and for those who did emigrate, the process was easy. One authority remarked, "pretty much any Irish man or woman who wanted to immigrate could just pick up and do so, with relative ease."[4] During the 1960s and early 1970s the Irish economy grew rapidly and few Irish desired to follow the millions of others who had gone to America. But then Ireland's economy turned sour. Prospective Irish migrants discovered that they lacked the skills or family connections to satisfy the provisions of the 1965 (Hart–Celler) Immigration Act. As a result they entered on visitors' visas and stayed after their visas expired, working and living as unauthorized immigrants. These New Irish, as they were called, organized the Irish Immigration Reform Movement to change the law so that it would facilitate their emigration to the United States. They found supporters in Congress who added a lottery to IRCA. Ireland's people were keenly aware of this provision, and they flooded the

Immigration and Naturalization Service (INS) with applications, winning 40 percent of the 10,000 visas. The lottery was repeated and then made part of the 1990 immigration act. To be eligible for the lottery, now called the "diversity visa" (DV), one had to come from a nation "adversely affected" by the Immigration Act of 1965 (the Hart–Celler Act).[5]

It was difficult to determine which nations had truly been disadvantaged by the 1965 Hart–Celler Act. A case for Ireland could be made, but was this true of other countries now permitted to participate in this lottery? Russia, for example, had sent few people to the United States after 1965, but this was mostly due to the policy of communist governments that controlled their citizens' movement, including the right of emigration, and not the 1965 Immigration Act. Nations such as Nigeria and Bangladesh had sent few immigrants before 1965 so that law did not adversely affect their migration. To determine which nations qualified for DVs the government simply decided that countries with little immigration after the Hart–Celler Act became fully operational in 1968 were eligible for the lottery. As a result the nations mentioned above turned to the new DV as a path to the United States. In the 1990 Immigration Act 40,000 slots were created for DVs, with Ireland guaranteed 40 percent of the places. After three years Ireland lost its favored position, but the DV slots were increased to 55,000.[6] In 2003 the diversity program was limited to nations which had fewer than 50,000 admissions during the preceding five years.[7] Ironically for the Irish the loss was not great because the Irish economy boomed again just as the DV became part of American immigration policy.[8] To apply for a DV, an applicant had to possess proof of a high school education or its equivalent, or prove two years of work experience in an occupation requiring at least two years of training or experience within the past five years. With the expectation that half of the winners would not follow through, the INS selected 100,000 winners instead of 50,000.[9] Over nine million applications were received for that year alone.[10] For the 2005 DV Bangladesh had 7,404 winners followed by Nigeria with 6,725 (Table 1).

Refugees and Asylum

Another important flow of immigrants consisted of refugees. Between 1946 and 2004 over three and one half million refugees entered the United States.[11] Prior to 1968 refugees were often admitted under special legislation, such as the Cuban Adjustment Act of 1966, or under Presidential orders. The Hart–Celler Act of 1965, as amended, placed a ceiling of 17,400 on refugees

Table 1. Recipients of Diversity Visas by Selected Countries by Year.

Nation	1998	2000	2001	2003
Bangladesh	2,835	1,720	1,509	745
Bulgaria	2,295	3,660	2,337	2,486
Ethiopia	2,090	1,778	2,194	3,382
Ghana	2,156	1,737	1,122	1,578
Nigeria	3,185	2,822	1,533	3,121
Pakistan	1,299	1,759	1,953	8
Romania	2,621	2,869	1,555	1,329
Soviet Union, former	5,067	42	30	25
Ukraine	2,095	3,970	2,749	3,034
Total	45,499	50,945	42,015	46,347

Note: The figures for the former Soviet Union were based on different criteria.
Source: The INS and the Department of Homeland Security (DHS), *Statistical Yearbooks*.

under the seventh preference. Even after 1965, however, special legislation was required to admit more than the worldwide ceiling. In addition, continued Presidential use of the parole power permitted several hundred thousand persons to enter. The largest number was South East Asians.[12] When it passed the Refugee Act of 1980, Congress attempted to regularize refugee admissions again. The law streamlined refugee policy and permitted refugees to become permanent resident aliens after one year.[13] From 1960 until the 1990s the vast majority of refugees hailed from Cuba and South East Asia. These major flows were reduced in the 1990s; indeed, the Clinton administration virtually repealed the Cuban Adjustment Act when a new surge of Cuban "raft people" appeared in 1994.[14] A 1989 amendment to the immigration laws introduced by Senator Frank Lautenberg opened the door for several hundred thousand refugees from the former Soviet Union.[15] Under this amendment individuals would not have to convince officials on a case-by-case basis that they were entitled to asylum in the United States.

Once they settled here, Ukrainians and Russians turned to family unification to bring in their relatives. Refugees from the Balkan wars also joined the flow. In addition, a growing number of refugees were African.[16] The large entrance of Cubans and South East Asians declined in the 1990s as did the total number of refugees, amounting to only 67,000 in 2001. After the World Trade Center was destroyed by terrorists in 2001, tightened security led to the admission of only 27,000 in 2002 and to 28,000 the following year.[17] However, President George W. Bush announced that refugee flows would be increased again and that 25,000 African

14   DAVID M. REIMERS

Table 2. Refugees and Asylees Granted Permanent Resident Status, by
Country of Origin and Year.

Nation	1981–1990	1991–2000	2002	2003
Cambodia	114,064	6,399	47	38
Cuba	113,367	144,612	24,893	7,047
El Salvador	1,383	4,073	187	194
Ethiopia	18,542	17,865	1,897	1,225
Laos	142,964	37,265	374	191
Poland	33,889	7,500	54	31
Romania	29,798	15,708	85	94
Russia	n/a	60,404	5,089	1,738
Somalia	70	16,837	4,084	126
Thailand	30,259	22,759	498	224
Vietnam	324,453	206,857	6,926	1,581
Total	1,013,620	1,021,266	126,084	44,027

Source: DHS, *Statistical Yearbook*, 2003, p. 69.

refugees were to be admitted in 2005, a figure that amounted to over one third of the total 70,000 refugees and nearly three times the number of Asians.[18] In 2005 "because of budget constraints" only 53,875 were admitted, but the President again announced the quota for 2006 would be 70,000 (Table 2).[19]

Africans, Cubans, and Asians were not the center of refugee debate during late 1970s through the 1990s. The focal point of the controversy was instead the status of Central Americans. In the 1970s and 1980s Central America was plagued by civil wars and natural disasters, but few fleeing the violence entered as refugees. The composition of refugee flows was shaped by anticommunism in spite of a broader definition of refugee spelled out in the 1980 Act. Nicaraguans, fleeing a left-wing government, were more likely to win either asylum or become refugees than were Guatemalans and Salvadorans, who were fleeing right-wing dictatorships, but even many Nicaraguans also found themselves rejected. As a result tens of thousands of Nicaraguans, Salvadorans, and Guatemalans took another route and sought asylum in the United States, crossing the border without inspection between the United States and Mexico.[20] Once in the United States they were permitted to apply for asylum. The problem for these unfortunate migrants was proving they were eligible for asylum, which unlike refugee status had to be documented on a case-by-case basis. This required individuals to demonstrate that they had a well-founded fear of persecution (based on race, national origin, religion or membership in certain groups) if they were forced to return to their homelands.

And there was also the issue of numbers. The 1980 law permitted up to 5,000 new asylum places annually, but hundreds of thousands persons requested asylum in the late 1980s and early 1990s. From 1986 to 1992, roughly half of the applications were Central Americans. Central Americans applying for asylum peaked in the mid-1990s, and began a decline in 1997. In response to the huge growth of persons asking for asylum in the 1980s Congress upped the figure to 10,000 in 1990, and the number of persons requesting asylum remained high. In 2003 the United States granted asylum to 15,000 persons, and the next year it dropped to 10,217.[21]

While awaiting their hearings, these applicants could remain in the United States, but could not receive a permanent resident visa or benefits that refugees received. However, they had the opportunity to find a job or obtain a green card through marriage. The chain migration of the family preference system offered hope. Even if they could not find a legal way to change their status, they could simply not appear when called to a hearing. The government might have rejected the vast majority of claims, but it did not chase down those rejected. It simply ordered them to leave the United States voluntarily, and many decided to remain as illegal immigrants rather than return home. Estimates about the number appearing before immigration officials vary, but apparently more than a majority of these newcomers never came to their hearings.[22]

Supporters of Central Americans insisted that these unfortunate persons were refugees and should be granted asylum in the United States, but immigration officials usually considered them to be economic migrants and thus not entitled to become refugees or successful asylum seekers. During the 1980s, only a small minority of Central Americans, less than 10 percent, were able to win asylum, and as late as 2001 only 13 percent of Central American applicants actually received asylum, which was well below the approval rate for most other nationality groups. Central Americans were not the only group to seek asylum in the United States after 1986; a number of Colombians, Chinese, Haitians, Burmese, and Somalis sought asylum and refugee states and were sometimes successful.[23]

Friends of Central Americans filed a class action suit that required the federal government to renew their claims. Under the ruling in *American Baptist Churches v. Thornburgh* (1991), thousands of Salvadorans and Guatemalans were permitted to apply again. Congress also responded in part to the refugee and asylum crisis by enacting the Nicaraguan Adjustment and Central America Relief Act in 1997. The law did not grant all Central

Americans residing illegally in the United States the right to become resident aliens, but it did suspend deportation orders and permitted many to become immigrants.[24] In addition Congress also passed the Haitian Refugee Immigration Fairness Act of 1998, which eased the requirements for Haitians requesting asylum.[25] Shortly before President Bill Clinton left the White House he signed the Legal Immigration and Family Unification Act (LIFE), which was not the blanket amnesty desired by Central Americans and others whose status was in limbo, but did offer many of these persons a chance to regularize their immigration status.[26] Many did so. Among LIFE's provisions was a section permitting unauthorized immigrants to remain in the United States if they were married to an American citizen instead of going home and applying for a green card. The window of opportunity was only a few months. Marriage bureaus in several cities reported a sharp increase in the number of new licenses. USA Today and other newspapers reported: "Newlyweds, INS race midnight."[27]

As a result of law suits, new hearings, and special laws enacted in the late 1990s many Central Americans were able to remain in the United States and adjust their status. The Department of Homeland Security (DHS) noted in 2003 that of the over 300,000 backlogged cases, 224,000 were Central Americans and Haitians who would eventually become permanent resident aliens under the special laws mentioned above.[28] El Salvador, the center of much political debate during the 1980s and 1990s, peaked as a sending nation at 31,272 immigrants in 2001. El Salvador's total placed it fifth among immigrants of that year.[29] Two years later, in 2003, 28,296 Salvadorans and 14,415 Guatemalans became immigrants.

About the same number of Salvadorans entered in 2004 along with over 17,000 Guatemalans. Of El Salvador's 2003 total only 294 were refugees or asylees; 3,458 were counted under the family preferences; and another 4,703 were immediate family members of United States citizens. 19,081 were due to the special legislation and court decisions.[30] Clearly while it was difficult for Central Americans to win individual asylum during the 1980s and early 1990s, a significant numbers of persons from that region were able to remain in the United States and adjust their status to resident aliens.

After 1995 the INS no longer guaranteed those requesting asylum permission to work, and Congress included tighter controls when passing the Illegal Immigration Reform and Immigrant Responsibility Act of 1996 (IIRIRA). The new law empowered asylum officers to assess the claims of those seeking asylum. These were not formal hearings but rather interviews to determine if the immigrants had credible fears of persecution and were eligible to apply for a hearing before an immigration judge. Aimed at heading off frivolous claims for asylum, these special INS authorities expedited cases, but did not put an end to asylum claims or controversy about asylum. Among the contested cases were battered women, Chinese fleeing the "one child per family" rule, and gays.[31]

Response to Terrorism

The Central American crisis was not the only foreign policy issue facing the government, and Congress and the INS instituted new procedures in response to the first attack on the World Trade Center in 1993 and the terrorist act that destroyed it in 2001 (9/11). Authorities instituted new rules after March 11, 2003, which came on top of growing concern about terrorism. Prompted by 9/11, the government announced its intention to detain people from Iraq and 32 other countries if they were seeking asylum. The nations singled out were Arab countries or nations with a substantial Muslim population in Asia or Africa. The new DHS cited several occasions in which terrorists had entered by winning asylum.[32] In particular, critics noted that Omar Abdel Rahman, the Egyptian sheik who was convicted of the first attack on the World Trade Center, entered as a refugee. The department's new regulations dictated that persons requesting asylum from these countries would automatically be detained while their applications were pending, a procedure that could take as long as six months.[33] A 2003 study by the U.S. Commission for International Religious Freedom revealed wide differences in how long persons were detained while awaiting the deposition of their cases. While incarcerated, the petitioners usually lacked access to lawyers to help them win their appeals.[34]

The difficulties of persons from Arab nations were by no means limited to potential asylum seekers. After 9/11 the government claimed that possibly 314,000 Middle Easterners lived in the United States without valid visas, and told them to come forth, at least for questioning. Some 82,000 men eventually agreed to register with the government, and in addition several thousand others were also called in for questioning. By 2003 the list of persons wanted for questioning had been shortened to approximately 13,000 from Muslim or Arab nations who were ordered to appear before authorities for possible deportation, an order that lasted until December 2003.[35] Federal authorities conducted closed hearings of many detained persons, including a few United States citizens, who were held months without a charge. The courts later overturned the policy of unlimited detention, and an internal Department of Justice report by the Inspector General was highly critical of those departmental policies.[36]

In 2003, Attorney General John Ashcroft announced that more sweeping changes were in store, not only affecting immigrants, but also millions of visitors to the United States. Under the rules proclaimed in April 2003, visitors from certain Middle Eastern and African countries, including Iran, Iraq, Libya, Sudan, and Syria, were singled out for processing through a new scheme called the Nationality Security Entry–Exit Registration System. Upon entry these nationals would be fingerprinted, photographed, and asked detailed questions. Plans were also announced to add other Middle Eastern or Islamic nations to the list.[37] Still tighter restrictions took effect in January 2004, including special scanning procedures. Nations that allowed Americans to visit without a visa were not included in the new procedures.[38]

Extended Voluntary Departure and Temporary Protected Status

There remained another way for persons who entered illegally or who were in the United States on nonimmigrant or temporary permits to remain in America. In the past the federal government had permitted persons to stay here when conditions in their homelands deteriorated due to civil war or other violence. The Attorney General granted such individuals Extended Voluntary Departure (EVD). Congress was not happy with these executive decisions, and the 1990 Immigration Act created Temporary Protected Status (TPS) to replace it. The Attorney General could grant TPS to nationals facing dire circumstances, such as a hurricane or civil war, if they had to return home when their temporary status expired. After 1990 the Attorney General granted TPS to a variety of nationality groups in the United States, especially Africans and Central Americans. At times the decision to grant TPS came at the eleventh hour. By 2003 nationals from Liberia, Sierra Leone, El Salvador, Guatemala, Honduras, Montserrat, Nicaragua, Somalia, and Sudan had TPS.[39] The President also had the authority to grant Deferred Enforced Departure (DED) for foreign policy reasons. Between 1994 and 2004, the President granted DED five times.

Like other temporary or non-immigrant persons, those with TPS had the opportunity to find a legal way to remain in the United States as resident aliens. The plight of Montserratians is a case in point. Originally granted TPS because of a volcanic eruption on this Caribbean island, TPS was ended by the State Department in June 2004. Conditions were still poor in Montserrat, and many of the 292 persons having TPS from that island had no desire to return home. But the federal government said otherwise, saying that these migrants should return home, or possibly head for Great Britain where they were British citizens because they lived in a British colony. Many did not like that option either. Thus the government began to deport Montserratians, which created individual hardships. At the same time, one third of these migrants had managed to stay in the United States legally when TPS expired.[40] That some Montserratians adjusted their status was not unusual; IRCA immigrants were already in the United States when they applied for the amnesties. The adjustment process was becoming common after 1990 and was not simply the product of IRCA as a majority of immigrants were in the United States when their applications were approved. In 2004, for example, 60 percent of persons becoming permanent resident aliens were already living in the United States.[41]

Closely related to refugee status is parole. When President Dwight Eisenhower was confronted with the refugee crisis stemming from the failed Hungarian revolution of 1956, he paroled over 30,000 Hungarians, making it possible for them to enter the United States. The parole power had been intended to admit individuals, such as those having a medical crisis, and not groups, but the President extended it to aid refugees. The parole power was used again to admit Cubans and Asians. According to the Immigration Act of 1990, TPS was intended to replace the parole of groups, just as the Refugee Act of 1980 was supposed to replace EVD. But parole remained part of American policy. The Attorney General (and in reality the President) retained the parole power to admit individuals on a case-by-case basis for urgent humanitarian reasons or "when that alien's entry is determined to be for significant public benefit." Parole confirmed "temporary status, and parolees are required to leave when the conditions supporting their admission are ended."[42] Such persons were treated as nonimmigrants, but they were not officially reported in the non-immigrant categories. The most common form of parole was issued to those legally in the United States but who had an unexpected need to travel abroad and when returning to the United States did not possess all of the necessary documents. These cases were resolved rapidly "when the documents are produced."[43]

Highly Skilled Workers

Adding diversity visas to immigration law and dealing with refugees were not the only challenges in the 1990s. Much of the debate centered on the need for highly skilled workers, and immigration critics, high-tech firms, and some economists insisted that immigration policy should be based more closely on occupations in demand in the United States. In 1990 the proponents of gearing immigration policy more towards economic needs managed to win an increase of the two occupational categories from 54,000 to 140,000. However, the nationalities that used family preferences (which from 1965 to 1990 accounted for 76 percent of all visas permitted under the preference system) did not wish to reduce family unification in order to add more immigrants based on occupational characteristics. While Congress did cut the preference for siblings of United States citizens, it also increased the size of the preference for the admission of family members of resident aliens. As a result of the debates and lobbying by ethnic and business groups, the Immigration Act of 1990 increased immigration by 35 percent. In the waning hours of the 101st Congress, the final bill was enacted with little debate and President George H. W. Bush signed it into law with little comment.[44] Even after its enactment, roughly 70 percent of all immigrants (outside of refugees) entered as family members under the preference system or as quota exempt immediate family members of U.S. citizens, a figure that amounted to over 400,000 persons in 2004 and amounted to 40 percent of all immigrants in that year.[45] Moreover, relatives of persons arriving under the occupation preferences were included in the total of those preferences. Families, not skills, continued to be the main route of immigration to America.

FLOWS OF IMMIGRANTS

Overall, IRCA, subsequent legislation, and administration action enabled many millions to immigrate to America. In 1990 IRCA participants began to appear in the immigration statistics, and the next year over 1.8 million immigrants were recorded, the highest one year figure in American history. A majority of those immigrants already resided in the United States but were waiting for their applications to be processed; their status was simply "adjusted" to permanent resident alien.

During the 1990s immigration averaged roughly one million entrants annually, and in the early 21st century immigration remained high. One million new immigrants were recorded in both 2001 and 2002.[46] In 2003, responding to tighter controls and delays due to 9/11, the figure dropped to only 705,827, a 34-percent decrease from the previous year.[47] However, in 2004 it increased to 946,142. Extensive backlogs still existed, so it remained an open question whether 9/11 was the beginning of a new, smaller trend.[48]

In the early 21st century, most newcomers – 63 percent – settled in six states: California, New York, Texas, New Jersey, Florida, and Illinois. The percentage was down from the proportion in the 1980s. Given the decrease in concentration and the increase of immigrants, it is not surprising that one of the dynamic changes in immigration is that large numbers of immigrants are heading for states that had relatively few immigrants prior to the 1980s. In the South, North Carolina and Georgia were such states. And in the Midwest, Minnesota, Iowa, and Missouri witnessed immigrants coming to work in small towns. Many were following "the chicken trail," finding employment in meat packing and chicken production. Yet skilled immigrants also settled in southern and midwestern states.[49]

Some nationalities that had dominated immigration figures before 1986 continued to do so. Mexico remained the main sending nation and, as noted, accounted for over half of those persons permitted to receive an amnesty under IRCA. In some years between 1995 and 2003, Mexicans comprised nearly one fifth of immigrants coming to America. In 2004 Mexico's 175,364 immigrants represented roughly one fifth of newcomers. The Philippines remained another large sender, accounting for 57,116 green card holders in 2004, but there were some shifts in the pattern of immigration to the United States.[50] Since the 1980s Indians and Chinese have moved into the top ranks of nations sending immigrants to the United States. As noted earlier, Central Americans increased their immigration while groups such as Koreans fell from their higher positions in the 1970s. Table 3 gives the origins of the leading sending nations.

Of course many immigrants leave the United States and return to their native lands. Around the turn of the 20th century, return emigration was especially high for Italians (roughly 50 percent) and for people from the Balkans. Jews had little incentive to return to Russia; consequently, their return rates were low.[51] From 1907 to 1957 the government reported that for every 100 immigrants entering, about one third returned. After 1957 the government ceased to compile emigration figures. However, scholars have estimated that the percentage grew after a low point in the 1950s, and was between one quarter and one-third of immigrants.[52] Among the undocumented population the figure for emigration was probably much higher.[53]

Immigrants vary widely in education, skills, and language ability. On the whole Hispanic migrants are less educated and skilled than Asian or African

Table 3.   Leading Nations Sending Immigrants to the US.

Countries	1981–1990	1990–2000	2001–2003
China, includes Taiwan	346,747	419,114	144,163
Dominican Republic	252,035	335,251	69,887
El Salvador	213,534	215,798	89,518
Hong Kong	98,215	109,779	23,279
India	250,786	363,060	180,537
Korea	333,746	164,166	53,224
Mexico	1,655,843	2,249,421	537,146
Philippines	548,764	503,945	143,102
Soviet Union	57,677	462,874	4,599
Vietnam	280,782	286,145	88,343
Total	7,338,062	9,095,417	2,833,877

Note: These are based on country of last residence.
Source: DHS, *Statistical Year Book*, 2003.

immigrants. However, within the "Hispanic" community there are important differences. Migrants from Mexico, Central America, and the Dominican Republic have low levels of education and incomes, but Cubans and South Americans are better off than these Hispanics.[54]

Asians too show variations. Among the elite of the new immigrants are Asians who held medical degrees. Foreign-born physicians account for over one-fifth of all American doctors.[55] By 2003 an estimated 35,000 Indian physicians practiced medicine in the United States. The Asian-Indian group coming after 1968 were college educated, many with advanced degrees, outside of medicine. Indians also became identified as entrepreneurs, running motels, gas stations, convenience stores, and newspaper stands.[56] Filipinos also entered as medical professionals, most as nurses, but some as physicians as well.[57] They were versed in American medical practices because the Philippines had been a colony of the United States for nearly a half century. After World War II, American hospitals aggressively recruited foreign nurses to fill their vacancies. A survey conducted by the Commission on Graduates of Foreign Schools in 2001 found that 41 percent of immigrant nurses were trained in the Philippines.[58] A substantial number of Korean immigrants were also nurses and physicians, but unlike Indians and Filipinos, acquisition of English language was a handicap for them, and as a result many highly educated Koreans opened small shops, such as greengroceries and dry cleaners. Of all Asians, in fact, Koreans were most likely to be owners of small businesses.[59]

Many Asians had originally been students in American colleges and universities. In the 1970s and 1980s, for example, over 100,000 Taiwanese headed for the United States to complete their studies. Many remained after further study, but some did return to utilize their skills in Taiwan. By the 1990s the number heading for America slowed and the number returning grew, finding new opportunities in facilities built for high-tech employment.[60] However, students from the People's Republic of China were taking their place. At the other extreme were Hmong refugees who had aided the United States during the Vietnam War. Largely agriculturalists, some were illiterate even in their native tongue.

African immigration, which grew due to an increasing number of refugees, persons winning the DV lottery, preferences for skilled immigrants, and eventually family unification, was also composed of a number of medical professionals as well as others with college degrees.[61]

Other Africans drove cabs or became street merchants who traveled to African-American fairs throughout the United States.[62]

Naturalization

The family unification preference system is one component of the chain migration of American immigration, but so is family migration outside of the preferences. Such sponsorship outside of the individual national and preference quotas requires American citizenship as did the sponsorship of the siblings of U.S. citizens within the preference system. Thus the need for naturalization was attractive to immigrants. Then when California passed Proposition 187 in 1994, denying social benefits, such as medical care and education to illegal aliens, many pro-immigrant spokespersons became alarmed, fearing that other measures might curtail the rights of immigrants.[63] Following passage of Proposition 187, Congress enacted the IIRIRA, which curtailed the benefits of legal immigrants arriving after 1996 who did not become U.S. citizens. Both of these measures increased the incentive for naturalization. Even before IIRIRA the Clinton administration had begun a program to encourage immigrants to naturalize, but in response to California's proposition and Congress's immigration law, the number of applications for citizenship surged with over one million becoming citizens in 1996, compared to 434,107 in 1994. They dropped after that peak, and only 450,000 immigrants became U.S. citizens in 2003, but the backlog was larger than that figure.[64] The fact that immediate family members of U.S. citizens are admitted above the nationality quota is crucial in explaining how nations such as Mexico, China, the Philippines, and India can send more than their seven percent of the total allocated of the preference categories.

UNAUTHORIZED IMMIGRATION

The Mexican-United States Border

While the growth of authorized immigration has been impressive since the early 1980s, so has the increase in the number of unauthorized immigrants, who now comprise about one quarter of the nation's foreign-born population. A paper by Jeffrey Passel will deal with undocumented immigration in detail, but some comments are in order here to include undocumented immigration in the context of overall migration to the United States.[65] Proponents of IRCA hoped that employer sanctions would stem future illegal immigration, but a decade later it was clear that unauthorized immigration composed a significant segment of the migration flow to the United States. In addition to employer sanctions, Congress voted additional funding in the 1990s for the INS, primarily in an attempt to seal the border between the United States and Mexico.[66]

Peter J. Gross, the director of the Central Intelligence Agency, raised a new issue after 9/11. He told a congressional committee in early 2005 that while no terrorists were known to have entered through Mexico, the agency was convinced that it possessed evidence that Al-Qaeda was considering this option.[67] While visiting Mexico in early 2005, Secretary of State Condoleezza Rice repeated the Bush administration's concern about terrorists crossing the border between Mexico and the United States.[68]

After 1990 the INS began two programs along the United States-Mexican border to stem the tide of unauthorized immigration. Proponents of a tighter border also claimed that more controls were required to halt the influx of drugs, and, after 9/11, to keep terrorists out. "Operation Blockade," which began in El Paso in 1993, consisted of intensive agent presence at the El Paso border. Silvestre Reyes, chief of the Border Patrol in El Paso, positioned 400 agents along the border in a virtual blockade. As a result the number caught trying to cross there dropped substantially, from 122,355 to 34,747 the next year. The name was later changed to "Operation Hold the Line," largely in deference to Mexican protests.[69] The tactic raised the possibility of severely cutting unauthorized immigration, but the El Paso crossing was only a tiny fraction of the nearly 2,000-mile boundary separating Mexico and the

United States.[70] Moreover, while the tactic successfully diminished the number of undocumented aliens trying to enter in El Paso, the city's downtown businesses reported a shortage of employees and a drop in receipts and fewer shoppers, which did not please all merchants.[71] Mexicans in turn began to apply for Border Crossing Cards (explained below), which would enable them to cross the border to El Paso.[72]

A few months later, in 1994, "Operation Gatekeeper" was instituted in the San Diego area. It was a beefed-up program along the border, and included high-intensity floodlights and an eight-foot steel fence running from the Pacific Ocean 14 miles inland. With increased funding from Congress, the INS also sent additional agents to the area.[73]

Like Operation Hold the Line, Operation Gatekeeper led to a sharp drop in the number of persons trying to enter the United States in the San Diego area. The INS reported that three years after the beginning of Operation Gatekeeper, the number of apprehensions along the San Diego border fell to 48 percent, which was similar to the success of Operation Hold the Line.[74] But critics said potential immigrants were channeled "to other, less visible locations along the two-thousand mile border," where physical conditions were harsher for crossing.[75] Such a place was the border between Arizona and Mexico. Border restrictions became even tighter after 9/11. By 2004, with new agents along that line, DHS reported that nearly one half million persons were intercepted attempting to slip into the United States via Arizona.[76] In 2002 the Mexican government maintained that between 1994 and 2002 2,000 persons had died trying to traverse the border, and in the first five months of 2003 another 98 persons attempting to enter the United States died of heat-related illnesses. A sensational case occurred in May 2003 when a Texas heat wave claimed the lives of 18 persons who had been locked in a trailer and abandoned by the "coyote" who smuggled them across the barren landscape.[77] Coyotes were those who assisted others to enter the United States illegally, for a fee of course. Alarmed by the growing number of deaths in the desert areas separating the United States and Mexico, the Mexican government published a guide intended for potential unauthorized immigrants that warned them of difficulties and gave helpful hints for border crossing.[78] Reports of deaths did not deter the administration from beefing up the governmental presence along the border. In December 2004, President George W. Bush signed into law the 9/11 commission's recommendation for hiring new Border Patrol agents and increasing funding for a huge increase in internal enforcement of immigration violations.[79] In 2005 Bush once again called for tighter controls along the border.[80]

Experts believe that the tighter restrictions might have had an unintended effect, namely, because it is more difficult to cross the border illegally, many of the unauthorized immigrants are reluctant to make trip home. Instead, they remain for longer periods of time in the United States. As three authorities noted, "a perverse consequence of draconian border enforcement is that it does not deter would-be migrants from trying to enter the country so much as it discourages those who are already here from returning home. The end result of a border building is typically longer trip durations, lower probabilities of return migration settlement."[81]

Others believe that the border measures have kept undocumented immigration from growing even larger, but they did little to catch those who became illegal workers by overstaying their visas. Ninety percent of those apprehended as undocumented immigrants were intercepted along the Mexican-United States boundary, but the INS estimated as many as 40 percent of the undocumented population in the United States were "visas abusers" – persons who overstayed their permits. Employer sanctions had proved to be ineffective for those working within the country's borders. Thus those remaining after their visa expired had little fear of being deported for working.[82] In trying to catch persons violating immigration laws, agents sometimes deported persons for very minor crimes, which caused hardship in families and triggered apprehension among immigrants, and heightened mistrust of the police.[83]

To plug the border was one issue, but even closely inspecting the legal flow of autos and trucks was difficult. The basic fact was that with such increases in legal traffic crossing the border, especially since the inauguration of North Atlantic Free Trade Agreement (NAFTA), it was impossible for INS agents to entirely halt illegal immigration or the importation of drugs. To inspect the millions of trucks coming to the United States from Mexico would have required a huge increase in the Border Patrol as well as Customs on top of the major additions of the post-1993 era. One senior Customs official put it, "if we examined every truck for narcotics [and undocumented aliens] arriving in the United States along the Southwest border ... Customs would back up the traffic bumper-to-bumper into Mexico City in just two weeks."[84]

Undocumented Immigrants Themselves

As a result of the inability to plug the border, undocumented immigration reached new heights in the 1990s. The 2000 Census led some governmental officials and scholars to suggest that nine to eleven million undocumented aliens lived in the United States.[85] Passel and his colleagues estimated that the figure was 9.2 million in 2002, 10.3 million in 2004, and by March 2005, the estimate was just short of 11 million, which was 29 percent of the foreign-born population in the United States.[86]

The undocumented population resembled authorized immigrants in many ways, but there were differences. Mexicans topped the list of both authorized and unauthorized immigration, but Mexicans were 57 percent of the illegal population, roughly three times their proportion of legal immigrants. Unauthorized persons settled in the same states as documented immigrants, with California being the leader in both cases, but Arizona and North Carolina also had substantial unauthorized populations. While women have been the slight majority of all resident aliens in the last forty years, among illegals, according to Passel, they account for only 29 percent. Undocumented immigrants tended to be young men, the vast majority of whom were in the work force.[87]

NON-IMMIGRANT BORDER CROSSERS

In addition to the growth of both authorized and unauthorized immigration after 1986, the number of Border Crossers also increased substantially. Some were daily crossers of the border between the United States and Mexico; they possessed a Border Crossing Card (BCC). They were not included in the official figures, and the INS did not count each trip across the border as either an immigrant or nonimmigrant. Such an inclusion would have led to a huge inflation of nonimmigrant or immigrant figures because of the frequency of their crossings.

In 2002 the United States issued Laser Visas, which was a new version of the BCC. Laser Visas were for those who were legal aliens or U.S. citizens living in Mexico but working in the United States; they could also use their green cards or passports to cross. By the early 1990s 17,000 persons alone were going from Mexico to the San Ysidro, California, border point daily, and according to Joseph Nevins and Caroline Moorehead, nearly 300,000 Mexican workers cross the boundary *legally* (italics from the original) on a daily or weekly basis to work in the United States.[88] Another category of Border Crossers were Mexicans entitled to admission "as a border crosser or non-immigrant visitor for a period not to exceed 72 hours to visit within 25 miles of the border."[89] These Border Crossers were entitled to shop, purchase supplies, deliver goods, visit relatives and friends, and do business with partners on the American side. Other than conducting business, these card holders were not supposed to work. Canadians are also allowed to cross for business or tourism for periods up to six months without obtaining a visa. But Canadian immigration to the United States is only a fraction of that from Mexico.

Scholars studying Border Crossers said that no accurate figure existed for the number of these migrants, but it was "safe to say that most of the millions of legal border crossings made each year between Juarez and El Paso are made by BCC holders."[90] Another estimate claimed that 800,000 people cross the Mexican-American border every day. In 2001 over 300 million two-way crossings took place, and the annual number was growing.[91] In 2002 the State Department reported that it issued 1.3 million BBCs of all kinds.[92] Jessica M. Vaughan stated that nearly seven million cards had been issued in recent years.[93]

Including BCCers in the official non-immigrant count would have driven this figure into the hundreds of millions. Most did not have permission to work, but it was an open secret that many of the BCC holders who legally crossed to shop or visit family and friends worked illegally in American border cities: women as household employees, men as casual laborers. Such labor was easy to find and immigration authorities did little to halt it. Its economic impact on border communities has not been the object of scholarly studies, but these BCCers, whether shopping, visiting or working do have some impact on these communities.

The question to be answered was why many more Mexicans did not apply for a BCC, given the fact that they were left largely unsupervised on the American side. Why should anyone cross illegally, paying coyotes large sums of money or risking injury or death attempting to enter the United States without inspection? In part the answer can be found in the limits on cardholders' employment opportunities in the United States, and in part because requirements for BCC included proving that one was solvent and not seeking employment in the United States, which means that they had Mexican employment, a Mexican bank account and proof of Mexican Social Security registration. But not all Mexicans were registered. In addition, while there is no limit on the number of BCCs, the procedure for obtaining a card is time consuming. The proof needed to obtain a BCC was often difficult to obtain, which discouraged applications, and as a result many choose to become unauthorized immigrants especially if they intend to work for only a brief time in American cities.[94]

NONIMMIGRANTS

Tourists and Businessmen

Nonimmigrants have no fixed ceiling, but certain categories of nonimmigrants do have limits. Overall, nonimmigrants increased substantially after World War II. In 2001 more than 32.8 million nonimmigrants were admitted to the United States; the vast majority of these were tourists. By contrast, before IRCA was passed during the early 1980s, the number averaged 9.5 million annually.[95] However, following 9/11, with passage of the U.S.A. Patriot Act (2001), the Enhanced Border Security and Visa Entry Reform Act (2002), and implementation of new rules and tighter screening, the number declined; by 2003 the total was 27.8 million. In 2004 it increased to over 30 million.[96] The United Kingdom, Mexico, Japan, and Germany account for nearly two-thirds of nonimmigrants (Table 4).

After 9/11 it became more difficult for citizens of some nations to visit the United States. Figures from African and Asian countries with large Islamic populations and nations in the Middle East dropped more sharply than did other regions. It should be noted that even before 9/11 in certain countries, such as the Philippines or the Dominican Republic, embassy officials carefully screened visitor applications because of the belief that natives of these nations were apt to stay on after expiration of their visas. American

Table 4. Selected Categories of Non-Immigrants, 2001–2003.

Category	2001	2002	2003
All Classes	32,690,082	27,907,139	27,849,443
Temporary visitors for business (B1)	n/a	4,376,935	4,215,714
For pleasure (B2)	n/a	19,967,281	20,142,909
Students (F1)	688,970	637,945	617,556
Students (M1)	43,326	41,490	38,049
Specialty occupations (H1B)	384,191	379,490	360,498
Agricultural workers (H2)	27,695	15,628	14,094
NATO officials and families (N1-7)	13,805	12,628	12,569
Artists or entertainers in culturally unique programs (Q1)	9,484	9,487	8,869
Workers in Irish peace process cultural and training program (Q)	299	466	664

Source: DHS, *Statistical Yearbook*, 2003.

embassies usually do not have enough personnel to interview all of those asking for an American visa. Before 9/11 roughly 20 percent applying for non-immigrant visitors' visas were interviewed by the staff in American overseas embassies. Even then, the interviews were very short, lasting only a few minutes. If their nation did not require a visa for entry from the United States, then the United States government did not require one for coming to America. Post-9/11 rules issued by the State Department in July 2003 stated that face-to-face interviews were to be required for all nonimmigrants coming from all nations except for Canada and Mexico and those in the Visa Waiver Program.[97]

Among nonimmigrants were persons needing to make business contacts in the United States and scholars and their families who were considered exchange visitors, who came to teach, to do research, or to study in the United States. They were the second largest category of nonimmigrants, second only to tourists. The United Kingdom and Germany are the leading sources for these exchange visitors.[98]

Students and Scholars

One of the largest non-immigrant categories is that of student. Like other nonimmigrants and immigrants the number of students grew substantially after the mid-1980s. In 1985 foreign-born students numbered 257,069, studying in a great variety of American colleges and universities. By 2001 the number peaked at 698,595.[99] The figure dropped after tougher, post-9/11 regulations went into effect, but the number of graduate students went up slightly in 2005.[100] Exchange visitors and vocational students at universities accounted for several hundred thousand more foreigners at American universities and colleges. Collectively they totaled nearly one million persons and were about four percent of all nonimmigrants in 2002.[101] Some educational institutions depended upon students for their tuition, and educational leaders believed that the foreign students are important for the American economy. In 2003 the Institute for International Education reported that international students contributed nearly 12 billion dollars to the U.S. economy.[102] In other cases, graduate students were receiving stipends for teaching undergraduates. While foreign students come from nearly all nations, those from Asia contributed the largest number. In 2003, Japan, Korea, India, and China topped the list of foreign-born students. Japan was number one with 81,558 and Korea was second with 74,115, followed by China with 56,870, and India with 50,884 that year.[103] Foreign students studying in scientific fields including computer science were a growing proportion of their fields, and it was not unusual for them to find a job in the American economy or to marry an American and adjust their status to resident alien. It is not known how many of those paying their own way worked in the off-the-books-economy, but the number was probably not small. Before 9/11, once students had a visa, they were not carefully tracked by either the United States government or the universities themselves. Economist George Borjas, an authority on immigration and critic of American immigration policy noted, "once enrolled in the United States, the educational institutions do not typically report to the INS if the student has, in fact, enrolled in the educational program."[104] After 9/11 the policy was changed.

The post-9/11 rules meant delays in obtaining a visa, especially for males from Arab and Islamic nations, such as Egypt, Pakistan, Saudi Arabia, and the United Arab Emirates. Certain fields also dropped. In 2003 students in computer science fell to 15 percent from the previous year.[105] While many universities reported a decrease, others held the number of foreign students constant or actually experienced a slight increase.[106] Students in fields such as science and technology had to be cleared by the Federal Bureau of Investigation and the Central Intelligence Agency, and all students were to be monitored more carefully.[107] While critics of immigration wanted tighter rules and fewer students, others warned that in the international search for talent, the United States was beginning to lose highly educated persons to other nations.[108]

Temporary Workers

One of the smaller programs for nonimmigrants was a K visa, granted to the fiancé of an American citizen. Fewer than 30,000 annually receive this particular visa. It was assumed the wedding would take place within three months of entering the United States; accordingly, the visa was only good for that time period. With a K visa, unlike many others, one could legally find a job.

Temporary visas for religious workers, entertainers, journalists, au pair women, and cultural exchange visas also did not account for large numbers. For example, religious workers can stay for up to five years, but only 20,272 persons entered in this category in 2003.[109] In many of the temporary categories family members were allowed to accompany the visa holders.

Another category falls under America's international obligations. It was for representatives of foreign governments and their families, including those with diplomatic ties to the United States or employees of international organizations such as the United Nations or the North Atlantic Treaty Organization (NATO). Collectively these categories constitute less than one percent of the foreigners entering as nonimmigrants.[110]

Under trade agreements with Canada and Mexico, several thousand persons, mainly Canadians, are admitted annually, but like nearly all immigrant and non-immigrants categories, the number fell in 2003.[111] It was under these agreements that some Canadian health professionals entered the United States easily.[112] This is a fairly new visa provided for under NAFTA, and totaled 66,129 in 2004. It could grow in the future, and down the road there is the potential for additional nonimmigrants to arrive under free trade agreements with other nations.[113]

The numbers of other temporary workers were also small. Much attention has been focused on non-immigrant nurses, who were believed to be in short supply. In 2001 the American Nursing Association claimed that America faced a shortage of 120,000 nurses across the United States, but others used a higher figure.[114] While Asian-Indian nurses rushed to fill this shortfall, Jamaicans, Irish, and especially Filipinos dominated the foreign-born nursing profession in the United States.[115] Most nurses entered under the regular immigration preferences, but under an H-1A program in existence from 1989 to 1995, 25,000 nurses entered to work temporarily in American hospitals and other health facilities. Only later did they adjust their status to become permanent resident aliens. After 2000 Congress kept a small temporary nursing program alive, and created the H-1C program to admit 500 nurses annually.[116] In 2003 only 924 arrived with H-1A visas and another 48 came as nurses under the Nursing Relief for Disadvantaged Areas Act.[117] Canadian nurses entered under NAFTA.[118]

Non-immigrant tourists, persons related to international obligations such as NATO, and temporary business visitors might have proven uncontroversial but several programs have come under attack and have been the subject of Congressional lobbying. Agribusiness won a victory in IRCA with inclusion of SAWs, many of whom had fraudulent claims. Immigration expert David North wrote, "many an urban resident claimed SAW status, many without justification. There were countless anecdotes of fur-coat wearing Europeans seeking SAW status in Manhattan, applicants who contended that the cotton they harvested was purple, or that cherries were dug out of the ground, or that one used a ladder to pick strawberries."[119] Clearly many SAWS were fraudulent claimants who had no intention of becoming poorly paid agricultural workers. The other victory won by agribusiness in 1986 opened the possibility of a large-scale temporary agricultural program: the Replacement (or Replenishment) Agricultural Worker program, which, if approved, would enable farm owners to replenish their supply of farm workers when needed. After 1986 agribusiness insisted that it lacked sufficient hands to harvest crops and that temporary farm laborers were required to harvest. However, the federal government has never granted these requests, and large-scale farms have increasingly employed unauthorized immigrants for these jobs.[120]

A small scale temporary farm worker program has been in use for years. The federal government began a limited program at the time of World War I. However, this program ended shortly after the war and did not involve many farm laborers. Beginning in World War II the Bracero program, which provided many farm workers for California (and later Texas and elsewhere), was in operation from the war until 1964 when it ended. While in existence it provided over 4.5 million workers, chiefly for agriculture.[121]

The temporary worker program replacing it was very modest. Under the H-2A program the government imported farm workers, chiefly West Indians, who were found along the East Coast picking apples in Vermont and tomatoes and other crops in Florida. At its height the Bracero program imported 400,000 workers annually in the late 1950s, compared to 33,292 H-2 workers in 2000; they amounted to only 14,092 persons in 2003.[122] While unable to convince the government of the need for a large-scale replenishment program for agricultural laborers as included in the IRCA, or a huge increase in H-2A workers, agribusiness felt the election of George W. Bush in 2000 promised a more positive policy response. Before 9/11 President Bush proposed that the United States should legalize undocumented immigrants provided that they had employment awaiting them in the United States. The permits were not limited to agriculture, but no doubt a large number would find employment in America's agricultural fields. Under the initial Bush proposal unauthorized migrants would be permitted to receive work permits for a three-year period. The President held out the possibility of a renewed three-year period, but in any event these workers were not to become permanent resident aliens. Obviously, President Bush did not want his program to be a general amnesty, and he pushed it again in 2005. The Bush proposals were vague and did not address how these workers were to be encouraged to go home. In addition, it was not made clear how many undocumented aliens were to be allowed to stay as temporary workers.[123] These proposals were by no means the only ones, and several members in Congress suggested amnesties, guest workers and tougher border controls.[124]

The border, as noted, was the subject of considerable debate and conflict between the United States and Mexico. Bush's proposal held out the hope of a different border strategy, which currently depended upon on what critics called the "militarization" of the Mexican-United States border. Scholars pointed out that during the Bracero period, the number of undocumented aliens grew apace because of laborers. If Mexicans were unable to become Braceros or get a green card, they simply crossed the border to work in California and Texas fields, picking the crops. Former INS Commission Doris Meissner wrote in 2004 that the Bracero program as enforced provided little protection for Braceros and that the program was riddled "with lax enforcement of its rules." Moreover, it "spawned and institutionalized networks and labor market relationships between Mexico and the United States. These ties continued and became the foundation for today's illegal migration from Mexico."[125] However, after 9/11 the President's suggestion received little support and the federal government instead moved to tighten border security.[126]

Highly Skilled Workers

If farm owners increasingly turned to undocumented aliens for their labor when they could not win support for another Bracero-type arrangement, other employers in the United States found more enthusiasm in Congress. Another section of the 1990 Immigration Act was a non-immigrant program to import highly skilled temporary workers under H-1B visas. No temporary worker program caused such controversy as did the H-1B program, set up to bring persons for scientific research, information technology, and the physical and life sciences. H-1B workers had to have at least a bachelor's degree. The permitted number grew from 65,000 to over 195,000 in 2001, though the actual figure of those arriving was slightly smaller.[127] After passage of the American Competitiveness in the Twenty-First Century Act, it was cut back to 65,000 admissions.[128] Under this program, popular overseas, the visas are quickly filled.[129] The H-1B workers came from nations around the world, but were dominated by Chinese, Filipinos, and especially Indians. In the eight-year period from 1996 to 2003 India topped the list of H-1B visas six times and accounted for nearly one half of those in this program. These workers are supposed to be employed in critical high-tech industries where shortages exist, and they were not to be employed at wages designed to undercut American workers. Critics insisted that employers were hiring these foreigners to pay wages below the prevailing one, while employers maintained that they faced shortages.[130] An attempt to increase these visas was killed in late 2005.[131]

Employers attempting to use the H-2B program for non-agricultural seasonal workers also complained that they could not find Americans willing to take on temporary jobs in their businesses. These workers were needed in the crab-processing trade and by those who maintained businesses in vacation spots such as ski or summer resorts. Over 100,000 were granted H-2B visas in 2003, but the number was cut to 66,000 in 2005.[132] The head of the National Restaurant Association remarked that employers would prefer to hire Americans, "but have not been able to get the personnel they need."[133]

CONCLUSION

Since 1986 immigrants, undocumented immigrants, Border Crossers, and nonimmigrants have all increased substantially. How to develop a coherent policy and how to determine who comes legally is elusive. Proponents of immigration praise the policy of uniting families, helping refugees and bringing persons with needed skills to America. In December 2005 the House of Representatives voted to eliminate the diversity visas, but what the Senate would do was uncertain. Even if it were to be eliminated, DVs amounted to only 50,000 visas annually.

When one examines governmental actions toward undocumented aliens and Border Crossers, it is clear that policies are often the product of debate or compromises, some of which have unintended consequences, such as undocumented aliens staying in the United States for longer periods. Enforcement of immigration law has been haphazard at best. After 1990 the government has more than doubled the size of the Border Patrol and has substantially increased its budget, but the unauthorized population still grows. Internally, employer sanctions have been ineffective in halting the employment of authorized immigrants.

As for nonimmigrants, the vast majority of these are tourists and persons conducting business, both of which are economically profitable to the United States. Another category of nonimmigrant, students, also benefits the United States. In addition, some experts are worried that the United States might be losing good students to other nations who are attracting them as the search for highly skilled workers becomes global.

Given the forces at play in regulating migrants to the United States, it is likely that governmental programs will continue to be shaped and impacted by politics, often without a clear resolution, at least in the near future. This means that the present flows of migrants to the United States will continue at a high rate. The subsequent events and government reaction to 9/11 seemed to point in the direction of tougher controls for immigrants, nonimmigrants and unauthorized persons, but the precise impact is too difficult to gauge at this time.

NOTES

1. See Nancy F. Rytina, "U.S. Legal Permanent Residents: 2004," U.S. Department of Homeland Security (DHS), June 2005. There are some minor categories, such as the adoption of foreign orphans, that are not counted in the total figures. In 2004, for example, 11,741 foreign children were adopted by Americans.

2. I use the terms "unauthorized," "illegal," and "undocumented" interchangeably to apply to persons who lack legal papers entitling them to be in the United States. No insult is intended by the use of any of these terms.

3. Roger Daniels, *Guarding the Door: American Immigration Policy and Immigrants since 1882* (New York: Hill and Wang, 2004), pp. 220–231. Another general account of the 1986 Act is found in Debra L. Delaet, *U.S. Immigration Policy in an Age of Rights* (Westport, Connecticut: Praeger, 2000), Chapter 3.

4. Quoted in Anna Law, "The Diversity Visa Lottery – A Case of Unintended Consequences in United States Immigration Policy," *Journal of American Ethnic History*, Vol. 21 (Summer 2002), p. 7. Law's article is an excellent account of the lottery or diversity visa.

5. Law, "The Diversity Visa," pp. 14–16. The 1965 Act consisted of amendments to the basic immigration laws of the 1920s.

6. The lottery did not mention Ireland by name. The law simply said that during the first three years, 40 percent of the diversity visas were to be granted to the country that had that many after IRCA's first lottery. The 55,000 spots were later decreased to 50,000, and 5,000 visas were reassigned for use under the Nicaraguan Adjustment and Central American Relief Act.

7. U.S. Department of Homeland Security (DHS), *Statistical Yearbook*, 2003, p. 5. No nation was permitted to have more than 3,850 places.

8. *New York Times*, Feb. 2, 2005. For a general account of the 1990 law, see DeLaet, *Immigration Policy*, Chapter 4.

9. *The Ghanaian Chronicle*, Nov. 23, 2004.

10. The U.S. State Department, Office of the Spokesman, July 21, 2004.

11. Immigration and Naturalization Service (INS), *Statistical Yearbook*, 2001, p. 110.

12. The McCarran–Walter Immigration Act of 1952 gave the parole power to the executive branch.

13. Many refugees chose not to become permanent resident aliens after only one year. The act set the "normal flow" of refugees at 50,000 yearly, but that figure was exceeded every year until 2002.

14. Daniels, *Guarding the Door*, pp. 207–208.

15. The Lautenberg amendment, which provided 300,000 places, favored Soviet Jews, but also included Armenians and Pentecostal Christians. See Philip G. Schrag, *A Well Founded Fear: The Congressional Battle to Save Political Asylum* (New York: Routledge, 2000), pp. 35, 52–53, 138–139.

16. Cuban refugees still arrived in the early 1990s, but after 1994 Cubans were more apt to be admitted under the regular immigration procedures. By that time, South East Asians were also arriving as regular immigrants rather than as refugees.

17. *Washington Post*, May 30, 2003; Deborah Meyers and Jennifer Yau, "U.S. Immigration Statistics in 2003," Migration Information Source, Nov. 1, 2004.

18. *USA Today*, Sept. 9, 2004.

19. David Martin, "The U.S. Refugee Program in Transition," Migration Information Source, May 1, 2005. The refugees listed are for the fiscal year.

20. Hurricane Mitch in 2001, rather than civil war, prompted many Hondurans to flee to the United States. The federal government has the power to allow them to remain temporarily in the United States.

21. Congressional Budget Office (CBO), *A Description of the Immigrant Population*, Nov. 2004, p. 4; Jeanne Batalova, "Spotlight on Refugees and Asylees in the United States," Migration Information Source, Aug. 1, 2005.

22. Bill Frelick, "U.S. Detention of Asylum Seekers and Human Rights," Migration Information Source, Mar. 1, 2005.

23. INS, *Statistical Yearbook*, 2001, pp. 89–110; DHS, *Statistical Yearbook*, 2003, pp. 69–71. For the struggle over asylum, see Schrag, *A Well-Founded Fear*.

24. INS, *Statistical Yearbook*, 2001, p. 89.

25. This law gave Haitians a status similar to Central Americans, though not entirely equal. In 2000, 22,003 Haitians became immigrants and another 40,000 did so in the next two years. The number fell as it did for nearly all groups in 2003. DHS, *Statistical Yearbook*, 2003, p. 14.

26. *New York Times*, Feb. 20, 2001. The exact provisions of the new law caused considerable confusion, but several hundred thousand undocumented aliens had the potential of becoming legal.

27. *USA Today*, May 1, 2001; *New York Times*, May 1, 2001.

28. DHS, *Statistical Yearbook*, 2003, p. 48.

29. DHS, *Statistical Yearbook*, 2003, p. 19.

30. DHS, *Statistical Yearbook*, 2003, p. 32; Rytina, "U.S. Legal Permanent Residents: 2004."

31. A few persons in these categories did win asylum. Congress even provided for 1,000 Chinese annually who were said to be fleeing China because of the one child per family rule.

32. In an effort to tighten security in 2002, the INS was placed under the newly created Department of Homeland Security (DHS) and given the authority to guard the borders. The newly formed U.S. Citizenship and Immigration Service (USCIS) was put in charge of immigration and naturalization services.

33. *New York Times*, Mar. 31, 2003.

34. *New York Times*, Feb. 8, 2005. The full report of this agency, which was created by Congress in 1998, can be found on their web site, www.uscirf.gov.

35. *USA Today*, Dec. 3, 2003; *New York Times*, Nov. 22, 2003.

36. *New York Times*, Apr. 30, 2003; June 3, 2003.

37. Maia Jachimowicz and Ramah McKay, "Spotlight on 'Special Registration' Program," Migration Information Source, Apr. 1, 2003. The rules applied only to men. North Korea was also on the list.

38. *San Francisco Chronicle*, May 20, 2003. Travel documents were also to be checked against a computer data bank; a partial finger proof test was to be used as well.

39. USCIS, TPS, Apr. 2004.

40. *New York Times*, Mar. 2, 2005.

41. Rytina, "U.S. Legal Permanent Residents, 2004."

42. INS, *Statistical Yearbook*, 2001, p. 129.

43. INS, *Statistical Yearbook*, 2001, p. 130. The annual number of parolees was between 250,000 and 300,000 in the late 1990s and early 2000s.

44. David M. Reimers, *Still the Golden Door: The Third World Comes to America* (New York: Columbia University Press, 2nd edition, 1992), Chapter 8.

45. Nancy F. Rytina, "U.S. Legal Permanent Residents, 2004," Office of Immigration Statistics, Department of Homeland Security (DHS), June 2004.

46. Jeffrey S. Passel and Roberto Suro, *Rise and Decline: Trends in U.S. Immigration, 1992–2004* (Washington: Pew Hispanic Center, 2005); *USA Today*, Dec. 12, 2005. The newspaper article was based on the Center for Immigration Studies investigation, which included both undocumented and documented aliens.

47. Meyers and Yau, "U.S. Immigration Statistics," p. 1.

48. Rytina, "U.S. Legal Permanent Residents: 2004."

49. Randolph Capps, Michael E. Fix, and Jeffrey S. Passel, "The Dispersal of Immigrants in the 1990s" (Washington: Urban Institute, Nov. 26, 2002).

50. Rytina, "U.S. Legal Permanent Residents: 2004."

51. For a discussion of return migration see Mark Wyman's excellent study, *Round-Trip to America: The Immigrant's Return to Europe, 1880–1930* (Ithaca: Cornell University Press, 1993).

52. U.S. Department of Justice, INS, and U.S. Department of Labor, Bureau of International Labor Affairs, *The Triennial Comprehensive Report on Immigration* (Washington: Government Printing Office, 1999), p. 53.

53. See Douglas S. Massey, Jorge Durand, and Nolan J. Malone, *Beyond Smoke and Mirrors: Mexican Immigration in an Era of Economic Integration* (New York: Russell Sage Foundation, 2002), pp. 135–136.

54. U.S. Bureau of the Census, Current Population Survey, "Overview of Race and Hispanic Origin," Issued Mar. 2001.

55. See Leon Bouvier and Rosemary Jenks, *Doctors and Nurses: A Demographic Profile* (Washington: Center for Immigration Studies, 1998).

56. For the role of role of Asians as small business owners, see U.S. Department of Commerce, Bureau of the Census, *Asian-and-Pacific Islander-Owned Businesses Number 900,000*, Public Information Office, May 22, 2001.

57. *New York Times*, Nov. 24, 2003.

58. *New York Times*, Nov. 24, 2003.

59. See U.S. Dept. of Commerce, *Asian Owned Businesses*.

60. Kevin O'Neil, "Brain Drain and Gain: The Case of Taiwan," Migration Information Source, Sept. 1, 2003.

61. *Washington Post*, Nov. 29, 2004; April Gordon, "The New Diaspora-African Immigration to the United States," *Journal of Third World Studies* (Spring 1998).

62. See Paul Stoller, *Money Has No Smell: The Africanization of New York City* (Chicago: University of Chicago Press, 2001).

63. Proposition 187 became a dead letter when the Ninth Circuit of the U.S. District Court struck it down. In addition, Governor Davis dropped the appeals process before the courts, effectively killing the law.

64. INS, *Statistical Yearbook*, 2001, pp. 201–205; DHS, *Statistical Yearbook*, 2003, pp. 2, 137.

65. A summary of estimates and characteristics can also be found in Jeffrey Passel, Jennifer Van Hook, and Frank D. Bean, "Unauthorized Migrants Living in the United States: A Mid-Decade Portrait," Pew Hispanic Center, Sept. 1, 2005.

66. See Peter Brownell, "The Declining Enforcement of Employer Sanctions," Migration Information Source, Sept. 1, 2005; David Dixon, "Spotlight on U.S. Immigration Enforcement," Migration Information Source, Sept. 1, 2005.

67. *New York Times*, Feb. 17, 2005; Tim Gaynor, "Mexico People Smuggling Ignores U.S. Security Fears," Reuters, Feb. 17, 2005.

68. *The Arizona Republic*, Mar. 11, 2005.

69. *New York Times*, Sept. 14, 1994.

70. *New York Times*, Sept. 14, 1994.

71. Frank Bean, et al., *Illegal Mexican Migration and the United States Border: The Effects of Operation Hold the Line on El Paso/Juarez* (Washington: Government Printing Office, U.S. Commission on Immigration Reform, 1990), pp. 37–42.

72. *New York Times*, Sept. 14, 1994. For an examination of border activities, see Wade Graham, "Masters of the Game: How the U.S. Protects the Traffic in Cheap Mexican Labor," *Folio: Harper's Magazine*, July, 1996, pp. 35–50. The Bean study (43–46) found that employers had little difficulty finding workers. The study concluded that the number of illegal workers had been small.

73. See Massey et al., *Beyond Smoke and Mirrors*, pp. 93–98; Joseph Nevins, *Operation Gatekeeper: The Rise of the "Illegal Alien" and the Making of the U.S.-Mexico Boundary* (New York: Routledge, 2002).

74. INS, "Fact Sheet," Oct. 1997.

75. Massey et al., *Beyond Smoke and Mirrors*, pp. 113–114.

76. *New York Times*, Mar. 14, 2005.

77. *USA Today*, May 15, 2003; *New York Times*, Mar. 13, 2005; Mar. 24, 2005. Desperate aliens even paid smugglers to take their children as well as themselves across the boundary. *New York Times*, Nov. 3, 2003. For the new border policies generally see Wayne A. Cornelius, "Death at the Border: Efficacy and Unintended Consequences of U.S. Immigration Control Policy," *Population and Development Review*, Vol. 27, No. 4 (Dec. 2001), pp. 661–685; Peter Andreas, *Border Games: Policing the U.S. Divide* (Ithaca: Cornell University Press, 2000).

78. *New York Times*, Feb. 9, 2005.

79. Terence P. Jeffrey, "Al Qaeda Threat Demands Border Funding," Human Events Online, Feb., 18, 2005.

80. *New York Times*, Nov. 30, 2005; Julia Gelatt, "Bush Puts Immigration Reform Back on Agenda, Approves Funding for DHS," Migration Information Source, Nov. 1, 2005.

81. Massey, et al., *Beyond Smoke and Mirrors*, pp. 128–129.
82. Jeffrey, "Al Qaeda Threat Demands Border Funding."
83. *New York Times*, Feb. 17, 2005; Feb. 20, 2005.
84. Quoted in Andreas, *Border Games*, p. 76.
85. *The Press-Enterprise (Riverside, California)*, Jan. 24, 2002; *The Orange County Register*, Jan. 24, 2002.
86. Jeffrey J. Passel, Randolph Capps, and Michael Fix, "Undocumented Immigrants: Facts and Figures," Urban Institute, Jan. 12, 2002; Jeffrey E. Passel, "Estimates of the Size and Characteristics of the Undocumented Population," Pew Hispanic Center, Mar. 21, 2005. Discussion of the undocumented population is based on these studies.
87. See Passel et al., "Undocumented Immigrants"; Passel, "Estimates of the Size." For a view that sees unauthorized immigrants as a drain on the American economy, consult Steven Camarota, *The High Cost of Cheap Labor: Illegal Immigration and the Federal Budget* (Washington: Center for Immigration Studies, 2004).
88. Nevins, *Operation Gatekeeper*, p. 5; Caroline Moorehead, *Human Cargoes: A Journey Among Refugees* (New York: Henry Holt and Co., 2005), p. 81.
89. Bean, et al., *Illegal Mexican Migration*, p. 13.
90. Bean et al., *Illegal Mexican Migration*, p. 14.
91. U.S. Bureau of Transportation Statistics, Siobhan Gorman, "A Nation Without Borders," *National Journal*, Dec. 1, 2001. Counting these persons as non-immigrants prompted the Congressional Budge Office to claim that aside from immigrants, asylees, and refugees, 181 million persons entered as non-immigrants in 2003. CBO, "The Immigrant Population," p. 4.
92. U.S. Department of State, Bureau of Consular Affairs, *Report of the Visa Office*, 2002, p. 19.
93. Jessica M. Vaughan, "Modernizing America's Welcome Mat: The Implementation of US-VISIT" (Washington: Center for Immigration Studies, Aug. 2005), p. 6.
94. Bean, et al., *Illegal Mexican Migration*, pp. 15–17.
95. INS, *Statistical Yearbook*, 2001, p. 125.
96. DHS, *Statistical Yearbook*, 2003, p. 101; Elizabeth M. Grieco, "Temporary Admissions of Non-immigrants to the United States in 2004," DHS, May 2005.
97. Maia Jachimowicz, "Government Widens Efforts to Scrutinize Foreign Visitors," Migration Information Source, Aug. 1, 2003.
98. Data on all non-immigrant categories can be found in DHS, *Statistical Yearbook*, 2003, pp. 86–137. Figures from the State Department's Bureau of Consular Affairs are greater than those reported by DHS.
99. DHS, *Statistical Yearbook*, 2003, p. 101.
100. *New York Times*, Nov. 7, 2005.
101. Maia Jachimowicz, "Foreign Students and Exchange Visitors," Migration Information Source, Sept. 1, 2003.
102. Jim Lobe, "U.S. Students Enrollments Hit By Muslim Stayaway," *Asia Times*, Nov. 5, 2003; Institute of Internal Education, "Open Doors," Nov. 3, 2003. George Borjas does not believe that students contribute significantly to the nation's economy. Borjas, *An Evaluation of the Foreign Student Program* (Washington: Center for Immigration Studies), pp. 6–7.

103. *USA Today*, May 6, 2003; DHS, *Statistical Yearbook*, 2003, pp. 89–90.

104. Borjas, *An Evaluation of the Foreign Student Program*, p. 2.

105. *The Scientist*, June 30, 2004.

106. *New York Times*, Nov. 10, 2004.

107. *New York Times*, Nov. 10, 2004; Jachimowicz, "Foreign Students and Exchange Visitors." For a critique of the new regulations, see John Paden and Peter Singer, "America Slams the Door (On Its Foot)," *Foreign Affairs*, Vol. 82 (May–June 2003), pp. 8–14.

108. David Heenan, *Flight Capital: The Alarming Exodus of America's Best and Brightest* (Mountain View, California: Davies-Black Publishing, 2005); Richard Florida, *The Flight of the Creative Class: The New Global Competition for Talent* (New York: Harper/Business, 2005).

109. DHS, *Statistical Yearbook*, 2003, p. 107.

110. DHS, *Statistical Yearbook*, 2003, pp. 89–96.

111. DHS, *Statistical Yearbook*, 2003, p. 96. In 2003, of the 59,446 North America Free-Trade Agreement Workers, 58,177 were from Canada (98 percent).

112. Jessica Vaughan, *Be Our Guest: Trade Agreements and Visas* (Washington: Center for Immigration Studies, 2003), p. 9.

113. Elizabeth M. Grieco, "Temporary Admissions of Non-immigrants to the United States in 2004," DHS, May 2005.

114. "Indian Nurses Come to U.S.," *India Abroad*, Dec. 2002. An excellent study of foreign-born health professionals is B. Lindsay Lowell and Stefka Georgieva Gerova's "Immigrants and the Healthcare Workforce," *Work and Occupations*, Vol. 31, No. 4 (Nov. 2004), pp. 474–498.

115. *New York Times*, Nov. 24, 2003.

116. Vaughan, *Be Our Guest*, p. 15; DHS, *Statistical Yearbook*, 2003, p. 190.

117. DHS, *Statistical Yearbook*, 2003, p. 101.

118. Vaughan, *Be Our Guest*, pp. 15–16.

119. David North, *Lessons Learned from the Legalization Programs of the 1980s* (Washington: Center for Immigration Studies, 2005), p. 5.

120. For agricultural labor see Philip L. Martin, *Promise Unfulfilled: Unions, Immigration, and Farm Workers* (Ithaca: Cornell University Press, 2003).

121. The number was not necessarily composed of different people, for some Braceros renewed their contracts and came to the United States several times.

122. DHS, *Statistical Yearbook*, 2003, p. 101.

123. *New York Times*, Nov. 29, 2005.

124. Eliot Turner and Marc R. Rosenblum, "Solving the Unauthorized Migrant Program: Proposed Legislation in the U.S.," Migration Information Source, Sept. 1, 2005; Julia Gelatt, "President Bush Pushes for Increased Enforcement and a Temporary Worker Program," Migration Information Source, Dec. 1, 2005.

125. Doris Meissner, "U.S. Temporary Worker Programs: Lessons Learned," Migration Information Source, Mar. 1, 2004.

126. *New York Times*, Mar. 23, 2005.

127. U.S. Department of State, Bureau of Consular Affairs, 2002, p. 109.

128. Maia Jachimowicz and Deborah W. Meyers, "Spotlight on Temporary High-Skilled Migration," Migration Information Source, Nov. 1, 2002.

42   DAVID M. REIMERS

129. Kevin Jernegan, "A New Century: Immigration and the US," Migration Information Source, Feb. 2005.

130. For a critical view of the whole temporary worker program, see Jessica Vaughan, *Shortcuts to Immigration: The "Temporary" Visa Program Is Broken* (Washington: Center for Immigration Studies, 2003).

131. *Mercury News*, Nov. 20, 2005.

132. DHS, *Statistical Yearbook*, 2003, p. 104; *USA Today*, Mar. 25, 2005.

133. *USA Today*, Mar. 25, 2005.

IMMIGRANT SKILL TRANSFERABILITY AND THE PROPENSITY TO INVEST IN HUMAN CAPITAL

Harriet O. Duleep

ABSTRACT

As immigrants live, learn, and earn in the US, the earnings of comparably educated immigrants converge regardless of their country or admission status. Indeed, controlling for initial human capital levels, there is an inverse relationship between immigrant entry earnings and earnings growth. Immigrants initially lacking transferable skills have lower initial earnings but a higher propensity to invest in human capital than natives or high-skill-transferability immigrants. Policies that bring in immigrants lacking immediately transferable skills, such as family-based admission policies, may provide an infusion of undervalued flexible human capital that facilitates innovation and entrepreneurship. Low-skill-transferability immigration may foster the development of immigrant employment that is distinct from native-born employment and possibly reduce employment competition with natives. Those who enter without immediately transferable skills are more likely to be permanent and permanence

Immigration: Trends, Consequences and Prospects for the United States
Research in Labor Economics, Volume 27, 43–73
© 2008 Published by Elsevier Ltd.
ISSN: 0147-9121/doi:10.1016/S0147-9121(07)00002-7

confers a variety of societal benefits. Because human capital that is not
valued in the host-country's labor market is still useful for learning new
skills, immigrants who initially lack transferable skills provide the host
country an undervalued, highly malleable resource that may promote a
vibrant economy in the long run.

If asked whether a graduating high school senior should get a job and earn
money right away, or attend college, most people would answer attend
college. Yet, the former rule – rapid assimilation versus long-term growth –
dominates discussions of the economic benefits of various immigration
policies. This paper seeks to broaden the lens through which we view
immigrant economic worthiness by shifting the focus from immigrants'
initial earnings to their propensity to invest in human capital. Under girding
the paper's arguments is an inverse relationship between the extent to which
immigrant skills transfer to the new country and the propensity for
immigrants to invest in human capital. Because human capital that is not
valued in the host-country's labor market is still useful for learning new
skills, immigrants who initially lack transferable skills provide the host
country an undervalued, highly malleable resource.

The paper begins by describing the initial earnings of US immigrants
divided by country of origin. Section 2 reviews evidence of an inverse
relationship between immigrant skill transferability and the propensity to
invest in human capital. Sections 3–9 describe various policy ramifications
of the inverse relationship. Key ideas within the context of immigration
policy are summarized in the conclusion.

1. IMMIGRANT EARNINGS ASSIMILATION AND ADMISSION POLICIES

A widely shared perspective is that desirable immigrants are those who
rapidly adjust to their host-country's labor market. The importance policy
makers and scholars ascribe to rapid earnings adjustment surfaces many
places. Much attention is paid, for instance, to whether immigrant earnings
approach or surpass those of natives with similar levels of human capital –
Is there a crossover point? The more quickly immigrant earnings equal those
of natives, the better. The historical decline in immigrant entry earnings, a
decline that mostly persists controlling for years of schooling and age, also

garners much attention. To some it denotes a decline in immigrant labor-market quality. Immigration scholars also use the gap between immigrant and native earnings to gauge the success of immigrant admission programs: the smaller the gap, the more successful the program (e.g. Bauer, Pereira, Vogler, & Zimmermann, 1998; Büchel & Frick, 2003).

The initial earnings of US immigrants vary enormously depending on where they come from (Fig. 1).[1] Immigrants from the source regions that dominate recent US immigration (Asia and Central and South America) earn about half or less than half what US natives earn, whereas the entry earnings of Western European immigrants resemble those of the US-born. Moreover, these differences persist within age and education categories (Table 1). Given their low initial earnings, policy makers and immigration scholars fear that Asian and Hispanic immigrants will not economically assimilate, as did earlier, European immigrants.

The level of economic development of immigrants' source countries is correlated with initial earnings. Immigrants from regions of the world with

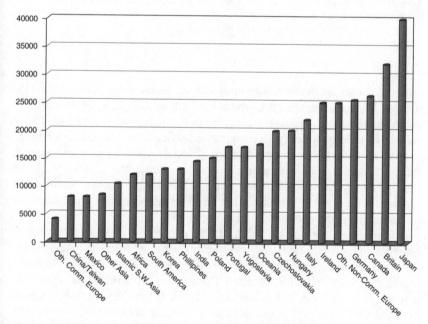

Fig. 1. Median 1989 US Earnings of Men Aged 25–54, Who Immigrated in the Years 1985–1990, by Country or Origin.

Table 1.   The Annual 1989 Earnings (as Measured by the 1990 Census)
of Immigrant Men Who Were Ages 25–54 in 1990 and Who Entered the
United States between 1985 and 1990[a].

	All	25–39 Years Old; 1–12 Years of School	25–39 Years Old; More than 12 Years of School	40–54 Years Old; 1–12 Years of School	40–54 Years Old; More than 12 Years of School
All immigrants	$12,367	11,062	15,977	9,833	22,122
Relative to US-born	0.406	0.529	0.485	0.381	0.500
By region of origin					
Asia	13,462	12,290	14,298	8,269	19,664
Relative to US-born	0.443	0.589	0.434	0.316	0.439
Central/South America[b]	11,062	10,570	14,748	9,833	17,949
Relative to US-born	0.364	0.506	0.447	0.376	0.401
Western Europe	30,726	23,966	30,726	22,123	61,452
Relative to US-born	1.010	1.147	0.931	0.845	1.372

Note: The estimates are based on the 1990 Census of Population, 5 percent and 1 percent Public
Use Samples combined.
[a]The statistics are given in 1995 dollars deflated by CPI.
[b]Mexico is included in Central America.

levels of economic development approaching or exceeding that of the US,
such as Western Europe and Japan, have initial earnings approaching or
exceeding those of comparably educated and experienced US natives. Those
hailing from economically developing countries have low initial earnings
relative to their US-born counterparts. Indeed, when we plot the median
1989 US earnings of immigrant men who entered the United States in
1985–1990 against the 1987 per adult GDP of each source country[2] a
positive relationship between immigrant entry earnings and level of
economic development emerges (Fig. 2).[3]

According to Chiswick's (1978, 1979) concept of skill transferability,
source-country variations in immigrants' initial earnings stem from
variations in the skills learned by growing up and working in different
source countries. Holding constant the level of human capital (years of
schooling and work experience), the skills of immigrants hailing
from economically developed countries transfer more easily to the US
because economically developed countries and the US have similar

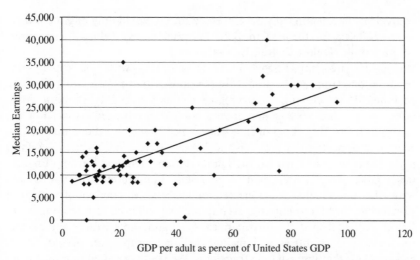

Fig. 2. The Relationship between Gross Domestic Product (GDP) per Adult and US Median Initial Earnings of Immigrants, by Country of Origin.

educational systems, industrial structures, and labor-market reward structures. The skills of immigrants from economically less developed countries are less transferable to the United States (resulting in lower US earnings) because the formal education and work experience in these countries are less applicable to the US economy (Chiswick, 1979; Mincer & Ofek, 1982).

> Skills attained in advanced, industrial economies are more easily transferable to the American labor market. After all, the industrial structure of advanced economies and the types of skills rewarded by those labor markets greatly resemble the industrial structure of the United States and the types of skills rewarded by American employers. In contrast, the industrial structures and labor markets of less developed countries require skills that are much less useful in the American labor market. The human capital embodied in residents of those countries is, to some extent, "specific" to those countries and is not easily transferable to the US labor market. (Borjas, 1992, pp. 428–429)

Another possibility is that immigrants from less developed countries have lower skill transferability because the limited opportunities in less developed countries make immigration worthwhile even when it entails substantial post-migration investments in new skills and credentials such as learning English, undertaking a US degree program, or starting a business. Their equivalents in economically developed countries would only migrate if there were positions for them in the US that immediately valued their source-country skills (Duleep & Regets, 1997a).

Consider two non-English-speaking scientists with the exact same training, one from an economically developed country, the other from an economically developing country. Since neither speaks English, both would have lower initial US earnings than a comparably trained native. For the scientist from the economically developed country, the similarity in economic opportunities between the United States and his home country make the costs associated with US immigration, including learning English, inadvisable. The greater relative economic opportunities in the United States for the scientist from the economically developing country make it worthwhile for him to migrate, even though he will need to learn English to become reestablished. In this manner, US immigrants from economically less developed countries will include a larger proportion of individuals lacking skills that immediately transfer to the US than will immigrants from economically developed countries.

This selection argument accommodates findings that the quality of schooling in some less economically developed countries is not inferior to that in the United States, and may be superior (Rivera-Batiz, 1996). Rather than the skills learned and used in less developed countries being less applicable to the United States, economic conditions in those countries make it worthwhile for persons to immigrate even when they lack skills that immediately transfer.

Several admission policies facilitate the immigration of persons with highly transferable skills who quickly earn on par with natives. One part of the US admission program admits immigrants to fill specific jobs as expressed by an employer's willingness to participate in a labor certification process. By the very nature of their admission, employment-based immigrants have specific skills that are immediately valued in the host-country's labor market. Quick earnings adjustment also occurs for those who enter via temporary work programs in response to specific US labor market needs. (Although not officially immigrants, the admission of temporary non-immigrants affects documented and undocumented immigration by fostering immigrant communities and information flows.) Guest-worker programs also exist in Germany and other European countries. Immigrant admission programs that emphasize fluency in the host-country's language(s) or credentials also encourage fast earnings adjustment.[4] Canada's admission program, for instance, awards points to prospective immigrants for fluency in English or French.

In contrast to policies that reward specific employment skills or other attributes fostering quick earnings adjustment, the predominant US immigration policy is family unification. The initial earnings of family-based immigrants are far below those of employment-based immigrants with comparable levels of education and experience (Duleep & Regets, 1992b, 1996a, 1996b; Jasso & Rosenzweig, 1995). Nevertheless, by looking beyond immigrants' initial earnings and considering what fuels human capital investment, "hidden" economic advantages may emerge that are associated with immigrants who begin their host-country economic journey at relatively low earnings, or no earnings at all.

2. IMMIGRANT SKILL TRANSFERABILITY AND THE PROPENSITY TO INVEST IN HUMAN CAPITAL

In a stream of papers, summarized in the May 1999 issue of the *American Economic Review*, Duleep and Regets (1992a, 2002) highlight two overlooked co-variates of low-skill-transferability. One, immigrants whose home-country skills transfer poorly to the new labor market will have a lower opportunity cost of human-capital investment than natives or immigrants with high-skill-transferability. Two, home-country skills that are not fully valued in the host-country labor market are still useful for learning new skills.[5] Combined, these factors imply that low-skill-transferability immigrants will have a higher propensity to invest in human capital and will do so over a longer period than otherwise similar natives or immigrants with skills that are initially more transferable. Because immigrants will invest more in US human capital than natives, and low-skill-transferability immigrants will invest more than high-skill-transferability immigrants (holding initial human capital levels constant), immigrants will experience higher earnings growth than natives and, among immigrants, there will be an inverse relationship between entry earnings and earnings growth.[6]

Empirical observations bolster this perspective. Duleep and Regets (1999) find that adult immigrants are more likely to be enrolled in school and at older ages than natives. In a study of Canadian immigrants, Green (1999) finds higher rates of occupational change, and at older ages, for immigrants than for natives.

Duleep and Regets (1992a, 1994a, 1996a, 1996b) examine the relationship between initial earnings and earnings growth by following with the 1960 through 1990 decennial censuses various entry cohorts of immigrants, defined by age, education, and country of origin. They find a strong inverse relationship between the entry earnings of immigrants and their earnings growth across countries, and over time for the same country.[7] Across groups, the lower the entry earnings, the higher the earnings growth; over time, as entry earnings fall (rise), earnings growth increases (decreases).

Similar results emerge, for both men and women, following individual immigrants using either snippets of longitudinal survey information (Duleep & Regets, 1997b) or longitudinal earnings information as recorded in the Social Security Administration (Duleep & Dowhan, 2002a, 2000b). The top two lines of Fig. 3 show the foreign-born to US-born earnings' growth ratios for five immigrant cohorts who entered the US between 1960 and 1982.[8] One line adjusts for foreign-born/native-born differences in age and schooling by weighting the two populations to have the same age and educational distribution. The bottom two lines show the unadjusted and adjusted cohort-specific ratios of foreign-born to native-born earnings at entry. An inverse relationship is apparent: as immigrant entry earnings have decreased, immigrant earnings growth has increased. Figs. 4 and 5 track the year-to-year earnings of more recent cohorts with immigrant cohorts defined by the first evidence of earnings in the Social Security records. These figures show that regardless of where immigrants begin, their earnings converge with time in the US consistent with the prediction that low-skill-transferability immigrants invest more in human capital (hence experience higher earnings growth) than high-skill-transferability immigrants.

Other methodological approaches support the central conclusion that, adjusting for education, immigrants starting at low earnings experience faster earnings growth than immigrants starting at higher earnings. Earnings convergence occurs among immigrant groups characterized by low- and high-skill-transferability. Controlling for education, family admissions are found to be associated with lower entry earnings, relative to those admitted on the basis of occupational skills, *but higher earnings growth* (Duleep & Regets 1992a, 1996a, 1996b; Jasso & Rosenzweig, 1995; DeSilva, 1996). Following immigrant cohorts with decennial census data, Duleep and Regets (1994b) also found that, the importance of country of origin as an explanatory variable decreases and the earnings of demographically comparable immigrants from the various countries and regions of the world converge with time in the United States.

Findings of faster earnings' growth attenuate concerns about the relatively low entry earnings of recent immigrants from economically

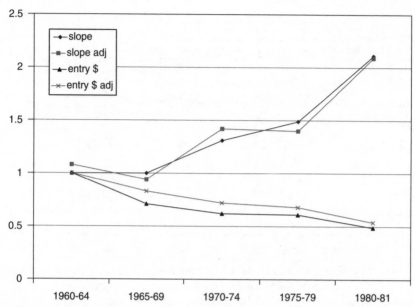

Fig. 3. Ratios of Foreign-Born to Native-Born Ten-Year Growth Rates and Entry Earnings. *Note:* Each point in the top two lines is the ratio of foreign-born to US-born 10-year earnings growth for five immigrant cohorts who entered the US between 1960 and 1982. Each point in the bottom two lines is the ratio of foreign-born to US-born entry earnings for the same five immigrant cohorts. In both the earnings growth and entry earnings series, one line adjusts for foreign-born/ native-born differences in age and schooling by weighting the two populations to have the same age and educational distribution. The estimates are based on longitudinal social security administration earnings data matched to the 1994 March current population survey (CPS). Year of immigration is defined by the CPS to which the longitudinal social security earnings data were matched.

developing countries.[9] Nevertheless, a perspective that measures immigrant economic worthiness by earnings would still conclude that immigrants lacking initially transferable skills are less beneficial to the host-country economy: with their low initial earnings, their life cycle earnings will also likely be lower than those of immigrants with initially transferable skills. Yet, the higher propensity of low-skill-transferability immigrants to invest in human capital may yield benefits to the host economy beyond immigrants' own earnings growth. These potential benefits are discussed in the following sections.

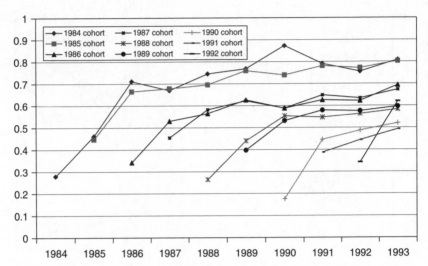

Fig. 4. Unadjusted Foreign Relative to Native-Born Annual Median Earnings. *Note:* The estimates are based on longitudinal social security administration earnings data matched to the 1994 March current population survey (CPS). Year of immigration is defined by the first evidence of earnings in the social security earnings records.

3. LOW-SKILL-TRANSFERABILITY, THE PROPENSITY TO INVEST IN HUMAN CAPITAL, AND FLEXIBILITY IN THE ECONOMY

In the original Chiswickian model, which introduced the idea of international skill transferability (Chiswick, 1978, 1979), immigrants initially earn less than natives because the skills they possess do not transfer completely to the US labor market. As English and other US-specific skills or credentials are gained, the value of the immigrant's home-country human capital is restored: the aerospace engineer, who could not get a job in aerospace engineering, or even engineering, now lands a job in his field.

With its emphasis on the low opportunity cost of human capital investment for immigrants lacking transferable skills paired with the value of home-country human capital for learning new skills, a distinguishing feature of the Duleep–Regets model is its more general conclusion that the higher incentive to invest in human capital pertains not only to US-specific human capital that restores the value of specific source-country human

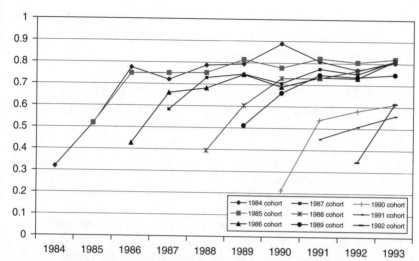

Fig. 5. Adjusted Foreign Relative to Native-Born Annual Median Earnings. *Note:* The estimates are based on longitudinal social security administration earnings data matched to the 1994 March current population survey (CPS). Year of immigration is defined by the first evidence of earnings in the social security earnings records. We adjusted for foreign-born/native-born differences in age and schooling by weighting the two populations to have the same age and educational distribution.

capital (the foreign-born aeronautical engineer who learns English so that he can pursue aeronautical engineering again), but to new human capital investment in general. When demand shifts requiring new skills to be learned, immigrants who initially lacked US-specific skills will be more likely to pursue the new opportunities than will natives or immigrants with highly transferable skills.

A native-born aerospace engineer well-launched into his career or an immigrant with highly transferable skills allowing him to immediately pursue a job in his field would be reluctant to undertake computer training or an MBA. This would be true even if the training facilitated an ultimately better paid line of work because of the lost wages that such training would incur. The low opportunity cost for a similarly educated immigrant who could not initially transfer his home-country human capital paired with the value of this undervalued human capital in producing new human capital might make pursuing further training an attractive option.

Thus, one potential benefit of immigrants lacking immediately transferable skills is a high rate of human capital investment that is not tied to restoring specific home-country skills. This gives such immigrants greater ability to adapt to changing skill needs in the economy, adding significant flexibility to the host-country economy.

4. IMMIGRANT SKILL TRANSFERABILITY, THE PROPENSITY TO INVEST IN HUMAN CAPITAL, AND INNOVATION

The labor market flexibility of immigrants who initially lack transferable skills may also encourage innovation. This insight appears by stepping through the looking glass and viewing the Duleep–Regets model from the employer's perspective.

To innovate is to introduce something new, such as a new method or product. In the US market economy, entrepreneurship is a principal route through which innovations occur. But what facilitates entrepreneurship?

In deciding whether to develop a new product or service, potential entrepreneurs examine the costs and returns of pursuing such an activity. Returns are affected by the potential demand for a new product or service. In addition to capital outlays, a crucial cost of any new venture is training the workforce that will create the new product or service. New businesses (and changes in existing businesses) require people who are willing to acquire new human capital. The extent to which this is true may be a function of how innovative the new business (or change) is. Indeed, a measure of innovativeness might be the distance between the skills needed to produce a new product or service and the existing set of skills – the greater the difference, the greater the innovation.

The cost of training employees to produce a new product or service is affected by the wage entrepreneurs have to pay employees while they are being trained and the return in terms of the value of the new human capital produced through the training. The wage entrepreneurs must pay employees while they are being trained is determined by the opportunity cost of potential employees. That is, what can they earn elsewhere? For US natives, the opportunity cost of training can be denoted as: $w \cdot H(1-\theta)$, where w is the market rate of return on a unit of human capital, H is the stock of human capital, and θ is the proportion of available time devoted to the training. The return to training can be expressed as $w \cdot f(H, \theta)$ where $f(H, \theta)$, the production of human capital, is a positive function of θ and H.

For immigrants, the opportunity cost of training can be denoted as $w \cdot \tau_M H (1-\theta)$ where τ_M denotes the proportion of source-country human capital initially valued in the labor market of the destination country. When $\tau_M < 1$, that is when immigrant skills are not fully valued in the US labor market, the opportunity cost of training is lower for immigrants than for US natives with the same level of human capital by $w \cdot H(1 - \tau_M)$.

An immigrant's initial stock of human capital may also not fully transfer to the production of new, destination-country, human capital. Language difficulties, differences in educational background, and lack of familiarity with US technologies and work processes may lower an immigrant's ability to learn new US-specific human capital relative to his or her US-born counterpart with comparable levels of previous training and education. To capture this feature, we include a transferability parameter τ_P in the production function for new human capital. The return to training for immigrants can then be expressed as $w\tau_P \cdot f(H, \theta)$.

If $\tau_M = \tau_P$, then the lower opportunity cost due to untransferred human capital to the labor market would be canceled out by a lower return to human capital due to untransferred human capital to the production of human capital. There would be no advantage to immigration in terms of training costs. However, immigrant human capital that is not valued in the labor market is still useful in producing new human capital. As long as some of the human capital that is not valued in the labor market is valuable for learning new human capital, then the training cost of immigrants lacking transferable human capital will be less than the training cost of natives or of immigrants with highly transferable human capital.

In comparing immigrants and natives with the same level of human capital, this model implies lower training costs for the immigrants. In comparing immigrants with the same level of source-country human capital, but different degrees of transferability of this human capital to the destination-country labor market, this model implies lower training costs for the immigrants with lower skill transferability. As skill transferability decreases, the opportunity cost of training falls more than does the return to training. This suggests that the immigration of low-skill-transferability immigrants would be more beneficial to the initiation of new businesses than the immigration of high-skill-transferability immigrants with similar levels of education and experience.[10]

Another implication of the above theory is that the more innovative a particular venture is, the lower the training costs of immigrants relative to US natives. To see this, return to the notion of skill transferability. Though an immigrant's initial stock of human capital might not fully transfer to the production of new, destination-country, human capital, it may also be true that the more innovative a product or service is, the greater the distance between the current set of available skills in the US native labor force and the skills that would be needed for a new firm or industry. Thus, the more innovative the venture is, the less the distance would be between τ_P for immigrants versus the US-born; the less advantage there is in applying native-born human capital to the production of the new skills. At the same time, the opportunity cost of training for natives would be unaffected. This implies that the more innovative the venture, the more helpful the availability of immigrant labor lacking transferable skills would be.

Part I describes two hypothetical causes of variation in skill transferability among immigrants originating from different countries. In one, variation in immigrant skill transferability stems from variation in what is taught and learned in other countries. In the other, variation in immigrant skill transferability stems from differences in economic opportunities between sending versus receiving countries; where the difference is small, few lacking transferable skills will choose to immigrate; the more the difference in opportunities, the greater the number of individuals lacking transferable skills who will find it worthwhile to immigrate. Of course, both scenarios are likely at work. However, the extent that the second versus the first scenario dominates has implications for the preceding models. The lower τ_M (the proportion of source-country human capital initially valued in the labor market of the destination country), the lower the opportunity cost of human capital investment, hence the higher the propensity to invest, ceteris paribus. Counterbalancing this effect is τ_P the proportion of source-country human capital that transfers to the production of destination-country human capital. The larger the τ_P is relative to τ_M, the greater the propensity to invest in new human capital for immigrants lacking transferable skills to the destination country's labor market. It is likely that the more that the second scenario is true, the larger τ_P is relative to τ_M.

In summary, the immigration of individuals lacking skills that immedi-ately transfer to the US labor market may encourage new business formation (or new directions in existing businesses) by providing a labor supply that is both willing and able to invest in new skills. An entrepreneur in an area or time period with immigrants will have a relative advantage in launching an innovation. Conditional on the level of human capital, the advantage will be greater the lower the skill transferability of immigrants and the more innovative the product. Policies that bring in immigrants lacking immediately transferable skills – such as family-based admission policies – may promote entrepreneurship and innovation by providing an infusion of undervalued, flexible human capital. Immigrants that enter to fill specific jobs, and paid accordingly, would have less of an incentive to invest in new human capital. Thus, immigrant admission programs that seek to fill specific labor market needs may be less likely to foster a flexible labor force. A caveat to this conceptual exploration is that the usefulness of immigrants lacking transferable skills to a given economy will depend upon the suppleness of an economic system – the flexibility of its wage structure and the extent to which it embraces mid-career educational and occupational changes. Without these ingredients, low-skill-transferability immigrants would not have a greater propensity to invest in human capital.

5. SKILL TRANSFERABILITY, THE PROPENSITY TO INVEST IN HUMAN CAPITAL, AND THE FAMILY

Family-based policies, as opposed to policies aimed at filling specific short-run skill needs, may also nurture human capital investment and immigrant entrepreneurship.

The research of Khandelwal (1996), Jiobu (1996), and Kim and Hurh (1996) provides case-study evidence of extended families and close-knit immigrant communities, fostered by kinship ties, supporting immigrant investment activities. Portes and Bach (1985), Waldinger (1986), Bailey (1987), and Gallo and Bailey (1996) have documented an immigrant sector in various industries characterized by mutually beneficial arrangements between recent immigrants and longer term immigrants in which recent immigrants working as unskilled laborers at low wages (or even no wages) in immigrant-run businesses are provided training and other forms of support eventually leading to more skilled positions.

The existence of close-knit communities – the development of which would be aided by the admission of immigrants on the basis of kinship – may also facilitate immigrant entrepreneurial activities (Bonacich & Modell, 1980; Kim, Hurh, & Fernandez, 1989; Light, 1972). Anecdotal and case-study evidence suggests that immigrant self-employment occurs within small concentrated pockets defined by ethnic identity and business activity. The clustering of entrepreneurial activities by ethnic group, geographic area, and detailed industry suggests that members of close-knit immigrant communities aid entrepreneurial activities. Local survey information (Waldinger, 1989; Kim & Hurh, 1996) indicates that such help comes not only in the form of financial assistance, but perhaps more importantly from the sharing of information.

To examine the relationship between admission criteria and self-employment, Duleep and Regets (1996a) used census data on individuals

Table 2. Admission Criteria and the Propensity to be Self-Employed: Correlation Coefficients (p Values in Parentheses).

Admission Criteria	Source Region		
	Asia	Central & South America[a]	Europe
Percent admitted on the basis of occupational skills	0.0050 (0.9132)	−0.0018 (0.6538)	0.0006 (0.9337)
Percent admitted as siblings of US citizens	0.1335* (0.0001)	0.0565* (0.0001)	0.0453* (0.0001)

Note: The estimates are based on the 1990 Census of Population, 5 percent and 1 percent Public Use Samples combined.
Source: Duleep and Regets (1996a).
*A p value of 0.0001 indicates that had the true correlation between the specific admission criteria and the propensity to be self-employed been 0, there would have only been a 0.0001 probability of obtaining correlation coefficients of this magnitude.
[a]Mexico is included in Central America.

matched to immigration and naturalization service (INS) data to measure the correlations between the percent of each country-of-origin/year-of-entry cohort that was self-employed and, respectively, the percent admitted via occupational skills and the percent admitted via the siblings' preference category. As shown in Table 2, there is no statistically significant correlation, for any of the regions of origin, between whether an immigrant is self-employed and the percent of his country-of-origin/year-of-immigration cohort admitted via the occupational skills criteria.[11] On the other hand, for all regions, there is a positive and highly statistically significant relationship between the propensity of individual immigrants to be self-employed and the percent of their cohort that gained admission through the siblings category.

To further probe the relationship between admission criteria and immigrant self-employment, we estimated for each region of origin the effect of the occupational skills and siblings admission criteria on the propensity to be self-employed controlling for human capital variables. The model we estimated is

$$P(\text{SelfEmp})_i = \alpha + X'\beta_1 + \beta_2\text{YSM} + \gamma_1\text{PerOcc}_{jk} + \gamma_2\text{PerSib}_{jk} + \Theta_1\text{PerOcc}_{jk} \cdot \text{YSM} + \Theta_2\text{PerSib}_{jk} \cdot \text{YSM} + \varepsilon_i$$

where $P(\text{SelfEmp})_i$ is the probability that immigrant i is self-employed, PerOcc_{jk} is the percent of immigrants in group j and cohort k who were admitted through the occupational skills preference categories, PerSib$_{jk}$ is the percent of immigrants in group j and cohort k who were admitted through the sibling-preference category, YSM is years since migration, and the vector X includes age, age squared, and seven education categories. (An eighth education category, 0–8 years, serves as the reference category.) The estimated coefficients from the logit model are shown in Table 3. [12] Once we control for education, age, and years since migration, we find that for European immigrants the percent of immigrants admitted as siblings is negatively associated and the percent admitted via occupational skills positively associated with the propensity to be self-employed, contrary

Table 3. Logistic Model of Immigrant Self-Employment (Asymptotic t-Test Statistics Are in Parentheses).

Explanatory Variables	Source Region		
	Asia	Central & South America[a]	Europe
Intercept	−7.8395 (25.17)*	−6.4335 (21.46)*	−4.4680 (10.40)*
9–11 years of schooling	0.3770 (4.86)*	0.1861 (4.12)*	0.2359 (2.26)*
12 years	0.5007 (8.13)*	0.2343 (4.82)*	0.2781 (2.98)*
Some college	0.3646 (6.02)*	0.4533 (9.31)*	0.3732 (3.97)*
Bachelor's degree	0.2384 (3.98)*	0.5239 (7.57)*	0.0865 (0.85)
Master's degree	−0.0547 (0.78)	−0.5835 (5.65)*	−0.0674 (0.63)
Professional degree	0.9565 (12.39)*	1.2590 (15.43)*	0.6987 (5.68)*
PhD	−0.6679 (6.09)*	−0.1383 (0.65)	−0.8865 (5.63)*
Age	0.2017 (13.91)*	0.1401 (9.40)*	0.0737 (3.58)*
Age^2	−0.00208 (12.84)*	−0.00137 (7.92)*	−0.0008 (3.43)*
Years since migration	0.0757 (20.74)*	0.0382 (8.84)*	0.1154 (18.73)*
Percent admitted on the basis of occupational skills	−0.4282 (1.97)*	0.0752 (0.19)	0.5854 (2.94)*
Percent admitted as siblings of US citizens	2.7850 (24.47)*	1.5436 (6.39)*	−0.9151 (4.87)*
−2 log likelihood			
Intercept only	34188.950	32601.964	15039.800
Intercept and covariates	31800.797	31701.502	14300.709
Sample size	42,723	63,038	18,724

Note: The estimates are based on the 1990 Census of Population, 5 percent and 1 percent Public Use Samples combined.
Source: Duleep and Regets (1996a).
*Statistically significant at 0.05 level assuming independent error terms.
[a]Mexico is included in Central America.

to our expectations. However, for the two largest immigrant groups, Asians and Hispanics, the percent admitted via occupational skills has either a negative effect on the propensity to be self-employed, or a statistically insignificant effect, and the siblings' effect is positive and large. In fact, the estimated effect on the propensity to be self-employed of the siblings' admission criterion exceeds that of any other variable in the analysis.[13]

6. LOW-SKILL-TRANSFERABILITY, ENCLAVES, AND THE DEVELOPMENT OF SPECIFIC KINDS OF BUSINESSES

Enclaves may provide havens for immigrants who lack the skills that would permit them to gain employment in the host country's general labor market. Empirical studies such as those of Chiswick and Miller (2002a) suggest that within groups, immigrants in enclaves have lower English proficiency than immigrants outside of enclaves.

The fact that immigrants lack skills that transfer to the economy at large may give enclave employers an advantage for developing certain types of businesses. In particular, the work performance of within-enclave employees may be more constrained than that of employees outside of the enclave.

Two factors work to increase the costs of doing substandard work and thereby reduce the performance variance of within-enclave hires. First, because of greater social cohesiveness within the ethnic enclave, than in society at large, substandard work by employees hired within the enclave is more likely to result in losing the right to work within the enclave because information on substandard work will travel to other prospective employers in the enclave. Second, the repercussions for persons hired within the enclave of doing substandard work is greater than for non-enclave members because enclave members have limited opportunities to work outside of the enclave due to poor English and other disadvantages associated with newcomer status.

As opportunities improve outside the enclave, the costs associated with doing substandard work decrease and the enforcement effect decreases. This would explain why enclave activity is most prevalent among immigrant groups and why it dwindles across generations. The more limited the outside opportunities of group members, due to low levels of US-specific skills such as English language proficiency, the smaller the performance variance of enclave hires.

Ethnic enclave entrepreneurs will thus have an advantage in developing businesses where a small variance in employee performance is crucial – where the cost of an employee performing below a certain level would be catastrophic for the firm. This would be true for small firms (the smaller the firm, the greater the share of each employee to the firm's total workforce and the more difficult it becomes for other employees to fill in for a delinquent employee), firms characterized by highly interconnected processes (the more interconnected a process is, the more damage a poor employee or a contractor can cause), and firms with low profit margins (the lower the profit margin, the more likely that a poor employee could cause the firm to go out of business).

In fact, these are the characteristics of enclave enterprises as depicted in case-study analyses. Enclave enterprises are most likely to be small businesses (Bates, 1996). They have also been documented in businesses that require highly interconnected processes or long lines of transactions. An example is the early 20th-century Japanese immigrants' development of specialty crops on marginal lands (Jiobu, 1996). Enclave hiring is also more likely to occur in businesses with low profit margins (Bates, 1996). Kim and Hurh (1996) describe Korean immigrants going into low-income minority areas to start businesses in Chicago. Bonacich and Light (1988) describe an extensive presence of Korean-owned businesses, particularly small scale retailing, in low-income Hispanic and African-American communities that is revitalizing deteriorating areas of inner-city Los Angeles. Waldinger (1986) documents extensive firm development and growth among New York City Chinese immigrants in a declining industry sector, garment manufacturing.

Via immigrant enclaves, low-skill-transferability may foster the development of businesses that would not otherwise exist, a tendency that increases the more socially cohesive the immigrant group is and the more its members lack readily transferable skills to the US labor market.

7. SKILL TRANSFERABILITY AND THE LABOR MARKET EFFECTS OF IMMIGRATION ON NATIVES

Economic theory suggests that depending on the extent to which immigrants are substitutes or complements for native-born labor, immigration may have a variety of effects on native-born employment. Ignoring potential effects of immigration on overall demand, the greater the extent to which immigrant workers are substitutes for native-born workers, the greater the potential for displacement. If low-skill-transferability fosters the development of immigrant employment that is distinct from native-born employment, then low-skill-transferability immigrants may pose less of an economic threat to natives than high-skill-transferability immigrants.

The preceding four sections suggest several ways that immigrants lacking readily transferable skills to the United States may either pursue or foster employment opportunities that are distinct from the employment opportunities of natives. When demand shifts requiring new skills to be learned, immigrants who initially lacked US-specific skills will be more likely to pursue the new opportunities than others. They may also encourage new business formation (or new directions in existing businesses) by providing a labor supply that is both willing and able to invest in new skills. Immigrants lacking readily transferable skills and enclaves composed of such immigrants may also foster the development of businesses that would not otherwise exist. In these respects, skill dissimilarity may be a virtue.

Lindsay Lowell (1996) comments: "Skill-based immigrants, in part because their admission depends on formal links to US employers ..., may enter directly into job competition with US workers ... . Conversely, the nature of the jobs that are initially filled by family-based immigrants, precisely because they are not as tightly linked to the primary labor market may mean that family-based immigrants compete less with US workers." Though empirically difficult to test, some light may be shed on the employment impact of low-skill-transferability versus high-skill-transferability immigration by comparing the impact on natives' employment of family-based versus employment-based immigration.

Using 1980 census data matched to INS data, Sorensen (1996) analyzed how the relative size of different admission-status immigrant groups in each SMSA affected the earnings and employment of native workers. Controlling for standard human-capital characteristics, such as education and years of work experience, Sorensen finds only small effects of immigration on the earnings and employment of natives when she combines all categories. Dividing by admission status, immigrants admitted because of occupational skills (employment-based immigrants) have a small but statistically significant negative effect on the employment opportunities of native-born white males. According to Sorensen, the estimated negative effect "implies that employment-related immigrants have skills that bring them into direct competition with white native males. This suggests that substantially increasing employment-related immigration may have small negative effects on the labor market opportunities (as measured by earnings and employment) of white native males." In contrast, family-preference immigrants have a statistically significant positive effect on the earnings and employment of US-born whites and on the earnings of US-born blacks.

8. SKILL TRANSFERABILITY AND PERMANENCE

Another potential correlate of low-skill-transferability is permanence. If immigrants who lack transferable skills are more likely to invest in human capital, then they will also be more likely to view the US as their permanent home: Why invest if the rewards of the investment cannot be reaped? Indeed, it would seem likely that immigrants who decide to come to the US with the idea of investing in human capital would, from the outset, be more likely to see the US as their permanent home than would immigrants coming with highly transferable skills who from the outset do not intend to invest in US-specific human capital.

In the absence of programs that bring in workers to fill specific labor market needs, immigrants from economically developing countries would tend to have lower US skill transferability than immigrants from regions of the world with US levels of economic development. The inverse relationship between skill transferability and propensity to invest in human capital suggests that immigrants from less economically developed countries would be more permanent than immigrants from countries similar to the US.

To inform this hypothesis, we used the 1980 and 1990 Census Public Use (5%) Microdata sets (PUMS) to estimate 10-year attrition rates for cohorts of immigrants which entered the US during 1975–1980, divided by age, gender, and economic development status of the source country.[14] That is, we counted the number of immigrants in the 1980 census data who reported immigration in 1975–1980 and then, using the 1990 PUMS, the number of immigrants in that cohort who were in the 1990 census. These 10-year attrition rates were adjusted by the expected 1980–1990 mortality of the cohorts: of the proportion that was missing, we subtracted the percent that we expect to have died, applying the 1998 US life tables, by sex and single year of age to the age/gender/economic development cohorts.[15] The resulting mortality-adjusted, 10-year attrition rates represent estimates of immigrant emigration (fifth column of Table 4). As predicted, the emigration rates of immigrants from economically developing countries are lower than for immigrants from economically developed countries, particularly at younger ages when the propensity to invest in human capital is greatest.

Whether well-educated immigrants stay permanently in the US or not, may have little impact on social welfare issues. On the other hand,

Table 4. Emigration Rates Over 10 Years Based on Analysis of 1980 and 1990 Census 5 Percent PUMS and National Mortality Data[a].

	1980–1990 Raw Attrition Rate [(Number of Immigrants in 1980 5 Percent PUMS)– (Number of Immigrants in 1990 5 Percent PUMS)]/ (Number of Immigrants in 1980 5 Percent PUMS)]		Ten-Year Mortality Rate from Gender and Age-Specific Mortality Applied to Individual 1980 Data		Residual Emigration Rate	
	Men	Women	Men	Women	Men	Women
Developed countries						
15–39 years old	0.3507	0.3292	0.0185	0.0089	0.3322	0.3203
40–56	0.3518	0.2590	0.0650	0.0403	0.2868	0.2186
57–69	0.4704	0.4592	0.2308	0.1568	0.2396	0.3023
Developing countries						
15–39 years old	0.0937	0.0609	0.0170	0.0080	0.0767	0.0529
40–56	0.1677	0.1062	0.0658	0.0415	0.1019	0.0646
57–69	0.3565	0.2803	0.2325	0.1534	0.1241	0.1269

[a]The mortality data are from Table 2: Life Table for Males: United States, and Table 3: Life Table for Females in Public Health Service, National Vital Statistics Report (2001).

expectations of permanence and upward mobility likely affect social behavior and the prevalence of pathologies otherwise associated with low-income individuals. The expectation of the US as a permanent home likely affects immigrants' propensity to learn English and to adopt the educational standards of US. There may also be intergenerational implications. Historically, groups that were permanently attached to the US showed greater intergenerational progress in educational attainment than groups who were less attached. Changes in permanence also brought about changes in intergenerational progress. With the closing of Southern and Eastern European immigration in 1920s, intergenerational progress increased for groups that were previously more tied to their original countries. A likely reason for this is that educational expectations are tied to the place that a group is attached to.

Those who enter without immediately transferable skills are more likely to be permanent and permanence confers beneficial aspects. Programs that seek to fill specific labor market needs are less likely to attract permanent entrants. These observations suggest that there may be hidden benefits of admission policies that attract permanent immigrants and hidden costs of policies that attract poorly educated immigrants to fill specific job needs temporarily while discouraging permanence.

9. IMMIGRANT ECONOMIC ASSIMILATION AND THE EDUCATION LEVELS OF IMMIGRANTS

In contrast to admission criteria and country of origin that appear to confer initial but not long-run advantages to immigrant economic assimilation, education confers an earnings advantage that persists over the life cycle of immigrants. Indeed, for adult immigrants younger than 40, the effect of education on earnings is most apparent in the long run. Table 5 shows the earnings ratio of immigrants with more than 12 years of schooling to those

Table 5. Earnings Ratio of High Education Immigrants to Low Education Immigrants at Entry and 10 Years Later, Immigrants 25–39 Years Old.

	1965–1970 Cohort[b,c]		1975–1980 Cohort[d,e]	
All	1.26	1.83	1.30	2.05
Central/South America[a]	1.29	1.53	1.17	1.75
Asia	1.25	2.18	1.27	1.68
Europe	1.29	1.67	1.50	1.61

Note: Estimates based on the 1970 Census of Population 1 percent State Public Use Sample based on the 5% questionnaire, the 1980 Census of Population 5 percent "A" Public Use Sample, and a 6 percent microdata sample created by combining and reweighting the 1990 Census of Population Public Use 5 percent and 1 percent Public Use samples.

Source: The ratios in this table are based on earnings estimates presented in Duleep and Regets, *The elusive concept of immigrant quality: Evidence from 1970–1990 (Revised version)*, Program for research on immigration policy. Discussion Paper no. PRIP-UI-41, Washington, DC: The Urban Institute.

[a]Mexico is included in Central America.
[b]The annual 1969 earnings, as measured by the 1970 Census, of immigrant men who entered the US between 1965 and 1970.
[c]The annual 1979 earnings, as measured by the 1980 Census, of immigrant men who entered the US between 1965 and 1970.
[d]The annual 1979 earnings, as measured by the 1980 Census, of immigrant men who entered the US between 1975 and 1980.
[e]The annual 1989 earnings, as measured by the 1990 Census, of immigrant men who entered the US between 1975 and 1980.

with 12 years or less at entry and 10 years later. For both the cohorts which entered in 1965–1969 and in 1975–1979, the beneficial effect of education on earnings increases markedly with time in the United States for immigrants from all source regions. For instance, among immigrants in the more recent cohort, the initial earnings of the more educated immigrants exceed the earnings of less educated immigrants by 30%. Ten years later, the earnings of the more educated are double those of the less educated.

The beneficial effects of education are also multifaceted. Chiswick and Miller (1996) find a strong and positive association between education and proficiency in host-country language proficiency. Their robust results lead them to note that an admissions policy that selects immigrants who are young and better educated would also select "immigrants who have, or who can be expected to acquire quickly, official language skills."

Simon and Akbari (1996) find that education is an important determinant of immigrant welfare use: holding constant other variables, halving schooling more than double the transfers received. Duleep and Sanders (1993) and Cobb-Clark (2004) find that, as with natives, education is positively associated with the propensity of immigrant women to work.

There are also interactive effects between skill transferability and education that may influence how education affects the propensity to invest in human capital.

In most human capital models, prior education or experience has an ambiguous effect upon investment decisions – increasing both the opportunity cost and the productivity of time spent in investing. In the Duleep–Regets model of immigrant human capital investment, source-country human capital that does not transfer to the destination-country labor market is still useful in gaining destination-country skills. Since low-skill-transferability reduces the opportunity cost of human capital investment more than it reduces its productivity, the lower the degree of skill transferability, the greater the likelihood that high-skill immigrants will invest more than low-skill immigrants. If natives were the special case of perfect skill transferability, we would expect education to have a more positive effect on further human capital investment for immigrants than for natives; the lower the skill transferability of immigrants, the more this would be true.

10. CONCLUSION: FOCUSING ON THE LONG TERM

Immigrants can be thought of as coming to the United States with two types of human capital: general human capital, as encompassed by years of schooling, and country-specific human capital that varies in the degree of its transferability to the US economy depending on the country of origin and admission category of the immigrant.

A compelling array of research suggests that earnings differences that stem from variations in skill transferability dissipate with time in the United States. Chiswick (1978, 1979), Duleep and Regets (1992a, 1994a, 1994b, 1996a, 1996b, 1996c, 1997a, 1997b), Jasso and Rosenzweig (1995) and others provide evidence that as immigrants live, learn, and earn in the US, the earnings of comparably educated immigrant men converge regardless of their country of origin or admission status. Furthermore, family-investment strategies may help offset the low earnings of immigrant men who initially lack skills for which there is a demand in the host-country labor market (Duleep & Sanders, 1993; Beach & Worswick, 1993; Ngo, 1994; Baker & Benjamin, 1997; Duleep, 1998). Extended families and close-knit immigrant communities nurtured by family admissions may aid the adjustment of immigrants who initially lack US-specific skills. Thus, viewed from a life cycle, family, and perhaps community/ethnic-group perspective, initial earnings differences associated with admission status or country of origin may not be of great importance.

Immigrants with low-skill-transferability, who start their US lives at low earnings, may also benefit the US economy by developing areas and businesses that would not otherwise be developed. Immigrants who initially lack transferable skills are more likely to invest in new human capital than are natives or immigrants with skills that readily transfer to the host economy. Policies that bring in immigrants lacking immediately transferable skills – such as family-based admission policies – may provide an infusion of undervalued human capital that increases the supply of flexible human capital. A flexible labor supply that is willing and able to invest in new skills may facilitate innovation and accompanying entrepreneurship. Via ethnic enclaves, low-skill-transferability immigration may foster the development of immigrant employment that is distinct from native-born employment and possibly reduce employment competition with natives. Those who enter without immediately transferable skills are more likely to be permanent and permanence promotes a variety of societal goods. For poorly educated immigrants, programs that foster long-term investment in human capital and permanence as opposed to temporarily filling labor shortages may be more likely to foster upwardly mobile immigrant communities.

In contrast to the short-lived effects of differences in skill transferability, the level of education that immigrants possess has an effect on economic assimilation that is large, persistent, and multifaceted. Moreover, the

Duleep–Regets model of immigrant human capital investment suggests a positive interactive effect between low-skill-transferability and education on the propensity to invest in human capital.

In thinking about what path US immigration policy should follow, it is instructive to examine the recent evolution of Canadian immigration policy as described in the paper by Charles Beach and Alan Green (2005).

In 1993, Canadian immigration policy evolved from a system that sought to achieve multiple objectives by giving points to prospective immigrants for a wide variety of attributes to one that simply gives points to immigrants for their level of schooling (the higher their schooling, the more the points), youthfulness, and language proficiency in English or French. Beach and Green (2005) write "... there was a major change in the point system ... away from specific occupational preferences and towards broader emphasis on educational credentials, language facility and young families ... with an eye to human capital and skill development of the host country."

An important aspect of the Canadian system's simplification was its abandonment of a policy of tailoring immigration to fill various perceived employment needs. As Beach and Green note, "... the weighting scheme [of the earlier system] ... focused on occupational needs in the economy at a particular point of time .... The occupational-based or gap-filling model used to guide admission was changed in the mid-nineties. In its place was substituted an earnings or human capital model perspective. Under this approach, specific occupational needs were reduced in the weighting scheme while additional points were awarded to education, age and language .... This shift in weights in Canada signaled a move towards a longer run view of immigration policy."

Beach and Green (2005) find that following the change, a huge increase in the educational level of Canadian immigrants occurred. Theoretically, this is what one would expect. As more objectives in an immigrant admission point system are added to the educational enhancement objective, the effectiveness of the educational enhancement objective is reduced. By dropping its emphasis on immigration as a tool for filling particular perceived labor shortages, the educational objective of the Canadian point system was enhanced. Quebec experienced less of an improvement in immigrant educational attainment than was true of the rest of Canada, perhaps reflecting a dilution of the educational objective with its greater emphasis on host-country language facility (Parent & Worswick, 2003; Beach & Green, 2005).

Policy analysts generally think of US immigration policy as serving two separate purposes. The principal goal is to unite families; a secondary goal is to meet labor market needs. Tailoring immigration to labor shortages is theoretically appealing, but difficult in practice. Admission based on kinship is often considered detrimental to the US economy but justified on humanitarian grounds. Yet, precisely because they lack specific skills that are immediately valued by the US labor market, family-based immigrants may meet labor market needs in an ongoing, flexible fashion that contributes to a vibrant economy and, at the same time, fosters permanence with its associated benefits.

As US policy makers put more emphasis on the economic effects of immigrants, an alternative route would be to focus on long-term goals. In this vein, an effective approach for the US to pursue might be to give points for both kinship ties and educational level both of which appear to have persistent economic benefits for immigrant economic assimilation and a dynamic economy.

NOTES

1. Fig. 1 shows by country of origin the 1989 median initial earnings of working-age immigrant men who entered the United States between 1985 and 1990. The 1989 median earnings estimates for the 1985–1990 cohort shown in Fig. 1 are based on a 6% microdata sample created by combining and reweighting the 1990 Census of Population Public Use 5% and 1% Public Use samples. Technical documentation may be found for the 1990 census data in Bureau of the Census (1992).

2. The 1987 per adult GDP of each source country is as a percent of the US per adult GDP. The observations in Fig. 2 on US median earnings for immigrant men and GDP per adult as a percent of US GDP per adult are for the following countries: Argentina, Australia, Bangladesh, Bolivia, Brazil, Canada, Chile, China, Colombia, Costa Rica, Czechoslovakia, Dominican Republic, Ecuador, Egypt, El Salvador, Fiji, France, West Germany, Greece, Guatemala, Guyana, Haiti, Honduras, Hong Kong, Hungary, India, Indonesia, Iran, Ireland, Israel, Italy, Jamaica, Japan, Jordan, The Republic of Korea, Laos, Malaysia, Mexico, Morocco, Myanmar, the Netherlands, New Zealand, Nicaragua, Nigeria, Pakistan, Panama, Peru, Philippines, Poland, Portugal, Romania, South Africa, Spain, Sri Lanka, Sweden, Switzerland, Syria, Taiwan, Thailand, Trinidad and Tobago, Turkey, U.S.S.R., United Kingdom, Venezuela, and Yugoslavia. All countries for which we had information on the GDP per adult were included. Median earnings for immigrant men in the 1985–1990 cohort from the aforementioned 65 countries were estimated using a 6% microdata sample created by combining and reweighting the 1990 Census of Population Public Use 5% and 1% Public Use samples. The statistics on GDP per adult as a percent of US GDP per adult are from Heston and Summers (1991).

3. When the median 1989 entry earnings of immigrant men in the 1985–1990 cohort are regressed on source-country GDP, the estimated coefficient indicates that the initial earnings of immigrant men increase $2,280 for each 10-percentage-point change in the country-of-origin GDP measure. The R^2 for this regression is 0.48.

4. The generally close link between earnings adjustment and fluency in the host-country's language is shown in various works of Chiswick and his colleagues. For example, Chiswick and Miller (2002b).

5. This concept of learning skills is akin to T. W. Schultz's (1975) concept of allocative efficiency – the ability to adjust or reallocate resources in response to changing circumstances.

6. The Duleep–Regets theoretical model is conditional on initial levels of human capital, as measured by education and age. Empirically, they find evidence of a very strong inverse relationship between initial earnings and earnings' growth conditional on education and age, as well as an unconditional relationship that generally holds up.

7. Our finding of a strong inverse relationship persists even when several methodological concerns are taken into account. In Duleep and Regets (1996a), a simple method to completely circumvent regression-to-the-mean bias in cohort analyses of entry earnings and earnings growth is introduced and used. In Duleep and Regets (1994a, 1996b), a method for testing the sensitivity of the estimated inverse relationship to the effects of emigration is introduced and applied.

8. In Fig. 3, year of immigration is defined by the CPS to which the longitudinal Social Security earnings data were matched.

9. A family response to immigration may also help offset the low earnings of immigrant men initially lacking skills specific to the US labor market. Duleep and Sanders (1993) found that the groups with the largest expected growth in immigrant men's earnings are also the groups with the highest unexplained labor force participation of married immigrant women.

10. A testable implication of this hypothesis is that immigrants, and re-entrants, are more likely to be in newer industries.

11. The p values in parentheses in the top part of Table 2 indicate statistical significance. Thus, a p value of 0.0001 on the siblings correlation coefficient of 0.1335 for Asians indicates that the probability of the true correlation being zero is <0.0001; a p value of 0.9132, as shown on the occupational-skills correlation coefficient of 0.005 for Asians, indicates that there is at least a 90% probability of measuring a correlation of that magnitude, given the absence of a correlation between occupational-skills admissions and self-employment in the population.

12. The logit model was estimated by maximum likelihood estimation.

13. A question of causality remains. Are siblings sponsored to provide a cheaper, more pliant source of labor? Does sibling migration result in self-employment or does self-employment result in sibling migration?

14. The emigration rates are from work with Dan Dowhan to inform a Social Security microsimulation model (Duleep & Dowhan, 2005).

15. The mortality data are from Table 2: Life Table for Males: United States, and Table 3: Life Table for Females in Public Health Service (2001). One could argue that we should apply race-specific mortality information to the attrition rates. As with immigrant emigration, little is known about immigrant mortality. However, recent studies, reviewed in Duleep and Dowhan (2005) hint that immigrants face lower mortality rates than their US-born racial/ethnic counterparts. For this reason, and in the absence of actual information on immigrant mortality, we chose to use the US gender- and age-specific national statistics to adjust our immigrant attrition rates for mortality.

ACKNOWLEDGMENTS

The author would like to thank Barry Chiswick, David Jaeger, Bob Lalonde, and Mark Regets for insightful comments.

REFERENCES

Baker, M., & Benjamin, D. (1997). The role of the family in immigrants' labor market activity: An evaluation of alternative explanations. *American Economic Review, 87*(4), 705–727.

Bates, T. (1996). Determinants of survival and profitability among Asian immigrant-owned small businesses. In: H. O. Duleep & P. V. Wunnava (Eds), *Immigrants and immigration policy: Individual skills, family ties, and group identities* (pp. 175–196). Greenwich, CT: JAI Press.

Bauer, T., Pereira, P. T., Vogler, M., & Zimmermann, K. F. (1998). *Portuguese migrants in the German labor market: Performance and self-selection.* Discussion Paper no. 20, IZA, Germany.

Beach, C. M., & Green, A. G. (2005). The impacts of the point system and immigrant class on skill characteristics of immigrant inflows: The experience of Canada. Paper presented at the conference on immigration: Trends, consequences and prospects for the United States, September.

Beach, C. M., & Worswick, C. (1993). Is there a double-negative effect on the earnings of immigrant women? *Canadian Public Policy, 19*(1), 36–53.

Bonacich, E., & Light, I. (1988). *Immigrant entrepreneurs: Koreans in Los Angeles 1965–1982.* Berkeley: University of California Press.

Bonacich, E., & Modell, J. (1980). *The economic basis of ethnic solidarity: Small business in the Japanese-American community.* Berkeley, CA: University of California Press.

Borjas, G. (1992). Immigration research in the 1980s: A turbulent decade. In: D. Lewin, O. S. Mitchell & P. Sherer (Eds), *Research frontiers in industrial relations and human resources* (pp. 417–446). Ithaca, NY: Industrial Relations Research Association.

Büchel, F., & Frick, J. R. (2003). *Immigrants in the UK and in West Germany – relative income position, income portfolio, and redistribution effects.* Discussion Paper no. 788, IZA, Germany.

Bureau of the Census. (1992). *Census of population and housing 1990: Public use microdata sample, U.S. technical documentation.* Washington, DC: U.S. Bureau of the Census.

Chiswick, B. R. (1978). The effect of Americanization on the earnings of foreign-born men. *Journal of Political Economy* (October), 897–922.

Chiswick, B. R. (1979). The economic progress of immigrants: Some apparently universal patterns. In: W. Fellner (Ed.), *Contemporary economic problems* (pp. 359–399). Washington, DC: American Enterprise Institute.

Chiswick, B. R., & Miller, P. W. (1996). Language and earnings among immigrants in Canada: A survey. In: H. O. Duleep & P. V. Wunnava (Eds), *Immigrants and immigration policy: Individual skills, family ties, and group identities* (pp. 39–56). Greenwich, CT: JAI Press.

Chiswick, R. B., & Miller, P. W. (2002a). *Do enclaves matter in immigrant adjustment?* Discussion Paper no. 449, IZA, Germany.

Chiswick, R. B., & Miller, P. W. (2002b). *The complementarity of language and other human capital: Immigrant earnings in Canada.* Discussion Paper no. 451, IZA, Germany.

Cobb-Clark, D. (2004). *Selection policy and the labour market outcomes of new immigrants.* Discussion Paper no. 1380, IZA, Germany.

DeSilva, A. (1996). *Earnings of immigrant classes in the early 1980's in Canada: A reexamination.* Working Paper. Human Resource Development, Canada.

Duleep, H. O. (1998). The family investment model: A formalization and review of evidence from across immigrant groups. *Gender Issues, 16*(4), 84–104.

Duleep, H. O., & Dowhan, D. (2002a). Insights from longitudinal data on the earnings growth of U.S. foreign-born men. *Demography, 39,* 485–506.

Duleep, H. O., & Dowhan, D. (2002b). *Revisiting the family investment model with longitudinal data: The earnings growth of immigrant and U.S.-born women.* Discussion Paper no. 568, IZA, Germany.

Duleep, H. O., & Dowhan, D. (2005). *Adding immigrants to microsimulation models.* Working Paper, Division of Economic Research, Social Security Administration, USA.

Duleep, H. O., & Regets, M. C. (1992a). The elusive concept of immigrant quality. Paper presented at the annual meeting of the American Economic Association.

Duleep, H. O., & Regets, M. C. (1992b). Some evidence on the effect of admission criteria on immigrant assimilation. In: B. Chiswick (Ed.), *Immigration, language and ethnic issues: Canada and the United States* (pp. 410–439). Washington DC: American Enterprise Institute.

Duleep, H. O., Regets, M. C. (1994a). *The elusive concept of immigrant quality.* Discussion Paper PRIP-UI-28. The Urban Institute, Washington, DC.

Duleep, H. O., Regets, M. C. (1994b). *Country of origin and immigrant earnings.* Discussion Paper PRIP-UI-31. The Urban Institute, Washington, DC.

Duleep, H. O., & Regets, M. C. (1996a). Family unification, siblings, and skills. In: H. Duleep & W. Phanindra (Eds), *Immigrants and immigration policy: Individual skills, family ties, and group identities.* Greenwich, CT: JAI Press.

Duleep, H. O., & Regets, M. C. (1996b). Admission criteria and immigrant earnings profiles. *International Migration Review* (Summer), 571–590.

Duleep, H. O., Regets, M. C. (1996c). Earnings convergence: Does it matter where immigrants come from or why? *Canadian Journal of Economics, 29*(April), S130–S134.

Duleep, H. O., & Regets, M. C. (1997a). The decline in immigrant entry earnings: Less transferable skills or lower ability? *Quarterly Review of Economics and Finance, 37*(Special Issue on Immigration), 189–208.

Duleep, H. O., & Regets, M. C. (1997b). Measuring immigrant wage growth using matched CPS files. *Demography, 34*(2 May), 239–249.

Duleep, H. O., & Regets, M. C. (1999). Immigrants and human capital investment. *American Economic Review* (May), 186–191.

Duleep, H. O., & Regets, M. C. (2002). *The elusive concept of immigrant quality: Evidence from 1970–1990.* Discussion Paper no. 631, IZA, Germany.

Duleep, H. O., & Sanders, S. (1993). The decision to work by married immigrant women. *Industrial and Labor Relations Review, 46*(4 July), 677–690.

Gallo, C., & Bailey, T. R. (1996). Social networks and skills-based immigration policy. In: H. Duleep & V. W. Phanindra (Eds), *Immigrants and immigration policy: Individual skills, family ties, and group identities.* Greenwich, CT: JAI Press.

Green, D. A. (1999). Immigrant occupational attainment: Assimilation and mobility over time. *Journal of Labor Economics, 17*(1 January), 49–79.

Heston, A., & Summers, R. (1991). The Penn World Table (mark 5): An expanded set of international comparisons, 1950–1988. *Quarterly Journal of Economics* (May), 327–368.

Jasso, G., & Rosenzweig, M. R. (1995). Do immigrants screened for skills do better than family-reunification immigrants? *International Migration Review, 29*(1), 85–111.

Jiobu, R. M. (1996). Explaining the ethnic effect. In: H. O. Duleep & P. V. Wunnava (Eds), *Immigrants and immigration policy: Individual skills, family ties, and group identities.* Greenwich, CT: JAI Press.

Khandelwal, M. (1996). Indian networks in the United States: Class and transnational identities. In: H. O. Duleep & P. V. Wunnava (Eds), *Immigrants and immigration policy: Individual skills, family ties, and group identities.* Greenwich, CT: JAI Press.

Kim, K. C., & Hurh, W. M. (1996). Ethnic resources utilization of Korean immigrant entrepreneurs in the Chicago minority area. In: H. Duleep & V. W. Phanindra (Eds), *Immigrants and immigration policy: Individual skills, family ties, and group identities.* Greenwich, CT: JAI Press.

Kim, K. C., Hurh, W. M., & Fernandez, M. (1989). Intra-group differences in business participation: Three Asian immigrant groups. *International Migration Review, 23*, 73–95.

Light, I. (1972). *Ethnic enterprises in America: Business and welfare among Chinese, Japanese, and Blacks.* Berkeley, CA: University of California Press.

Lindsay Lowell, B. (1996). Skilled and family-based immigration: Principles and labor markets. In: H. O. Duleep & P. V. Wunnava (Eds), *Immigrants and immigration policy: Individual skills, family ties, and group identities* (pp. 353–372). Greenwich, CT: JAI Press.

Mincer, J., & Ofek, H. (1982). Interrupted work careers: Depreciation and restoration of human capital. *Journal of Human Resources, 17*, 1–23.

Ngo, H.-Y. (1994). The economic role of immigrant wives in Hong Kong. *International Migration, 32*(3), 403–423.

Parent, D., & Worswick, C. (2003). *Qualificaitons et immigrations: Réforme de la grille d'admissions du Québec et composition de la population d'immigrants s'établessant au Québec.* Research paper prepared for the Department of Finance, Government of Québec.

Portes, A., & Bach, R. (1985). *Latin journey: Cuban and Mexican immigrants in the United States.* Berkeley, CA: University of California Press.

Public Health Service. (2001). *National vital statistics report, 48*(18).

Rivera-Batiz, F. (1996). English language proficiency, quantitative skills and the economic progress of immigrants. In: H. Duleep & V. W. Phanindra (Eds), *Immigrants and immigration policy: Individual skills, family ties, and group identities.* Greenwich, CT: JAI Press.

Schultz, T. W. (1975). The value of the ability to deal with disequilibria. *Journal of Economic Literature, 13*(3 September), 827–846.

Simon, J., & Akbari, A. (1996). Determinants of welfare payment use by immigrants and natives in the United States and Canada. In: H. O. Duleep & P. V. Wunnava (Eds), *Immigrants and immigration policy: Individual skills, family ties, and group identities* (pp. 79–102). Greenwich, CT: JAI Press.

Sorensen, E. (1996). Measuring the employment effects of immigrants with different legal statuses on native workers. In: H. Duleep & V. W. Phanindra (Eds), *Immigrants and immigration policy: Individual skills, family ties, and group identities.* Greenwich, CT: JAI Press.

Waldinger, R. (1986). *Through the eye of the needle: Immigrant enterprise in New York's garment trades.* New York, NY: New York University Press.

Waldinger, R. (1989). Structural opportunity or ethnic advantage? Immigrant business development in New York. *International Migration Review, 23*, 48–72.

MODELING IMMIGRANTS' LANGUAGE SKILLS

Barry R. Chiswick and Paul W. Miller

ABSTRACT

One in nine people between the ages of 18 and 64 in the US, and every second foreign-born person in this age bracket, speak Spanish at home. And whereas around 80 percent of adult immigrants in the US from non-English-speaking countries other than Mexico are proficient in English, only about 50 percent of adult immigrants from Mexico are proficient. The use of a language other than English at home, and proficiency in English, are both analyzed in this paper using economic models and data on adult males from the 2000 US Census. The results demonstrate the importance of immigrants' educational attainment, their age at migration, and years spent in the US to their language skills. The immigrants' mother tongue is also shown to affect their English proficiency; immigrants with a mother tongue more distant from English being less likely to be proficient. Finally, immigrants living in ethnic–linguistic enclaves have lesser proficiency in English than immigrants who live in predominately English-speaking areas of the US. The results for females are generally very similar to those for males. The findings from an ordered probit approach to estimation are similar to the findings from a binary probit model, and the conclusions drawn from the analyses mirror those in studies based on the 1980 and 1990 US Censuses. Thus, the model of

Immigration: Trends, Consequences and Prospects for the United States
Research in Labor Economics, Volume 27, 75–128
ISSN: 0147-9121/doi:10.1016/S0147-9121(07)00003-9

language skills presented appears to be remarkably robust across time and estimation techniques, and between the genders.

1. INTRODUCTION

Immigrants typically fare quite poorly in the labor market in the US and in other immigrant receiving countries in the immediate post-arrival period. Using data from the 1990 US Census, Miller and Neo (2003) show that the earnings in 1989 of adult male recent arrivals in the US were up to 28 percent below the earnings of comparable native-born workers. This disadvantage arises because of the less-than-perfect international transferability of immigrants' human capital, their lack of knowledge of the institutions of the US labor market, and perhaps through discrimination. The earnings disadvantage is temporary for most groups: Immigrants tend to rapidly catch up with the native born, and much of the empirical research into immigrant labor market outcomes has focused on the factors that enhance this adjustment process (Chiswick, 1978, 1979).

Attention has been directed at post-arrival investment in human capital in general, and destination-specific language capital in particular. Among immigrants in the US labor market, English language skills attract considerable wage premiums: Chiswick and Miller (1995) show that the earnings gain in 1989 associated with proficiency in English among adult male immigrants was approximately 17 percent, or the equivalent of around 3 years of schooling. This earnings increase is similar to that associated with dominant language proficiency in Canada, and is more than twice the increase in earnings associated with English language proficiency among immigrants in Australia. Destination language skills have been found to be important in non-English-speaking destinations, such as Germany and Israel (Chiswick & Miller, 1998). Moreover, part of immigrants' economic progress captured by duration of residence variables may be linked to improvements in their English language skills (see, for example, McManus, Gould, & Welch, 1983).

Presumably largely reflecting these rewards, the English language skills of the foreign-born in the US improve rapidly with duration of residence. Among adult male workers who had lived in the US for fewer than four years, the 1990 US Census reveals that as few as 13 percent spoke English only. A further 44 percent spoke a language other than English at home, but spoke English very well. However, fully 43 percent of this group spoke a language other than English at home and reported that they spoke English "not well" or "not at all" (Chiswick & Miller, 1996). Among those who had resided in the US for 21–30 years, however, monolingual English speakers were more prevalent (31 percent), and those with either limited or no English skills (i.e., they spoke English "not well" or "not at all") were far less prevalent (14 percent).

This paper examines the processes associated with the acquisition of English language skills among the foreign-born in the US. It has a special focus on the role that ethnic networks and linguistic distance play in the acquisition of dominant language skills, and employs alternative measures of ethnic networks to that pioneered in Chiswick and Miller (1998, 2002, 2005a). Extensions of the analysis of language practice to consider origin language retention are also presented. The paper also gives attention to females as well as to male immigrants, and consolidates a series of modifications to the language model made in various papers. Being based on data from the 2000 US Census, it permits an update of the evidence using the 1990 Census reported in Chiswick and Miller (1998, 2002, 2005a).

The structure of the paper is as follows. Section 2 outlines briefly the model of dominant language acquisition, introduced in Chiswick (1991) and Chiswick and Miller (1992), and subsequently developed in Chiswick and Miller (1995, 1998, 2005a). Section 3 outlines the dataset to be used, the US 2000 Census of Population, and presents estimates of models of dominant language proficiency for males. Estimates from Binary Probit and Ordered Probit models are considered. Similar sets of estimates for females are presented in Section 4. Section 5 contains the analyses of origin language retention among immigrants, that is, the propensity among immigrants to speak their non-English mother tongue at home. These are also presented for both males and females. Concluding comments are provided in Section 6.

2. MODEL OF DOMINANT LANGUAGE PROFICIENCY

Immigrant decision making in relation to the learning of dominant language skills can be analyzed using a human capital framework. Destination language proficiency among immigrants is a form of human capital that is productive in consumption and/or labor market activities, it is costly to acquire, in terms of time and out-of-pocket expenditures and it is embodied in the person. Thus, the optimal investment in destination language proficiency

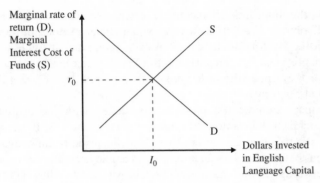

Fig. 1. Supply and Demand for Funds for Investment by Immigrants from Non-English-Speaking Countries in English Language Capital.

for immigrants is determined in the same manner as for other human capital investments: as the level of investment that will equate the marginal rate of return on the investment to the marginal interest cost of the funds they invest. This decision-making process is outlined in Fig. 1 (which is based on Becker & Chiswick, 1966) for immigrants from a non-English-speaking country.

The demand for language skills (D) is given by the marginal rate of return on the investment in these skills. The position of this curve depends on the costs of, and benefits from, the investment in language skills. The demand (or marginal return schedule) will be higher the lower are the costs and the greater are the benefits from investment in language capital. The costs of the investment include the direct costs of language classes, as well as the indirect costs of foregone earnings. The benefits from destination language acquisition include higher wages, lower chances of being unemployed, greater efficiency in consumption, and greater participation in social activities and political processes.

The demand curve is downward sloping for several reasons. First, individuals will invest first in those dimensions of language skills that have the highest payoff (marginal returns) in labor market and non-labor market activities. These are followed by less productive investments. Second, as previous investments raise the opportunity cost of time, the marginal rate of return declines even if the dollar value of the benefit is unchanged. Third, since investments take place over time, the greater the investments already made, other things the same, the fewer the time periods remaining in the future and hence the lower the return on additional investments. And, finally, as with most activities, whether investment, production or consumption, beyond some point diminishing returns set in greater the intensity of the activity. The marginal product of an hour of language learning per day will, at some point, start declining the greater the number of hours in language study.

The supply of funds for investment in language skills (S) is given by the marginal interest cost of funds. This curve will be upward sloping because immigrants will use lower-cost sources of finance (own savings, family, and friends) before they access more expensive sources. For these reasons, this curve will also be lower for those with greater access to resources, including greater wealth, for financing the investment in language capital.

The intersection of the demand-and-supply curves gives an optimal level of English language proficiency (I_0) for the immigrant.

The estimating equation to be developed below can be thought of as a reduced form equation incorporating both the supply and demand conditions for funds for investment in language capital. The actual dollar amounts invested cannot be estimated, but other variables being the same, the immigrants' level of English language proficiency can serve as a proxy for the dollars invested. The explanatory variables considered below (e.g., age at migration, educational attainment, years of residence in the US) may, for example, shift the demand curve outward or inward, resulting in higher or lower proficiency in English.[1]

For an immigrant from an English-speaking country, however, the marginal rates of return on investments in English language training are so low that no or minimal investments would be made. This is illustrated in Fig. 2, where there are no investments in post-migration English language training. Given the trivial magnitude of the investments by this group, models of English language acquisition among immigrants in English-speaking destinations have generally been applied only to non-English-speaking background immigrants.

The demand-and-supply curves will shift for a variety of reasons. The demand curve will shift to the right if an immigrant is more efficient in the production of language capital (D_1 compared to D_0 in Fig. 3). This might be associated with a higher educational attainment, or being of a younger age at the time of migration. The supply curve for an immigrant with greater wealth will be lower or to the right of that for an immigrant with relatively little wealth (S_1 compared to S_0 in Fig. 3).

Variations in English proficiency among the immigrant population will therefore be linked to factors that shift the demand-and-supply curves in Fig. 3. Chiswick and Miller (1992, 1995, 1998, 2005a) categorize these as exposure, efficiency, and economic incentive factors. Hence, destination

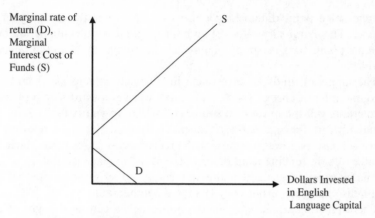

Fig. 2.   No Investment in English Language Capital.

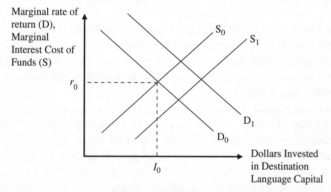

Fig. 3.   Shift in Supply and Demand for Funds for Investment by Immigrants from Non-English Language Capital.

language proficiency (LANG) can be expressed as:

$$\text{LANG} = f(\text{Exposure, Efficiency, Economic Incentives}) \qquad (1)$$

2.1. Language Measures

Three measures of language practice are used in the statistical analyses. The first is a binary measure (LANG2), which is set equal to one for individuals who speak only English at home, or if a language other than English is spoken at home, the individual speaks English either "very well" or "well".

The variable is set to zero where a language other than English is spoken at home and the respondent speaks English either "not well" or "not at all". The second measure (LANG5) is also a measure of proficiency, and it is a polychotomous (five categories) variable, defined to include all proficiency categories contained in the relevant Census variables: (i) speaks only English at home; speaks a Language other than or in addition to English at home and speaks English (ii) very well; (iii) well; (iv) not well; and (v) not at all. The third language variable (MT) is a binary variable that records whether the individual speaks a language other than English at home (MT = 1) versus speaking only English at home (MT = 0). Where a language other than English is spoken at home it is assumed, for ease of discussion, to be the individual's mother tongue. This is a measure of origin language retention.

2.2. Exposure Factors

Exposure to the destination language can occur before or after immigration. The degree of pre-immigration exposure depends, in large part, on the extent to which English is used in the origin country. This could be due to a British/US colonial past, or a major US military presence, though with advances in telecommunications and the world-wide spread of American and British media and movies, and more recently the internet, it would seem that pre-immigration exposure could become reasonably widespread. A dichotomous variable for whether the origin was a colony of the United States or the United Kingdom (COLONY) is used to capture some of these influences.

Post-immigration experience will depend on two main factors. First, there is the time unit of exposure to English. This is the extensive margin, and can be measured by the number of years since the immigrant came to the US to stay. A quadratic specification (YSM and YSMSQ) is used to allow the effect of an extra year in the United States to be larger in the early years than in subsequent years.[2] The variable assumes that the immigrant has lived continuously in the US from the time of arrival. Some immigrants, however, spend time outside the US after the initial migration. The potential effects of this sojourner migration, or to-and-fro migration, on English language skills can be assessed for those immigrants who arrived before 1995 by a dichotomous variable (ABROAD5) which is unity where the immigrant lived abroad five years ago, and is zero otherwise.

Second, there is the intensive margin, which is the intensity of exposure per unit of time. The intensity of exposure per unit of time depends on the immigrant's neighborhood and family experiences. Ethnic enclaves can be expected to play a major role in the immigrant's language skills. An immigrant who lacks English language skills can avoid having to learn English by living in an area in which many others use his or her origin language. Similarly, working in a linguistic enclave can limit the benefits from acquiring English skills. These effects can be measured by the proportion of the population of the area, regardless of nativity, that speaks the immigrant's origin language (CONC). The top 25 non-English languages spoken at home are utilized in the construction of the CONC variables. These cover about 91 percent of the sample of immigrants from non-English-speaking countries used in the analyses reported below.[3] Language rather than birthplace or ancestry is used as the defining element of an enclave on the grounds that it better measures the cultural linguistic concept developed in Chiswick and Miller (2005b). For example, the use of birthplace in the construction of this measure would encounter difficulties with bilingual (e.g., Belgium) and multilingual countries (e.g., India), and areas over which there is a common language used in many countries (e.g., Spanish in Mexico, Central America, and much of South America).

Of special interest in the work reported below is the most appropriate definition of "area" when attempting to capture these ethnic enclave effects in a model of destination language proficiency. Three alternatives are employed, and these are distinguished by the level of geographic identifiers used in their construction. The first is based on the state (50 States and the District of Columbia) of residence (CONC-STATE, which was used in earlier Chiswick and Miller research). The second is based on the Super Public Use Microdata Areas (Super-PUMAs) used in the 1 percent Public Use Microdata Sample (PUMS) of the 2000 US Census (CONC-Super).[4] All 532 separate areas are utilized for the construction of this variable. The third variable is constructed using the information on Metropolitan Statistical Areas (CONC-MSA).[5] The 106 separate regions are used in forming this measure using the 1 percent sample. In this instance, immigrants living outside metropolitan areas are assigned the value of the concentration measure constructed for the non-metropolitan components of their state of residence. The CONC variable is set equal to zero in all three definitions for those reporting a language that is not among the top 25 languages on the grounds that the density or concentration of speakers of these languages is too low to matter.

The CONC variables constructed may not capture the intended influences outside metropolitan areas. This is for several reasons, depending on the particular measure employed. First, where the CONC variable is computed at the state level, it would be expected that it would over-estimate the minority language concentration in non-metropolitan areas. Second, where the CONC variable is computed from the more disaggregated data on MSA-PMSAs, there is insufficient detail on the Census files to permit identification of non-metropolitan areas in each of the states. Accordingly, a single non-metropolitan dichotomous variable (NON-MET) is included in the estimating equation. A variable for the southern states (SOUTH) is also included to capture regional influences. An alternative specification (described below) of regional variables is used when the regression analysis is limited to those born in Mexico.

Language practice within the family will also influence the individual's dominant language proficiency. Chiswick, Lee, and Miller (2005a, 2005b) show that, due to similarities in the observed and unobserved characteristics of family members, there are links between their dominant language fluency. These factors include assortative mating, genetic and home investment linkages between parents and children, language learning in the family, migration as a family unit and systematic reporting errors within a household, as well as the similarity in the processes governing dominant language proficiency for family members. The correlations in language proficiency are stronger for spouses than for parent–offspring combinations. The similarities in the underlying factors that give rise to these outcomes would be expected to be more apparent for those married prior to immigration (where marriage is more likely to be to a spouse from the same country of birth with the same linguistic background) than for those married after immigration. Where marriage takes place after immigration, it is more likely to be to a person who is not proficient in the immigrant's mother tongue. This may encourage the use of the dominant language. Accordingly, a marital status variable (MARRIED is unity if married, spouse present) is also employed in the model. It is not possible in the 2000 Census data to distinguish between pre- and post-migration marriages.[6]

The presence of children in the household could have a range of effects on immigrants' dominant language proficiency. Four channels have been identified in the literature. The first concerns children as teachers, based on the greater ability of children to learn new languages, and the intense exposure to the destination language in schools (Long, 1990; Newport, 1990; Service & Clark, 1993).[7] The rapid learning of the dominant language among children enables them to assist the development of the dominant language skills of their parents.

The second is children as translators. As children learn the dominant language, they move into a position where they can serve as translators for their parents. This possibility lessens the need for parents to acquire dominant language skills, at least from the perspective of consumption and home production. Children are unlikely to be able to serve this function in the workplace, other than possibly having a role in the context of the self-employed. This effect is likely to be stronger for mothers than for fathers.

Third, children can affect labor supply, particularly among females. To the extent that investments in language skills are made in anticipation of labor market activity, and to the extent that the workplace provides an environment conducive to the further development of dominant language skills, reduced labor supply can dampen dominant language proficiency. This effect is also likely to be stronger for mothers than for fathers.

Fourth, where parents seek to transmit the culture of their country of origin, they may encourage the learning of their origin language among their children. Origin language use within the home may therefore compete with dominant language use, with the potential to limit the development of dominant language skills among all family members.

Thus, while the learning of dominant language skills from their children will have a positive influence on the dominant language skills of their parents, the remaining three factors will tend to dampen the incentives for parents to acquire dominant language skills. As such, the sign of the overall effect of children on parental language skills is ambiguous. The effects of children on parental language skills would be expected to differ between the mother and the father, being less positive or more negative for the mother than for the father.

2.3. Efficiency Factors

There are four important measurable efficiency factors that can influence the development of dominant language skills among immigrants: age at migration, educational attainment, refugee status, and linguistic distance.

The young appear, for biological reasons, to have a greater capacity to learn a new language than do older individuals (Long, 1990; Newport, 1990; Service & Clark, 1993).[8] Age at migration (AGE) would therefore be expected to have a negative impact on dominant language skills. The effect of age at migration is measured by the partial effect of age (AGE) when years since migration are held constant. The age variable is entered in quadratic form, Age and Age^2, in the analysis reported in the text.[9]

Similarly, educational attainment is expected to be closely related to dominant language outcomes. The better educated may have technically superior language production functions. This could arise through the better educated having greater innate learning ability or unmeasured characteristics that enhance both forms of human capital. Or it could be that having greater knowledge of one's own language enhances the ability to learn other languages. It is also possible that the destination language, particularly where it is an international language such as English, may have been learned as part of the curriculum in either secondary school or tertiary studies abroad.[10]

The difficulty in learning a second language depends in part on the person's mother tongue. The argument here can be put as follows: it should be more difficult for a Chinese speaker to learn French than it is for a Spanish speaker to learn French because the differences between the languages are that much greater. In other words, the "linguistic distance" between Chinese and French is greater than the distance between Spanish and French. The greater the linguistic distance between the destination and origin language, the lower would be the efficiency of an immigrant for learning the destination language.

This concept of linguistic distance has been developed by Chiswick and Miller (1998, 2005b). Their measure is based on the ability of Americans to learn a variety of languages in fixed periods of time. The lower the scores on a standardized proficiency test, the greater the assumed distance between these languages and English. The equivalences outlined in Table 1 of Chiswick and Miller (2005b) are used in the data analyses reported below. In the case of those who report that they speak only English at home, the mean of the linguistic distance scores of immigrants in the US from the person's country of origin was used. Fully 97 percent of the sample has valid data for this measure. The remaining individuals are assigned the sample mean (their exclusion from the analyses yields similar results).

Linguistic distance may also be related to the degree of self-selection in immigration. Individuals with a mother tongue more distant from English, perceiving greater difficulty learning English, may only migrate if they have relatively high levels of unobservables that are related to the ability to learn English, and with immigrant adjustment in general.

Admission criteria may be relevant for understanding immigrant adjustment (see Chiswick, Lee, & Miller, 2006). Unfortunately, the US Census does not provide information on the visa used at entry, or the current visa status, other than whether the immigrant has become a naturalized citizen. Yet, research suggests that refugees experience a different adjustment than family or economic immigrants. Refugee status may impact on dominant language skills because refugees tend to be less favorably selected for a successful adjustment in the destination than are economic migrants. The less-intense selection arises because of the greater importance of factors in the migration

BARRY R. CHISWICK AND PAUL W. MILLER

Table 1. Probit Estimates of Language Models, Adult Foreign-Born Men by Origin, 2000.

Variables	Total Sample		Immigrants from All Countries Except Mexico	Immigrants from Mexico
	Probit	Ordered probit	Probit	Probit
Constant	−0.584	0.882	0.293	−0.920
	(6.31)	(13.43)	(2.21)	(6.07)
Education	0.107	0.084	0.122	0.082
	(88.89)	(95.84)	(68.18)	(47.48)
	[0.032]		[0.024]	[0.033]
Age at migration	−0.008	−0.008	−0.044	−0.001
	(1.84)	(2.62)	(7.16)	(0.09)
	[−0.010]		[−0.010]	[−0.009]
Age at migration Squared/100	−0.025	−0.021	0.009	−0.028
	(4.83)	(5.94)	(1.30)	(3.36)
	[−0.010]		[−0.010]	[−0.009]
Years since migration (YSM)	0.073	0.053	0.080	0.071
	(43.83)	(48.54)	(34.92)	(28.00)
	[0.020]		[0.017]	[0.022]
YSM Squared/100	−0.052	−0.017	−0.063	−0.054
	(12.09)	(6.46)	(10.75)	(8.46)
	[0.020]		[0.017]	[0.022]
Abroad 5 years ago	−0.358	−0.242	−0.415	−0.293
	(10.80)	(9.80)	(8.65)	(6.43)
	[−0.121]		[−0.102]	[−0.116]
Married	0.143	0.074	0.120	0.172
	(11.61)	(8.46)	(6.81)	(9.90)
	[0.044]		[0.024]	[0.069]
With own children under 6 years only	−0.055	−0.082	−0.024	−0.037
	(3.09)	(6.57)	(0.91)	(1.45)
	[−0.017]		[−0.005]	[−0.015]
With own children 6 to 17 years only	−0.066	−0.076	−0.062	−0.027
	(4.60)	(7.62)	(3.15)	(1.27)
	[−0.020]		[−0.013]	[−0.011]
With own children under 6 years and 6–17 years	−0.093	−0.112	−0.022	−0.074
	(5.55)	(9.27)	(0.85)	(3.30)
	[−0.029]		[−0.005]	[−0.030]
Non metropolitan	0.053	0.024	0.301	0.090
	(1.09)	(0.67)	(2.63)	(1.68)
	[0.016]		[0.050]	[0.036]
SOUTH	0.072	0.068	0.103	0.002
	(6.04)	(8.15)	(5.89)	(0.14)
	[0.021]		[0.020]	[0.001]
	0.258	0.243	0.227	−0.153

Table 1. (*Continued*)

Variables	Total Sample		Immigrants from All Countries Except Mexico	Immigrants from Mexico
	Probit	Ordered probit	Probit	Probit
Miles ('000) from origin	(19.11) [0.029]	(26.82)	(13.73) [0.016]	(1.25) [−0.030]
Miles ('000) from origin Squared	−0.022 (14.85) [0.029]	−0.027 (27.62)	−0.021 (12.62) [0.016]	0.038 (0.74) [−0.030]
Linguistic distance	−1.305 (25.03) [−0.395]	−0.943 (26.61)	−1.396 (25.88) [−0.278]	(a)
Minority language Concentration CONC-STATE	−0.014 (18.75) [−0.004]	−0.016 (29.45)	−0.013 (9.42) [−0.003]	−0.010 (6.24) [−0.004]
Colony	0.800 (30.21) [0.189]	0.591 (42.69)	0.797 (28.81) [0.123]	(a)
Refugee	−0.236 (9.31) [−0.077]	−0.072 (3.85)	−0.236 (8.87) [−0.053]	(a)
μ_1	(a)	1.082 (224.10)	(a)	(a)
μ_2	(a)	1.982 (410.08)	(a)	(a)
μ_3	(a)	3.369 (475.70)	(a)	(a)
χ^2	30226.76	37258.38	16965.45	6217.43
Prediction success rate	77.95	46.17	84.10	67.99
Sample size	85865	85865	54001	31864

Note: Figures in parentheses are 't' statistics, and the figures in square brackets for the binary probit models are partial effects, with effects for variables entered into the model in quadratic form being evaluated at the mean and listed for both terms of the quadratic; (a) Variable not relevant.

Source: US Census of Population, 2000, Public Use Microdata Sample, 1 Percent Sample.

decision other than the expectation of economic success. Also, refugees often have less time to prepare for the move. The refugee variable (REFUGEE) is based on country of birth, period of immigration, and age at migration. The latter criterion permits refugee status to influence dominant language outcomes only where the person entered the US as an adult.[11] A variable for US citizenship is not included since a degree of proficiency in English is generally required to become a naturalized citizen.

2.4. Economic Factors

Economic incentives for dominant language proficiency are central to the model outlined above. However, finding empirical counterparts to this set of factors is difficult. Only variables that broadly correspond to the underlying influences can be considered. Hence, from the theoretical perspective, it is desirable to include the expected increments in earnings for each individual in the empirical applications. While this is not possible, it is known that there are strong links between educational attainment and the economic returns from becoming proficient in the dominant language, and this suggests that the individual's level of education (EDUC) may serve as a proxy for the expected economic returns for the investment in dominant language skills.

The incentive for an immigrant to acquire English proficiency will be greater the longer the expected duration in the US, as this will be associated with greater returns from any given investment. It is expected that the degree of return migration and the degree of favorable self-selection in immigration will vary with the distance of the origin country from the US. Greater geographic distance implies a higher cost of migration and of return migration. This should deter the less able and be associated with better dominant language skills among those who do immigrate. It also implies a lower propensity for return migration which should also be associated with greater proficiency in English. This distance effect is captured through a variable for the number of thousands of miles (MILES) from the major city in the origin country to New York, Miami or Los Angeles, whichever is the shorter. A quadratic specification is used.

When the analysis is limited to immigrants from Mexico, the geographic distance variable is computed with reference to the capital of their state of residence, and three cities in Mexico, namely Mexico City, Tijuana, and Ciudaf Juarez. Two alternative continuous measures were considered, namely the distance between Mexico City and the capital of the immigrant's current state of residence, and the minimum of the direct-line distance between the capital of their current state of residence and either Tijuana or Ciudaf Juarez. The latter measure is used in the statistical analyses reported below as it yielded slightly stronger results. Moreover, in the analysis limited to immigrants from Mexico, an alternative measure of the regional variable for the US is employed. Further comment on these is provided below.

Hence, the empirical counterpart to Eq. (1) that is the basis for the analysis that follows is:

$$
\begin{aligned}
\text{LANG} = f(&\text{Educational Attainment, Age at Migration, Age at Migration} \\
&\text{Squared, YSM, YSMSQ, ABROAD5, MARRIED, Children,} \\
&\text{NON-MET, SOUTH, MILES, MILESQ, Linguistic Distance,} \\
&\text{CONC, COLONY, REFUGEE})
\end{aligned}
\tag{2}
$$

Following Chiswick and Miller (2001), the estimating equation includes five variables based partly on country of birth, namely the proportion of individuals living in the same region as the immigrant who speaks his home language (CONC), whether the person is a refugee (REFUGEE), whether the origin is a former British or American colony (COLONY), linguistic distance, and miles of the country of origin from the US (MILES).[12] Unlike dichotomous variables for country of birth, these variables have behavioral interpretations, and they provide for greater understanding of the factors affecting language practice among immigrants. Chiswick and Miller (2001) show that the behavioral variables based on birthplace provide almost as much explanatory power as the birthplace dummy variables. Accordingly, birthplace fixed effects are not included in the model.

The data for the estimations presented below are from the 2000 Census of Population, PUMS, and are for the 1 percent sample of the foreign-born adult (25–64 year old) men and women from non-English-speaking countries.[13] This age bracket is the group of immigrants for whom the issues surrounding language choice are most acute. Separate analyses are conducted for men and women, and the extent to which this is necessary is examined. The analyses are performed overall and separately for immigrants from Mexico and all other countries. Mexico is the largest single source country, providing over one-third of the men and women in the sample. Moreover, Mexican migrants have much lower levels of skills (among adult males they have 8 years of schooling compared to 13 years for other immigrants) and a much greater proportion of illegal aliens than migrants from other countries. They may be of special interest for these reasons. Moreover, Mexico and Canada are the only countries sharing a land border with the United States. The variables are defined in detail, and the means and standard deviations are reported, in Appendix A.

3. ESTIMATES: MALE IMMIGRANTS

Table 1 reports the basic regression analyses for foreign-born men. The first column of this table lists estimates of a probit model examining variations in the summary measure of English proficiency given by the binary variable LANG2 described above. Three figures are reported in each cell for the binary probit models. The first is the estimated coefficient for the probit index; the second the associated 't' statistic; and the third the marginal effect of the variable on the probability of being proficient in English. As there are multiple marginal effects with the ordered probit model (one for each of the language categories), only the estimated coefficient for the probit index and the 't' statistic are presented in Table 1, column (ii).

The probit model estimates in Table 1, column (i) are consistent with the results reported in previous studies using the 1990 Census (see, for example, Chiswick & Miller, 2005a). English proficiency increases with years of schooling, with the partial effect of an additional year of education being an improvement of 3.2 percentage points in the predicted probability of being proficient in English.[14] In comparison, English proficiency decreases at an increasing rate with age at migration. That is, the older an immigrant is at the time of entry into the US the less likely he is to become proficient in English, and this effect gets stronger with age. This is a reflection of the phenomenon established in the linguistics literature of language skills being more difficult to acquire for older than for younger individuals. Separate analyses (Chiswick & Miller, 2006) indicate that the pattern of age effects established in Table 1 carries across to an alternative specification of the estimating equation based on year-specific dichotomous variables for age at migration.

The immigrant adjustment process summarized in the years since migration variable is a strong influence on English proficiency. According to the estimates, English proficiency improves at a decreasing rate with duration of residence in the US.[15] This improvement is observed for all durations in the US. In the first few years after arrival, the improvement in English proficiency is about 2.5 percentage points per year. At 10 years of residence, English proficiency improves by close to 2 percentage points per year. Even at 20 years there is improvement in the rate of English proficiency of around 1.8 percentage points per year of residence in the US. The relationship between English language proficiency and years in the US is portrayed in Fig. 4. The profiles in this figure have been calibrated so that each one passes through the mean rate of English proficiency for the particular group when that group's duration of residence is equal to the group-specific mean.

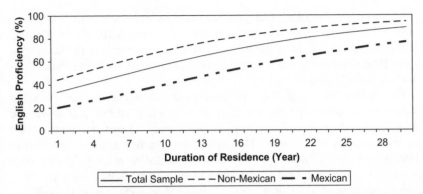

Fig. 4. Predicted English Proficiency by Duration of Residence in the US, Adult Foreign-Born Men by Origin, 2000 US Census. *Source:* Author' Calculations Based on Table 1.

Table 2. Partial Effect of Years since Migration on English Proficiency, Adult Foreign-Born Men by Origin, 1980, 1990, and 2000.

Years Since Migration	1980		1990		2000	
	Non-english-speaking countries	Mexico	Non-english-speaking countries	Mexico	Non-english-speaking countries	Mexico
5	1.62	2.15	1.95	2.50	2.41	2.61
10	1.34	1.80	1.70	2.20	2.23	2.39
15	1.06	1.45	1.45	1.90	2.05	2.18
20	0.78	1.10	1.20	1.60	1.86	1.96
25	0.50	0.75	0.95	1.30	1.68	1.74

Source: 1980: Chiswick and Miller (1992); 1990: Chiswick and Miller (1998); 2000: This paper, Table 1.

Analyses performed for the 1980 Census and the 1990 Census (Chiswick & Miller, 1992, 1998) show a similar pattern of a steeper rise in proficiency rates in the early years after immigration, with the rate of increase diminishing with duration. Selected partial effects of years since migration on English proficiency for male immigrants aged 25–64 years from non-English-speaking countries and for those from Mexico are listed in Table 2. Across each year of data, the effect of years since migration is stronger for immigrants from Mexico. The effects of years since migration also get stronger across cohorts. That the increase in proficiency with duration repeats itself in successive censuses suggests that it is reflecting a longitudinal phenomenon, rather than merely a decline in the linguistic proficiency of more recent cohorts or selective emigration of the least proficient immigrants in each arrival cohort.

Just as the length of time an immigrant has spent in the US has a pronounced positive impact on English proficiency, spending time abroad after immigration diminishes English proficiency. Hence immigrants who came to the US to stay more than five years ago but who lived abroad in 1995 have a rate of English proficiency around 12 percentage points less than otherwise similar immigrants who were living in the US five years ago. This impact is the equivalent of the improvement that comes about through the first four years of residence in the US (see Fig. 4). The intermittent nature of the stay among sojourners, and perhaps the expectation of a relatively short future stay in the US among them, should be viewed as a major negative influence on immigrants' English language skills.

Immigrants who are married have a rate of English proficiency that is 4 percentage points above that of their non-married counterparts. As noted above, while it is desirable when modeling dominant language proficiency to be able to distinguish between marriage prior to migration (expected negative effect on dominant language skills) and marriage after migration (expected positive effect on dominant language skills where the marriage is to a dominant language speaker), this cannot be done with the 2000 Census data. The positive coefficient of the marriage variable on the rate of dominant language proficiency shows that the positive factors dominate.

Children are associated with a slight reduction in the English language skills of their fathers. Where the family has only a child (or children) under 6 years of age, or where it has only a child (or children) 6–17 years of age, the rate of English proficiency is reduced by 1.7–2.0 percentage points, respectively, compared to having no children. This is the same magnitude of impact that would be associated with a reduction in educational attainment of around two-thirds of one year. In each of these cases there may be one or more children in the family, though only child families cannot be distinguished from multiple child cases. However, where the family has children under 6 years and between 6 and 17 years (i.e., there are at least two children present), the English proficiency of the adult males is reduced by 2.9 percentage points, an effect that is equivalent to a reduction of about one year of education.

Residence in the southern states is also shown to be associated with greater rates of English proficiency. The small positive influence of living in the

South is similar to the effect recorded in Chiswick and Miller (2005a). As is apparent from the results presented in Table 1, columns (iii) and (iv), this finding only holds for immigrants from source countries other than Mexico.

Five additional variables with behavioral interpretations that are constructed using birthplace information are included in the model – the miles of the origin country from the US, linguistic distance, minority language concentration, and the colony and refugee variables. While the two language-related variables are constructed using information on the language other than English that is spoken in the immigrant's home, birthplace is also used to assign values for English-only speakers. The results show that English language skills improve with miles from the origin country, up to around 6,000 miles. The changes in English skills with miles from the origin country beyond this point to the maximum observed in the data (Indonesia, 8,985 miles) are relatively minor. Fig. 5 portrays this relationship. To assist reading the figure, a number of source countries are identified on the graph. As with Fig. 4, the diagram has been calibrated so that the predicted relationship passes through the mean rate of English proficiency when the miles from the origin are at the sample mean (3,672 miles).

As argued when providing the conceptual background for the model of dominant language skills, the further the country of origin from the US the more intense the self-selection in migration and the less likely is the return migration – both of which should be associated with higher rates of English language proficiency. This is exactly the relationship depicted in Fig. 5.

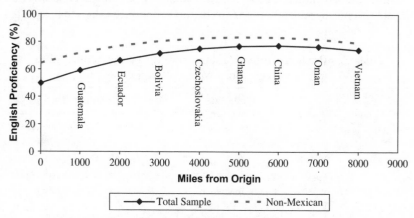

Fig. 5. Predicted English Proficiency by Miles of Origin Country from the US, Adult Foreign-Born Men by Origin, 2000 US Census. *Source:* Authors' Calculations Based on Table 1.

The language scores that form the basis for the linguistic distance measure range in value from 1.0 (Korean) to 3.0 (Swedish, Norwegian – see Table 1 of Chiswick & Miller, 2005b). The measure of linguistic distance included in the model is the reciprocal of these language scores. The variable in the model will range from 0.3 to 1.0, with a value of 1 indicating a home language quite far from English and 0.3 indicating a value close to English.[16]

The linguistic distance measure has a marked influence on English language proficiency. There is a potential difference of 0.66 in the linguistic distance measure, and this is associated with a difference of −0.861 in the probit index – an impact that is the equivalent of 8.1 years of education. In other words, the linguistic distance measure has a major impact on English proficiency. The predictions in Table 3 highlight this further.

The minority language concentration variable in this first set of results is formed using state-level data (CONC-STATE). The results indicate that living in an area with a high representation of others who speak the same home language has a negative impact on an immigrant's English language proficiency. The minority language concentration variable ranges in value from 0 to 30 (percent), and so the variable, with a coefficient of −0.014 is associated with a change of up to 0.42 in the probit index. This is the equivalent of the impact on the probit index of four years of education. While this effect is far less than that associated with the linguistic distance measure, it is quite a pronounced effect, particularly considering that it is a neighborhood characteristic rather than an individual characteristic.

While the estimated impact of the minority language concentration variable is considerable, it appears to be less pronounced than that reported

Table 3. Predicted English Fluency by Linguistic Score, Adult Foreign-Born Men by Origin.

Linguistic Score	Linguistic Distance	Illustrative Languages	Predicted English Proficiency (%)	
			Total sample	Excluding immigrants from Mexico
1.0	1.00	Korean, Japanese	44.01	57.65
1.5	0.67	Vietnamese, Arabic	61.20	74.49
2.0	0.50	Polish, Indonesia	69.22	81.36
2.5	0.40	Portuguese, Italian	73.65	84.87
3.0	0.33	Norwegian, Swedish	76.41	86.95

Note: All other variables evaluated at their means.
Source: Authors' calculations based on Table 1.

in the research based on the 1990 Census by Chiswick and Miller (2005a). Chiswick and Miller (2005a) estimate only a model that included birthplace fixed effects. Hence, to facilitate comparisons, a similar specification was estimated using the 2000 Census data. The estimated coefficient in this instance was −0.006. Comparison of this estimate with that presented in Chiswick and Miller (2005a) needs to be sensitive to the changes between the 1990 and 2000 Censuses in both the rate of proficiency and the mean of the measure of minority language concentration. Hence, an elasticity is computed. The elasticity of English language proficiency with respect to the minority language concentration was 4.3 using the 1990 US Census (Chiswick & Miller, 2005a) and 3.0 using the 2000 US Census. Estimation of the model in Table 1 stratified by age and period of residence suggested the effect of a minority language concentration was greater (by about 15 percent) among those aged 35–64 years than among 25–34 year olds, and also among those resident in the US for 10 or more years (by about 45 percent) than for those who have resided in the US for less than 10 years. This suggests there has been a dilution of the negative impact of minority language concentration on English language proficiency among the more recent immigrants.

The final sets of variables in Table 1 record the influence on English language skills of being from a former British or US colony, or being a refugee. Coming from a former US/British colony is associated with higher rates of English proficiency, with the marginal effect being a substantial 19 percentage points.[17] Being classified as a refugee is associated with poorer English skills, the marginal effect being −8 percentage points. This is the equivalent of over two years of schooling.

Separate models were estimated in Table 1 for adult male immigrants from Mexico (column (iv)) and for all immigrants other than those from Mexico (column (iii)). For these disaggregated analyses, the estimating equations are modified as follows. First, for immigrants from Mexico the COLONY, REFUGEE, and Linguistic Distance variables are not relevant.[18] Second, as noted above, the model for immigrants uses geographic distance variables defined with reference to the state of residence and Mexico City, Tijuana and Ciudaf Juarez. An alternative that was considered involved the use of dichotomous variables for US states that are near Mexico. Four groups are considered: California (benchmark); Texas; Arizona, New Mexico, Nevada; and Rest of the US. Neither the geographic distance nor the state dichotomous variables have much explanatory power when the sample is confined just to immigrants from Mexico. The estimates presented are based on a geographic distance variable defined as the minimum of the distance between the capital of the immigrant's current state of residence and either Tijuana or Ciudaf Juarez, whichever is shorter. While the distance variables are insignificant, they are included for consistency with the other model specifications.

The estimates show that the effects discussed above are reasonably robust with respect to this disaggregation of the data between Mexico and all other countries. There are two exceptions though. First, the effects of age at migration on English proficiency follow different patterns, though in each instance the partial effect of age is negative across all relevant age groups. For immigrants other than those from Mexico, the linear age term is negative and the squared term positive. Both are statistically significant. The partial effect on English proficiency is around −1.04 percentage points at 40 years of age. For immigrants from Mexico, however, only the square of age is statistically significant. The partial effect of age on English proficiency for this group at 40 years of age is −0.92 percentage points, only marginally less than for the non-Mexican immigrants. With the estimated pattern of effects, however, it is apparent that migrating at an older age has a relatively larger negative effect on the English proficiency of immigrants from Mexico compared to the effect for other immigrants. This pattern is illustrated in Fig. 6.

The second difference between the results for immigrants from Mexico and all other immigrants is in the influence of children on the English skills of their fathers. While the effects of children on their father's English proficiency are always negative, these effects are much weaker in the

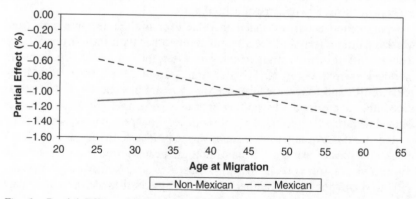

Fig. 6. Partial Effect of Age at Migration on English Proficiency among Adult Foreign-Born Men, by Origin, 2000 US Census. *Source:* Authors' Calculations Based on Table 1.

disaggregated analysis, with the effect of the variable for living with children under 6 and 6–17 years being significant only for immigrants from Mexico. Among other immigrants the negative effect of children is significant only for the group of fathers with children only in the 6–17 age category. Note, however, that, taken as a set the children variables are negative and statistically significant in both the Mexican and other analyses in Table 1.

Table 1, column (ii) lists results from the estimation of an ordered probit model with the full range of data on immigrants' language skills recorded in the LANG5 measure discussed above. The main feature of these results is that the estimated effects on the underlying ordered probit index are very much the same as for the index function in the binary probit model.

The effects of variables in the ordered probit model are difficult to assess, as the sign of a coefficient indicates unambiguously only the direction of the effect on the highest and lowest English proficiency groups. Accordingly, to illustrate the variation in membership of the five language categories distinguished in the LANG5 variable, predicted probabilities of being in a language category can be computed for the regressors included in the estimating equation. Sets of prediction are presented in Table 4 for education and duration of residence. These predictions have been computed using the mean values of all variables in the estimating equation other than for the specific variable that is the focus of the panels in the table.

The data in Panel A of Table 4 show that increases in the level of education are associated with marked shifts away from the "not at all" and "not well" categories to the "very well" and "only English" categories. For education levels above the mean, there is also a shift away from the "well" category with more schooling. Comparison of the predicted distributions at 8 and 20 years of schooling shows that the change in proficiency, as measured by the binary scale adopted above, from 64 to 91 percent is also associated with quite pronounced shifts within the two groups "not proficient" and "proficient".

The predictions in Table 4, Panel B, for duration of residence, show a similar trend towards improvement in English skills with length of time in the US. Comparison of the two extreme duration of residence levels represented in Table 4 indicates that the improvements in English skills with duration of residence are more pronounced than those associated with educational attainment.

In each case illustrated in Table 4, and in general, it is seen that the marked improvements in English proficiency associated with particular characteristics, such as educational attainment, duration of residence in the US and a younger age at migration, do not result in major changes in the proportion of

Table 4.   Predicted Distribution across Language Proficiency Categories
by Level of Education and Duration of Residence, Adult Foreign-Born
Men, 2000.

	Speaks Language Other than English at Home				Speaks Only English	Total
	Not at all	Not well	Well	Very well		
A. *Level of education*						
8	7.51	28.54	34.61	26.67	2.68	100.00
10	5.41	24.57	34.66	31.47	3.90	100.00
12	3.80	20.62	33.80	36.24	5.54	100.00
14	2.60	16.87	32.12	40.73	7.68	100.00
16	1.74	13.44	29.72	44.69	10.40	100.00
18	1.14	10.44	26.79	47.87	13.76	100.00
20	0.72	7.91	23.52	50.06	17.79	100.00
B. *Duration of residence*						
1	15.81	37.35	30.48	15.46	0.90	100.00
5	11.34	33.61	33.09	20.42	1.54	100.00
10	7.23	28.07	34.66	27.24	2.81	100.00
15	4.45	22.34	34.29	34.17	4.76	100.00
20	2.65	17.03	32.21	40.54	7.57	100.00
25	1.54	12.50	28.89	45.74	11.34	100.00
30	0.87	8.88	24.88	49.30	16.07	100.00

Note: Rows may not sum to 100.00 due to rounding. All other variables are evaluated at their means.
Source: Authors' calculations based on Table 1.

immigrants becoming monolingual English speakers at home. Rather, there is an extremely strong tendency for the mother tongue to be retained, so that most of the improvement in English proficiency is associated with increased representation in the category "speaks a language other than English at home and speaks English very well". This phenomenon of mother tongue retention is analyzed in Section 5.

Finally, each of the thresholds (μ's) in the ordered probit model is highly significant, indicating that the language categories coded in the Census are distinct, and as such analysis using an ordered polychotomous probit model may offer advantages over a study using the binary probit model. The similarity of the findings with the two approaches, and Kominski's (1989) caution that there is an absence of a clear differentiation between each of the four levels of English-speaking ability used in the US Census, suggests that the binary and polychotomous approaches to modeling English language proficiency offer similar findings.

Among the many strong influences on immigrants' English proficiency documented above, one that is of particular interest is associated with the minority language concentration variable. This variable captures an influence on English language skills of the "neighborhood" in which the immigrant lives. It was argued that living among others with whom the immigrant has a non-English language in common raises the cost of learning English and lowers the benefit from becoming proficient in English.

In the analysis reported in Table 1, the minority language concentration variable was constructed using state-level data. Two alternative geographic units are available for use in the construction of this variable: the Super-PUMAs (CONC-Super) and the CONC-MSA. As discussed above, over 500 separate areas are identified with the Super-PUMA data, and over 100 with the MSA data, representing, respectively, a 10-fold increase and a doubling of the number of separate geographic entities compared to the state-level data. This more refined information may be important to use where the effect on English language proficiency of the neighborhood is more local than captured by the state-level aggregates.

Table 5 presents the coefficients for the alternative minority language concentration variables for the series of models presented in Table 1. There are two broad features of the results summarized in this Table. First, the impact of a minority language concentration on English language proficiency tends to be weaker when estimated with more disaggregated data

Table 5. Estimates of Minority Language Concentration Variables, Language Models for Adult Foreign-Born Men by Origin, 2000.

Minority Language Concentration Variable: (Number of Areas)	Total Sample		Immigrants from All Countries Except Mexico	Immigrants from Mexico
	Probit	Ordered probit	Probit	Probit
State data (51)	-0.0138 (18.75) [-0.0042]	-0.0163 (29.45)	-0.0135 (9.42) [-0.0027]	-0.0096 (6.24) [-0.0038]
MSA (106)	-0.0079 (18.57) [-0.0024]	-0.0116 (36.04)	-0.0086 (12.78) [-0.0017]	-0.0079 (10.57) [-0.0032]
Super PUMA (532)	-0.0060 (17.88) [-0.0018]	-0.0071 (27.79)	-0.0084 (14.43) [-0.0017]	-0.0041 (9.16) [-0.0016]

Note: For notes to table, see Table 1.

than when state-level data are used, though the differences in the estimates do not affect in any way the overall interpretation that can be attached to this concentration or enclave effect. Second, the effects of a minority language concentration obtained with the more disaggregated data, reflecting the greater variability in the explanatory variable, appear to be estimated more precisely in the analyses disaggregated by birthplace region. With 't' values of six or more with the state-level data, however, obtaining even greater precision in estimation is not a major consideration. While it is not obvious which level of aggregation among the three is the "best" from an analytical point of view, and while it is not obvious which is the "best" from a measurement perspective (measurement errors), they all point to the negative association of ethnic/linguistic enclaves and immigrants' English language proficiency.[19]

4. ESTIMATES: FEMALE IMMIGRANTS

Tests were conducted as to whether the data for males and females could be pooled and the effects on English proficiency represented by a single set of parameters common to both males and females. In each case, the hypothesis of a common set of parameters was rejected. Table 6 presents estimates of the models of English language proficiency for females.[20] In cases where the estimated effects of a variable for females and males differ significantly, these are denoted by an asterisk against the estimated impact for females. These tests of statistical significance are based on equations estimated on a pooled sample of males and females with a full set of interaction terms for females.

In general, the direction of impact given by the estimated coefficients for female immigrants are the same as those established for males. For most variables, the magnitudes of the estimated effects for females are of the same order as the estimated effects for males. Where significant differences arise, the differences (with the exception of the miles from the origin country variable) are small, though interesting. Five main differences arise.

First, educational attainment is shown to have a slightly stronger (more positive) effect on the English skills of female immigrants than it has on the English skills of male immigrants. The differences in the partial effects, however, are all less than 1 percentage point. Educational attainment is included in the language model on the ground that it will capture efficiency factors. An implication of the current finding, therefore, is that these efficiency factors are more closely related to educational attainment in the

Table 6. Probit Estimates of Language Models, Adult Foreign-Born Women by Origin, 2000.

Variables	Total Sample		Immigrants from All Countries Except Mexico	Immigrants from Mexico
	Probit	Ordered probit	Probit	Probit
Constant	−0.694	0.893	−0.096	−0.298
	(7.24)	(13.26)	(0.75)	(1.74)
Education	0.114*	0.084	0.126*	0.086
	(89.64)	(91.97)	(72.51)	(43.41)
	[0.037]		[0.030]	[0.034]
Age at migration	−0.006	−0.011	−0.032	−0.009
	(1.30)	(3.35)	(5.52)	(1.16)
	[−0.011]		[−0.011]	[−0.009]
Age at migration Squared/100	−0.029	−0.017	−0.006	−0.016
	(5.53)	(4.74)	(0.90)	(1.81)
	[−0.011]		[−0.011]	[−0.009]
Years since migration (YSM)	0.073	0.054	0.086*	0.060*
	(43.19)	(49.44)	(39.48)	(21.60)
	[0.022]		[0.020]	[0.021]
YSM Squared/100	−0.041*	−0.020	−0.067	−0.019*
	(9.77)	(7.95)	(12.24)	(2.87)
	[0.022]		[0.020]	[0.021]
Abroad 5 years ago	−0.238*	−0.154*	−0.333	−0.095*
	(6.25)	(5.50)	(6.75)	(1.59)
	[−0.083]		[−0.092]	[−0.037]
Married	−0.057*	−0.057*	−0.048*	−0.054*
	(4.88)	(7.00)	(3.10)	(2.92)
	[−0.018]		[−0.011]	[−0.021]
With own children under 6 years only	−0.099*	−0.101	−0.080	−0.068
	(5.28)	(7.72)	(3.32)	(2.15)
	[−0.033]		[−0.020]	[−0.027]
With own children 6–17 years only	−0.116*	−0.099*	−0.110*	−0.055
	(8.19)	(10.09)	(6.23)	(2.27)
	[−0.038]		[−0.027]	[−0.022]
With own children under 6 years and 6–17 years	−0.209*	−0.175*	−0.166*	−0.137*
	(12.27)	(14.32)	(6.86)	(5.26)
	[−0.071]		[−0.042]	[−0.054]
Non-metropolitan	0.004	−0.016	0.552	−0.092*
	(0.08)	(0.40)	(4.78)	(1.36)
	[0.001]		[0.097]	[−0.036]
SOUTH	0.123*	0.103	0.119	0.095*
	(10.13)	(12.24)	(7.36)	(4.72)
	[0.039]		[0.027]	[0.038]

Table 6. (*Continued*)

Variables	Total Sample		Immigrants from All Countries Except Mexico	Immigrants from Mexico
	Probit	Ordered probit	Probit	Probit
Miles ('000) from origin	0.315*	0.209*	0.297*	−0.696*
	(23.53)	(22.69)	(18.45)	(4.97)
	[0.023]		[0.014]	[−0.123]
Miles ('000) from origin	−0.031*	−0.025	−0.032*	0.192*
Squared	(22.01)	(25.93)	(19.65)	(3.16)
	[0.023]		[0.014]	[−0.123]
Linguistic distance	−1.204	−0.762*	−1.282	(a)
	(26.54)	(24.22)	(27.49)	
	[−0.391]		[−0.304]	
Minority language	−0.019*	−0.022*	−0.017*	−0.021*
concentration	(23.57)	(36.63)	(12.01)	(11.49)
	[−0.006]		[−0.004]	[−0.008]
Colony	0.830	0.596	0.841	(a)
	(34.74)	(43.73)	(33.86)	
	[0.215]		[0.157]	
Refugee	−0.224	−0.101	−0.203	(a)
	(9.02)		(7.85)	
	[−0.077]	(5.48)	[−0.052]	
μ_1	(a)	1.041	(a)	(a)
		(217.58)		
μ_2	(a)	1.848	(a)	(a)
		(381.65)		
μ_3	(a)	3.184	(a)	(a)
		(457.46)		
χ^2	33990.68	37940.77	21084.55	5826.60
Prediction success rate	78.99	46.19	83.05	71.27
Sample size	83832	83832	58000	25832

Note: For notes to table, see Table 1.
Source: 2000 US Census.
*estimate significantly different from that for males.

case of females than in the case of males. It may also capture labor supply effects, as educational attainment is a far more important determinant of labor supply for women than for men, and greater labor supply implies a stronger incentive to acquire English language skills.

The second variable where reasonably consistent differences emerge from the analyses for female and male immigrants is the "lived abroad 5 years ago" variable. The sojourner behavior captured through this variable has a less negative impact on the English skills of female immigrants than it has on the English skills of their male counterparts. This difference may be a reflection of tied mobility, in which case the sojourner behavior would be more reflective of male intentions concerning length of stay in the US than it would be of female intentions.

Consistent with the discussion in Section 2, children have a much more negative effect on the English skills of female immigrants than they have on the English skills of male immigrants. The partial effects for the samples pooled across birthplace regions are almost twice as large (in absolute value) for female immigrants as they are for male immigrants, and the gender differences are statistically significant. Indeed, the negative effect of children on female English language proficiency is highly significant for all the children variables, even when separate analyses are done for Mexican and other immigrants.

The minority language concentration variable is also associated with a more negative impact on English language proficiency for female immigrants than it has for male immigrants. This finding could be associated with the lesser involvement of female immigrants in market work, an activity that is likely to offset some of the negative effects associated with living in a language enclave.

The final variable where a difference between males and females is apparent is for the geographic distance of the origin country from the US. The main difference here arises in the analysis for immigrants from Mexico. Among male immigrants from Mexico, the distance variable (the distance between the capital city of the immigrants' current state of residence and either Tijuana or Ciudal Juarez, whichever was shorter) was not a significant determinant of their English proficiency. Among female immigrants from Mexico, however, the geographic distance variable is statistically significant. Surprisingly, over the relevant range of distances represented in the data, immigrants living further from the border with Mexico are less likely to be proficient in English than those who live close to the border, other measured variables the same. To put this another way, female immigrants living close to the border, for example in Texas, are more likely to be proficient in English than their counterparts who, say, live in Illinois.

When the geographic distance variable was replaced by a number of dichotomous variables for residence of a state that borders Mexico, similar findings were generated: the states that border Mexico are associated with much higher rates of English proficiency for female immigrants from Mexico than are states in the rest of the US. When similar variables for state of residence are entered into the estimating equation for male immigrants from Mexico, they are typically statistically insignificant, or where significant, are associated with very small impacts.

The reasons for this finding are unclear, and the most likely possibilities cannot be tested with the census data used in the current analysis. For example, it is possible that immigrants who live close to the border with Mexico originate from different regions of Mexico, possibly in border regions, compared to Mexican immigrants who live elsewhere in the US, who may originate from a broader catchment area.[21] To the extent that they originate from border regions in Mexico, those resident in the states in the US near Mexico may have had greater exposure to English through more frequent trips to the US and US media prior to migration.

5. ANALYSES OF MOTHER TONGUE RETENTION

The discussion of the results from the estimation of the ordered probit model showed that as years of residence in the US increase, immigrants' English language skills improve considerably. This improvement largely comes about through shifts to the better English ability categories ("well", "very well") from the poorer English ability categories ("not at all", "not well") among immigrants who speak a language other than English at home. While there is an important increase in the percentage of immigrants speaking only English at home, mother tongue retention is the dominant feature of the analysis of the five-category language proficiency variable (LANG5).

This section sharpens the focus on mother tongue retention by estimating language models where the dependent variable is a dichotomous variable (MT), set equal to one where the immigrant speaks a language other than English at home, and set equal to zero where the immigrant speaks only English at home.[22] Around 90 percent of each of the samples of immigrants studied (from non-English-speaking origins), speak a language other than English at home. Even with such high rates of mother tongue retention, interesting patterns emerge from the analysis. Tables 7 and 8 list results from the model for males and females, respectively. The specification of the estimating equation that was used for the study of English skills in the previous section is employed in this analysis.

Many of the broad patterns from the study of mother tongue retention for males (Table 7) are the complement of those reported from the analysis of English proficiency. There are, however, a number of cases where the

Table 7. Probit Estimates of Model of Mother Tongue Retention, Adult Foreign-Born Men by Origin, 2000.

Variables	Total Sample	Immigrants from All Countries Except Mexico	Immigrants from Mexico
	Probit	Probit	Probit
Constant	1.331	1.057	1.150
	(11.78)	(7.51)	(5.15)
Education	−0.005	−0.015	0.014
	(3.49)	(7.13)	(5.42)
	[−0.001]	[−0.002]	[0.002]
Age at migration	−0.007	−0.007	0.014
	(1.30)	(1.15)	(1.37)
	[0.002]	[0.001]	[0.000]
Age at migration Squared/100	0.026	0.034	−0.018
	(4.21)	(4.49)	(1.49)
	[0.002]	[0.001]	[0.000]
Years since migration (YSM)	−0.006	−0.015	0.009
	(3.64)	(6.97)	(2.55)
	[−0.004]	[−0.006]	[0.000]
YSM Squared/100	−0.056	−0.052	−0.029
	(14.95)	(11.76)	(3.52)
	[−0.004]	[−0.006]	[0.000]
Abroad 5 years ago	0.035	0.093	−0.081
	(0.81)	(1.67)	(1.21)
	[0.005]	[0.014]	[−0.009]
Married	0.141	0.147	0.096
	(9.37)	(7.89)	(3.56)
	[0.021]	[0.024]	[0.010]
With own children under 6 years only	0.133	0.184	0.035
	(5.92)	(6.51)	(0.90)
	[0.018]	[0.027]	[0.004]
With own children 6–17 years only	0.091	0.102	0.027
	(5.23)	(4.83)	(0.83)
	[0.013]	[0.016]	[0.003]
With own children under 6 years and 6–17 years	0.149	0.160	0.092
	(6.75)	(5.46)	(2.61)
	[0.020]	[0.024]	[0.009]
Non-metropolitan	−0.081	−0.376	0.033
	(1.38)	(4.25)	(0.39)
	[−0.012]	[−0.076]	[0.003]
SOUTH	−0.041	−0.038	0.046
	(2.86)	(2.13)	(1.68)
	[−0.006]	[−0.006]	[0.005]

Table 7. (*Continued*)

Variables	Total Sample	Immigrants from All Countries Except Mexico	Immigrants from Mexico
	Probit	Probit	Probit
Miles ('000) from origin	−0.226	−0.095	−0.138
	(14.57)	(5.20)	(0.77)
	[0.009]	[0.021]	[0.004]
Miles ('000) from origin	0.035	0.025	0.086
Squared	(21.06)	(13.71)	(1.08)
	[0.009]	[0.021]	[0.004]
Linguistic distance	0.372	0.359	(a)
	(6.11)	(5.77)	
	[0.053]	[0.057]	
Minority language	0.020	0.034	0.000
concentration CONC-	(19.26)	(17.57)	(0.13)
STATE	[0.003]	[0.005]	[0.001]
Colony	−0.677	−0.675	(a)
	(31.40)	(30.63)	
	[−0.133]	[−0.136]	
Refugee	−0.071	−0.091	(a)
	(1.77)	(2.18)	
	[−0.011]	[−0.015]	
χ^2	6138.56	5755.66	104.86
Prediction success rate	90.77	88.65	94.71
Sample size	85865	54001	31864

Note: For notes to table, see Table 1.
Source: 2000 US Census.

impact of variables on mother tongue retention diverge from that which might have been expected, given the results from the study of English proficiency.

In the analyses pooled across birthplace regions, mother tongue retention is less likely among the better educated than it is among the less well-educated. However, in the separate analyses conducted for the broad birthplace regions, it is found that the impact of educational attainment differs markedly for immigrants from Mexico and for immigrants from other countries. For non-Mexican male immigrants, mother tongue retention is less likely among the better educated. In comparison, for male immigrants from Mexico, mother tongue retention is more likely among the better educated.

Table 8. Probit Estimates of Model of Mother Tongue Retention, Adult Foreign-Born Women by Origin, 2000.

Variables	Total Sample	Immigrants from All Countries Except Mexico	Immigrants from Mexico
	Probit	Probit	Probit
Constant	0.928	0.772	0.152
	(8.25)	(5.74)	(0.64)
Education	0.008	−0.003	0.023
	(4.91)	(1.56)	(8.15)
	[0.001]	[−0.001]	[0.003]
Age at migration	0.000	0.005	0.002
	(0.09)	(0.74)	(0.21)
	[0.002]	[0.002]	[−0.000]
Age at migration Squared/100	0.016	0.017	−0.006
	(2.61)	(2.37)	(0.52)
	[0.002]	[0.002]	[−0.000]
Years since migration (YSM)	−0.009	−0.016	0.009
	(5.25)	(8.06)	(2.51)
	[−0.004]	[−0.005]	[0.000]
YSM Squared/100	−0.039*	−0.037*	−0.023
	(10.63)	(8.67)	(2.71)
	[−0.004]	[−0.005]	[0.000]
Abroad 5 years ago	0.006	0.065	−0.154
	(0.13)	(1.17)	(1.87)
	[0.001]	[0.010]	[−0.020]
Married	0.103*	0.147	−0.320*
	(7.61)	(9.20)	(1.18)
	[0.016]	[0.025]	[−0.004]
With own children under 6 years only	0.108	0.115	0.044
	(4.79)	(4.36)	(0.96)
	[0.016]	[0.018]	[0.005]
With own children 6–17 years only	0.109	0.124	0.023
	(6.65)	(6.48)	(0.66)
	[0.016]	[0.020]	[0.003]
With own children under 6 years and 6–17 years	0.136	0.159	0.046
	(6.36)	(5.77)	(1.22)
	[0.019]	[0.024]	[0.005]
Non metropolitan	−0.035	−0.340	0.267
	(0.57)	(4.13)	(2.58)
	[−0.006]	[−0.069]	[0.026]
SOUTH	−0.077*	−0.076	−0.085*
	(5.50)	(4.58)	(2.93)
	[−0.012]	[−0.013]	[−0.010]

Table 8. (*Continued*)

Variables	Total Sample	Immigrants from All Countries Except Mexico	Immigrants from Mexico
	Probit	Probit	Probit
Miles ('000) from origin	−0.128*	−0.056	1.172*
	(8.18)	(3.06)	(6.25)
	[0.015]	[0.023]	[0.056]
Miles ('000) from origin	0.027*	0.021	−0.358*
Squared	(16.25)	(11.62)	(4.20)
	[0.015]	[0.023]	[0.056]
Linguistic distance	0.024*	−0.002*	(a)
	(0.46)	(0.03)	
	[0.004]	[−0.000]	
Minority language	0.026*	0.035	0.029*
concentration CONC-	(24.45)	(18.46)	(11.99)
STATE	[0.004]	[0.006]	[0.003]
Colony	−0.688	−0.696	(a)
	(32.40)	(32.17)	
	[−0.142]	[−0.146]	
Refugee	−0.009	−0.080	(a)
	(0.24)	(2.05)	
	[−0.001]	[−0.014]	
χ^2	5192.54	5064.45	255.83
Prediction success rate	89.97	88.40	93.74
Sample size	83832	58000	25832

Note: For notes to table, see Table 1.
Source: 2000 US Census.

The reasons for these differences are not clear. While Mexican immigrants appear to have higher rates of repeat migration than other immigrants, among both groups the rate appears to decline with a higher level of schoolings.[23] Married Mexican men are more likely to be married to a woman born in Mexico than are other men to a woman born in their country of origin, and the Mexican men are more likely to have a US-born spouse. However, rates of same origin marriages decline with level of schooling, while marriages to a person born in the US increases sharply with educational attainment among men born in Mexico and other countries.[24] Alternatively, it might be a reflection of non-linearities in the effect of education on mother tongue retention, and the sharply different educational distribution between the Mexican (mean schooling 8.3 years) and non-Mexican (13.3 years) immigrants. There is support for this hypothesis as the inclusion of an education-squared term in the analysis for Mexico reveals a positive effect of education on mother tongue retention among the less well-educated (up to 12.7 years of schooling for males and 13.6 years for females) and a negative relation among the better educated. Among other immigrants, however, there was no evidence of a positive relationship between mother tongue retention and education among the less well-educated.

The impact of age at migration on mother tongue retention also differs between male immigrants from Mexico and those from other countries. For immigrants from countries other than Mexico, the older the age at migration, the more likely the immigrant is to retain his mother tongue. Age at migration, however, is not a significant determinant of mother tongue retention among immigrants from Mexico. Immigrants from Mexico are more likely to have lived abroad (presumably in Mexico) 5 years ago than are other immigrants. They presumably are characterized by much more to-and-fro migration between their country of origin and the US than are other immigrants. This could be associated with incentives to retain the origin country language that dominate the age at migration influences.

Similar to the patterns associated with education and age at migration, the duration of residence effects on mother tongue differ between immigrants from Mexico and immigrants from other countries. For immigrants from countries other than Mexico, the probability of retaining the mother tongue declines with duration of residence. The partial effect of duration of residence on the probability of speaking a language other than English at home is 0.4 percentage points, when evaluated at 15 years of residence. Among immigrants from Mexico, however, there is virtually no change with duration of residence in the probability of speaking a language other than English at home, as illustrated in Fig. 7.

The family structure variables have strong impacts on the probability of mother tongue retention. Mother tongue retention is greater among those who are married and who have children. However, the partial effects of these significant variables are double in magnitudes for Mexican immigrants compared to immigrants from other countries. This difference could arise from the importance of Spanish in the US (see Appendix Table A.1).[25] In this situation, where these general neighborhood influences appear so strong, the more immediate neighborhood effect associated with the family might be expected to have less influence.

In Table 7, column (i), for the pooled sample, the probability of mother tongue retention declines with the distance of the country of origin from the

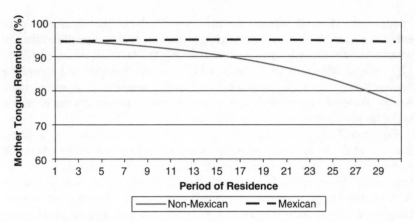

Fig. 7. Predicted Probability of Speaking a Language other than English at Home, Adult Foreign-Born Men by Origin, 2000 US Census. *Source:* Authors' Calculations Based on Table 7.

US up to around 3,500 miles, and increases thereafter. This result is reasonably consistent with the finding for the ordered probit model (Table 1), where the probability of speaking only English at home rises with geographic distance over the first 4,700 miles, and declines thereafter.

The results for the linguistic distance variable indicate that immigrants whose mother tongue is closer to English (and hence who should find it easier to learn English) are most likely to shift from speaking their mother tongue to English. This finding is in the expected direction. Note that the sizes of the estimated partial effects are much smaller than the results in the study of English proficiency (Table 1). Given the motivation in the design of the linguistic distance variable, as a measure of how easy it is for foreign language speakers to learn English, the relative magnitudes of these estimated effects make sense.

The minority language concentration variable is intended to capture the ease with which conversation in a language other than English is possible. According to the results in Table 7, the likelihood of immigrants speaking a language other than English at home rises with the extent to which the immigrant lives among others who speak the same (non-English) home language as the immigrant. However, this effect does not carry across to immigrants from Mexico.[26] With the dominant position of Spanish in the US (see Appendix Table A.1) and the proximity to Mexico, and hence to Mexican media, this may not be as important a consideration for mother tongue retention among Mexican immigrants.

Finally, it is seen that immigrants from a former colony of the US or UK, and those who are likely to have been refugees, are less likely to speak a language other than English at home. The former may reflect their greater comfort with English and the latter may reflect a lower prospect of return migration.

Similar conclusions can be drawn from the study of mother tongue retention among adult female immigrants. These results, presented in Table 8, have four main features.

First, the estimates of the model of mother tongue retention for females are, as a set, statistically different from the estimates for males.[27]

Second, the way educational attainment impacts on mother tongue retention differs for males and females. In particular, while mother tongue retention decreases with educational attainment among non-Mexican male immigrants, educational attainment is not a significant determinant of mother tongue retention among female immigrants from these countries. Like their male counterparts, the better educated female immigrants from Mexico are more likely to speak a language other than English at home than is the case for less well-educated female immigrants. However, also similar to the case for males, when the education variable is entered in the model in quadratic form, the results indicate that mother tongue retention initially increases with educational attainment, but after around 13.6 years of schooling, additional years of education are associated with decreases in the likelihood of a language other than English being spoken at home.

Third, the marital status variable and the three variables for the presence of children are insignificant in the model of mother tongue retention for female immigrants from Mexico.

Fourth, among female immigrants from Mexico, the geographic distance variables are significant, whereas they were insignificant among male immigrants from Mexico. The estimated coefficients indicate that, over the range of distances represented in the sample for immigrants from Mexico, the likelihood of speaking a language other than English at home increases at a decreasing rate the further the female immigrants live from Mexico. While this is an unexpected finding, it sits comfortably alongside the finding reported earlier to the effect that the probability of being proficient in English decreases with distance from the border between US and Mexico.

Finally, the linguistic distance variable is not statistically significant in any of the models estimated for females. While this variable was statistically significant in the models for males, the estimated impacts were far less than those found in the model for English proficiency. The linguistic distance variable therefore appears to be more relevant to models capturing shifts to English than it is to models of origin language retention.

It is apparent from this discussion of the incidence of immigrants speaking a language other than English at home that the influences of both the personal characteristics and the behavioral variables included in the model vary between immigrants from Mexico and those from other countries. Given the extent to which Spanish is used in the US – as noted above, one in nine people between the ages of 18 and 64, and every second foreign-born person in this age bracket, speaks Spanish at home – differences of this nature might be expected. However, the high degree of mother tongue retention among adult immigrants (of 90 percent or more) suggests that the appropriate research questions might be focused on the language use of the children of immigrants. Chiswick et al. (2005a, 2005b) show how the family setting can be incorporated into the study of English-speaking skills. Applying the same framework to the study of mother tongue retention is an appropriate direction for future research.

6. SUMMARY AND CONCLUSION

One in nine people between the ages of 18 and 64 in the US, and every second foreign-born person in this age bracket, speaks Spanish at home. And whereas around 80 percent of adult immigrants in the US from non-English-speaking countries other than Mexico are proficient in English, only about 50 percent of adult immigrants from Mexico are proficient.

A theoretical model, grounded in human capital theory, is presented in this paper to account for these empirical facts. Variations in English proficiency are shown to be linked to factors that shift the supply and demand for funds for investment in English language capital. The model has three key sets of factors: exposure, efficiency and economic incentives.

The exposure factors are separated into exposure to English before immigration (e.g., living in a former US or British colony), and exposure after immigration. Exposure after immigration has both extensive and intensive margins. The extensive margin can be measured by the number of years since the immigrant arrived in the US, taking into account sojourner effects. The intensive margin is the intensity of exposure per unit of time in the US, and this will depend on the immigrant's neighborhood and family experiences. Special attention is given in the study to the most appropriate measure of neighborhood or enclave in the context of models of English proficiency.

Four measurable efficiency factors that can influence the development of language skills among immigrants are age at migration, educational attainment, refugee status, and linguistic distance. The conceptual basis for the measure of linguistic distance is the ease with which immigrants of particular linguistic backgrounds (mother tongues) can learn English: It is argued that it should be more difficult for a Chinese speaker than for a Spanish speaker to learn English.

The economic factors included in the conceptual framework are the wage, consumption and social gains associated with English proficiency, and the expected duration in the destination. Several proxies for these are considered, including educational attainment and the geographical distance between the country of origin and the US.

The empirical analyses are conducted using the 2000 US Census 1 percent Public Use Microdata file. The research is limited to adults (aged 25–64 years) from non-English-speaking countries, though in contrast to most of the literature which focuses on males, the language practices of both male and female immigrants are considered. Binary probit analysis of a dichotomous proficiency index, and ordered probit analyses of a five-category language skills variable, are presented. As well, a binary measure of mother tongue retention is analyzed.

The analyses show that immigration at a younger age, increases in the level of education and a longer duration in the US are associated with a higher probability of being proficient in English. English language proficiency tends to be lower the greater the age at migration.

English proficiency improves at a decreasing rate with duration of residence. Analyses performed for the 1980 and 1990 Censuses show a similar pattern, although it is noted that the effects of years since migration get slightly stronger across cohorts. That the pattern repeats itself suggests that it is reflecting a longitudinal phenomenon rather than merely a decline in the linguistic ability of more recent cohorts, or selective emigration of the least proficient immigrants in each arrival cohort. That the relationship gets stronger in the more recent data may be linked to the slightly lower measured proficiency in English of recent arrival cohorts: there is a well established pattern in the immigrant adjustment literature of faster rates of adjustment among those with the fewest skills at arrival.

Spending time abroad after immigration diminishes English proficiency. Thus, the intermittent nature of the stay in the US among those who came to the US to stay more than five years ago, but who lived abroad in 1995, and perhaps the expectation among them of a relatively short future stay in the US, appears to have a major negative influence on immigrants' English skills.

A greater geographic distance between the country of origin and the US was associated with greater proficiency in English, and a greater linguistic distance between the immigrant's mother tongue and English was associated with lesser proficiency in English. Both patterns are consistent with the theoretical model, and with results reported in previous research. The estimated effect is also very large: the estimated differences in English proficiency of the immigrants with mother tongues at the extremes of the measure of linguistic distance (e.g., Korean, Japanese versus Norwegian, Swedish) are the equivalent of over eight years of schooling.

The proportion of individuals living in the same region as the immigrant that speak his or her mother tongue was also shown to have a major influence on the immigrant's English skills. Three measures of minority language concentration were used. The first was constructed using state-level data. As in previous research, 51 separate areas are used in the construction of this variable. The second was constructed using MSA (106 separate areas), and the third was based on the Super-PUMA (532 separate areas). The impact of a minority language concentration on English language proficiency tends to be weaker when estimated with more disaggregated data than when state-level data are used. It was not possible to assess which level among the three is the best from an analytical point of view, or even from a measurement perspective. However, the results with each of the three alternative measures point to a negative association of ethnic/linguistic enclaves and immigrants' English language proficiency.

The directions of impact of variables in the models of English skills for females were remarkably similar to those for males. The estimated coefficients for females as a set were, however, statistically different from those for males. Among the variables giving rise to different results by gender are the minority language concentration variable and the variables for children. There is a more negative impact on English proficiency of living in a minority language concentration for female immigrants than for male immigrants. It was suggested that this difference could be associated with the lesser involvement of female immigrants in market work.

Children have a much more negative effect on the English skills of their immigrant mothers than they have on their immigrant fathers. It was argued that this difference may arise because of the negative effect of children on mother's labor supply and children serving as translators for their mothers in consumption activities.

The analysis of mother tongue retention showed that many of the variables that affected immigrants' proficiency in English were significant determinants of their likelihood of retaining their mother tongue in the US.

In many cases variables that are associated with greater proficiency in English (e.g., years since migration, fewer children) are associated with a lower probability of speaking a language other than English at home. However, in some cases variables have impacts of the same sign on both English proficiency and mother tongue retention (e.g., years of education among male immigrants from Mexico) or were significant in one set of analyses and insignificant in the other (e.g., the linguistic distance variable for female immigrants). These differences indicate that additional information can be gained from the separate study of mother tongue retention.

The results from study of mother tongue retention, however, showed much more variability across birthplace groups and between males and females than was the case with the study of English proficiency. The differences between immigrants from Mexico and other countries are presumably associated with the dominant role of Spanish in the US. The differences between males and females could be associated with females having a more influential role than males in the transmission of the language and culture of the origin country within the family. Study of mother tongue retention using the family as the unit of observation may therefore be a priority in research. In this context, the very high rates of mother tongue retention among adult immigrants (of 90 percent or more) suggest that the appropriate focus in this research would be on the home language use of the children of immigrants. This will provide information on the determinants of the extent to which the use of languages other than English at home is more than a one-generational phenomenon, and whether this varies by country of origin or mother tongue.

There are two main lessons from this research. First, English proficiency varies across immigrants in predictable ways. Immigrants with higher educational attainment, who migrate at a younger age, who live in predominately English-speaking areas of the US, and who have a mother tongue close to English or who had been exposed to English prior to immigration are more likely to be proficient in English than other immigrants. These findings could be used in immigrant selection (e.g., in a points system such as that used in Australia). The similarity of the estimated impacts across the separate groups analyzed above (males, females, immigrants from Mexico, and immigrants from other countries) suggests that the application of the findings in this way would be neutral across these broad groups. The results also have implications for settlement policy, suggesting a focus on areas of ethnic language concentrations. Moreover, comparisons between men and women and with the 1980 and 1990 Census suggest that the results are robust across the two genders and across time.

Second, mother tongue retention also varies across immigrants in predictable ways. The overall rate of mother tongue retention among adult immigrants in the US is very high, at around 90 percent. Perhaps the more interesting issues that arise from this are the retention of the mother tongue within the household of married couples, including linguistic inter-marriages, and the transmission of the mother tongue from adult immigrants to their children, and the labor market implications of bilingualism among the children of immigrants. These issues are the topics for future research.

ACKNOWLEDGMENTS

We thank Derby Voon for research assistance. Chiswick acknowledges research support from the Smith-Richardson Foundation, IZA-Institute for the Study of Labor and the Institute of Government and Public Affairs, University of Illinois. Miller acknowledges financial assistance from the Australian Research Council.

NOTES

1. For example, due to greater efficiency in language acquisition, an immigrant who arrived in the US at 10 years of age would be expected to develop greater proficiency in English from any dollar investment than one who arrived in the US at 50 years of age. Thus, age at migration would be a shift variable in the demand for funds equation and affect investment levels and proficiency.

2. While improvements in English skills can be expected with practice, most investment in language skills should occur just after migration, since investments in language skills tend to be more profitable if the period over which the benefits will be received is longer, since the opportunity cost of investment in language training is lower in the early period when wages are lower, and since the returns are greater if investments with high rates of return are made sooner rather than later. The complementarity in the labor market of language skills and schooling and post-migration labor market experience also encourages earlier investments. Consequently, a non-linear specification for duration of residence should be used.

3. See Appendix A for a list of these languages and their shares of the immigrant population.

4. A Super-PUMA is a geographic entity that comprises at least 400,000 people.

5. A metropolitan area is one of a large population nucleus, together with adjacent communities that have a high degree of economic and social integration with that nucleus. Where a metropolitan area has 1 million people or more, two or more primary metropolitan statistical areas (PMSAs) may be defined within it.

Information on the MSA and PMSAs contained in the variable MSA-PMSA1 is used in the construction of the CONC-MSA variable.

6. Year of first marriage was last asked in the 1980 Census.

7. However, Fathman's (1975) review of the evidence indicated that "younger children are not necessarily better second language learners than adults in all respects", with her research showing that "after puberty the ability to learn rules, to make generalizations or to memorize patterns may be more fully developed".

8. Although, see Fathman (1975) for an alternative perspective.

9. See Chiswick and Miller (2006) for an analysis of the precise shape of the negative effect of age at migration and whether there is a discontinuity or "critical period".

10. This last factor could not explain the greater level of Hebrew language proficiency of immigrants with a higher level of secular schooling in Israel (Chiswick & Repetto, 2001).

11. As an example, adult immigrants from Cuba would be classified as refugees for this analysis if they entered the US after Castro came to power in 1959, but not earlier Cuban immigrants, or those who came to the US as children.

12. The emigration rate variable employed by Chiswick and Miller (2001) is not used here, as the information is dated and more recent comparable data do not appear to be available. These data were also affected by the presence of illegal immigrants in 1980 and their receiving amnesty by 1990.

13. Immigrants from the main English-speaking countries (UK, Ireland, Canada, Australia, New Zealand, and the Caribbean) are excluded as, for the reasons given in Section 2, the language issues do not exist to any great extent for this group.

14. The partial effects have been computed using the formula $\phi(X\beta)\beta_k$ for continuous variables (where ϕ is the standard normal density function), and as differences in predictions for groups distinguished within the dichotomous variables. For example, the partial effect for marital status is the difference between the predicted rate of proficiency for those who are married and that for those who are not married, where these predictions are sample averages.

15. As Age = (Age at Migration + YSM), the model is $\text{LANG} = \beta_0 + \beta_1$ (Age at Migration + × YSM) + β_2YSM + ⋯, and so $\partial \text{LANG}/ \partial \text{YSM} = \beta_1 + \beta_2$, or the effect of one year in the US plus the effect of an extra year of age. As the effects associated with years in the US are far stronger than those associated with age, the same pattern as established here carries over to the interpretation based on both β_1 and β_2, though as $\beta_1 < 0$ the years since migration effects are smaller. The discussion here has a focus on β_2.

16. The reciprocal of the original score was employed in the early research by Chiswick and Miller, as a means of assigning a score for English only speakers had not been developed and a zero value was used. In the current research, where the mean of the valid scores for the individual's birthplace is assigned where the individual speaks only English at home, there is less need to use the reciprocal functional form. While it is used here for consistency with past research, it is noted that entering the linguistic scores from Chiswick and Miller (2005b) in the probit index in linear form yields results similar to those listed in Tables 1 and 6.

17. Recall that immigrants from Canada, Australia, New Zealand, the UK, and the English-speaking islands in the Caribbean have been deleted from the dataset.

18. While some immigrants from Mexico report speaking indigenous languages at home, there are no measures for the linguistic distance of Native American languages from English. Among the adult male immigrants from Mexico, 94.3 percent report speaking Spanish, 5.4 percent report only English, and 0.3 percent all other languages.

19. See Chiswick and Miller (2005a) for an "ethnic goods" model that hypothesizes this negative relationship.

20. Females are generally shown to have an initial rate of learning advantage over males in first language acquisition. The limited evidence available suggests that this may carry over to second language acquisition (see, for example, Larsen-Freeman & Long, 1991, pp. 204–205).

21. The Census does not include information on the areas in Mexico in which the immigrants lived prior to migrating to the US.

22. For a multivariate analysis of mother tongue retention of Hispanics, see Linton (2004).

23. The percent of foreign-born men in the US in 2000 who immigrated in 1995 or earlier who lived abroad 5 years ago is:

Education (years)	Source Country		
	Mexico	Non-Mexico	Total
0–8	3.67	2.75	3.39
9–12	3.26	2.61	2.89
Over 12	2.99	2.33	2.41

24. The percent of foreign-born married men from non-English-speaking countries whose spouse was born in various countries is:

Level of Education	Men Born in Mexico: Spouse Born in:			Men Born in Other Countries: Spouse Born in:		
	Mexico	US	Elsewhere[*]	Same country	US	Elsewhere[*]
0–8 yrs	86.18	11.77	2.04	80.85	5.87	13.28
9–12 yrs	77.92	18.61	3.47	70.92	15.08	14.00
Over 12 yrs	67.76	27.59	4.65	66.98	19.23	13.79
Total	80.46	16.59	2.95	69.43	16.77	13.80

[*]Individuals born in Puerto Rico included under "Elsewhere"; row totals may not sum up to 100.00 due to rounding.

25. In the US, in 2000, fully, 11 percent of individuals aged 18–64, and 60 percent of the foreign-born of the same age group, speak Spanish at home. The next most frequently reported language is French, spoken at home by 0.6 percent of the adult population and by 3.4 percent of the foreign-born.

26. The mean value of the minority language concentration (State) variable is 20.6 for immigrants from Mexico compared to a value of only 4.9 for other immigrants.

27. The χ^2 test of whether the female shift variable and female interaction terms on all slope variables were jointly significantly different from zero was highly significant in each sample.

REFERENCES

Becker, G. S., & Chiswick, B. R. (1966). Education and the distribution of earnings. *American Economic Review, 56*(2), 358–369.

Chiswick, B. (1978). The effects of Americanization on the earnings of foreign born men. *Journal of Political Economy, 86*, 897–921.

Chiswick, B. (1979). The economic progress of immigrants: Some apparently universal patterns. In: W. Fellner (Ed.), *Contemporary economic problems 1979* (pp. 357–399). Washington, DC: American Enterprise Institute.

Chiswick, B. R. (1991). Speaking, reading and earnings among low-skilled immigrants. *Journal of Labor Economics, 9*(2), 149–170.

Chiswick, B. R., Lee, Y. L., & Miller, P. W. (2005a). Family matters: The role of the family in immigrants' destination language acquisition. *Journal of Population Economics, 18*(1), 1–17.

Chiswick, B. R., Lee, Y. L., & Miller, P. W. (2005b). Parents and children talk: English language proficiency within immigrant families. *Review of Economics of the Household, 3*(3), 243–268.

Chiswick, B. R., Lee, Y. L., & Miller, P. W. (2006). Immigrants' language skills and visa category. *International Migration Review, 40*(2), 419–450.

Chiswick, B. R., & Miller, P. W. (1992). Language in the immigrant labour market. In: B. R. Chiswick (Ed.), *Immigration, language and ethnicity: Canada and the United States* (pp. 229–296, 471–476). Washington, DC: American Enterprise Institute.

Chiswick, B. R., & Miller, P. W. (1995). The endogeneity between language and earnings: An international analysis. *Journal of Labor Economics, 13*(2), 246–288.

Chiswick, B. R., & Miller, P. W. (1996). The languages of the United States: Who speaks what and what it means. *READ Perspectives, 3*(2), 5–41.

Chiswick, B. R., & Miller, P. W. (1998). English language fluency among immigrants in the United States. *Research in Labor Economics, 17*, 151–200 (JAI Press).

Chiswick, B. R., & Miller, P. W. (2001). A model of destination-language acquisition: Application to male immigrants in Canada. *Demography, 38*(3), 391–409.

Chiswick, B. R., & Miller, P. W. (2002). Immigrant earnings: Language skills, linguistic concentrations and the business cycle. *Journal of Population Economics, 15*, 31–57.

Chiswick, B. R., & Miller, P. W. (2005a). Do enclaves matter in immigrant adjustment? *City and Community, 4*(1), 5–35.

Chiswick, B. R., & Miller, P. W. (2005b). Linguistic distance: A quantitative measure of the distance between English and other languages. *Journal of Multilingual and Multicultural Development, 26*(1), 1–11.

Chiswick, B. R., & Miller, P. W. (2006). *The cultural period hypothesis: What the 2000 US Census says.* Department of Economics, University of Illinois at Chicago.

Chiswick, B. R., & Repetto, G. (2001). Immigrant adjustment in Israel: Literacy and fluency in Hebrew and earnings. In: S. Djajic (Ed.), *International migration: Trends, policy and economic impact* (pp. 204–228). New York: Routledge.

Fathman, A. (1975). The relationship between age and second language productive ability. *Language and Learning, 25*(2), 245–253.

Fitzpatrick, G. L., & Modlin, M. J. (1986). *Direct-line distances: United States edition.* Metuchen, NJ: The Scarecrow Press Inc.

Hart-Gonzalez, L., & Lindermann, S. (1993). *Expected achievement in speaking proficiency, 1993.* School of Language Studies, Foreign Service Institute, US Department of State.

Kominski, R. (1989). How good is "how well"? An examination of the census English-speaking ability question. *American Statistical Association 1989 Proceedings of the social statistics section* (pp. 333–338).

Larsen-Freeman, D., & Long, M. H. (1991). *An introduction to second language acquisition research.* New York: Longman.

Linton, A. (2004). A critical mass model of bilingualism among U.S.-born Hispanics. *Social Forces, 83*(1), 279–314.

Long, M. H. (1990). Maturational constraints on language development. *Studies in Second Language Acquisition, 12*(3), 251–285.

McManus, W., Gould, W., & Welch, F. (1983). Earnings of Hispanic men: The role of English language proficiency. *Journal of Labor Economics, 1*(2), 101–130.

Miller, P. W., & Neo, L. (2003). Labour market flexibility and immigrant adjustment. *Economic Record, 79*(246), 336–356.

Newport, E. L. (1990). Maturational constraints on language learning. *Cognitive Science, 14*(1), 57–77.

Service, E., & Clark, F. I. M. (1993). Differences between young and older adults in learning a foreign language. *Journal of Memory and Language, 32*, 608–623.

APPENDIX A. DEFINITIONS OF VARIABLES

The variables used in the statistical analyses are defined below. Mnemonic names are also listed where relevant.

Data Source: 2000 Census of Population of the United States, PUMS, 1 percent sample of the foreign-born, except where noted otherwise.

Definition of Population: Foreign-born men and women aged 25–64, born in countries other than the main English-speaking countries (UK, Ireland, Canada, Australia, New Zealand and the English-speaking Caribbean), territories of the United States, at sea or born abroad of American parents. Only residents of the 50 States and the District of Columbia are considered.

Dependent Variables:

English Language Fluency (LANG2 and LANG5): LANG2 is set equal to one for individuals who speak only English at home, or if a language other than English is spoken at home, who speak English either "very well" or "well". The variable is set to zero where a language other than English is spoken at home and the respondent speaks English either "not well" or "not at all". LANG5 is a polychotomous dependent variable (five categories), defined to include all proficiency categories: (i) speaks only English at home; speaks a Language other than English at home and speaks English (ii) very well; (iii) well; (iv) not well; (v) not at all.

Mother Tongue Retention (MT): This is a binary variable, set equal to one for individuals who speak a language other than English at home (assumed to be their mother tongue). It is set equal to zero for individuals who speak only English at home.

Explanatory Variables:

Minority Language Concentration (CONC): Each respondent is assigned a measure equal to the percentage of the population aged 18–64 in the region in which he/she lives, who reports the same non-English language as the respondent. In the construction of this variable, only the 25 largest non-American Indian language groups nationwide and the top 5 Indian language groups are considered. (Details are provided in Table A.1.). These constitute 92 percent of all responses where a language other than English is used at home. Representation in the other language groups is so small numerically that the proportions are approximately zero, and this value is assigned. Those who reported speaking only English are assigned the mean value of the CONC measure for other-language speakers of their birthplace group.

Three separate regional classifications and hence measures of CONC are considered. CONC-STATE is based on the state (50 States and the District of Columbia) of residence – a measure that corresponds to that used by Chiswick and Miller (2005a). The second is based on the Super-PUMA data available on the 1 percent file (CONC-Super). In all, 532 separate regions are distinguished in the empirical analysis. The third measure is an intermediate case and is constructed using the information on CONC-MSA. Overall, 106 separate regions are used in forming this measure.

Location: The three location variables record residence in a non-metropolitan area (NON-MET) or in the southern states (SOUTH).

The states included in the latter are: Alabama, Arkansas, Delaware, District of Columbia, Florida, Georgia, Kentucky, Louisiana, Maryland, Mississippi, Missouri, North Carolina, Oklahoma, South Carolina, Tennessee, Texas, Virginia, and West Virginia. In the analyses for Mexico, four dichotomous variables for US states that are near Mexico are used: California (benchmark); Texas; Arizona, New Mexico, Nevada; Rest of the US.

Colony (COLONY): Countries that are current or former colonies of English-speaking countries are coded one. All other countries are coded zero. Dependencies of the UK, US, Australia, New Zealand and South Africa are coded as colonies under this definition.

Years Since Migration (YSM): This is computed from the year the foreign-born person came to the United States to stay.

Lived Abroad Five Years Ago (ABROAD5): This is set equal to one if the individual had resided in the US for more than 5 years and lived abroad in 1995, otherwise it is set equal to zero. Note that ABROAD5 is zero for immigrants in the US for five or fewer years.

Marital Status (MARRIED): This is a binary variable that distinguishes individuals who are married, spouse present (equal to 1) from all other marital states.

Years of Education (EDUC): This variable records the total years of full-time equivalent education. It has been constructed from the Census data on educational attainment by assigning the following values to the Census categories: completed less than fifth grade (2 years); completed fifth or sixth grade (5.5); completed seventh or eighth grade (7.5); completed ninth grade (9); completed tenth grade (10); completed 11th grade (11); completed 12th grade or high school (12); attended college for less than one year (12.5); attended college for more than one year or completed college (14); bachelor's degree (16); master's degree (17.5); professional degree (18.5); doctorate (20).

Refugee (REFUGEE): This variable is constructed to identify the major sources of post–World War II refugees to the US It is defined only for immigrants who migrated at age 25 and older. It takes a value of one for individuals who migrated from Cambodia, Laos or Vietnam in 1975 or later, Iran in 1980 or later, Cuba in 1960 or later, the Former Soviet Union

(USSR) in 1950 or later, from China between 1950 and 1990, and Somalia or the former Yugoslavia between 1990 and 2000. All other immigrants are assigned a value of zero.

Linguistic Distance (DISTANCE): This is a measure of the difficulty of learning a foreign language for English-speaking Americans. It is based on a set of language scores (LS) measuring achievements in speaking proficiency in foreign languages by English-speaking Americans at the US Department of State, School of Language Studies, reported by Hart-Gonzalez and Lindermann (1993). It is described in detail in Chiswick and Miller (2005b).

In the construction of this variable, foreign-born persons who speak only English at home are assigned the mean value of the linguistic score measure for individuals reporting a foreign language from their birthplace group. For the 3 percent of the sample who report a language for which there is no linguistic score, the sample mean value is assigned as the language score.

The variable in the regression equations is linguistic distance, which is one divided by the linguistic score, $DISTANCE = 1/LS$.

Direct-Line Distances (MILES): The miles between the major city in the immigrant's country of origin and the nearest large port of entry in the United States (New York, Miami, and Los Angeles) are constructed from data in Fitzpatrick and Modlin's (1986) *Direct Line Distances, United States Edition.* For the analysis limited to immigrants from Mexico the distance from the capital in their state of residence in the US and Tijuana or Ciudad Juarez (whichever is shorter) is used.

Means and standard deviations for these variables are reported in Table A.2 (for men) and Table A.3 (for women).

Table A.1. Frequency of Language Use among Adults in the
United States, 2000[a].

Language	Percent of All Languages		Percent of All Languages Other than English	
	Frequency	Cumulative frequency	Frequency	Cumulative frequency
Spanish	11.228	11.228	59.743	59.743
French	0.632	11.860	3.364	63.107
Chinese, Min	0.623	12.483	3.316	66.423
Tagalog/Filipino	0.557	13.040	2.962	69.385
German, Austrian, Swiss	0.505	13.545	2.689	72.074
Vietnamese	0.433	13.978	2.302	74.376
Korean	0.383	14.361	2.038	76.414
Italian	0.329	14.690	1.751	78.165
Russian	0.274	14.964	1.459	79.624
Arabic	0.258	15.222	1.371	80.995
Portuguese	0.252	15.474	1.343	82.338
Polish	0.226	15.700	1.202	83.540
Japanese, Ainu	0.185	15.885	0.983	84.523
French Creole, Haitian Creole	0.175	16.060	0.932	85.455
Hindi	0.150	16.210	0.800	86.255
Persian, Dari, Farsi, Pushto	0.136	16.346	0.725	86.980
Greek	0.135	16.481	0.719	87.699
Urdu	0.109	16.590	0.580	88.279
Cantonese, Toishan	0.106	16.696	0.562	88.841
Gujarati	0.099	16.795	0.529	89.370
Kru, Ibo, Yoruba, Akan, Ashanti, Ewe, Fanti, Ga, Igbo, Nigerian, Twi	0.086	16.881	0.457	89.827
Hebrew	0.083	16.964	0.442	90.269
Mandarin	0.077	17.041	0.408	90.677
Mon-Khmer, Cambodian, Khmer	0.069	17.110	0.365	91.042
Armenian	0.069	17.179	0.365	91.407

Table A.1. (*Continued*)

Language	Percent of All Languages		Percent of All Languages Other than English	
	Frequency	Cumulative frequency	Frequency	Cumulative frequency
Navajo[b]	0.073	17.252	0.386	91.793
Dakota, Assiniboine, Lakota, Oglala, Sioux[b]	0.008	17.260	0.042	91.835
Cherokee[b]	0.008	17.268	0.041	91.876
Yupik[b]	0.006	17.274	0.033	91.909
Apache[b]	0.006	17.280	0.032	91.941
Other languages specified	1.514	18.794	8.056	99.997
Other languages not specifically listed	0.001	18.795	0.004	100.00
Not reported	0.000	18.795	0.002	100.00
English only	81.206	100.00	–	–

Source: 2000 US Census of Population, PUMS, 1 percent sample.
[a]All persons, regardless of nativity, aged 18–64 as reported in the 2000 Census; refers to language spoken at home if English is not the only language.
[b]American Indian Language.

Table A.2. Means and Standard Deviations of Variables in Language Models, Adult Foreign-Born Men by Origin, 2000.

Variables	Total Sample	Immigrants from All Countries Except Mexico	Immigrants from Mexico
Proficient in English (LANG2)	0.695 (0.46)	0.800 (0.40)	0.507 (0.50)
Education	11.525 (4.96)	13.323 (4.20)	8.279 (4.55)
Age at migration	40.053 (10.30)	41.506 (10.47)	37.429 (9.44)
Age at migration^2	1710.296 (882.51)	1832.273 (911.21)	1490.107 (781.40)

Table A.2.   (*Continued*)

Variables	Total Sample	Immigrants from All Countries Except Mexico	Immigrants from Mexico
Years since migration	16.135	16.413	15.634
(YSM)	(11.04)	(11.51)	(10.13)
YSM^2	382.307	401.889	346.956
	(472.27)	(503.57)	(407.38)
Abroad 5 years ago	0.023	0.020	0.028
	(0.15)	(0.14)	(0.16)
Married	0.622	0.644	0.583
	(0.48)	(0.48)	(0.49)
With own children under 6 years only	0.129	0.119	0.147
	(0.33)	(0.32)	(0.35)
With own children 6–17 years only	0.259	0.251	0.274
	(0.44)	(0.43)	(0.45)
With own children under 6 years *and* 6–17 years	0.152	0.107	0.233
	(0.36)	(0.31)	(0.42)
Non metropolitan	0.010	0.005	0.020
	(0.10)	(0.07)	(0.14)
SOUTH	0.282	0.273	0.299
	(0.45)	(0.45)	(0.46)
Miles ('000) from origin	3.672	4.906	0.701
	(2.64)	(2.56)	(0.39)
Miles ('000) from origin Squared	20.443	30.614	0.644
	(23.11)	(23.24)	(0.81)
Linguistic distance	0.508	0.543	(a)
	(0.13)	(0.15)	
Minority language concentration CONC-STATE	10.447	4.798	20.645
	(11.10)	(7.92)	(8.40)
Minority language concentration CONC-MSA	12.880	7.369	22.829
	(16.13)	(14.38)	(14.24)
Minority language concentration CONC-Super	15.746	8.799	28.287
	(19.64)	(16.13)	(19.19)
Colony	0.150	0.233	(a)
	(0.36)	(0.42)	

Table A.2. (*Continued*)

Variables	Total Sample	Immigrants from All Countries Except Mexico	Immigrants from Mexico
Refugee	0.053	0.082	(a)
	(0.22)	(0.27)	
Sample size	85,865	54,001	31,864

Note: Figures in parentheses are standard deviations; (a) Variables not relevant.
Source: US Census of Population, 2000, PUMS, 1 percent sample.

Table A.3. Means and Standard Deviations of Variables in Language Models, Adult Foreign-Born Women by Origin, 2000.

Variables	Total Sample	Immigrants from All Countries Except Mexico	Immigrants from Mexico
Proficient in English	0.666	0.762	0.440
(LANG2)	(0.47)	(0.43)	(0.50)
Education	11.483	12.815	8.344
	(4.73)	(4.12)	(4.60)
Age at migration	41.074	42.157	38.523
	(10.62)	(10.69)	(9.99)
Age at migration	1799.821	1891.493	1583.786
Squared	(922.16)	(938.83)	(843.12)
Years since migration	16.573	16.762	16.127
(YSM)	(11.46)	(11.76)	(10.70)
YSM Squared	405.906	419.201	374.577
	(501.44)	(519.07)	(455.67)
Abroad 5 years ago	0.018	0.017	0.020
	(0.13)	(0.13)	(0.14)
Married	0.670	0.672	0.667
	(0.47)	(0.47)	(0.47)
With own children	0.120	0.116	0.130
under 6 years only	(0.33)	(0.32)	(0.34)
With own children 6–17	0.296	0.279	0.338
years only	(0.46)	(0.45)	(0.47)
	0.155	0.107	0.269

Table A.3. (*Continued*)

Variables	Total Sample	Immigrants from All Countries Except Mexico	Immigrants from Mexico
With own children under 6 years and 6–17 years	(0.36)	(0.31)	(0.44)
Non metropolitan	0.009	0.006	0.017
	(0.09)	(0.07)	(0.13)
SOUTH	0.277	0.276	0.280
	(0.45)	(0.45)	(0.45)
Miles ('000) from origin	3.883	4.919	0.650
	(2.65)	(2.53)	(0.35)
Miles ('000) from origin Squared	22.086	30.575	0.546
	(23.29)	(23.04)	(0.73)
Linguistic distance	0.520	0.552	(a)
	(0.15)	(0.16)	
Minority language concentration CONC-STATE	9.860	4.803	21.778
	(11.04)	(7.91)	(7.70)
Minority language concentration CONC-MSA	12.670	7.433	25.012
	(16.76)	(14.48)	(15.21)
Minority language concentration CONC-SUPER	15.526	8.763	31.466
	(20.28)	(16.10)	(20.18)
Colony	0.160	0.228	(a)
	(0.37)	(0.42)	
Refugee	0.056	0.080	(a)
	(0.23)	(0.27)	
Sample size	83,832	58,000	25,832

Note: Figures in parentheses are standard deviations; (a) Variables not relevant.
Source: US Census of Population, 2000, PUMS, 1 percent sample.

SECTION II:
IMMIGRANT LIFE

GREEN CARDS AND THE LOCATION CHOICES OF IMMIGRANTS IN THE UNITED STATES, 1971–2000

David A. Jaeger

ABSTRACT

This paper examines the determinants of the initial location choices of immigrants who enter the U.S. with different kinds of visas ("green cards"). Conditional logit models with the 48 contiguous U.S. states as the choice set are estimated using population data on immigrants from the Immigration and Naturalization Service between 1971 and 2000 matched to data on state characteristics from the Integrated Public Use Microsamples of the U.S. Census. As in previous research, it is estimated that immigrants have a higher probability of moving to states where individuals from their region of birth are a larger share of the state population, with relatives of legal permanent residents responding most to this factor. In addition, it is estimated that immigrants in all admission categories respond to labor market conditions when choosing where to live, but that these effects are the largest for male employment-based immigrants and, surprisingly, refugees. These relationships are relatively stable across models that include state fixed effects as well as those that allow the coefficients to vary across the four decades available in the data.

Immigration: Trends, Consequences and Prospects for the United States
Research in Labor Economics, Volume 27, 131–183
Copyright © 2008 by Elsevier Ltd.
All rights of reproduction in any form reserved
ISSN: 0147-9121/doi:10.1016/S0147-9121(07)00004-0

1. INTRODUCTION

Since 1971, approximately 25 million immigrants have entered the U.S. as legal permanent residents. These immigrants have tended to locate on both coasts and along the southern border, with labor market and fiscal impacts of immigrants concentrated in those areas. That immigrants tend to locate near the border might suggest that immigrants are relatively insensitive to economic conditions in the interior of the U.S. even though many come to the U.S. for economic reasons.

Given the continued large flow of immigrants that began in 1965 with the change in U.S. immigration law from a geographic quota system to one determined primarily by the goal of reuniting families, the determinants of immigrant location choice should be important considerations in designing immigration policy. The capacity of the U.S. to absorb immigrants is potentially much greater if they are more likely to respond to disperse economic opportunities rather than clustering solely in "traditional" immigrant-receiving areas.

The literature on the determinants of immigrant locations in the U.S. provides mixed evidence on the responsiveness of immigrants to geographic variation in labor market conditions. Bartel (1989), using individual-level data of the 1980 U.S. Census, estimated a conditional logit model and found that the foreign-born tend to locate in metropolitan areas with large ethnic populations and that more highly-educated immigrants tend to be less geographically concentrated than less-educated immigrants. She also found that immigrants are relatively insensitive to economic conditions, a result that has been frequently cited in the literature on the impact of immigration on the labor market outcomes of native workers (see Borjas, 1999 for an overview). Dunlevey (1991), using aggregated data from the Immigration and Naturalization Service (INS) from 1986 and 1987, focused solely on the location patterns of Caribbean- and Latin-born resident aliens. He found that new immigrants are attracted to locations with relatively large concentrations of similar immigrants. Zavodny (1999) followed a similar estimation strategy using aggregate data from annual INS and Office of Refugee Resettlement reports from 1989 to 1994 and found that flows of new immigrants respond both to demographic factors like the share of the foreign-born in a state as well as economic factors like the unemployment rate. She found that these influences vary by visa type, with employment immigrants being affected most by economic factors and family reunification immigrants being more influenced by high concentrations of the foreign-born. Bauer, Epstein, and Gang (2002) used individual level data from the Mexican Migration Project and estimated a model similar to that of Bartel (1989) and Jager (2000). They examined the importance of immigrant concentrations in greater detail and found that Mexican immigrants respond both to recent flows as well as the stock of immigrants from their village when deciding where to locate in the U.S. They also presented some evidence that local unemployment rates affect immigrants' choices, particularly for those who are in the U.S. illegally. Borjas (2001), using Census and Current Population Survey data from the 1990s, found that immigrants were more responsive than natives to differences in economic conditions and that they "grease the wheels" of the labor market by bringing workers to where they can be used most efficiently.

In this paper, I revisit the issue of immigrants' location choice by using INS data on nearly every legal immigrant who came to the U.S. to reside permanently between 1971 and 2000. Unlike most past research, I stratify by one of the primary policy levers used to alter the character flow of the legal immigrant flow to the U.S.: green card categories. I also look at a much longer time frame than previous research. Because I have information on *nearly every legal immigrant* that has come to the U.S. since 1971, my samples are quite a bit larger than those used previously. Matching these data to samples of the U.S. population from the 1970 through 2000 U.S. Censuses, I find that labor market conditions (measured by unemployment and expected wages) affect immigrant location choices across time and across admission categories, but are most important in determining employment-related immigrants' locations. Like past research, I find that concentrations of similar immigrants (defined by region of birth) are also important determinants of where immigrants decide to live, particularly for relatives of past green card recipients.

The next section of the paper briefly discusses the admission categories that are used to determine the eligibility of a foreign national to emigrate to the U.S. and which form the core of the analysis in the paper. I then present, in Section 3, some descriptive statistics on the origin of immigrants in broad admission categories and where they locate in the U.S. I discuss the skills of immigrants in different admission categories in Section 4. In Section 5, I describe the stochastic choice model and present estimates of the parameters of that model for immigrants in different admission categories. I offer some conclusions in Section 6.

2. A BRIEF OVERVIEW OF ADMISSION CATEGORIES

The Immigration and Naturalization Services Act of 1965 abolished national origin as the primary basis of U.S. immigration law and replaced it with a system based mainly on three objectives: to reunite families, to fill jobs with skilled or needed workers, and to provide safe haven for refugees. Of these, the first is by far the most important and a majority of legal immigrants enter the U.S. through this channel. The law distinguishes between admission categories that have annual limits on the number of visas that can be issued and those that do not. Immediate relatives of U.S. citizens (spouses, parents, and unmarried children under 21) are not subject to quotas on the number of available visas while all other admission categories, or "green cards,"[1] are subject to annual quotas. Limits are imposed both by the type of green card and by the country of "chargeability," which is usually an immigrant's country of birth. Refugees and asylum seekers face different limitations than other visa categories.

While reuniting families, filling jobs, and providing safe haven have remained the primary goals of U.S. immigration policy, the absolute number of numerically limited green cards as well as the relative share of those green cards in different categories have changed at various points since 1965. Most notably, the Immigration Act of 1990 increased both the total number of numerically limited green cards as well as the share of those devoted to employment immigrants. The "diversity" category was also introduced by the Immigration Act of 1990, with the objective of increasing the number of immigrants from "underrepresented" countries, those that sent fewer than 50,000 individuals to the U.S. during the previous five years.[2] These visas are allocated by a lottery; in 2005, the U.S. Department of State received 6.3 million valid applications for 50,000 diversity green cards.

In this paper, I divide immigrant entrants into seven primary categories: immediate family of U.S. citizens not subject to quotas (spouses, unmarried children under 21, and parents), family of U.S. citizens subject to quotas (unmarried children over 21, siblings, and married children), family of legal permanent residents (i.e. current green card holders), employment-based visas,[3] "diversity" visas,[4] refugees and asylees, and a vestigial category of entrants from the Western Hemisphere.[5] There are many different kinds of visas within each of these categories, but they represent the basic outline of U.S. immigration policy.[6]

The entry requirements vary by visa type and therefore we might expect the location choices of immigrants in different admission categories to vary as well. Family reunification immigrants must have a sponsoring relative already in the U.S. who files a petition with U.S. Citizenship and Immigration Services (CIS, formerly one of the constituent parts of the INS). Employment-based immigrants must, in general, already have secured a job in the U.S. and their prospective employer must file a petition with CIS for them to be admitted. In addition, for most employment visas, the U.S. Department of Labor must certify that no qualified U.S. worker is available to fill the job. Unlike family-reunification and employment-based immigrants, immigrants entering on a diversity green card do not necessarily have prior connections to individuals or firms in the U.S. They therefore provide, perhaps, the best measure of how a random individual from outside the U.S. would respond to various factors that determine location choice. Refugees, in general, enter the U.S on temporary visas first and then can apply for legal permanent residence.[7]

An immigrant who desires to enter the U.S. under a visa category that is subject to numerical limits may have to wait in a queue until an appropriate visa becomes available. The length of this wait can vary substantially by visa category and the immigrant's country of chargeability. For example, in May 2006, the "priority date" for individuals from the Philippines waiting to enter as a sibling of a U.S. citizen was 15 October 1983, meaning that their application for admission must have been approved on or before that date for them to eligible for a visa of that type. For all other countries other than Mexico and India, the "priority date" for a visa for a sibling of a U.S. citizen was 1 January 1995 – still a substantial wait. Of course, immigrants can potentially avail themselves of more than one potential sponsor, particularly for family-reunification visas, and may strategically choose under which category to apply. Because I have no way of knowing who an immigrant's potential sponsors are, I will not try to model this choice, but merely note that an immigrant may have more than one legal path of entry into the U.S.

Two final distinctions made by U.S. policy should be noted. First, an immigrant whose relationship to an individual or firm in the U.S., refugee status, or lottery success allows them to enter the U.S. is considered the "primary" immigrant. Their immediate family (spouse and minor children) may, in general, also enter the U.S. at the same time. If they do, they are considered "beneficiaries" of the primary immigrant because their visa status is a "derivative" of the status of the primary immigrant.[8] Second, individuals may apply for legal permanent residency while they are either inside or outside of the U.S. Those who are already in the country must "adjust" their status from temporary (e.g. a student, J, or temporary employment, H, visa) to permanent. Those who are outside of the U.S. enter as "new" immigrants, although, of course, they are very likely to have ties to individuals or firms in the U.S. For the regression analysis later in the paper, I will examine the location choices of newly arrived primary immigrants to minimize potential endogeneity issues.

3. DATA

Data on nearly every immigrant admitted legally to the U.S. between 1971 and 2000 are available in the various *Immigrants Admitted to the United States* files produced by the former INS (now split into several sub-agencies of the Department of Homeland Security). I use all of the data available from 1971 to 2000 for the descriptive statistics in the paper. The key variable available in the INS data that is not available in other data sources such as the Census or Current Population Survey is the type of visa under which an immigrant was admitted to the U.S. Reflecting the complexity of U.S. immigration law, there is a substantial amount of detail available about visa type in the INS data. But to simplify the analysis and provide consistency over time, I divide the immigrant population into the seven broad visa categories discussed above: immediate relatives of U.S. citizens not subject to quota limitations, other family of U.S. citizens subject to quota limitations, family of resident legal aliens, employment-related, diversity (for the years after 1991), Western Hemisphere immigrants (for the years prior to 1977), and refugees. The descriptive graphs also present a residual category of "other." Categorization of the detailed visa types available in the INS data into these seven areas generally follows the classification outlined in the documentation to the 2000 INS data file (U.S. Department of Justice, 2000). The INS data are made available by fiscal year but I present results by calendar year.[9]

In this paper, I use states as the geographic units of analysis. I define the geography this way for a variety of reasons. First, this allows me to examine the behavior of all of the immigrants who locate in the contiguous 48 states, rather than excluding those who live outside of some arbitrary number of large cities.[10] Second, inclusion of all 48 contiguous states provides a "control" group of states, partially absent from analyses that use only large metropolitan areas (e.g. Bartel, 1989), which do not include large numbers of immigrants that entered the U.S. previously. Using a choice set of 48 states is both computationally feasible in the conditional logit analysis described below while also providing a substantial amount of variation in the right hand side variables. Third, and most important, state boundaries are constant and permit direct comparisons over time without concerns about how differing definitions of metropolitan areas might alter the descriptive statistics or the estimated coefficients of the models. In the INS data, the observed "location" is the address to which the immigrant's green card was mailed. While this may or may not be the exact location in which the immigrant initially lived, for my purposes there will be no mismeasurement of their location as long as the immigrant received their green card in the state in which they first resided.

For the regression analysis, data on state characteristics (e.g. unemployment, wages, and concentrations of the foreign-born) are drawn from the Integrated Public Use Microsamples of the U.S. Census, or IPUMS (Ruggles, et al., 2004) from 1970, 1980, 1990, and 2000. Each Census provides a snapshot of the U.S. population on 1 April of that year. These data are then matched to the information on individual immigrants from the INS data. To estimate the stochastic choice models, I use data on non-refugee immigrants who entered the U.S. from June to December 1971 (the earliest data available), May to December 1980, May to December 1990, and May to September 2000, matched to data from the 1970, 1980, 1990, and 2000 IPUMS, respectively. Thus, I measure the location decisions of immigrants just after the labor market conditions and socio-demographic distributions are observed. I estimate the models for non-refugees only using "new" immigrants who were (presumably) not in the U.S. at the time of the Census. These two restrictions reduce, as much as possible, the possibility of endogeneity bias that is present in some previous estimates (e.g. Bartel, 1989), in the sense that the observed information about a state would include the immigrant herself, while still giving a strong temporal link between the observed U.S. conditions and the location choices of immigrants.

Because refugees are observed only when they change their status from temporary to permanent, I must treat them differently when defining the regression samples.[11] The INS data record only the year, but not the month, in which "adjustees" first entered the U.S. on a temporary visa. To avoid endogeneity issues, I match the 1980 Census data to individuals in the INS data who first entered the U.S. in 1981 and received their green card in 1981 or 1982; the refugee population matched to the 1990 Census is defined similarly. The refugee population matched to the 1970 Census data includes "new" refugees who received their green cards in the latter half of 1971 or the first half of 1972 as well as "adjusting" refugees who first entered the U.S. in 1971 and received their green card between 1971 and 1974. Because the INS data are available only until fiscal year 2000 (October 1999 to September 2000), I do not have data on any refugees who I am certain entered the U.S. after the Census data of 1 April 2000. I must also assume that the location of a refugee when entering U.S. was same as the location when they received their green card, as the INS data do not record the immigrants' initial locations. The populations are chosen to limit the amount of time between initial entry and when I observe the immigrant's location. Because of these data limitations, the temporal and perhaps spatial

link between the observed conditions in the U.S. and the location choice of
refugees may not be as close as for the other admission categories.

I impose two other restrictions on the population used for the regression
analysis. First, I limit the data to individuals who were 25–60 years old at the
time they received their green cards and who did not report their occupation
as a student, to insure that they have some potential connection to the labor
market. Second, I conduct the regression analysis only on "primary"
immigrants – that is, the immigrants whose status permitted their immediate
family (if any) to enter the U.S. This abstracts from issues of intra-
household correlation of unobserved characteristics and insures that only
one individual per family is used for the regression analysis.[12]

4. HOW MANY IMMIGRANTS? FROM WHERE? TO WHERE?

The flow of immigrants to the U.S. since 1971 has not been constant,
peaking in the mid-1990s then declining until 2000. Fig. 1 shows the flow of
immigrants from 1972 to 1999 (the first and last years in which data for the
full calendar year are available) in the seven admission categories discussed
above. These figures include both "new" immigrants as well as those who
were adjusting their status from a temporary to permanent legal residency.
The number of immigrants admitted to the U.S. more than doubled between

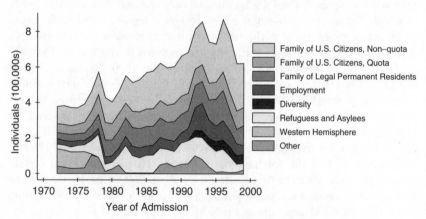

Fig. 1. Number of Immigrants Admitted to the U.S.
Note: 48 Contiguous States.
Source: Author's Tabulations of INS Data.

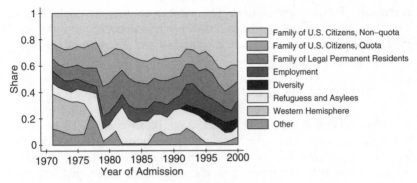

Fig. 2. Share of Admission Categories of Immigrants Admitted to the U.S.
Note: 48 Contiguous States.
Source: Author's Tabulations of INS Data.

1972 and 1996, from just less than 400,000 to a peak of about 870,000, and then decreased to around 625,000 in 1999.[13]

Fig. 2 presents the share of each green card group in total immigrant admissions from 1971 to 2000. Immediate relatives of U.S. citizens, who are not subject to quota limitations, are always the largest group, with a share that has been generally increasing from around 25 percent in the early 1970s to around 40 percent in the late 1990s and 2000. The number of other relatives of U.S. citizens, which is subject to a quota, has fluctuated somewhat, but has usually remained between 12 and 18 percent of the total. Not surprisingly, given the increasing number of green card holders, the share of relatives of legal permanent residents increased fairly substantially from the early 1970s (when it was around 10 percent) to the mid-1980s (when it was around 20 percent). The share of this group then declined somewhat in the 1990s and by 2000 was around 15 percent. Total family-related admissions (relatives of U.S. citizens and legal permanent residents) have been at least half of the entire flow of immigrants since 1973, at times exceeding 70 percent of the flow. This has been in spite of the legislative changes in 1990 that increased the number of employment-based visas and introduced employment-creation and "diversity" green cards (winners of the visa lottery). Reflecting those changes, employment-based entrants (including those entering as beneficiaries of the job holder) increased from less than 10 percent of the total in 1971 to a peak of 18 percent in 1992, falling back to an average of around 11 percent from 1995 to 2000. Refugee admissions have fluctuated substantially depending on the conditions around the world that warrant awarding refugee status, from a minimum of 6 percent in 1999 to a maximum of 28 percent in 1982. The number of diversity admissions has remained fairly constant at around 50,000 per year since their introduction in 1992, but as a share have fluctuated between 4 and 8 percent of the total.

4.1. Where Did the Immigrants Come from?

Past research (e.g. Bartel, 1989; Jaeger, 2000; Bauer et al., 2002) has shown that concentrations of similar immigrants are important determinants of location choice. To the extent that immigrants in different admission categories originate in different countries, we would expect that settlement patterns would also differ across those categories. Given the different requirements of the various types of green cards, it is not surprising that immigrants entering the U.S. under different visas come from different areas of the world. In Figs. 3–8, I present the share of green card recipients from each of 13 regions of origin in each of the seven primary admission categories.[14] Relative to other visa groups, immediate relatives of U.S. citizens (Fig. 3) have had a roughly constant distribution across the 13 regions of origin over time. The biggest changes have been an increase in entrants from Eastern Europe after 1985 and an increase in the share of entrants from Mexico and Central America after the mid-1990s.

Compared to immediate family of U.S. citizens, both family of U.S. citizens subject to quotas (Fig. 4) and relatives of legal permanent residents

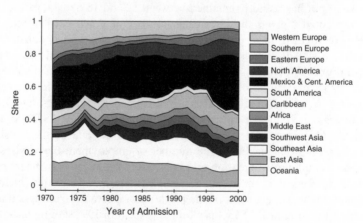

Fig. 3. Share by Country of Birth of Relatives of U.S. Citizens, Non-Quota.
Note: 48 Contiguous States.
Source: Author's Tabulations of INS Data.

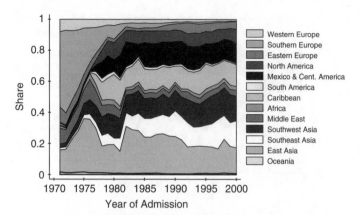

Fig. 4. Share by Country of Birth of Relatives of U.S. Citizens, Quota.
Note: 48 Contiguous States.
Source: Author's Tabulations of INS Data.

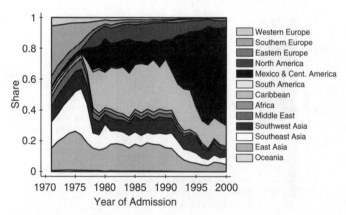

Fig. 5. Share by Country of Birth of Relatives of Legal Permanent Relatives.
Note: 48 Contiguous States.
Source: Author's Tabulations of INS Data.

(Fig. 5) have experienced much greater shifts in the distribution across region of origin. For relatives of U.S. citizens, the largest changes came after 1975, when immigrants from the Western Hemisphere (i.e. from North America, Mexico and Central America, the Caribbean, and South America) were required to enter the U.S. through the "normal" admission categories from which they had previously been exempt. At the same time that the

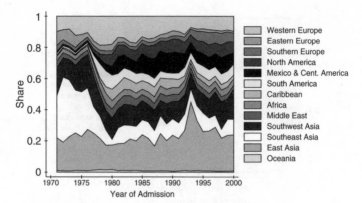

Fig. 6.   Share by Country of Birth of Employment Immigrants.
Note: 48 Contiguous States.
Source: Author's Tabulations of INS Data.

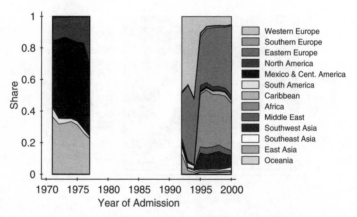

Fig. 7.   Share by Country of Birth of Western Hemisphere Immigrants, 1971–1977,
and Diversity Immigrants, 1992–2000.
Note: 48 Contiguous States.
Source: Author's Tabulations of INS Data.

share of Western Hemisphere immigrants was increasing, that of immigrants
from Western and Southern Europe was decreasing. Relative to the 1970s,
the share of Eastern Europeans and Southeast Asians increased in the early
and mid 1980s. Since 1985, however, the shares from the various country
groups have been quite stable. This has not been the case for relatives of

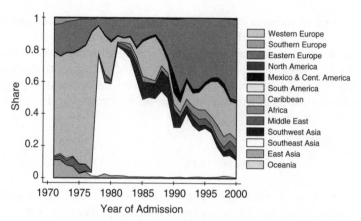

Fig. 8. Share by Country of Birth of Refugees and Asylees.
Note: 48 Contiguous States.
Source: Author's Tabulations of INS Data.

legal permanent residents. As with numerically limited relatives of U.S. citizens, there was a large increase in the share of immigrants from Mexico and Central America and South America when Western Hemisphere immigrants were required to enter under "normal" categories after 1976. What is more striking, however, is the substantial increase in the share of immigrants from Mexico and Central America after 1990. The timing of this large increase coincides with the legalization of illegal aliens following the 1986 Immigration Reform and Control Act (IRCA), which were largely of Mexican and Central American origin, suggesting that the overall impact of IRCA on the number of legal immigrants was substantially greater than just the 2.8 million who were admitted directly.

The change in the region-of-origin composition after 1976 is also evident in the distribution of employment-based green cards. Fig. 6 shows the time pattern of these flows. On the whole, the shares were fairly stable after 1980, with a notable spike of East Asians in 1993 and an increase in Eastern Europeans following the fall of the Iron Curtain.

The region-of-origin distributions of Western Hemisphere and diversity immigrants are shown in Fig. 7.[15] The most notable feature here is the change in the composition of the flow of diversity immigrants in 1995. This is because in 1995 the countries from which diversity immigrants could come was substantially increased; prior to 1995, citizens of Ireland and Poland were the main beneficiaries of the diversity visa program.

The origin of refugees is determined both by political and humanitarian situations around the world. Fig. 8 presents the region-of-origin shares of refugees. Refugees were predominantly from Cuba in the early 1970s. The share of refugees from Southeast Asia increased following the end of the Vietnam War and since approximately 1980 there has been a steady increase in the share of refugees from Eastern Europe, particularly just prior to, and after, the break up of the Soviet Union.

4.2. Where Did the Immigrants Go?

It is well known that immigrants tend to be more geographically concentrated than natives. I present Herfindahl indices of concentration for the flow of immigrants to the U.S. (measured annually from 1971 to 2000 in the INS data) and the stocks of foreign- and native-born individuals (measured at 10 year intervals from 1970 to 2000 in the IPUMS data) in Fig. 9. The Herfindahl index is given by

$$H_{it} = \sum_{j=1}^{48} \theta_{ijt}^2 \tag{1}$$

where θ_{ij} is the share of group i that is located in state j, in year t, with $0 \leq H_{it} \leq 1$. Smaller values of H_{it} indicate lower degrees of geographic

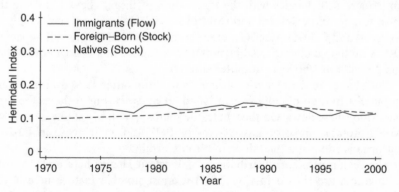

Fig. 9. Geographic Concentration of Stock of Foreign-Born and Natives, Flow of Immigrants.
Note: 48 Contiguous States.
Source: Author's Tabulations of IPUMS and INS Data.

concentration. The geographic concentration of natives was essentially constant, while that for both the flow of immigrants and the stock of the foreign-born peaked around 1990 and then declined by 2000. The flow of immigrants appears to have been less geographically dispersed than the stock of the foreign-born in 1970 and 1980, but they were essentially concentrated to the same degree by 1990 and 2000.

Fig. 10, for family reunification visas, and Fig. 11, for all other admission categories, repeat this exercise. Immediate family of U.S. citizens

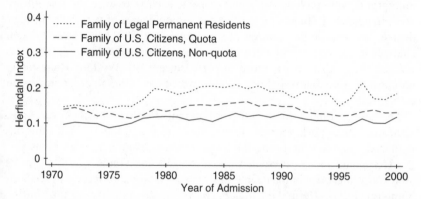

Fig. 10. Geographic Concentration of Family Reunification Immigrants.
Note: 48 Contiguous States.
Source: Author's Tabulations of INS Data.

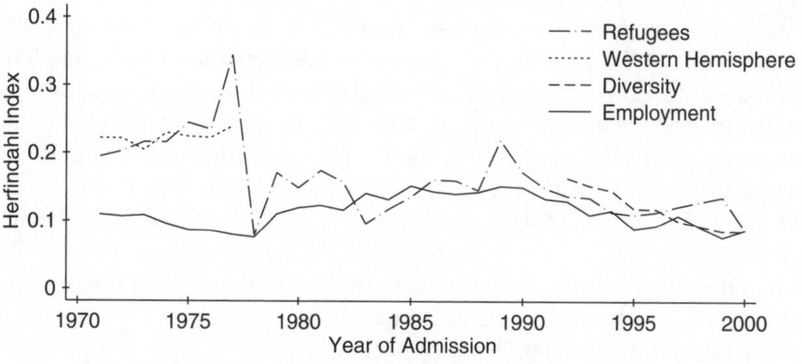

Fig. 11. Geographic Concentration of Employment, Refugee, and Western Hemisphere Immigrants.
Note: 48 Contiguous States.
Source: Author's Tabulations of INS Data.

(mostly spouses) are, less concentrated than other relatives of U.S. citizens, but are, still substantially more concentrated than the total native-born population, in comparison to Fig. 9. Relatives of legal permanent residents are less dispersed than the relatives of U.S. citizens, which is not surprising, given that the foreign-born are more concentrated than the native-born. As with the overall flow of immigrants, the geographic concentration of employment-visa immigrants peaked between 1985 and 1990. The increase in geographic dispersion since 1990 is also evinced by diversity immigrants, who have grown more disperse each year since the visa lottery was introduced. Refugees have exhibited a high degree of variability in their degree of geographic concentration, reflecting the sometimes sudden changes in the country of birth composition of refugees. Overall, however, refugees have also grown more disperse since 1990. Western Hemisphere immigrants were relatively highly concentrated compared to other admission categories.

The conventional wisdom is that immigrants locate primarily in six states: California, New York, Florida, Texas, New Jersey, and Illinois. While this has remained roughly true during the 30 years under examination in this paper, the Herfindahl indices presented above suggest substantial variation across admission categories in the degree to which these six states receive the bulk of immigrants. The Herfindahl indices, however, do not capture the shifting location choices of immigrants. To examine where immigrants choose to live in greater detail, in Figs. 12–19 I present maps of the geographic distribution of natives, the foreign born, and the various immigrant groups across the 40 years of this study. Figs. 12 and 13 show the distribution of the stock of the native and foreign-born populations, respectively, in each of the four Census years. Figs. 14–19 present the geographic distribution of the cumulative immigrant flow for each green card category during the three decades under study. In each map, the share of the stock or flow is grouped into five categories, with the each break point between categories being double the previous break point, i.e. the categories are [0%, 0.5%], (0.5%, 1.0%], (1.0%, 2.0%], (2.0%, 4.0%], (4.0%, 8.0%], (8.0%, 16.0%], and (16.0%, 100.0%].

It was clear from Fig. 9 that natives are geographically less concentrated than the foreign born. This can also be seen by comparing Figs. 12 and 13 for natives and the foreign born, respectively. Between 1970 and 2000 both populations shifted away somewhat from northern states like New York and Michigan. While the "Big 6" states were important locations in all four decades for immigrants, they also started moving to non-traditional locations like Arizona, Nevada, North Carolina, and Utah in the latter

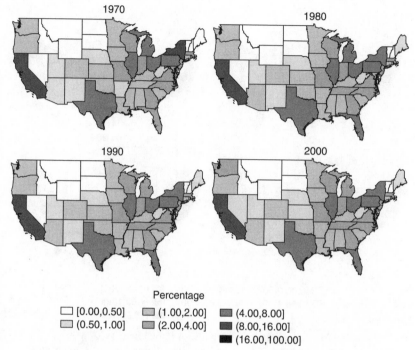

Percentage

☐ [0.00,0.50]   ☐ (1.00,2.00]   ▨ (4.00,8.00]
☐ (0.50,1.00]   ▨ (2.00,4.00]   ▨ (8.00,16.00]
                                  ■ (16.00,100.00]

Fig. 12. Locations of Native Population, 1970–2000.
Note: Map Shows Share of Native Population Living in Each State.
Source: Author's Tabulations of IPUMS Data.

two decades. Unlike in 1970, Texas and Florida were roughly as important locations for the foreign-born as New York in 2000.

Like the geographic distribution of natives, the location choices of immediate relatives of U.S. citizens, shown in Fig. 14, have also changed relatively little in the three decades between 1971 and 2000. The same could also be said of other relatives of U.S. citizens, shown in Fig. 15, except for a slight shift toward the south- and northwestern states. There have been substantial changes, however, in the location choices of relatives of legal permanent residents, as shown in Fig. 16. Given the large increase in the share of this group coming from Mexico and Central America, as shown in Fig. 5, it is perhaps not surprising that Texas became an increasingly important destination. There was also been a distinct shift toward states relatively near to Texas and California (Arizona, New Mexico, Nevada, Utah, Oklahoma, Kansas, and Colorado) as well as the northwest (Washington and Oregon).

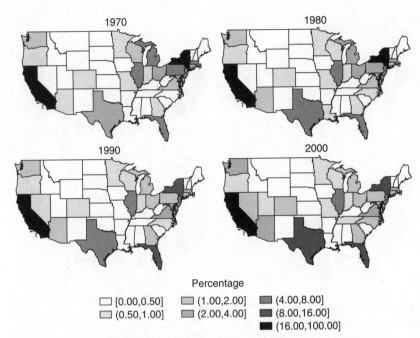

Fig. 13. Locations of Foreign-Born Population, 1970–2000.
Note: Map Shows Share of Foreign-Born Population Living in Each State.
Source: Author's Tabulations of IPUMS Data.

There was variation across non-family-reunification admission categories as well. Employment visa immigrants, shown in Fig. 17, were less concentrated in all three decades than the family of legal permanent residents and non-immediate family of U.S. citizens. In all three periods, they were more likely to locate in the upper Midwest and the Southeast than either family of legal permanent residents or non-immediate family of U.S. citizens. The most notable changes among employment immigrants were shifts away from Illinois after 1980 and New York after 1990. Fig. 18 shows that Western Hemisphere immigrants were highly concentrated in the "Big 6" states, and avoided locating in much of the country. Diversity immigrants were less highly concentrated than those from the Western Hemisphere 20 years earlier, but still much more concentrated than natives or immediate family of U.S. citizens, with the "Big 6", particularly New York, figuring prominently in their location choices. In general, the geographic distributions of refugees, shown in Fig. 19, were fairly similar to those of non-immediate family of U.S.

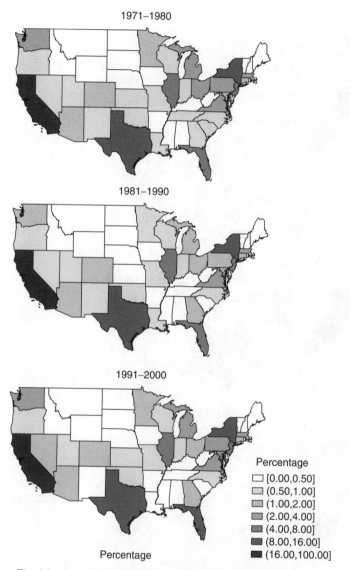

1971–1980

1981–1990

1991–2000

Percentage

Percentage
☐ [0.00,0.50]
☐ (0.50,1.00]
▨ (1.00,2.00]
▨ (2.00,4.00]
■ (4.00,8.00]
■ (8.00,16.00]
■ (16.00,100.00]

Fig. 14. Locations of Relatives of U.S. Citizens, Non-Quota.
Note: Map Shows Share of Cumulative Flow in Decade Locating in Each State.
Source: Author's Tabulations of INS Data.

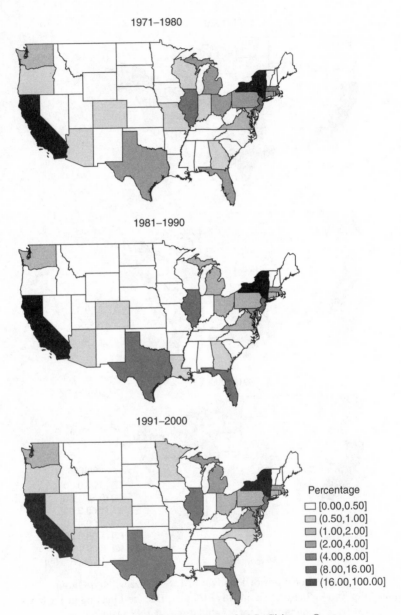

Fig. 15. Locations of Relatives of U.S. Citizens, Quota.
Note: Map Shows Share of Cumulative Flow in Decade Locating in Each State.
Source: Author's Tabulations of INS Data.

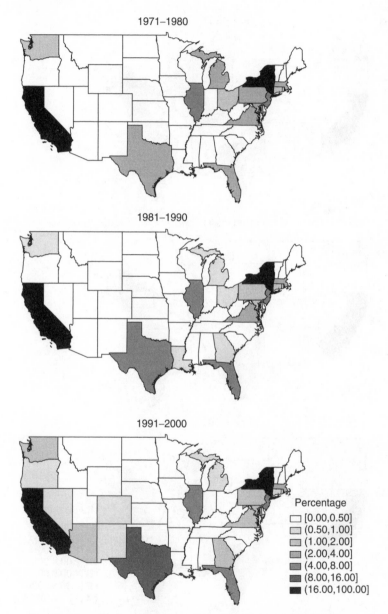

Fig. 16. Locations of Relatives of Legalized Permanent Residents.
Note: Map Shows Share of Cumulative Flow in Decade Locating in Each State.
Source: Author's Tabulations of INS Data.

1971–1980

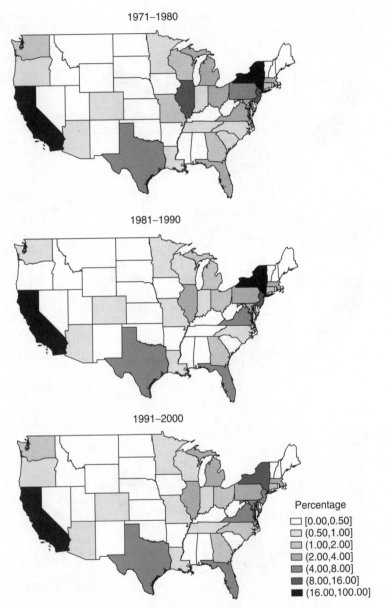

1981–1990

1991–2000

Percentage

☐ [0.00,0.50]
☐ (0.50,1.00]
☐ (1.00,2.00]
☐ (2.00,4.00]
☐ (4.00,8.00]
☐ (8.00,16.00]
■ (16.00,100.00]

Fig. 17.   Locations of Employment Visa Immigrants.
Note: Map Shows Share of Cumulative Flow in Decade Locating in Each State.
Source: Author's Tabulations of INS Data.

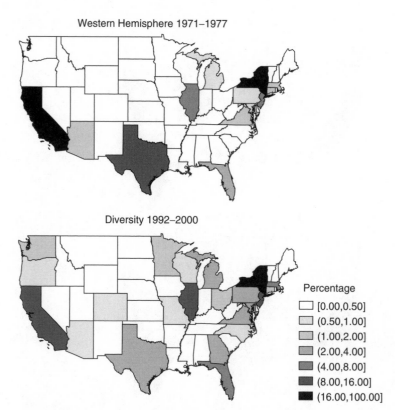

Fig. 18.   Locations of Western Hemisphere and Diversity Immigrants.
Note: Map Shows Share of Cumulative Flow in Decade Locating in Each State.
Source: Author's Tabulations of INS Data.

citizens. Refugees were somewhat more likely to locate in the Southeast in 1991–2000 than in 1971–1980, and were somewhat less likely to locate in Louisiana and Arkansas. Washington and Oregon also became more popular, while New York was less so in the middle decade than in the first and last. Over the 30-year period of the data, however, the changes in the geographic distributions of refugees have been relatively minor.

Taken as a whole, these figures indicate that there are substantial differences in location choices among immigrants in different admission categories and, to some extent, over time within admission category. This is due, in part, to the different countries of origin and varying skills of immigrants in the various admission categories.

1971–1980

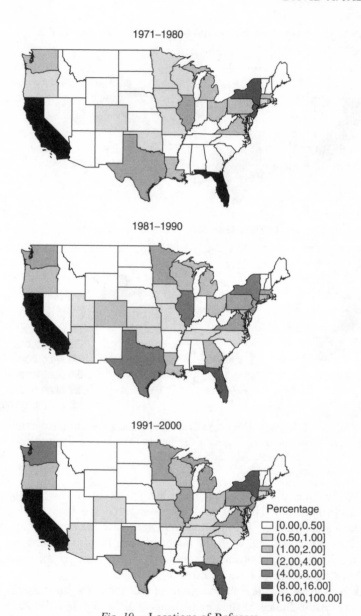

1981–1990

1991–2000

Percentage
□ [0.00,0.50]
□ (0.50,1.00]
▨ (1.00,2.00]
▨ (2.00,4.00]
▨ (4.00,8.00]
▨ (8.00,16.00]
■ (16.00,100.00]

Fig. 19. Locations of Refugees.
Note: Map Shows Share of Cumulative Flow in Decade Locating in Each State.
Source: Author's Tabulations of INS Data.

5. GREEN CARDS AND THE SKILLS OF IMMIGRANTS

While concentrations of individuals from their country of birth are likely to be an important determinant of where an immigrant decides to live, Bartel (1989) has noted that the more highly educated foreign-born tend to be more geographically disperse than those with lower levels of education. Skills and their interaction with labor market conditions may also play an important role in determining location choice. The INS data unfortunately do not contain information on educational attainment. They do, however, contain information on occupation, which should be directly related to the human capital that immigrants bring to the U.S.

Occupation in the INS data is self-reported. For primary employment visa immigrants, the recorded occupations are those of the immigrants' jobs in the U.S. All other immigrants are free to record whatever occupation they want. From the responses in the INS data it is impossible to tell whether the recorded occupation is the one they will or want to do in the U.S. or one that they performed in their home country. The responses to the occupation question are therefore likely to be better used as a general measure of human capital rather than a strong indication (except for primary employment-based immigrants) of what occupation the immigrant will hold in the U.S. The coding used by the INS was also, until recently, fairly idiosyncratic. Occupation codes vary across time in the INS data and between the INS and IPUMS data. The "lowest common denominator" for the occupation codes was those used in the INS data between 1983 and 1998. This yields a variable with 18 categories after dropping students and combining a few occupations with small cell sizes.[16]

I combine the data on occupation along with information on the immigrant's region of origin and demographic information to generate a prediction of the skills that the immigrant brings to the U.S. Pooling data on the foreign-born from the 1980 and 1990 Censuses in which both occupation and demographic information as well as educational attainment are observed, I estimated separate ordered logit regressions for men and women with three broad education categories as the dependent variable: less than 12 years (low skill), 12–15 years (medium skill) and 16 or more years of education (high skill). In addition to indicator variables for occupation, the regressions included indicators for each of the 13 region of origin groups, an indicator for being married, and a quadratic in age. To abstract from schooling and retirement issues, I dropped individuals who were in school as well as those who were less than 25 years old or greater than 60 years old. The coefficients from these models were then used to create a predicted probability that the individuals in the INS data were in each of the three skill categories. More information on the results of the ordered logit regressions and the prediction procedure can be found in the Data Appendix.

To evaluate the changing skill composition of immigrants within admission categories, I plot the distribution across the three skill groups in Figs. 20–25. For each year, I summed the predicted probability of being in each of the three skill groups across individuals; i.e. each individual contributed some fraction to each of the three skill group shares. This procedure amounts to assigning fixed weights to occupation, region-of-origin, age, and marital status based on the coefficients of the mens' and womens' ordered logit regressions. Changes over time in the imputed skill distribution of immigrants in each admission category derive completely from changes in the occupational, region-of-origin, age, and marital status distributions.

For family of U.S. citizens, shown in Figs. 20 (immediate family) and 21 (other relatives), the distribution across skill groups was relatively constant. Roughly 22 percent of both immediate and other relatives of U.S. citizens were assigned to the lowest skill category, although this declined to 15 percent between 1998 and 2000. About 30 percent of immediate family and 35 percent of other family were assigned to the highest skill category (college graduates), although this increased for immediate relatives, ending at 37 percent in 2000.

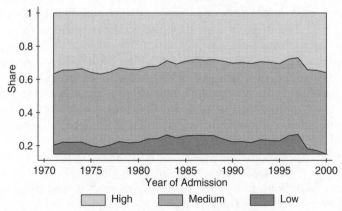

Fig. 20. Share of Skill Group Relatives of U.S. Citizens, Non-Quota.
Note: 48 Contiguous States.
Source: Author's Tabulations of INS Data.

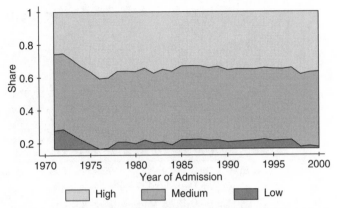

Fig. 21. Share by Skill Group of Relatives of U.S. Citizens, Quota.
Note: 48 Contiguous States.
Source: Author's Tabulations of INS Data.

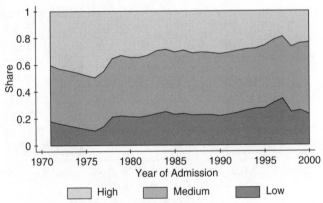

Fig. 22. Share by Skill Group of Relatives of Legal Permanent Residents.
Note: 48 Contiguous States.
Source: Author's Tabulations of INS Data.

The average skill of individuals who entered as family of legal permanent residents (Fig. 22) declined continuously after 1976. In 1971, 40 percent of the families of legal permanent residents were imputed to be in the highest skill category while this was only 23 percent in 2000. Similarly, in the mid 1970s,

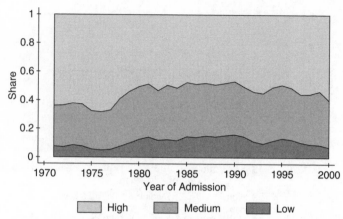

Fig. 23. Share by Skill Group of Employment Immigrants.
Note: 48 Contiguous States.
Source: Author's Tabulations of INS Data.

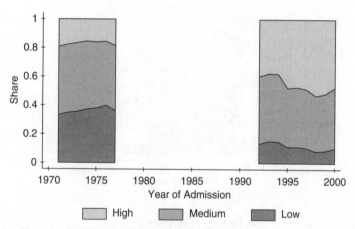

Fig. 24. Share by Skill Group of Western Hemisphere Immigrants, 1971–1977, and
Diversity Immigrants, 1992–2000.
Note: 48 Contiguous States.
Source: Author's Tabulations of INS Data.

only about 12 percent were assigned to the lowest skill category, while
35 percent were in 1997, falling somewhat to 23 percent in 2000.

Since most primary employment visa immigrants are required to be well-
educated or have substantial work experience, it is not surprising that Fig. 23

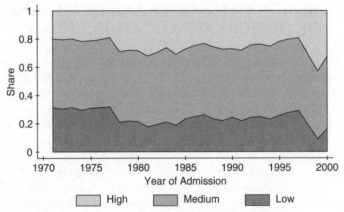

Fig. 25.   Share by Skill Group of Refugees and Asylees.
Note: 48 Contiguous States.
Source: Author's Tabulations of INS Data.

shows that a much larger share of employment-based immigrants were highly skilled than in the family reunification admission categories. Over the entire period, roughly 50–60 percent of employment-based green card holders were in the highest skill group while another 30–40 percent were in the middle skill group and between 5 and 15 percent were in the lowest skill category. The average skill level declined somewhat in the late 1980s, rebounding afterwards. Diversity immigrants are also required to have at least a high-school diploma, and the skill distribution in Fig. 24 reflects this. Western Hemisphere immigrants generally had lower skills than the other admission categories, with less than 20 percent in the high-skill category.

The skill level of refugees, shown in Fig. 25, improved somewhat after the 1970s, when roughly one-third were in the low-skill group, while more recently this share has been closer to 20 percent. Also, in the late 1980s the share allocated to the highest skill group increased substantially, reflecting, perhaps, the shift toward Eastern Europeans.

While these skill measures are relatively coarse, they do roughly capture the administrative requirements of the various admission categories. Given the differing skills and region of origin across the various admission categories, we might expect that different groups will respond differently to changing economic and socio-demographic conditions when deciding where to locate in the U.S.

6. ADMISSION CATEGORIES AND DETERMINANTS OF IMMIGRANTS' LOCATION CHOICE

What determines where immigrants decide to live? Proximity to kin and country-specific networks surely play an important role. While the past evidence is mixed, it is also almost certainly true that labor market conditions affect where immigrants decide to live, even for family-reunification entrants. In this section, I present regression results that attempt to resolve the extent to which various socio-demographic and labor market factors influence where immigrants live.

I employ a standard discrete choice model for the analysis. This framework is similar to those employed by Bartel (1989), Jaeger (2000), and Bauer et al. (2002). I assume that immigrants have an additive stochastic utility function of the form

$$U_{ij} = \mathbf{L}_j \Theta + \mathbf{X}_{ij} \Pi + \varepsilon_{ij} \tag{2}$$

where $\mathbf{L}_j$ is a vector of state characteristics (including, potentially, state fixed effects) and $\mathbf{X}_{ij}$ a vector of interactions between state and individual characteristics. I assume that immigrants choose the location that maximizes their expected utility. If the stochastic term $\varepsilon_{ij} \sim$ i.i.d. Weibull, the parameters of the model can be estimated using a conditional logit model (McFadden, 1984). The probability of individual i choosing to live in state l is then

$$P(y_i = l) = \frac{\exp(\mathbf{L}_j \Theta + \mathbf{X}_{ij} \Pi)}{\sum\limits_{j=1}^{48} \exp(\mathbf{L}_j \Theta + \mathbf{X}_{ij} \Pi)} \tag{3}$$

where y_i is individual i's location choice and there are 48 states in the choice set for all immigrant groups. This analysis requires estimation using $48 \times N$ observations, where N is the number of individuals in the data. The marginal effect of a change in some characteristic, z, of a state, l, on the probability that an immigrant will choose to live in that state is just the derivative of (3), i.e.

$$\frac{\partial P(y_i = l)}{\partial z_l} = \left[P(y_i = l)(1 - P(y_i = l)) \right] \theta_z \tag{4}$$

While the effect of any covariate will vary with l (because the share of immigrants choosing to live in any given state, $P(y_i = l)$, is different),

I present "average" effects of z on $P(y_i = l)$, i.e.

$$\frac{\partial \hat{P}(y_i = l)}{\partial z_l} = [(1/48) - (1 - (1/48))]\hat{\theta}_z \qquad (5)$$

These are just a rescaling of the underlying conditional logit coefficients so that they can be interpreted as marginal effects on a probability.

The variables in **L** and **X** are designed to capture a variety of state characteristics that possibly affect both the pecuniary and non-pecuniary aspects of immigrants' utility. I include two variables to measure labor market conditions: the unemployment rate for all workers aged 25–60 and the immigrant's expected log wage. The unemployment rate for all workers (both natives and immigrants) is used as a general indicator of labor demand in the state. The expected wage is calculated by taking a weighted average of log median wages for all workers (both immigrants and natives) aged 25–60 in each of the skill categories discussed above, calculated from the IPUMS data, with the weights being $\hat{P}(S = k)_i$, derived from the results of the conditional logit estimation and the individual characteristics of the immigrants in the INS data. I use median rather than mean wages to avoid issues of different nominal topcode values across Censuses. The choice of using the wages of all workers rather than just those of immigrants is motivated by the small or non-existent samples of immigrants in some of the less populous states in some skill categories, particularly in 1970 and 1980. The median log wage is calculated separately for men and women in each state and year. Thus, the "expected" wage varies by state, year, and the characteristics of the immigrant.

While it might be possible to use occupation-specific wages (although sample size reasons would prevent one from using immigrant-specific wages within occupations in states with few immigrants), the measurement of occupation in the INS data makes this somewhat questionable. The INS occupation data can refer either to the immigrant's occupation in the U.S. or in their home country. With the exception of primary employment immigrants, whose reported occupation is from their job in the U.S., however, it is impossible to tell whether the reported occupation refers to the immigrant's job in their home country, an actual job in the U.S. or merely in what occupation the immigrant thinks they will work in the U.S. In addition, given that home country occupation-specific skills may not be immediately transferable to the U.S., using occupation-specific wages might substantially mismeasure the wages available to an immigrant upon arrival. Using "expected" wages probabilitistically weights the log median wages from all the three skill categories. So, for example, an unmarried 28-year-old female Russian engineer entering the U.S. may not work as an engineer, or even in a high-skill job, upon arrival. Given the experiences of past immigrants, she faces some probability of working in a high-skilled job, and a smaller probability of working in a lower-skilled job. The "expected" wage will encompass these opportunities (or lack thereof) better than using the occupation-specific wage.

Past research (e.g. Bartel, 1989; Dunlevey, 1991; Jaeger, 2000; Bauer et al., 2002) has clearly shown that immigrants are drawn to locations with concentrations of immigrants who are like them. This may be due to network externalities, herd effects, linguistic considerations, or some combination of all three. For sample size reasons in the IPUMS (particularly in low-immigrant states in 1970 and 1980), I measure immigrant concentrations using region of birth rather than country of birth. These concentrations enter the regressions in three ways. First, I include the share of the immigrant's region of birth group in the state population. This controls for the relative size of the potential network and, to some extent, for the size of linguistic community available to the immigrant. Second, as a measure of the absolute size of the population of an immigrant group in a state, I include the share of the total population in the U.S. of the immigrant's region of birth that lives in the state.[17] And, finally, I include the share of the state's population that was born outside of the U.S. Immigrants may prefer, for cultural and economic reasons, to live in areas with more "international" neighbors, without regard to their country of origin. For instance, these places may be more tolerant of immigrants in general or they may offer more services to immigrant children in schools. This variable is most similar to the concentration variables employed by both Bartel (1989) and Zavodny (1999).

Bauer et al. (2002) argued that there are diminishing returns to the size of immigrant networks and so their "magnetic" effect should also show diminishing or even declining returns. I therefore include both a linear and quadratic term for all three of the immigrant concentration measures. I also include the natural log of the state's population and (in models without state fixed effects) the natural log of the land area of the state, which together control for the population density.

Many immigrants still maintain ties with their "home" country even after receiving a green card. To proxy for costs of visiting kin (or perhaps permanently returning home), I include a quadratic in the straight-line distance from the most populous city in the immigrant's country of birth to the geographic center of the state.[18] In addition, Cragg and Kahn (1997) show that amenities like climate are important determinants of migration propensities. I include in the models a quadratic in the absolute difference between the average temperature in the state and the immigrant's country of birth and a quadratic in the absolute difference between the average annual precipitation in the state and the immigrant's country of birth.[19] While past research (Bartel, 1989; Zavodny, 1997; Zavodny, 1999; Kaushal, 2005) has examined how social safety net programs like general assistance or welfare affect immigrants location choices, the evidence suggests that state-level variation in these program has no influence on where immigrants choose to live. I therefore do not include these measures in the analysis.

I first estimate models where I pool the four samples from the INS data matched to IPUMS data from 1970, 1980, 1990, and 2000 and include state fixed effects. These fixed effects control for time-invariant characteristics of the state, e.g. the land area of the state, and the "gateway" effects of places like California and New York, which naturally attract immigrants because they are on the coasts. In addition, fixed effects capture the "initial" endowment of immigrants that determined where past migrants chose to live. Identification with state fixed effects comes from within-state variation over time in the covariates. Entries in the tables are marginal effects of a change in the characteristic of state j on the probability that an immigrant will locate in state j, evaluated at the "average" probability of location (i.e. $1/48 = .0208\bar{3}$), per Eq. (5). Recall that the population used for the estimation is limited to individuals who were 25–60 years old at the time that they received their green card and who, except for refugees, are newly arrived in the U.S. Given the extremely large sample sizes in these regressions it is prudent to be conservative with the nominal level of significance when conducting hypothesis tests. I will use a nominal one percent level when discussing statistical significance, giving a nominal non-rejection region for the z-ratios of $(-2.5758, 2.5758)$ for a two-tailed test that the parameter in question is equal to zero.

Table 1 presents results of estimating (3) on the population of "primary" male immigrants. Focusing first on labor market conditions, I find that they have mixed effects on the location propensities of family-reunification immigrants. For all three family-reunification groups, the unemployment rate is not statistically significant at the one percent level, while expected log wages have a strong positive effect for immediate relatives of U.S. citizens and a marginally statistically significant and positive effect for relatives of legal permanent residents. For other relatives of U.S. citizens, higher wages *negatively* affect the probability of locating in a state.

For employment-based immigrants, higher unemployment rates have a negative and statistically significant effect on location probabilities,

Table 1. Determinants of Location Choice: Men Pooled between 1971 and 2000 with State Fixed Effects.

Variable	Visa Category				
	Relatives of U.S. citizens		Relatives of LPR	Employment	Refugees (1971–1990)
	Non-quota	Quota			
Expected log(wage)	.0256	−.0180	.0121	.0232	.0648
	(8.19)	(4.77)	(2.86)	(4.34)	(11.51)
Unemployment rate	−.0003	.0004	.0008	−.0017	.0018
(percentage points)	(1.77)	(1.68)	(2.45)	(4.74)	(4.36)
Region of birth as percent of	.0066	.0110	.0059	.0017	.0210
state population	(22.26)	(26.44)	(13.00)	(3.03)	(17.29)
Region of birth as percent of	−.0305	−.0606	−.0332	−.0069	−.0533
state population sq.÷100	(17.07)	(21.54)	(11.19)	(1.66)	(2.83)
Percent of region of birth	.0014	.0007	.0003	.0007	.0030
population in state	(24.43)	(8.52)	(3.95)	(6.33)	(15.54)
Percent of region of birth	−.0021	−.0014	.0001	−.0005	−.0062
pop. in state sq.÷100	(25.33)	(11.81)	(1.24)	(2.94)	(20.76)
Foreign-born percent of state	−.0013	.0004	.0011	.0030	−.0044
population	(5.89)	(1.53)	(3.17)	(9.45)	(5.22)
Foreign-born percent of state	.0022	−.0028	−.0048	−.0074	.0063
pop. sq.÷100	(4.38)	(4.86)	(6.29)	(10.03)	(3.30)
Log(state population)	.0162	.0199	.0301	.0363	.0005
	(10.09)	(9.64)	(11.54)	(12.98)	(0.08)
Distance from country of	−.0162	−.0263	−.0347	−.0080	−.0077
birth (1,000 miles)	(20.72)	(24.42)	(29.12)	(6.52)	(2.48)
Distance from country of	.0660	.1329	.1948	.0166	.0446
birth sq.÷100	(10.37)	(16.04)	(20.92)	(1.71)	(2.08)
|State−country of birth	.0009	.0000	.0004	−.0005	−.0003
temperature|(°F)	(13.94)	(0.40)	(4.69)	(5.05)	(2.31)
|State−country of birth	−.0016	.0008	.0001	.0024	.0005
temperature sq.|÷100	(8.24)	(3.82)	(0.29)	(8.51)	(1.67)
|State−country of birth	−.0004	−.0003	−.0004	−.0003	−.0003
precipitation|(inches)	(15.32)	(10.92)	(13.94)	(8.20)	(6.32)
|State−country of birth	.0003	.0002	.0005	.0003	.0001
precipitation sq.|÷100	(9.32)	(6.68)	(11.14)	(4.58)	(1.26)
Pseudo-R^2	.355	.397	.479	.307	.352
Number of individuals	30,419	25,384	24,597	11,755	16,267
Number of observations	1,460,112	1,218,432	1,180,656	564,240	780,816

Note: Estimated via conditional logit with robust standard errors. Choice set is 48 contiguous U.S. states; Own-state marginal effects, z-ratios in parentheses.
Source: Author's calculations using INS and IPUMS data.

while wages have a positive and statistically significant effect. This suggests that employment immigrants locate in places with better labor markets, *ceteris paribus*. Because employment immigrants must normally have a job and be sponsored by a firm to enter the U.S., interpreting these coefficients as purely causal effects of the labor market on the immigrants' choices alone is somewhat problematic. The estimate also reflects actions by *firms* in high-wage, low-employment states. When labor markets are tight, firms will be more likely to look outside of the U.S. for labor. That the region-of-birth variables are also statistically significant suggests that when firms decide to look outside of the U.S., they may look for immigrants who are similar to those that already work for the firm. Government or private agencies often resettle refugees, so it is somewhat surprising that expected wages are even more important in determining location for them than for employment immigrants. For refugees, the unemployment rate is also perversely signed and statistically significant.

Broadly speaking, the results confirm the previous literature that finds that concentrations of similar immigrants have a magnetic effect on immigrants' location choices. This is true for all family reunification groups with two of the three measures of immigrant concentrations, i.e. the percentage of the state that is from the immigrant's region of birth, and percent of the total U.S. population from the immigrant's region of birth that is living in the state. Of these two, the former is much more important. This suggests that immigrants would prefer a smaller state in which individuals from their region of birth make up a larger percentage even if there are other states that have larger absolute numbers of individuals born in the same region as they were. Immigrant concentrations are more important for refugees than for either employment or family reunification immigrants. The magnitude of the third concentration variable, the percent of foreign born in the state population, is much smaller than the other concentration variables, except for employment-based immigrants. This suggests that there are areas of the country that are "immigrant-hiring" and those that are not. Lastly, given that the "Big 6" are populous states, it is not surprising that I estimate that immigrants are more likely to locate in states with larger populations. This is likely due to immigrants' preferences for urban areas, where it is easier for them to take advantage of existing employment and linguistic networks. The effect of population is strongest for employment immigrants, followed by relatives of legal permanent residents, and family of U.S. citizens. Population size does not affect the location probabilities of refugees.

The geographic and weather variables have differing effects across the admission categories. Distance has a negative effect for all groups (even though the coefficients on the quadratic terms are positive, over the relevant range the net effect of both variables is negative), but this is largest for relatives of legal permanent residents and smaller and statistically insignificant for refugees. The weather variables are of little quantitative importance and are often statistically not significant.

I repeat the same estimation for immigrant women in Table 2. Here the labor market effects are sometimes perversely signed, statistically insignificant, or both. Perhaps most puzzling is the negative and relatively large coefficients on expected wages for employment immigrants. Even though the population used for the estimation is primary immigrants, the location choices of female immigrants may be more likely to be a joint decision or affected more by their spouse's labor market possibilities than those of male immigrants.[20] Only for refugees are the coefficients on the labor market variables statistically significant with the expected signs. As with men, the share of the state's population that comes from the immigrant's region of birth is the most important of the three immigrant concentration variables. Distance from the "home" country is a more important determinant of location for family of legal permanent residents than for the other admission categories.

In general, across all 10 groups for men and women, I find confirmation of Bauer et al.'s (2002) results that the magnetic effects of immigrant concentrations have diminishing effects, although the coefficients on the quadratic terms are generally not large enough to lead to an inverted U-shape over the relevant ranges of the immigrant concentration variables.

In Tables 3–6, I present estimates of the same model, with the addition of the natural logarithm of the state's land area as a regressor and without state fixed effects, for immediate family of U.S. citizens, other family of U.S. citizens, family of legal permanent residents, and employment immigrants, respectively. In each table, I estimate the models separately for each of the four years under examination (1971, 1980, 1990, and 2000) and for men and women. Unlike the models in Tables 1 and 2, these are identified by both cross-state and within-state variation in the regressors. The within-state variation comes from having immigrants from different regions- and countries-of-birth as well as different occupations. In general, I find that the coefficients for men and women are remarkably similar within year and admission category.

Taking the results in Table 3–6 as a whole, it appears that labor market conditions do significantly affect location choices across all four groups, with immigrants choosing higher-wage, lower-unemployment areas. Labor market conditions are most consistently important for employment-based

Table 2. Determinants of Location Choice: Women Pooled between 1971 and 2000 with State Fixed Effects.

Variable	Visa Category				
	Relatives of U.S. citizens		Relatives of LPR	Employment	Refugees (1971–1990)
	Non-quota	Quota			
Expected log(wage)	−.0005	−.0269	.0357	−.0664	.0068
	(0.17)	(6.57)	(9.18)	(8.21)	(6.76)
Unemployment rate	−.0006	.0013	−.0003	−.0004	−.0030
(percentage points)	(3.26)	(4.63)	(0.97)	(0.58)	(6.12)
Region of birth as percent of	.0060	.0098	.0048	−.0048	.0022
state population	(27.15)	(23.20)	(14.80)	(5.98)	(1.11)
Region of birth as percent of	−.0257	−.0544	−.0215	.0503	.1772
state population sq. ÷ 100	(20.03)	(18.56)	(11.94)	(8.29)	(3.87)
Percent of region of birth	.0013	.0008	.0009	.0011	.0058
population in state	(29.12)	(9.68)	(14.01)	(8.25)	(28.09)
Percent of region of birth	−.0017	−.0014	−.0007	−.0008	−.0099
pop. in state sq. ÷ 100	(25.88)	(11.42)	(6.96)	(3.56)	(28.19)
Foreign-born percent of state	.0004	.0014	.0005	.0044	−.0053
population	(2.85)	(4.93)	(1.69)	(7.69)	(7.48)
Foreign-born percent of state	−.0009	−.0056	−.0026	−.0118	.0090
pop. sq. ÷ 100	(2.55)	(9.33)	(4.25)	(8.98)	(4.81)
Log(state population)	.0057	.0201	.0231	.0423	.0554
	(4.92)	(9.05)	(10.91)	(8.84)	(9.45)
Distance from country of	−.0122	−.0268	−.0321	−.0065	.0087
birth (1,000 miles)	(19.92)	(24.44)	(30.24)	(3.08)	(6.53)
Distance from country of	.0497	.1365	.1737	−.0048	−.0362
birth sq. ÷ 100	(9.77)	(15.86)	(20.69)	(0.26)	(3.36)
|State−country of birth	.0003	.0001	.0002	−.0008	−.0003
temperature|(°F)	(7.39)	(0.90)	(2.15)	(5.51)	(2.28)
|State−country of birth	−.0003	.0008	.0005	.0044	.0002
temperature sq.| ÷ 100	(1.95)	(3.40)	(2.39)	(9.07)	(0.47)
|State−country of birth	−.0004	−.0003	−.0004	−.0004	−.0001
precipitation|(inches)	(19.52)	(9.66)	(14.92)	(7.22)	(2.15)
|State−country of birth	.0003	.0002	.0004	.0002	.0002
precipitation sq.| ÷ 100	(11.95)	(4.33)	(9.42)	(3.36)	(1.26)
Pseudo-R^2	.312	.400	.452	.406	.353
Number of individuals	54,273	24,597	31,299	6,921	9,250
Number of observations	2,605,104	1,180,656	1,502,352	332,208	444,000

Note: Estimated via conditional logit with robust standard errors. Choice set is 48 contiguous U.S. states; Own-state marginal effects, z-ratios in parentheses.
Source: Author's calculations using INS and IPUMS data.

Table 3.   Determinants of Location Choice: Family of U.S. Citizens (Non-Quota).

Variable	Men				Women			
	1971	1980	1990	2000	1971	1980	1990	2000
Expected log(wage)	.0275	.0385	.0426	.0253	.0011	.0118	.0254	.0259
	(4.57)	(9.37)	(12.89)	(5.12)	(0.27)	(2.73)	(6.08)	(6.79)
Unemployment rate	−.0027	−.0009	−.0009	−.0002	−.0015	−.0011	.0001	.0003
(percentage points)	(4.33)	(3.77)	(3.07)	(0.31)	(4.11)	(4.39)	(0.38)	(0.57)
Region of birth as percent	.0280	.0245	.0144	.0096	.0246	.0213	.0112	.0073
of state population	(12.93)	(21.59)	(25.31)	(14.82)	(14.49)	(19.23)	(16.73)	(17.26)
Region of birth as percent	−.6314	−.3147	−.1060	−.0446	−.5253	−.2528	−.0766	−.0277
of state pop. sq. ÷ 100	(10.34)	(16.35)	(22.11)	(12.80)	(10.83)	(14.02)	(14.13)	(12.10)
Percent of region of birth	.0010	−.0003	−.0003	.0002	.0005	−.0002	.0003	.0009
population in state	(7.12)	(2.37)	(3.12)	(0.97)	(4.33)	(1.45)	(2.25)	(7.45)
Percent of region of birth	−.0014	.0007	.0008	.0003	−.0002	.0005	.0000	−.0012
pop. in state sq. ÷ 100	(6.30)	(2.63)	(4.39)	(0.77)	(1.31)	(2.27)	(0.11)	(5.10)
Foreign-born percent of	.0065	.0037	.0032	.0019	.0033	.0028	.0024	.0019
state population	(10.02)	(9.24)	(17.80)	(8.32)	(8.45)	(9.05)	(13.10)	(12.91)
Foreign-born percent of	−.0321	−.0092	−.0063	−.0029	−.0150	−.0093	−.0068	−.0043
state pop. sq. ÷ 100	(7.44)	(4.03)	(8.44)	(3.55)	(5.73)	(5.12)	(8.61)	(7.98)
Log(state population)	.0146	.0174	.0156	.0165	.0153	.0192	.0158	.0156
	(19.75)	(28.18)	(29.13)	(20.87)	(31.76)	(37.28)	(29.62)	(31.63)
Distance from country of	−.0159	−.0113	−.0160	−.0131	−.0144	−.0096	−.0123	−.0118
birth (1,000 miles)	(8.21)	(7.79)	(12.77)	(6.74)	(9.34)	(7.12)	(8.78)	(9.44)
Distance from country of	.0598	.0360	.0727	.0573	.0692	.0369	.0644	.0559
birth sq. ÷ 100	(3.31)	(2.88)	(7.31)	(3.73)	(4.94)	(3.21)	(5.67)	(5.62)
Log(state land area)	.0065	.0030	.0032	.0003	.0037	.0011	.0022	−.0002
	(11.40)	(8.71)	(8.32)	(0.66)	(9.62)	(3.69)	(6.06)	(0.75)
|State−country of birth	.0011	.0008	.0003	.0003	.0006	.0006	−.0001	.0001
temperature|(°F)	(6.03)	(6.17)	(3.27)	(1.95)	(5.31)	(6.68)	(1.00)	(0.68)
|State−country of birth	−.0017	−.0013	.0004	.0001	−.0013	−.0013	.0010	.0002
temperature sq.| ÷ 100	(3.24)	(3.41)	(1.23)	(0.28)	(3.88)	(4.81)	(3.62)	(0.62)
|State−country of birth	−.0005	−.0006	−.0004	−.0001	−.0003	−.0005	−.0003	−.0002
precipitation|(inches)	(6.92)	(10.51)	(9.92)	(1.67)	(6.33)	(10.15)	(7.12)	(5.46)
|State−country of birth	.0005	.0005	.0003	−.0002	.0003	.0006	.0002	−.0000
precipitation sq.| ÷ 100	(4.22)	(6.24)	(5.88)	(2.04)	(4.12)	(8.80)	(3.95)	(0.53)
Pseudo-R^2	.402	.358	.356	.324	.262	.303	.327	.326
Number of individuals	4,787	8,258	11,745	5,629	8,020	11,460	10,367	10,421
Number of observations	229,776	396,384	563,760	270,192	384,960	550,080	497,616	500,208

Note: Estimated via conditional logit with robust standard errors. Choice set is 48 contiguous U.S. states; Own-state marginal effects, z-ratios in parentheses.
Source: Author's calculations using INS and IPUMS data.

immigrants, where the unemployment rate, in particular, has a much larger effect than for other groups. The magnitude of the coefficients on the labor market variables, while changing somewhat from decade to decade, are fairly constant over time within admission category. Given these results it is

Table 4. Determinants of Location Choice: Family of U.S. Citizens (Quota).

Variable	Men				Women			
	1971	1980	1990	2000	1971	1980	1990	2000
Expected log(wage)	.0557	.0307	.0605	.0287	.0754	.0543	.0752	.0546
	(6.13)	(7.96)	(17.18)	(4.99)	(8.28)	(10.14)	(12.35)	(7.71)
Unemployment rate	−.0006	−.0009	−.0007	.0034	−.0016	−.0002	.0014	.0033
(percentage points)	(0.78)	(3.33)	(2.24)	(4.38)	(2.35)	(0.58)	(2.61)	(3.54)
Region of birth as percent	.0281	.0317	.0158	.0104	.0269	.0285	.0143	.0097
of state population	(10.59)	(24.66)	(21.10)	(11.53)	(10.16)	(21.97)	(14.47)	(10.69)
Region of birth as percent	−.4042	−.4242	−.1040	−.0499	−.4066	−.3784	−.0999	−.0424
of state pop. sq. ÷ 100	(7.65)	(22.66)	(18.28)	(10.25)	(7.74)	(19.75)	(13.08)	(8.57)
Percent of region of birth	.0023	−.0014	−.0001	−.0001	.0032	−.0012	.0000	−.0000
population in state	(6.55)	(8.53)	(0.63)	(0.26)	(8.44)	(7.50)	(0.23)	(0.15)
Percent of region of birth	−.0035	.0021	.0001	.0004	−.0056	.0019	.0000	.0001
pop. in state sq. ÷ 100	(4.48)	(8.15)	(0.50)	(0.93)	(6.91)	(7.09)	(0.08)	(0.30)
Foreign-born percent of	.0067	.0032	.0039	.0028	.0079	.0032	.0029	.0020
state population	(6.54)	(8.06)	(19.87)	(10.23)	(7.58)	(7.59)	(10.88)	(7.99)
Foreign-born percent of	−.0494	−.0009	−.0115	−.0059	−.0634	−.0002	−.0096	−.0048
state pop. sq. ÷ 100	(7.06)	(0.37)	(13.22)	(5.92)	(9.32)	(0.07)	(8.35)	(4.96)
Log(state population)	.0182	.0261	.0220	.0236	.0148	.0235	.0229	.0260
	(14.07)	(33.92)	(33.20)	(22.59)	(11.71)	(28.26)	(25.61)	(25.81)
Distance from country of	.0102	−.0312	−.0225	−.0271	−.0023	−.0290	−.0272	−.0271
birth (1,000 miles)	(2.23)	(18.89)	(14.70)	(11.87)	(0.55)	(17.70)	(13.05)	(12.54)
Distance from country of	−.0761	.1898	.1144	.1414	.0103	.1801	.1478	.1226
birth sq. ÷ 100	(2.04)	(14.89)	(9.95)	(8.10)	(0.30)	(13.76)	(9.38)	(7.47)
Log(state land area)	−.0040	−.0022	.0011	−.0040	−.0021	−.0027	.0007	−.0031
	(3.90)	(6.06)	(2.87)	(7.01)	(2.09)	(6.72)	(1.36)	(5.86)
|State−country of birth	.0001	−.0003	−.0004	−.0005	.0001	−.0001	−.0004	−.0003
temperature|(°F)	(0.51)	(2.25)	(3.55)	(2.76)	(0.60)	(1.18)	(2.76)	(1.95)
|State−country of birth	−.0006	.0026	.0018	.0017	−.0010	.0025	.0020	.0020
temperature sq.| ÷ 100	(0.79)	(8.24)	(6.02)	(3.55)	(1.12)	(7.66)	(5.25)	(4.21)
|State−country of birth	−.0005	−.0004	−.0003	−.0002	−.0004	−.0003	−.0003	−.0002
precipitation|(inches)	(4.67)	(7.27)	(7.69)	(2.96)	(3.39)	(5.53)	(6.35)	(3.99)
|State−country of birth	.0009	.0003	.0002	.0001	.0008	.0002	.0002	.0001
precipitation sq.| ÷ 100	(4.51)	(4.95)	(4.52)	(1.22)	(3.87)	(3.25)	(3.90)	(1.41)
Pseudo-R^2	.397	.397	.405	.388	.406	.403	.405	.381
Number of individuals	2,723	9,214	12,798	5,090	2,562	8,354	7,052	4,006
Number of observations	130,704	442,272	614,304	244,320	122,976	400,992	338,496	192,288

Note: Estimated via conditional logit with robust standard errors. Choice set is 48 contiguous U.S. states; Own-state marginal effects, z-ratios in parentheses.
Source: Author's calculations using INS and IPUMS data.

hard to argue that labor market conditions do not influence where immigrants decide to live. The results presented here are consistent with Zavodny (1999), who found, using a different methodology, that employment visa immigrants are generally more sensitive to economic conditions

Table 5. Determinants of Location Choice: Family of Legal Permanent Residents.

Variable	Men				Women			
	1971	1980	1990	2000	1971	1980	1990	2000
Expected log(wage)	.0439	.0374	.0665	.0287	.0642	.0456	.0770	.0298
	(3.48)	(8.43)	(16.28)	(3.57)	(6.72)	(8.41)	(10.71)	(5.65)
Unemployment rate	−.0008	.0008	−.0007	.0095	−.0018	.0006	.0009	.0045
(percentage points)	(0.75)	(2.77)	(1.65)	(8.57)	(2.60)	(2.10)	(1.30)	(5.57)
Region of birth as percent	.0190	.0300	.0098	.0121	.0266	.0337	.0079	.0087
of state population	(4.90)	(19.52)	(12.22)	(10.85)	(8.75)	(23.96)	(7.66)	(15.06)
Region of birth as percent	−.1422	−.4967	−.0836	−.0522	−.4123	−.4952	−.0677	−.0437
of state pop. sq. ÷ 100	(1.72)	(23.56)	(12.93)	(8.94)	(6.19)	(25.38)	(7.93)	(13.53)
Percent of region of birth	.0021	−.0020	−.0007	−.0001	.0020	−.0018	−.0004	.0011
population in state	(4.90)	(10.72)	(4.88)	(0.27)	(6.08)	(10.20)	(2.20)	(6.06)
Percent of region of birth	−.0044	.0046	.0023	.0000	−.0034	.0037	.0018	−.0016
pop. in state sq. ÷ 100	(5.26)	(15.90)	(10.20)	(0.08)	(5.12)	(13.72)	(6.03)	(4.23)
Foreign-born percent of	.0088	.0064	.0065	.0032	.0045	.0050	.0056	.0020
state population	(6.19)	(12.80)	(26.89)	(8.69)	(4.72)	(11.26)	(17.94)	(7.36)
Foreign-born percent of	−.0502	−.0149	−.0182	−.0081	−.0343	−.0139	−.0166	−.0039
state pop. sq. ÷ 100	(5.32)	(5.30)	(19.00)	(6.20)	(5.41)	(5.52)	(13.41)	(3.96)
Log(state population)	.0231	.0289	.0264	.0250	.0225	.0286	.0250	.0160
	(12.49)	(28.14)	(27.39)	(17.16)	(17.18)	(31.29)	(21.09)	(20.06)
Distance from country of	.0037	−.0344	−.0274	−.0166	.0187	−.0288	−.0304	−.0169
birth (1,000 miles)	(0.63)	(18.87)	(18.17)	(5.69)	(3.73)	(16.23)	(14.54)	(8.61)
Distance from country of	−.0898	.2198	.1546	.0816	−.2300	.1773	.1827	.0495
birth sq. ÷ 100	(1.93)	(14.66)	(12.84)	(3.58)	(5.98)	(12.49)	(10.64)	(3.07)
Log(state land area)	−.0036	−.0039	−.0016	−.0067	−.0052	−.0020	−.0017	−.0037
	(2.77)	(8.58)	(2.96)	(8.43)	(6.20)	(4.91)	(2.63)	(8.43)
|State−country of birth	.0011	−.0005	−.0002	.0004	.0002	−.0004	−.0002	−.0008
temperature|(°F)	(3.24)	(3.88)	(1.87)	(1.47)	(0.60)	(2.75)	(1.23)	(4.55)
|State−country of birth	−.0016	.0037	.0027	−.0005	−.0008	.0030	.0024	.0034
temperature sq.| ÷ 100	(1.70)	(9.63)	(8.50)	(0.65)	(1.08)	(8.44)	(5.50)	(6.78)
|State−country of birth	−.0009	−.0006	−.0004	−.0005	−.0008	−.0005	−.0003	−.0007
precipitation|(inches)	(6.22)	(11.31)	(11.05)	(5.58)	(6.67)	(10.50)	(6.68)	(10.80)
|State−country of birth	.0013	.0005	.0003	.0005	.0009	.0005	.0002	.0004
precipitation sq.| ÷ 100	(6.51)	(7.75)	(6.76)	(4.13)	(5.55)	(7.22)	(2.64)	(4.35)
Pseudo-R^2	.437	.510	.466	.435	.407	.472	.455	.433
Number of individuals	1,508	9,087	11,043	2,959	2,388	9,500	6,015	7,451
Number of observations	72,384	436,176	530,064	142,032	114,624	456,000	288,720	357,648

Note: Estimated via conditional logit with robust standard errors. Choice set is 48 contiguous U.S. states; Own-state marginal effects, z-ratios in parentheses.
Source: Author's calculations using INS and IPUMS data.

than immigrants in other admission categories, and Borjas (2001), who found that immigrants are more sensitive than natives to labor market conditions when deciding where to live. That the results are fairly similar across decades, while relative economic conditions across states were

Table 6. Determinants of Location Choice: Employment-Based Immigrants.

Variable	Men				Women			
	1971	1980	1990	2000	1971	1980	1990	2000
Expected log(wage)	.0378	.0191	.0502	.0521	.0305	.0416	.1737	.0364
	(4.12)	(3.13)	(5.69)	(7.14)	(2.16)	(2.97)	(10.99)	(2.54)
Unemployment rate	−.0051	−.0020	−.0085	−.0104	−.0044	.0009	−.0162	−.0011
(percentage points)	(6.83)	(5.01)	(9.25)	(10.10)	(4.45)	(1.34)	(7.69)	(0.65)
Region of birth as percent	.0122	.0102	−.0015	−.0028	.0166	.0217	−.0030	−.0046
of state population	(3.35)	(4.32)	(0.89)	(1.93)	(1.90)	(7.08)	(1.68)	(2.04)
Region of birth as percent	−.1438	−.1116	.0233	.0049	−.2155	−.3795	.0652	.0320
of state pop. sq. ÷ 100	(1.63)	(2.73)	(1.58)	(0.53)	(1.10)	(7.93)	(4.31)	(2.46)
Percent of region of birth	.0027	−.0000	.0011	.0019	.0039	−.0021	.0007	.0026
population in state	(8.04)	(0.01)	(3.55)	(5.77)	(5.81)	(5.51)	(2.15)	(4.99)
Percent of region of birth	−.0049	−.0001	−.0007	−.0022	−.0085	.0042	−.0007	−.0036
pop. in state sq. ÷ 100	(6.98)	(0.18)	(1.29)	(3.63)	(6.18)	(6.08)	(1.20)	(3.99)
Foreign-born percent of	.0031	.0006	.0047	.0022	.0061	−.0007	.0048	.0032
state population	(3.86)	(1.10)	(10.02)	(7.25)	(4.77)	(0.70)	(7.44)	(6.29)
Foreign-born percent of	−.0226	.0068	−.0138	−.0062	−.0483	.0192	−.0197	−.0109
state pop. sq. ÷ 100	(4.10)	(1.92)	(6.83)	(5.13)	(5.79)	(3.23)	(6.85)	(5.58)
Log(state population)	.0192	.0250	.0231	.0219	.0310	.0410	.0432	.0199
	(16.27)	(22.71)	(13.93)	(18.12)	(15.40)	(18.13)	(11.61)	(10.41)
Distance from country of	.0132	−.0109	−.0120	−.0039	.0236	−.0208	−.0213	−.0041
birth (1,000 miles)	(3.51)	(5.10)	(3.94)	(1.39)	(3.16)	(4.91)	(5.25)	(0.89)
Distance from country of	−.1781	.0367	.0664	.0035	−.2667	.0988	.1200	.0356
birth sq. ÷ 100	(6.15)	(2.18)	(2.67)	(0.16)	(4.79)	(2.43)	(3.54)	(1.08)
Log(state land area)	−.0038	−.0002	−.0026	.0007	−.0089	−.0141	−.0016	−.0020
	(4.65)	(0.37)	(2.48)	(0.98)	(6.37)	(11.83)	(1.21)	(1.89)
|State−country of birth	−.0005	−.0003	−.0006	.0000	−.0014	.0008	−.0001	−.0004
temperature|(°F)	(2.23)	(1.63)	(2.67)	(0.01)	(3.15)	(2.66)	(0.50)	(1.33)
|State−country of birth	.0019	.0023	.0021	−.0001	.0040	−.0004	.0008	.0010
temperature sq.| ÷ 100	(3.28)	(4.70)	(2.77)	(0.22)	(4.05)	(0.49)	(0.90)	(1.05)
|State−country of birth	−.0009	−.0003	−.0001	−.0001	−.0006	−.0005	−.0004	−.0001
precipitation|(inches)	(6.96)	(3.41)	(1.60)	(1.41)	(2.62)	(4.81)	(4.19)	(0.44)
|State−country of birth	.0008	.0001	−.0001	.0003	.0007	.0001	.0001	−.0001
precipitation sq.| ÷ 100	(5.45)	(1.03)	(0.72)	(2.53)	(2.37)	(0.89)	(0.58)	(0.38)
Pseudo-R^2	.277	.295	.380	.246	.343	.420	.454	.242
Number of individuals	2,478	3,175	1,949	1,710	1,233	1,672	1,539	634
Number of observations	118,944	152,400	93,552	82,080	59,184	80,256	73,872	30,432

Note: Estimated via conditional logit with robust standard errors. Choice set is 48 contiguous U.S. states; Own-state marginal effects, *z*-ratios in parentheses.
Source: Author's calculations using INS and IPUMS data.

changing, suggests that the results are not just picking up an artifact of low unemployment rates in California (for example) at one point in time.

Examining the immigrant concentration variables, I find strong evidence that these are more important for the family reunification groups than for immigrants entering under an employment visa. As in the models with fixed effects, the share of a state's population from the immigrant's region is the most important of the three immigrant concentration variables for all groups. Moreover, for all four admission categories, the coefficients on the share of the state's population from the immigrant's region of birth are smaller in 1990 and 2000 than they are in 1971 and 1980, suggesting that immigrants started seeking "non-traditional" locations during the last 20 years.

With the geographic and weather variables, as with the pooled fixed effects models, distance from country of birth is most important for relatives of legal permanent residents and least important for employment immigrants. The coefficients are fairly similar over time, except that for some groups the linear and quadratic terms switch signs in 1971. For all groups, the coefficient on log(state population) is positive and for all groups except immediate family of U.S. citizens the coefficient on log(state land area) is negative. This is the pattern we would expect, *ceteris paribus*, if immigrants prefer to live in states with a higher population density (like New Jersey). Because the coefficients on both variables are positive for immediate family of U.S. citizens, it would appear that they prefer to live in less dense states. The sizes of the coefficients on the weather variables are generally quite small and of varying signs, although for some groups in some years they are statistically and significantly different from zero.

I only observe Western Hemisphere and diversity immigrants in 1971 and 2000, respectively, and so cannot include them in the pooled analysis with state fixed effects. In Table 7, I present results from estimating the now-familiar model on these two groups. Both groups provide, in some sense, a better test of the hypothesis that labor markets matter in addition to network and kinship effects, because individuals in neither group needed formal ties like family or employment in the U.S. prior to entering. Diversity immigrants, in particular, were chosen at random, and had a very low probability of actually winning the visa lottery. Their arrival in the U.S. can therefore be seen almost as a natural experiment, at least conditional on having applied for the lottery. Western Hemisphere and, particularly, diversity immigrants are substantially less unconstrained in their choice set than immigrants entering with other types of green cards.

For both groups, I find that labor market conditions are important determinants of their location choice. In particular, for diversity immigrants, higher wages in a state positively affect the probability of locating there, while higher unemployment are a deterrent. For both men and women these effects are statistically and significantly different from zero. This is perhaps

Table 7. Determinants of Location Choice: Western Hemisphere and Diversity Immigrants.

Variable	Men		Women	
	Western Hemisphere	Diversity	Western Hemisphere	Diversity
	1971	2000	1971	2000
Expected log(wage)	.0096	.0366	.0510	.0650
	(1.54)	(5.07)	(8.41)	(5.72)
Unemployment rate (percentage points)	−.0097	−.0042	−.0017	−.0044
	(11.39)	(5.14)	(3.46)	(3.32)
Region of birth as percent of state population	.0458	.0088	.0423	.0101
	(23.43)	(3.39)	(24.21)	(4.10)
Region of birth as percent of state population sq. ÷ 100	−1.1533	−.0889	−1.0855	−.0775
	(23.07)	(2.43)	(25.38)	(2.80)
Percent of region of birth population in state	−.0012	.0030	−.0005	.0026
	(6.64)	(7.39)	(3.83)	(5.28)
Percent of region of birth population in state sq. ÷ 100	.0029	−.0041	.0011	−.0036
	(9.86)	(5.59)	(5.22)	(4.36)
Foreign-born percent of state population	.0062	.0028	.0058	.0021
	(10.91)	(9.39)	(12.84)	(5.86)
Foreign-born percent of state population sq. ÷ 100	−.0086	−.0105	−.0129	−.0096
	(2.20)	(8.59)	(4.12)	(6.80)
Log(state population)	.0196	.0199	.0193	.0234
	(21.81)	(16.91)	(23.56)	(14.53)
Distance from country of birth (1,000 miles)	−.0243	−.0292	−.0342	−.0269
	(8.75)	(7.55)	(12.12)	(5.81)
Distance from country of birth sq. ÷ 100	.1131	.1613	.0656	.1681
	(2.44)	(5.56)	(1.51)	(4.88)
Log(state land area)	.0073	.0005	.0050	.0018
	(14.25)	(0.53)	(11.51)	(1.43)
|State−country of birth temperature|(°F)	.0004	.0009	.0007	.0008
	(2.42)	(4.75)	(4.07)	(3.17)
|State−country of birth temperature sq.| ÷ 100	.0022	−.0008	.0004	−.0014
	(4.62)	(1.54)	(0.89)	(2.11)
|State−country of birth precipitation|(inches)	−.0005	−.0003	−.0004	−.0002
	(8.68)	(4.56)	(7.29)	(2.26)
|State−country of birth precipitation sq.| ÷ 100	.0001	.0002	.0003	.0001
	(1.61)	(2.16)	(3.74)	(0.89)
Pseudo-R^2	.564	.266	.541	.278
Number of individuals	7,851	3,049	9,913	2,029
Number of observations	376,848	146,352	475,824	97,392

Note: Estimated via conditional logit with robust standard errors. Choice set is 48 contiguous US states; Own-state marginal effects, z-ratios in parentheses.
Source: Author's calculations using INS and IPUMS data.

the cleanest test and clearest refutation of the hypothesis that labor markets are relatively unimportant in determining where immigrants live.

Immigrant concentrations are much more important for Western Hemisphere immigrants than for diversity immigrants, reflecting, perhaps that they come from relatively few countries. Both groups, however, prefer to locate closer to their country-of-origin than not. Both groups also appear to prefer less densely populated states. As with other groups, weather matters comparatively little.

Lastly, Table 8 presents the marginal effects estimates for refugees in 1971, 1980, and 1990. As with the pooled fixed effects models, I find very strong evidence that refugees locate in areas with good labor markets. These effects were strongest in 1971 for men and in 1971 and 1980 for women, but in all years the magnitude of the coefficients on the labor market variables are similar to those for employment-based immigrants. The impact of immigrant concentrations was stronger for both men and women in 1980 and 1990 than in 1971. Effects of the other variables were roughly constant over time and consistent with other groups.

7. CONCLUSIONS

This paper comprehensively examines the determinants of location choice of legal immigrants between 1971 and 2000. From the preponderance of data and coefficients, a fairly clear picture emerges. Immigrants are generally responsive to labor market conditions, and locate (in most cases) in areas with higher wages and lower rates of unemployment. The magnitude of this relationship differs across admission categories, however, with the most consistent relationship being found for male employment-based immigrants. This is perhaps not surprising: employment-based immigrants must enter the U.S. with a job. Given the cost of recruiting overseas, firms will likely look only for foreign workers if they are in markets in which native workers are scarce, expensive, or both. In general, the results on the effect of labor market conditions on immigrant location choice would seem to refute strongly any notion that immigrants do not respond to labor market conditions. The results also cast doubt on the extensive literature that uses geographic variation in the concentration of immigrants to try to identify the relative demand curves of immigrants and natives. It is clear from these results that immigrants' locations cannot be treated as exogenous to labor demand.[21]

Table 8. Determinants of Location Choice: Refugees.

Variable	Men			Women		
	1971	1980	1990	1971	1980	1990
Expected log(wage)	.1585	.0355	.0398	.1300	.1359	.0401
	(8.81)	(6.13)	(9.13)	(8.13)	(13.23)	(4.30)
Unemployment rate (percentage points)	−.0016	−.0034	−.0019	−.0028	−.0086	−.0040
	(1.37)	(10.08)	(5.42)	(2.44)	(19.52)	(6.40)
Region of birth as percent of state	.0064	.0210	.0181	.0043	.0160	.0254
population	(1.01)	(6.69)	(12.11)	(0.56)	(4.82)	(9.50)
Region of birth as percent of state	.0069	−.3091	−.0440	.0672	−.0336	−.0990
population sq. ÷ 100	(0.06)	(3.22)	(2.12)	(0.51)	(0.44)	(2.91)
Percent of region of birth population in	.0040	.0040	.0000	.0034	.0025	.0009
state	(5.34)	(16.20)	(0.20)	(3.99)	(6.96)	(2.58)
Percent of region of birth population in	−.0093	−.0066	−.0006	−.0079	−.0037	−.0024
state sq. ÷ 100	(5.34)	(13.88)	(1.94)	(4.04)	(5.84)	(4.52)
Foreign-born percent of state	.0009	.0004	−.0006	.0072	-.0017	−.0030
population	(0.48)	(0.87)	(2.78)	(3.53)	(2.76)	(7.38)
Foreign-born percent of state	.0058	−.0122	.0038	−.0419	−.0028	.0073
population sq. ÷ 100	(0.46)	(4.67)	(4.15)	(3.02)	(0.77)	(4.21)
Log(state population)	.0125	.0149	.0160	.0157	.0125	.0195
	(6.41)	(22.97)	(26.66)	(7.58)	(14.04)	(17.51)
Distance from country of birth	−.0711	.0561	−.0395	−.0596	.0284	−.0372
(1,000 miles)	(4.08)	(12.93)	(10.41)	(3.42)	(4.56)	(6.36)
Distance from country of birth sq. ÷ 100	.5142	−.3935	.2652	.4065	−.2268	.2821
	(3.60)	(13.26)	(9.57)	(2.88)	(5.27)	(6.76)
Log(state land area)	.0057	.0062	.0090	.0026	.0042	.0062
	(3.57)	(11.27)	(15.80)	(1.76)	(6.69)	(7.17)
|State−country of birth	−.0003	−.0007	−.0001	−.0006	−.0010	−.0008
temperature|(°F)	(0.68)	(4.35)	(0.59)	(1.47)	(4.07)	(2.80)
|State−country of birth temperature	.0000	.0021	−.0001	.0020	.0025	.0016
sq.| ÷ 100	(0.01)	(4.99)	(0.15)	(1.20)	(4.31)	(2.38)
|State−country of birth	−.0000	−.0006	−.0002	−.0003	−.0007	−.0005
precipitation|(inches)	(0.24)	(8.88)	(2.51)	(1.48)	(8.01)	(4.42)
|State−country of birth precipitation	.0003	.0001	−.0002	.0007	.0002	.0002
sq.| ÷ 100	(0.73)	(1.56)	(1.72)	(2.05)	(1.93)	(1.22)
Pseudo-R^2	.576	.326	.331	.535	.275	.331
Number of individuals	2,283	7,477	8,790	1,432	4,199	8,790
Number of observations	109,584	358,896	421,920	68,736	201,552	421,920

Note: Estimated via conditional logit with robust standard errors. Choice set is 48 contiguous U.S. states; Own-state marginal effects, z-ratios in parentheses.
Source: Author's calculations using INS and IPUMS data.

Like previous researchers, I also found that foreign-born concentrations had a magnetic effect on newly arrived immigrants. This magnetism is most strongly felt by relatives of legal permanent residents, although all groups are somewhat subject to it. Individuals in most admission categories are drawn to states in which individuals from their region of birth make up a higher percentage of the state population. The effects of the share of the foreign-born in the state population as well as the state's share of the total U.S. population of individuals from the immigrant's region of birth are much smaller for most admission groups in most years.

One surprising, but consistent, finding is the degree to which refugees' location choices seem to be influenced by labor market conditions; refugees are often relocated by government agencies or private charities, and I expected that refugees' responsiveness to labor market conditions would therefore be particularly low. One possibility is that resettlement agencies are aware of which labor markets are best and then seek to place refugees in those places.

Diversity immigrants and to some extent Western Hemisphere immigrants provide a quasi-natural experiment as they do not need to have any formal ties to the U.S. prior to arrival. The estimates of their responses to immigrant concentrations and labor market conditions most closely approximate what would happen if the U.S. shifted to a policy that required only that immigrants meet certain skill requirements but not have any formal link through kin or employment to the U.S. It is clear from these results that immigrants are naturally drawn to areas with good labor markets that bring the prospect of lower unemployment and higher wages, as well areas in which individuals born in their home region are a larger share of the population.

How might these results inform immigration policy? If, as the results here suggest, immigrants are responsive to labor market conditions and increase labor market efficiency by being the margin on which labor markets equilibrate geographically (Borjas, 2001), then it stands to reason that this "greasing the wheels" function of immigrants would be most enhanced by admitting more of the immigrants who are most responsive to labor market conditions. While the results suggest that all immigrants are, to some extent, sensitive to labor market conditions when deciding where to locate, employment visa immigrants and, surprisingly, refugees, are the most consistently sensitive to higher wages and lower rates of unemployment. Admitting more of these types of immigrants and, perhaps, fewer family reunification immigrants, would likely increase labor market efficiency.

NOTES

1. They were so-called because the paper on which the documentation that showed the immigrant was a legal permanent resident of the U.S. was green, although now the card is predominantly white.

2. While the initial set of countries from which diversity immigrants could come was relatively limited, since 1995 diversity visas have, in general, been open to individuals from most countries in the world. For example, in fiscal year 2007, only individuals from Canada, China (mainland-born), Colombia, Dominican Republic, El Salvador, Haiti, India, Jamaica, Mexico, Pakistan, Philippines, Poland, Russia, South Korea, and the United Kingdom (except Northern Ireland) were ineligible for a diversity visa.

3. I include employment-creation, or "investor," immigrants in the employment-related category. The employment-creation immigrant category was created in Immigration Act of 1990. "Investor" immigrants must agree to invest $1,000,000 ($500,000 in a targeted employment area) and create at least 10 jobs. Since the program's creation, there have been on average 446 immigrants per fiscal year who enter the U.S. with an employment-creation visa.

4. Diversity entrants only appear after 1991.

5. Prior to 1976, Western Hemisphere immigrants were not subject to the same admission categories as Eastern Hemisphere immigrants nor were they subject to per-country limitations, although the overall number of Western Hemisphere immigrants was limited after 1965. Thus, Western Hemisphere immigrants mainly appear in the other admission categories only after 1976.

6. The one exception is formerly illegal aliens who were legalized as part of the Immigration Reform and Control Act (IRCA) of 1986. More than 2.6 million illegal aliens have been given green cards since 1989 under the IRCA amnesty, with all but approximately 35,000 legalizations occurring between 1989 and 1992. Information on individuals who received a green card via IRCA legalization is not available in the INS data files.

7. Both refugees and asylees are granted admission to the U.S. because they fear persecution, injury, deprivation, or death if they were to return to their home country. Refugees and asylees differ only in where they seek protection by the U.S. Refugees are those who seek protection while outside of the U.S., while asylees are those who seek protection while already in the U.S. I will refer to both groups as "refugees" for the rest of the paper.

8. Both of these words are sometimes used to describe the status of non-primary immigrants.

9. The fiscal year was July-June for years prior to 1976 and October-September for fiscal years after 1976. There is also a file for the "transition quarter" of July-September 1976.

10. I treat Washington, D.C. as part of Virginia for the analysis.

11. Prior to 1976, some refugees were permitted to enter the U.S. with a green card in hand rather than waiting one year with a temporary visa before applying for one.

12. Unfortunately, one cannot identify members of the same family entering the U.S. to link the "primary" immigrant to his or her "beneficiaries."

13. Note that these statistics are for the calendar year, not the federal government's fiscal year, and so will not match exactly the statistics reported by the Immigration and Naturalization Service. They also do not include amnesty legalizations authorized by the 1986 Immigration Reform and Control Act. After 2000, the flow of immigrants increased again. From fiscal years 2000 to 2004, the number of immigrants admitted to the U.S. averaged about 925,000, with a peak of just over 1,000,000 in 2002 (United States Census Bureau, 2006, Table 6).

14. The regions of origin are: Western Europe, Southern Europe, Eastern Europe, North America excluding Mexico, Mexico and Central America, South America, Caribbean, Africa, Middle East, Southwest Asia, Southeast Asia, East Asia, and Oceania. See the Data Appendix for more information about which countries are included in each region.

15. The small number of European-born immigrants that appear for Western Hemisphere visas is due to individuals who were born in Europe but who could be "charged" to a Western Hemisphere country, presumably because they had become citizens there.

16. One of the categories is a residual category of individuals who are unemployed, out of the labor force, retired, or are homemakers, which are not separately identified in the IPUMS data. The rest of the categories are listed in Appendix Table A1.

17. Note that this is just the population of a region of birth group in a state divided by the total population of that region of birth group in the U.S. Since this denominator is the same for all states, the variable measures the effect of the absolute size of the group, but in a way that permits easier comparison to the other immigrant concentration variables.

18. The Data Appendix discusses how these distances were calculated in greater detail.

19. Note that because neither distance nor weather relies on the IPUMS data, I use the actual country of birth rather than the general region of birth in calculating these variables.

20. That labor market conditions are more important for the male spouses of female U.S. citizens than they are for female spouses of male U.S. citizens suggests that, perhaps, female immigrants are more likely than their male counterparts to marry for love than for money.

21. See Chiswick (1992, 1993) for early critiques of identifying the impacts of immigration using cross-metropolitan area variation.

ACKNOWLEDGEMENTS

The author thanks Seth Sanders and an anonymous referee for comments and IZA for financial support.

REFERENCES

Bartel, A. (1989). Where do the new U.S. immigrants live? *Journal of Labor Economics, 7*, 371–391.

Bauer, T., Epstein, G., & Gang, I. (2002). *Herd effects or migration networks? The location choice of Mexican immigrants in the U.S.* Institute for the Study of Labor Discussion Paper 551, August.

Borjas, G. J. (1999). The economic analysis of immigration. In: O. C. Ashenfelter & D. Card (Eds), *Handbook of labor economics* (Vol. 3A, pp. 1697–1760). Amsterdam: North-Holland.

Borjas, G. J. (2001). Does immigration grease the wheels of the labor market? *Brookings Papers on Economic Activity, 1,* 1–51.

Chiswick, B. R. (1992). Review of Immigration, Trade, and the Labor Market. In: John M. Abowd & Richard B. Freeman (Eds), *Journal of Economic Literature* (Vol. 30, pp. 212–213).

Chiswick, B. R. (1993). Review of Immigration and the Work Force: Economic Consequences for the United States and Source Areas. In: George J. Borjas & Richard B. Freeman (Eds), *Journal of Economic Literature* (Vol. 31, pp. 910–911).

Cragg, M., & Kahn, M. (1997). New estimates of climate demand: Evidence from migration. *Journal of Urban Economics, 42,* 261–284.

Dunlevey, J. A. (1991). On the settlement patterns of recent Caribbean and Latin immigrants to the U.S. *Growth and Change, 22,* 54–67.

Jaeger, D. A. (1997). Reconciling educational attainment questions in the CPS and the Census. *Monthly Labor Review, 1218,* 36–40.

Jaeger, D. A. (2000). *Local labor markets, admission categories, and immigrant location choice.* Hunter College and Graduate Center, City University of New York. Unpublished mimeo.

Kaushal, N. (2005). New immigrants' location choices: Welfare without magnets. *Journal of Labor Economics, 23,* 59–80.

McFadden, D. (1984). Econometric analysis of qualitative choice models. In: Z. Griliches & M. D. Intriligator (Eds), *Handbook of econometrics* (Vol. 2, pp. 1396–1456). Amsterdam: North-Holland.

Ruggles, S., Sobek, M., Alexander, T., Fitch, C. A., Goeken, R., Hall, P. K., King, M., & Ronnander, C. (2004). *Integrated public use microdata series: Version 3.0* [machine-readable database]. Minneapolis, MN: Minnesota Population Center [producer and distributor]. URL: http://www.ipums.org

Sinnot, R. W. (1984). Virtues of the haversine. *Sky and Telescope, 68*(2), 159.

United States Census Bureau. (2006). *Statistical abstract of the United States.* Washington, DC: Government Printing Office. URL: http://www.census.gov/statab/www

United States Department of Justice. (2000). *Immigrants admitted to the United States* [documentation to machine-readable database]. Washington, DC: Immigration and Naturalization Service [producer]. Inter-University Consortium for Political and Social Research version, 2002, Ann Arbor, MI [distributor]. URL: http://webapp.icpsr. umich.edu/cocoon/ICPSR-STUDY/03486.xml

Zavodny, M. (1997). Welfare and the location choices of new immigrants. *Economic Review* (Federal Reserve Bank of Dallas), *2nd quarter,* 2–10.

Zavodny, M. (1999). Determinants of recent immigrants' locational choices. *International Migration Review, 33,* 1014–1030.

DATA APPENDIX

1. Region of Birth Groups

Region of birth groups are defined in both the Immigration and Naturalization Service data and in the various Censuses from the IPUMS.

Codes for the different countries vary across different years of the INS data and between the INS data and the IPUMS. In addition, the names of some geographic areas have changed over time (e.g. the breakup of the Soviet Union). This list, therefore, is not exhaustive, but should be sufficient so that the reader knows which countries are included in which grouping.

Western Europe: Austria, Belgium, Denmark, Finland, France, Germany, Iceland, Ireland, Liechtenstein, Luxembourg, Monaco, Netherlands, Norway, Sweden, Switzerland, United Kingdom.

Southern Europe: Gibraltar, Greece, Italy, Malta, Portugal, San Marino, Spain, Vatican City.

Eastern Europe: Albania, Andorra, Bulgaria, Czechoslovakia, Estonia, Hungary, Latvia, Lithuania, Poland, Romania, Soviet Union, Yugoslavia.

North America: Bermuda, Canada, Greenland, St. Pierre and Miquelon.

Central America and Mexico: Belize, Costa Rica, El Salvador, Guatemala, Honduras, Mexico, Nicaragua, Panama.

South America: Argentina, Bolivia, Brazil, Chile, Colombia, Ecuador, Falkland Islands, French Guyana, Guyana, Paraguay, Peru, Suriname, Uruguay, Venezuela.

Caribbean: Anguilla, Antigua, Aruba, Bahamas, Barbados, British Virgin Islands, Cayman Islands, Cuba, Dominican Republic, Dominica, Grenada, Guadeloupe, Haiti, Jamaica, Martinique, Montserrat, Netherlands Antilles, St. Kits-Nevis, St. Lucia, St. Vincent and the Grenadines, Trinidad and Tobago, Turks and Caicos Islands.

Africa: Algeria, Angola, Benin, Botswana, Burkina Faso, Burundi, Central African Republic, Cameroon, Cape Verde, Chad, Comoros, Congo, Djibouti, Egypt, Equatorial Guinea, Ethiopia, Gabon, Gambia, Ghana, Guinea, Guinea-Bissau, Ivory Coast, Kenya, Lesotho, Liberia, Libya, Madagascar, Malawi, Mali, Mauritania, Mauritius, Morocco, Mozambique, Namibia, Niger, Nigeria, Reunion, Rwanda, Sao Tome and Principe, Senegal, Seychelles, Sierra Leone, Somalia, South Africa, St. Helena, Sudan, Swaziland, Tanzania, Togo, Tunisia, Uganda, Western Sahara, Zaire, Zambia, Zimbabwe.

Middle East: Bahrain, Cyprus, Iraq, Israel, Jordan, Kuwait, Lebanon, Oman, Qatar, Saudi Arabia, Syria, Turkey, United Arab Emirates, Yemen.

Southwest Asia: Afghanistan, Bangladesh, Bhutan, India, Iran, Maldives, Nepal, Pakistan, Sri Lanka.

Southeast Asia: Brunei, Burma, Cambodia, Indonesia, Laos, Malaysia, Philippines, Singapore, Thailand, Vietnam.

East Asia: China, Hong Kong, Japan, Korea, Macau, Mongolia, Taiwan.
Oceania: Australia, Christmas Island, Cocos Island, Cook Island, Fiji,
French Polynesia, French Southern Antarctic, Kiribati, Nauru, New
Caledonia, New Zealand, Niue, Papua New Guinea, Pitcairn Island,
Solomon Island, Tonga, Tuvalu, Vanuatu, Wallis and Futuna Islands,
Western Samoa.

2. Distance

Distance from country of birth to the state of intended residence is
calculated as the straight line distance from the most populous city in the
country of birth in 1991 to the geographic center of each state (taken from
http://geography.about.com/library/weekly/aa120699a.htm). Distance, d, in
1,000s of miles is calculated following Sinnot (1984):

$$d = \frac{2 \cdot 3956}{1000} \arcsin\left(\min\left(1, \sqrt{a}\right)\right) \qquad (A.1)$$

where

$$a = \sin\left(\frac{lat_2 - lat_1}{2}\right)^2 + \cos(lat_1) \cdot \cos(lat_2) \cdot \sin\left(\frac{lon_2 - lon_1}{2}\right)^2 \qquad (A.2)$$

lat_2 and lon_2 are the coordinates of the destination (in radians), lat_1 and
lon_1 the coordinates of the origin (in radians) and 3,956 is the diameter
of the earth in miles. This method treats the Earth as a perfect sphere,
resulting in less measurement error than if the earth were treated as a flat
plane.

3. Ordered Logit Estimates and Skill Imputation

Skill categories for individuals in the INS data were predicted on the basis
of reported occupation, age, and marital status. I estimated an ordered
logit using pooled data from the 1980 and 1990 IPUMS on foreign-born
individuals aged 25–64, separately for men and women. The dependent
variable has three categories: less than 12 years of school, 12–15 years of
school, and 16 or more years of school. The method suggested by Jaeger
(1997) was used to code the schooling categories. Results of the ordered
logit regressions are presented in Appendix Table A1. This method correctly
predicts the within-sample educational category about 64% of the time
in the IPUMS data. The predicted probabilities of being in each skill category

for individual i are then

$$\hat{P}(S<12)_i = (1 + \exp(X_i\hat{\beta} - \hat{\mu}_1))^{-1}$$
$$\hat{P}(12 \leq S<16)_i = (1 + \exp(X_i\hat{\beta} - \hat{\mu}_2))^{-1} - (1 + \exp(X_i\hat{\beta} - \hat{\mu}_1))^{-1} \quad \text{(A.3)}$$
$$\hat{P}(S \geq 16)_i = 1 - \hat{P}(S<12)_i - \hat{P}(12 \leq S<16)_i$$

where $\hat{\mu}_1$ and $\hat{\mu}_2$ are the estimated cut points, X_i is the vector of characteristics (age, age squared, occupational dummy variables, and a dummy variable for being married), and $\hat{\beta}$ is the vector of estimated coefficients.

Table A1.   Skill Level Imputation between 1980 and 1990 Census Pooled Sample of Foreign-Born.

Variable	Men		Women	
	Coeff.	Std. err.	Coeff.	Std. err.
Southeast Asia	reference		reference	
Southwest Asia	0.909	0.025	0.761	0.028
Africa	0.686	0.032	0.220	0.032
East Asia	0.260	0.019	0.147	0.017
Western Europe	0.029	0.018	−0.113	0.016
Eastern Europe	−0.177	0.017	−0.233	0.015
Oceania	−0.300	0.044	−0.392	0.038
Middle East	−0.325	0.026	−0.436	0.030
North America	−0.385	0.019	−0.392	0.019
South America	−0.387	0.021	−0.434	0.018
Caribbean	−0.831	0.017	−0.809	0.016
Southern Europe	−1.277	0.018	−1.254	0.018
Mexico and Central America	−2.020	0.016	−1.974	0.015
Writers, artists, entertainers and athletes	reference		reference	
Physicians	5.774	0.187	4.901	0.242
Lawyers	4.728	0.256	3.373	0.197
Post-secondary teachers, social scientists, librarians	3.189	0.078	2.133	0.063
Mathematical, computer, and natural scientists	1.928	0.053	1.575	0.064
Teachers except post-secondary	1.885	0.063	1.281	0.042
Engineers, surveyors, and architects	1.837	0.038	1.644	0.086
Nurses, health assessment, diagnosing, and treating	1.605	0.066	0.574	0.037

Table A1. (*Continued*)

Variable	Men		Women	
	Coeff.	Std. err.	Coeff.	Std. err.
Counselors, social, recreation and religious workers	1.398	0.067	1.053	0.063
Executives, administrative, and managerial	0.212	0.030	−0.225	0.035
Technologists and technicians	0.192	0.034	0.026	0.039
Sales	−0.555	0.031	−1.273	0.034
Administrative support	−0.665	0.032	−0.937	0.033
Precision production, craft, and repair	−1.700	0.030	−2.331	0.038
Service	−1.900	0.031	−2.206	0.034
Laborers	−2.057	0.030	−2.886	0.034
Unemployed, out of labor force, retired, homemaker	−2.191	0.037	−2.251	0.033
Farming, forestry, and fishing	−2.681	0.036	−3.263	0.049
Age	0.043	0.003	0.009	0.003
Age^2	−0.001	0.000	−0.000	0.000
Married	−0.014	0.008	0.061	0.008
Cut point 1	−2.511	0.073	−3.564	0.070
Cut point 2	0.324	0.073	−0.367	0.070
Pseudo-R^2	0.292		0.237	
N	387,050		429,672	

Note: Estimated with ordered logit; sample limited to non-students aged 25-60. Entries in table are logit coefficients and standard errors. Dependent variable categories are: less than 12th grade, 12th-15th grade, 16th grade and higher.
Source: Authors tabulations of 1980 and 1990 IPUMS data.

IMMIGRANT AND NATIVE ASSET ACCUMULATION IN HOUSING

Sherrie A. Kossoudji

ABSTRACT

Purchasing a home is the largest expenditure many people will make during their lifetime, as well as their greatest source of wealth. There is a homeownership gap between natives and immigrants well documented in the literature. I examine the determinants of homeownership, the value of purchased homes (a measure of potential housing wealth), and the equity owned for those who have purchased a home (a measure of actual housing wealth) for immigrants and natives. When immigrants are separated by citizenship status the homeownership gap between natives and immigrants is shown to be a gap between natives and non-citizen immigrants. Immigrant citizens have ownership outcomes as good or better than natives. Further, the gap reflects a problem in ownership, brought about by age and income distributional differences, not in value or equity for homeowners. All immigrants are predicted to have higher home value and home equity than natives.

INTRODUCTION

Wealth means economic security. For many people, purchasing a home is the largest expenditure they will make during their lifetime, as well as their

Immigration: Trends, Consequences and Prospects for the United States
Research in Labor Economics, Volume 27, 185–213
Copyright © 2008 by Elsevier Ltd.
ISSN: 0147-9121/doi:10.1016/S0147-9121(07)00005-2

greatest source of wealth. Homeownership is also associated with a host of positive social behaviors, from voting and political activity to community connection that are associated with membership in a community. The social benefits of homeownership are consistently recognized by the federal government by the number of federal programs designed to facilitate home purchases and the mortgage interest deduction for federal taxes.

Questions about immigrant wealth are not often asked – even in the face of thousands of articles about immigrant assimilation. Yet, just as there is an earnings gap between immigrants and natives, there is also an overall homeownership gap. According to Borjas (2002) there was a 20 percentage point difference in homeownership rates in 2000. There are a number of possible explanations for the measured homeownership gap. Immigrants may lack access, knowledge, and confidence in U.S. financial institutions. Financial institutions, in turn, may be less accommodating to immigrants, particularly non-citizens, or see them as less credit worthy applicants than natives.[1] Immigrants may choose to invest in the home country as well as in the United States. Some of the same factors that explain the earnings gap may also explain the housing gap. How do the myriad of differences in education, legal status, family type, race, and location influence home-ownership?

In this chapter I ask about wealth differences between immigrants and natives by focusing on the acquisition of a single asset – one's home.[2] I examine the determinants of homeownership, the value of purchased homes (a measure of potential housing wealth), and the equity owned for those who have purchased a home (a measure of actual housing wealth).

While past authors have concentrated on immigrant status, immigrant nativity, and residential location to explain homeownership differences, citizenship and income and age effects are allowed to differ for immigrants and natives in this chapter. The findings in this chapter indicate that immigrant and citizenship status are, themselves, not associated with the probability of homeownership, home value, and home equity, but work through critical age and income effects.

The results of this study have important economic as well as policy implications. Given that the distribution of wealth is much more unequal than that of income and homeownership represents a high proportion of wealth, policies that promote immigrant homeownership are a means of reducing wealth gaps. If homeownership is an important aspect of community participation and neighborhood stability, then homeownership by immigrants is good for the community. Closer community ties through homeownership may mean that immigrants are more likely to retain steady employment, become politically integrated, improve language skills and provide better education for their children. Whether homeownership is the cause or effect of these related outcomes, it is important to understand better the factors that influence the housing decisions of immigrants.

HOMEOWNERSHIP ISSUES

Homeownership is considered a hallmark of life in the United States. Bostic, Calem, and Wachter (2004, p. 13) review the literature and identify income, wealth, and credit constraints as the principal reasons (from the demand side) that people are unable to purchase a home. They note the declining credit quality of renters over time and say it is possible that "successive waves of immigrants have had larger proportions with credit quality below the critical threshold levels". They also note that race-based discrimination and predatory lending are possible explanations for the homeownership gap. In an investigation of the impact of affordable lending efforts, Quercia, McCarthy, and Wachter (2003) identify the populations associated with such constraints as minority, low to moderate income, central city residents, and young households – all stereotypical characteristics of immigrants – but do not mention immigrants specifically.

People in minority populations and immigrants may find that the most difficult barrier to homeownership may well be the decision by mortgage lenders to deny loan applications. The impact of a bias in those decisions is felt by families over the long run because of housing's unique features. It is both a consumption and asset good. Some kind of shelter is necessary and the marginal payments on a mortgage are often similar in size to rental payments. While rental payments are sufficient to acquire shelter, mortgage payments provide shelter while also acting as savings, improving one's welfare through wealth accumulation. In a now famous study of mortgage lending, Munnell, Browne, and McEneaney (1996, p. 39) found that "even after accounting for the applicant's obligation ratios, wealth, credit history, and loan-to-value ratio, and property, neighborhood and lender characteristics, as well as the stability of income, and whether he or she received private mortgage insurance, the race of the applicant still plays an important role in the lender's decision to approve or deny the loan". Race is not often discussed in the context of economic gaps between immigrants and natives, but may trigger discriminatory practices on the part of lenders.

Although there is a much smaller literature on the impact of immigration on housing, Chiswick and Miller (2003) document immigrant residential and mobility patterns in an analysis of future housing trends in the United States. They, and all authors, reveal a significant difference in homeowner-ship rates for natives and immigrants. Borjas (2002) notes that the "homeownership gap" has been increasing since 1980. Coulson (1999) finds that immigrants consistently reduce the rates of homeownership of different ethnic groups by 10–16 percentage points and that Latino immigrants are less likely to own their own home, while the results for Asian immigrants are mixed. Painter, Gabriel, and Myers (2001) get similarly negative results on immigrant status, but also include several ethnicity variables that emphasize the role that ethnicity plays in housing decisions.

Several authors claim that although homeownership rates for immigrants are more similar to African American than white rates, the causes for the difference may be quite different. While discrimination in housing markets often sits squarely in the middle of the explanation of differential home-ownership rates for African Americans, and may provide some explanation for immigrants, questions about immigrants' familiarity with US financial institutions, the role of time horizons, and the question of credit constraints more often arise when immigrants are studied. Krivo (1995) considers potential problems with credit markets and also notes that less than fluent English may lead to difficulty negotiating contracts. She finds that the individual characteristics of immigrants are important to explain the ownership differential but may be more important in the aggregate as a "neighborhood context". She is also one of the few authors to consider housing value. She finds that the foreign born have higher valued houses, but she does not adequately control for the size of the city of residence, which plays an important role in housing values. Coulson (1999) claims that lower rates of homeownership are largely explained by being immigrants, living in large metropolitan places where homeownership rates are generally low, having less education and by being younger than native household heads. Alba and Logan (1992) found strong support for the importance of individual characteristics' effect on homeownership, especially age, house-hold composition, and socioeconomic position. Many authors find that homeownership rates differ by nationality or broad sending region. There is little discussion about why those differences arise. Borjas (2002, p. 20) makes several claims: that only a small part of the native/immigrant homeownership gap is a result of differences in characteristics, that the different locations of residence of natives and immigrants are important to explain the homeownership gap, and changes in national origin, combined with lower wages for "newer" national origin groups, drive the differences. But he does not know if lower homeownership rates stem from discrimination against "newer" groups, or if "the way the population is self selected from each source country's population could be responsible for the remaining differences".

Perhaps because immigrant housing literature is still relatively new, homeownership rates typically remain the point of analysis (with the exception of Krivo). Many of the characteristics that are associated with homeownership militate against immigrant homeownership. City dwellers, those with lower income, and younger adults are less likely to own homes and immigrants have a high rate of urban residence, earn less money on average than natives, and are younger on average. Immigrants, unlike most natives, are likely to have family and community connections abroad and may choose to invest in housing or other assets in the home country rather than in the United States. At every age, immigrants may have spent fewer years in the U.S. labor market, and so may have less money to use as a down payment on a home. Further, immigrants' lack of knowledge of financial institutions, combined with potential cultural, ethnic, or racial biases on the part of lending institutions could both act to reduce immigrant home-ownership rates.

THE EMPIRICAL STRATEGY

I investigate three housing outcomes that are related to wealth: whether or not the household owns a home, because mortgage payments contribute to wealth accumulation as well as providing shelter; home value, because the long-run potential wealth accumulation from housing is related to the value of the home; and home equity because it is a measure of current wealth. When I use the phrase "homeownership rates" or "homeowners", I refer, as most people do, to people who own their homes, whether or not there is a mortgage on the property.

Three important characteristics are given special consideration in this chapter. Citizen immigrants are considered separately from non-citizen immigrants. Citizenship, and all it entails, is likely to both increase the desire for homeownership and to ease lender constraints to homeownership. While there is no official discrimination by citizenship, lenders may be more cautious when lending money to non-citizens. It is also possible that non-citizens have not made a commitment to the United States and choose to invest their money elsewhere (a home in the home country, for example). Immigrants are also younger than the native population and they earn lower incomes on average. They may also choose a very different investment strategy for their income than natives. Immigrants, particularly non-citizens, may prefer fungible investments over a home. At the same time, the economic myth exists that immigrants mark their success by owning their home in the United States. The differences in the age and income distribution, along with a potential differential impact of age and income on home outcomes, suggest that interacting those terms with immigrant citizenship status is necessary.

Both value and equity are contingent on having purchased a home, which means they are estimated on a select sample. I jointly estimate two sets of bivariate equations that account for selection in homeownership. I estimate homeownership and value jointly and then estimate homeownership and equity jointly using maximum likelihood methods. The first equation in each set estimates the probability of homeownership using a probit equation whose dependent variable distinguishes between those who do and do not own a home. The estimates from this equation are used to construct a selection bias correction in the second equation, which is either the home value or the home equity equation. This procedure is now a common way to correct for selection bias.[3]

Data

The data come from the 1996 Survey of Income and Program Participation (SIPP) for the United States. The 1996 panel contains 12 waves of interviews conducted over the period from 1996 to 2000. This chapter does not include a panel analysis, but utilizes information from every wave in the 1996 panel, since waves include different information. Although this data set has individual level information as well as household level information for some variables, the housing information was asked of the reference person only; the same housing information was entered into the records of all individuals in the household. Thus, data for spouses or other family members is not independent information.[4] Each observation is the reference person of the household, who I will refer to as the householder.[5] Because only householders, and not the entire adult population, are used in the sample, the sample is older than the adult population.

The sample was restricted to householders age 25–70, those not living in mobile homes, and those not living in institutional group homes. Each householder must be in both the migration history universe (to ascertain immigration status) and the assets universe.[6] Any biases that result from this data selection strategy are present in these analyses. The final, unweighed, sample has 19,583 natives, and 2,559 immigrants.[7]

Variables

The analysis compares three groups of people: natives, immigrant citizens, and immigrant non-citizens.[8] Immigrant citizens are people who have become naturalized citizens by passing the citizenship requirements and making a formal application. Non-citizens are those immigrants who have not obtained U.S. citizenship even though they may be eligible.[9] Although a person can apply for citizenship after five years, delays in processing can make the non-citizenship period longer even if someone has applied for citizenship. For the purposes of this analysis, immigrants who have been in the United States for less than seven years are new non-citizens who either are not yet eligible for citizenship or who, because of processing, are unlikely to have taken the citizenship oath even if the person has applied. People who have been in the United States for more than seven years are clearly eligible for citizenship. For all immigrants, the number of years since coming to the United States is an independent variable in all equations.

Earned income, because its level and stability are fundamental to mortgage lenders' decisions, helps explain housing outcomes. Mortgage lenders rely on income in their credit scores and householders rely on it when making housing decisions. The permanent earned household income is calculated as the average household earned income over all 12 waves of the panel (or waves in which that household was observed), but given the short panel of SIPP it is more appropriately called "smoothed income".[10] The square of income is also included and both are interacted with immigrant status to ascertain whether there are differences in behavior by immigrants and natives at the same income levels, allowing for the possibility that immigrants choose to spend and invest their income differently than natives. This is of particular interest for homeownership, since remittances or savings sent to the home country are important for many immigrants, but not natives.

It has been argued that more educated individuals behave differently in the housing market than their less educated counterparts (Segal & Sullivan, 1998). Dummy variables are included for householders with a high school diploma or less education, and with some college. The comparison category is householders with at least a four-year college degree. Married householders are identified separately by gender and are compared to all householders that are not part of a married couple (see Kossoudji, 2005). Race dummy variables are white, African American, Asian, and Native American. White is the omitted race category.

Housing prices and the desire to own homes vary by location. Rural or small town residents are defined as those who do not live in any of the approximately 100 identified MSA cities or city groups in the United States. Immigrants are more likely than natives to live in large cities that are often called gateway cities. The identified gateway cities constitute a group of 14 large cities that have significant immigrant populations.[11] The omitted residence location is MSA, but not Gateway city, residence. To control for differences in housing prices by market, the poverty income index (a measure of the income required to be above the poverty line for each household in each residential location), which is based on local housing and rental prices, is included. Following the literature, the age-life-cycle association with the choice of homeownership is acknowledged by including age and age squared in the homeownership probability equation. They are interacted with native, immigrant citizen, and immigrant non-citizen dummies to investigate life cycle differences in homeownership. The number of children in the household is included since the decision to purchase a home often depends on this aspect of family structure and because mortgage lenders calculate an obligation ratio based partly on this information.[12]

For identification purposes, the determinants of the outcomes in the jointly estimated equations must be different. The number of children in the household and the age of the householder are included in the regression on homeownership. The length of time the house has been owned and whether the home was purchased with an FHA mortgage were included in the value and equity regressions. Although the existence of FHA mortgages could influence the probability of homeownership, the measured variable in SIPP is whether the house was purchased with an FHA mortgage, which will affect the size of the loan and the size of the down payment (and hence the value and equity).[13]

The length of time the house has been owned influences value through rising home prices over time and equity by mortgage pay down (the longer a home is owned the more equity one has conditional on value). Although age may also play a role in value (older people may well purchase higher valued homes) it probably does so because of higher income, a variable already in the regression.

A dummy variable for people who have ever retired from a job is included in the homeownership equation (since retirement may alter preferences for ownership over renting), but not in the value or equity equations (retirement itself should not influence those values). The equity equation includes an instrument for value (so that equity comparisons do not also include value differences).[14]

Homeownership, and its self-reported characteristics, is taken from the latest housing information available from SIPP, which pertains to 1999 or

2000.[15] Both home value and equity are measured in 1999/2000 dollars. Home equity is the total property value minus any mortgage debt. The cross-section weights of that time period are used for all predictions and descriptive statistics.

HOMEOWNERSHIP, IMMIGRATION, AND CITIZENSHIP

Two sources of differences in homeownership between immigrants and natives stand out: citizenship status and residential location. Citizenship, and all it proxies, matters. Eligible non-citizen immigrants are only two-thirds as likely to own homes as immigrant citizens. When one compares immigrant citizens and natives, the homeownership differences between immigrants and natives disappear. Location matters for homeownership, itself, and is important because a high proportion of immigrants live in large "gateway" cities where home values are high.

Table 1 documents the rates of homeownership among natives, immigrant citizens, and non-citizens (eligible for citizenship and not eligible for citizenship). About 67 percent of native householders are homeowners as are 54 percent of immigrant householders, a finding consistent with other studies. That is, natives are about 30 percent more likely to be homeowners than immigrants. This large gap has driven much of the past discussion

Table 1. Proportion of Homeowners by Residential Location for Natives, Immigrant Citizens, and Non-citizens.

	Native	Immigrant Citizen	Ineligible Non-citizen	Eligible Non-citizen
Entire sample	0.672	0.662	0.304	0.434
	(100%)	(100%)	(100%)	(100%)
Non-MSA residents	0.636	0.595	0.293	0.339
	(47.6%)	(29.3%)	(45.9%)	(33.0%)
MSA (not Gateway) residents	0.705	0.767	0.457	0.519
	(30.7%)	(18.7%)	(19.5%)	(17.5%)
Gateway city residents	0.706	0.663	0.263	0.533
	(21.6%)	(52.0%)	(34.6%)	(49.5%)

Note: Percent of each group in each location in parentheses.
Source: 1996 SIPP panel and author's calculations. Sample weights are used in the table.

about asset accumulation and assimilation for immigrants. But this gap principally exists because of a dearth of homeownership among non-citizen immigrants. Natives are no more likely to own homes than immigrant citizens (of whom 66 percent are homeowners) but are 55 percent more likely to own homes than eligible non-citizens (of whom 43 percent are homeowners) and 121 percent more likely than ineligible non-citizens (of whom 30 percent are homeowners). To be sure, time in the United States is a factor in this outcome, but eligible non-citizens have been in the United States for an average of 16.5 years. Even before standardizing on numerous characteristics, then, the "homeownership gap" has been significantly explained by simply conditioning on citizenship.[16]

Two further observations stand out in Table 1. Home ownership rates vary by residential location for all groups. Just under three-fourths of natives and more than three-fourths of citizen immigrant householders who live in an MSA – but not a Gateway city – are homeowners. That is, except in the Gateway cities, immigrant citizens who live in cities are *more* likely to own their own homes than natives. About 30 percent of natives, but less than 20 percent of immigrants, live in these MSAs. In Gateway cities, a higher proportion of natives are homeowners (70.6 percent) and a slightly lower proportion of immigrant citizens are homeowners (66.3 percent) but while only 21.6 percent of natives live in Gateway cities, more than one-half of immigrant citizens live in these large cities. Homeownership is lower for all groups in non-MSA residences. Only a small proportion of immigrant citizens and eligible non-citizens live in non-MSA areas, but 46 percent of new immigrants live there – highlighting a shift in immigrant residences. Non-citizens are unlikely to own homes. A minority of all non-citizens (who are about one-half of immigrants) are homeowners, whether they are in the group that is eligible for citizenship or not. It may be, but this is unsubstantiated, that immigrant farm workers or other low-skilled immigrants are living disproportionately in rural areas and they are unlikely to purchase homes.

Table 2 documents the characteristics of immigrant citizens, immigrant non-citizens, and natives. Immigrant homeowners, whether citizen or non-citizen, have higher value homes than natives but only the difference for immigrant citizens is significant. Larger housing values probably come from the fact that housing values are higher in the large cities where immigrants live. The equity differences are similar proportionately, but, again, only immigrant citizens have significantly more equity than do natives. Non-citizens, have slightly less equity value than do natives. This table reveals other important differences between immigrants and natives, and between immigrant citizens and non-citizens. In particular, while immigrant citizens

Table 2. Descriptive Statistics by Immigration Status.

	Native	Immigrant Citizen	Ineligible Non-citizen	Eligible Non-citizen
Property value	$145,414	$182,843	$159,324	$147,301
	($107,550)	($117,991)	($121,584)	($99,371)
Equity	$92,296	$117,255	$85,144	$87,702
	($94,027)	($105,072)	($106,182)	($94,747)
FHA or VA	17.6	15.4	20.8	21.0
Loan (%)	(38.0)	(36.0)	(40.6)	(40.7)
Years owned	12.1	10.9	4.5	8.8
home	(11.2)	(10.5)	(6.0)	(8.3)
Years in the US	–	25.0	3.0	16.5
		(12.2)	(2.0)	(8.2)
Price index	$1,096	$1,199	$1,283	$1,350
(month)	($3,541)	($3,976)	($4,306)	($4,660)
Age	46.4	47.9	39.0	43.5
	(11.4)	(10.9)	(9.6)	(10.3)
Retiree	19.1	19.2	6.6	7.8
	(39.3)	(39.4)	(24.8)	(26.9)
Monthly HH	$4,222	$4,315	$2,990	$3,195
earnings	($3,539)	($3,599)	($2,807)	($3,140)
High school	41.4	41.0	50.9	69.3
diploma or	(49.3)	(49.2)	(50.0)	(46.1)
fewer years of				
school (%)				
Some college	30.8	27.2	17.3	16.8
(%)	(46.2)	(44.5)	(37.8)	(37.4)
College	27.9	31.8	31.8	13.9
graduate (%)	(44.8)	(46.6)	(46.6)	(34.6)
# Kids	0.9	1.0	1.2	1.5
	(1.2)	(1.2)	(1.3)	(1.5)
Married woman	18.3	17.8	22.6	16.6
(%)	(38.6)	(38.3)	(41.8)	(37.2)
Married man	39.9	48.9	47.4	46.9
(%)	(49.0)	(50.0)	(49.9)	(49.9)
African	15.6	11.5	9.4	10.6
American/	(36.3)	(31.9)	(29.2)	(30.8)
Black				
Asian	0.9	29.5	24.1	14.0
	(9.1)	(45.5)	(42.8)	(34.7)
Native	1.1	–	–	–
American	(10.3)			
N (unweighted)	19,583	1,070	447	1,042

Note: Standard deviations are given in parentheses.
Source: 1996 SIPP panel and author's calculations. Sample weights are used in the table.

are about the same age as natives, immigrant non-citizens are much younger. While immigrant citizens and natives have similar monthly household incomes, non-citizens' incomes are only three-fourths as high. Immigrant citizens have an educational distribution similar to that of natives' but eligible non-citizens are much less likely to have gone to college. Ineligible non-citizens reflect newer migration patterns and are likely to have little or a lot of education.

ANALYTICAL RESULTS

Preliminary Analysis and Discussion

It has already been noted that citizenship plays a key role in determining housing outcomes. The differences in the age and income distributions for immigrants and natives also play an important role in the discussion of the home–asset gap between them. Fig. 1A documents the age distribution for natives, immigrant citizens, and eligible and non-eligible immigrant non-citizens while Fig. 1B documents the income distribution for the same groups. As Fig. 1A shows, immigrant citizens are slightly older than natives but the two distributions are very similar. The age distribution for non-citizens is highly skewed to younger ages, especially for the ineligible non-citizens. Ineligible non-citizens are much younger than all of the other groups. Similarly, as Fig. 1B shows, immigrant citizens have an income distribution that is similar to natives', but non-citizens have an income distribution that is highly skewed to lower incomes. There is almost no difference in the income distributions of eligible and ineligible non-citizens but they are both radically different from that of natives and immigrant citizens. Approximately three-fourths of all non-citizens earn below the median native income. Since homeownership varies by age and income, immigrant non-citizens, who are younger and poorer, may be less likely to purchase a home (conditional on time in the United States) than other immigrants and natives as a result of income and age differences, not because they are immigrants.

Because this analysis uses an atypical set of interactions, and finds atypical results, a series of preliminary analyses were conducted to make sure that the results did not stem from an unusual sample, methodology, etc. A summary of these preliminary regressions is in Table 3. As in past studies (with no age or income interaction), preliminary analysis shows that being an immigrant is negatively correlated with homeownership. Most past

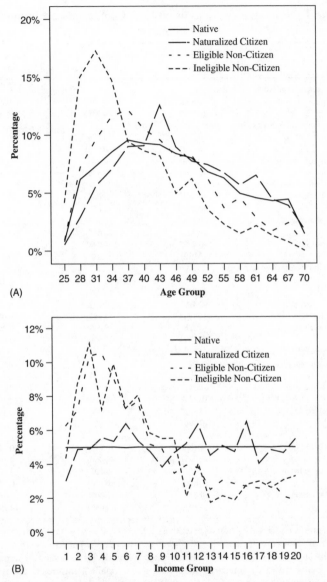

Fig. 1. (A) Age Distribution for All Groups. (B) Income Distribution for All Groups. *Source:* 1996 SIPP Panel and Author's Calculations. *Note:* There are 20 income groups. The income range is set so that 5 percent of natives are in each group. Sample weights are used in the graph.

Table 3. Preliminary Analysis and the Coefficients on Immigrant Status.

	Home Ownership Equation	Home Value Equation[a]	Home Equity Equation
No earnings interaction/No age interaction			
Immigrant	−0.802*	0.136*	0.298*
	(0.055)	(0.039)	(0.061)
No earnings interaction/No age interaction			
Immigrant citizen	−0.514*	0.075	0.181*
	(0.073)	(0.050)	(0.079)
Immigrant non-citizen	−0.824*	0.140*	0.387*
	(0.056)	(0.039)	(0.061)
No earnings interaction/No age interaction			
Immigrant citizen	−0.444*	0.046	0.114
	(0.086)	(0.053)	(0.085)
Ineligible non-citizen	−0.924*	0.194*	0.432*
	(0.721)	(0.055)	(0.086)
Eligible non-citizen	−0.727*	0.098*	0.212*
	(0.072)	(0.048)	(0.075)
No earnings interaction/Age interacted			
Immigrant citizen	−0.331	0.418	0.107
	(0.737)	(0.053)	(0.084)
Ineligible non-citizen	−2.429*	0.192*	0.419*
	(1.164)	(0.055)	(0.086)
Eligible non-citizen	−0.270	0.093*	0.200*
	(0.697)	(0.048)	(0.075)
Earnings interacted/No age interaction			
Immigrant citizen	−0.646*	0.110	0.159
	(0.110)	(0.066)	(0.105)
Ineligible non-citizen	−1.187*	0.110	0.620*
	(0.137)	(0.110)	(0.171)
Eligible non-citizen	−0.803*	0.006	0.143
	(0.096)	(0.066)	(0.150)
Earnings interacted/Age interacted			
Immigrant citizen	−0.363	0.111	0.160
	(0.740)	(0.066)	(0.105)
Ineligible non-citizen	−2.469*	0.101	0.605*
	(0.416)	(0.110)	(0.171)
Eligible non-citizen	0.325	0.005	0.136
	(0.697)	(0.066)	(0.105)

Note: Standard deviations are given in parentheses. An asterisk means significant at a standard 5%. These regressions also include all of the other variables detailed in Table 4. In no case were variables unrelated to immigrant status affected, except slightly, by these model changes. These regression results are easily compared with those in the extant literature. Entire results are available from the author until 2008. The coefficients in the final panel come from the model specified in Table 4.

Source: 1996 SIPP panel and author's calculations.

[a]The natural log of home value or home equity is the dependent variable.

studies do not examine home value or home equity but using only the immigrant dummy variable leads to a positive impact on home value and a positive and significant differences between immigrants and natives in home equity (row 1). That is, using these results, the immigrant/native home-ownership wealth gap is a problem of "getting one's foot in the door". The same pattern is retained when using citizen or non-citizen (the omitted category is native-row 2) and when using citizen, eligible non-citizen and ineligible non-citizen, while coefficients on value and equity lose their significance for citizens (row 3). But when age is interacted with immigrant status, the immigrant effect on homeownership disappears for citizens and eligible non-citizens (row 4). When income is interacted with immigrant status (but not age), the immigrant effect on value disappears and the effect on equity disappears for all but ineligible non-citizens (row 5). When both are interacted, there is no independent effect of immigrant status on homeownership, home value, or home equity except for that on ineligible non-citizens (row 6). This final set of regressions, with both age and income interactions, form the basis of the rest of the chapter.

Homeownership

Once age and income effects are allowed to vary for immigrants and natives, there is no independent effect of being an immigrant citizen on home-ownership, value, or equity. Similarly, there is no independent effect of being an immigrant for eligible non-citizens for any of those outcomes. It appears, then, that differences between immigrant and native home-ownership are not driven by unobservable characteristics associated with immigrants themselves or with the choice to become a citizen. Ineligible non-citizens are, however, much less likely to buy a home and likely to have more equity if they do buy a home. This independent effect for those who are not yet eligible for citizenship (this is after controlling for time in the United States) could either reflect uncertainty on the part of the immigrant or on the part of the mortgage lender. The fact that the effect is so large (remember that these people have only been in the United States for only a few years and have likely very recently purchased their home) suggests that lenders may require a larger down payment (hence equity) and that credit constraints are important for new immigrants after conditioning on the typical characteristics that determine homeownership.

The homeownership column of Table 4 documents the full set of marginals from the probit specification on homeownership in the bivariate

Table 4. Coefficients from Bivariate Regressions.

	Home Ownership	Home Value[a]	Home Equity[b]
Immigrant citizen	-0.1378	0.1105	0.1595
	(0.2920)	(0.0660)	(0.1045)
Ineligible non-citizen	-0.6702*	0.1014	0.6045*
	(0.0763)	(0.1098)	(0.1709)
Eligible non-citizen	0.1075	0.0048	0.1359
	(0.2086)	(0.0657)	(0.1046)
Years in the US	0.0079*	0.0026	0.0014
	(0.0013)	(0.0019)	(0.0031)
Earnings*native[b]	0.0070*	0.0031*	-0.0031*
	(0.0020)	(0.0003)	(0.0006)
Earnings^2*native	-0.0002*	-0.0000	0.0002*
	(0.0000)	(0.0000)	(0.0000)
Earnings*citizen	0.0082*	0.0007	-0.0052*
	(0.0010)	(0.0012)	(0.0019)
Earnings^2*citizen	-0.0002*	0.0000	0.0003*
	(0.0000)	(0.0000)	(0.0000)
Earnings*ineligible non-citizen	0.0089*	0.0051	-0.0109*
	(0.0016)	(0.0034)	(0.0055)
Earnings^2*ineligible non-citizen	-0.0003*	-0.0000	0.0006
	(0.0001)	(0.0002)	(0.0003)
Earnings*eligible non-citizen	0.0068*	0.0067*	-0.0005
	(0.0010)	(0.0017)	(0.0027)
Earnings^2*eligible non-citizen	-0.0002*	-0.0001	0.0000
	(0.0000)	(0.0000)	(0.0001)
Age*native	0.0340*		
	(0.0025)		
Age^2*native	-0.0002*		
	(0.0000)		
Age*citizen	0.0347*		
	(0.0110)		
Age^2*citizen	-0.0003*		
	(0.0001)		
Age*ineligible non-citizen	0.0666*		
	(0.0202)		
Age^2*ineligible non-citizen	-0.0007*		
	(0.0002)		
Age*eligible non-citizen	0.0666*		
	(0.0202)		
Age^2*eligible non-citizen	-0.0007*		
	(0.0002)		
Years owned the home		-0.0079*	0.0114*
		(0.0005)	(0.0097)
FHA loan		-0.1254*	-0.4232*
		(0.0138)	(0.0248)

Table 4. (*Continued*)

	Home Ownership	Home Value[a]	Home Equity[b]
Non-MSA residence	−0.0532*	−0.0303*	0.0774*
	(0.008)	(0.0139)	(0.0206)
Gateway city residence	−0.0434*	0.3017*	0.2947*
	(0.009)	(0.0147)	(0.0369)
Price index	0.0001*	−0.0000	0.0001
	(0.0000)	(0.0000)	(0.0001)
Kids under 18	−0.0067		
	(0.0041)		
Retiree	0.1896*		
	(0.0095)		
African American/Black	−0.1125*	−0.3129*	−0.1378*
	(0.0103)	(0.0177)	(0.0434)
Native American	−0.1448*	−0.2266*	0.0762
	(0.0354)	(0.0608)	(0.0990)
Asian	−0.0295	0.1052*	0.1014
	(0.0216)	(0.0353)	(0.0567)
Married woman	0.1863*	0.0046	−0.1273*
	(0.0082)	(0.0170)	(0.0277)
Married man	0.2008*	−0.0239	−0.1889*
	(0.0081)	(0.0150)	(0.0242)
High school diploma or fewer years of school	−0.0751*	−0.3427*	−0.0742
	(0.0093)	(0.0139)	(0.0407)
Some college	−0.0443*	−0.1986*	−0.0747*
	(0.0098)	(0.0141)	(0.0306)
Predicted value index			0.3501*
			(0.0895)
Constant	NA	12.0441*	9.6500*
		(0.0252)	(0.5173)

Note: Standard deviations are given in parentheses. An asterisk means significant at a standard 5%. Wald χ^2 for equity/ownership1888.77 ($p = 0.000$), for value/ownership 3649.13 ($p = 0.0000$). The coefficient ρ for equity/homeownership = −0.7784. The likelihood ratio test of independent equations ($\rho = 0$) is $\chi^2 = 207.04$ ($p = 0.0000$). The ρ for value/homeownership = −0.6763. The likelihood ratio test of independent equations ($\rho = 0$) is $\chi^2 = 456.77$ ($p = 0.0000$).
[a]The natural log of home value or home equity is the dependent variable.
[b]The coefficients on all earnings measure marginal changes per $100 per month.

regressions.[17] The differences between native and immigrant homeownership rates are driven by dramatic differences in the age and income distributions (both critical variables in the decision to become a homeowner and in the decision of lenders to provide funds for homeownership) and differences in the impact of those variables on homeownership. Non-citizens are younger and poorer than natives and this helps explain the home-ownership gap. It is in the relationship between age and homeownership and income and homeownership that explains much of the observed home-ownership gap between immigrants and natives. As the combination of coefficients on age reveals, the age effect, which is nearly the same for natives and immigrant citizens, leads to a higher probability of home-ownership at every age for non-citizens when compared to native house-holders. Non-citizens who are in the oldest age groups have rapid fall in homeownership probabilities. Thus, much of the homeownership difference between natives and non-citizens exists because non-citizens are so much younger. The marginal effect of income is strongest for immigrant citizens and ineligible non-citizens. Looking at this effect alone, they are more likely to purchase a home at every income and the effect widens with age. Eligible non-citizens, however, have the same income effect as natives.

There are several other important homeownership determinants that need to be highlighted. First, residence in a Gateway city or in a rural/small town area leads to a lower probability of homeownership than residence in a non-Gateway city. The marginal effect of location is not small. Living in a Gateway city reduces homeownership probability by a marginal 4.3 percentage points and living in a rural/small town area reduces it by a marginal 5.3 percentage points (compared to living in an MSA that is not a gateway city). Both African Americans/blacks and Native Americans have lower probabilities of homeownership, but Asian Americans do not (see Kossoudji, 2005 for a discussion of race in homeownership). Married householders are more likely to be homeowners, as are those with more education. The number of years in the United States is an important predictor, leading to an increase in the probability of homeownership by 8.0 percentage points for each additional decade in the United States.

The overall impact of these differences is revealed in Figs. 2A and 2B, which show the predicted probability of homeownership by age and by income group for native, immigrant citizen and immigrant non-citizen householders.[18] As Fig. 2A shows, after the effect of all characteristics has been taken into account, Native and immigrant citizen householders are predicted to have nearly identical probabilities of homeownership up until about age 52, when the immigrant citizen probability does not continue to rise like the native probability and, in fact, declines significantly at older ages. Non-citizen householders lag far behind at every age, with the gap growing larger until about age 48. Eligible non-citizens have probabilities that essentially flatten out after this age – mimicking the probability curve for natives but ineligible non-citizens have probabilities that plummet, going

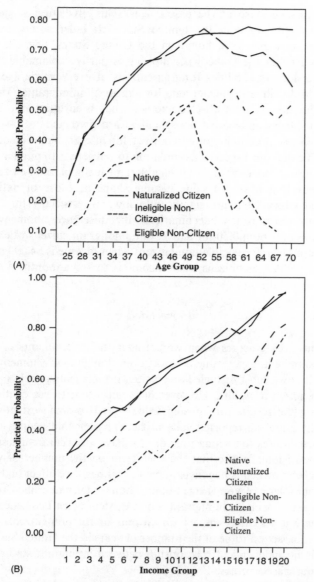

Fig. 2. (A) Predicted Probability of Homeownership by Age. (B) Predicted Probability of Homeownership by Income. *Source:* 1996 SIPP Panel and Author's Calculations. *Note:* There are 20 income groups. Income ranges are set so that 5 percent of natives are in each group. Sample weights are used in the graph. This graph includes all sample householders whether or not they are homeowners.

down to close to zero at the oldest ages. This prediction suggests that immigrants who arrive in the United States as older adults are highly unlikely to own their own homes in the United States. Overall, this age graph reveals that the homeownership gap is partly explainable by lower homeownership probabilities for non-citizens at every single age and by declining probabilities at higher ages for almost all immigrants. As Fig. 2B shows, after the effect of all characteristics has been taken into account, immigrant citizen and native householders are predicted to have almost exactly the same probability of homeownership at every single income level. It is possible that one aspect of assimilation for citizens is to purchase homes at the same rate as natives. Both eligible and ineligible non-citizens have probabilities that have the same income shape as those of natives and naturalized citizens but are significantly lower – especially for ineligible non-citizens. As a rough benchmark of the differences, homeownership probabilities are about 0.50 for natives and immigrant citizens when income is $2,490 a month, for eligible non-citizens when income is $4,090 a month, and for ineligible non-citizens when income is $5,740 a month.

Home Value

A different story emerges when we consider the determinants of housing value. I examine housing value because, even though many homeowners do not actually own most of their home value, it represents people's potential long-term access to wealth. However, it is important to use caution when interpreting the results for housing value – and to some extent equity – because these are self-reported values. It is apparent that people who have owned their houses for a long time do not have an accurate assessment of their home's value. Notice that the coefficient on the number of years the home has been owned is negative. Some of this negative effect undoubtedly results from a lack of knowledge about a home's current value. Again, the direct impact of being an immigrant is non-existent when I consider housing value. There is no direct impact for citizens or for non-citizens. Further, there is no impact on value of the number of years in the United States. That is, there is no independent relationship between immigrant status and the value of purchased homes.

Neither immigrant citizens nor eligible non-citizens exhibit any impact of income on home value. This unusual result is compounded by the strong linear impact of income on value for natives and the even stronger, and also linear impact of income on value for ineligible non-citizens. This strong effect, combined with low homeownership probabilities, suggests that low income is a critical constraint for ineligible non-citizens.

Housing value is closely related to location and to race. As expected, there is a large increase in value for Gateway city residents (30.2 percent) over those in other MSAs but only a small decrease in value between those in rural/small towns compared to those in non-Gateway MSAs (–3.0 percent). Thus, the higher housing values of immigrant citizens compared to natives results almost exclusively from residential differences. African American/ black householders have housing values that are 31.3 percent lower than those of white householders and for native Americans the value is lower by 22.7 percent. Asians have housing values that are 10.5 percent higher than those of white householders. It is possible that some of the Asian effect is picking up immigrant behavior. As expected (given that housing value is limited for FHA loans), householders who got an FHA loan to purchase their home have lower valued homes than those who use conventional mortgages.

Now when we put all impacts together and examine predicted probabilities of home value (see Figs. 3A and 3B), we observe predicted probabilities that show that all immigrants have a higher predicted home value at every age when compared to natives. The pattern among immigrants is surprising. Naturalized citizens and ineligible non-citizens are predicted to have the highest home values until about age 50, when the predicted home value for ineligible non-citizens collapses. Again, caution is warranted when considering age and housing value. The decline in predicted value for natives after age 52 probably reflects a lack of knowledge about housing value from long-time homeowners. Similarly, immigrant citizens and non-citizens are also predicted to have higher home values by income than do natives. When considering value, however, there is no significant difference between predicted home values for naturalized citizens, ineligible non-citizens and eligible non-citizens until immigrants are in the highest income brackets. Only natives lag far behind.

Equity

Equity is an indicator of current wealth and represents the amount that an individual could recover from the home by selling it. The same caveat that applies to value also applies to equity. Some people who have owned their homes for a long period of time do not make a good assessment of the current values of their homes and hence the increase in their equity

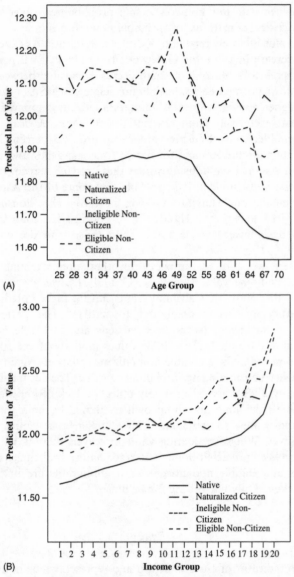

Fig. 3. (A) Predicted Home Value (ln) by Age. (B) Predicted Home Value (ln) by Income. *Source:* 1996 SIPP Panel and Author's Calculations. *Note:* There are 20 income groups. Income ranges are set so that there are 5 percent of natives in each group. Sample weights are used in the graph. This graph includes all householders whether or not they are homeowners.

investment from rising home values. Once again, there is no independent impact for naturalized citizens or eligible non-citizens on equity but ineligible citizens have equity that is 60 percent higher than others after controlling for all other variables. Again, it is possible that mortgage lenders require a larger down payment from immigrants still ineligible for citizenship. It is also possible that, without citizenship, immigrants may be more cautious about their housing investment compared to others. If this were true, however, eligible non-citizens would also have higher predicted equity. Such behavior may instead be reflective of new immigrants, rather than simply immigrants without citizenship.

The relationship between income and equity is unexpected but explainable. The marginal relationship between income and equity is negative. It is possible that this sign reflects two common occurrences from the 1990s: people buying higher value homes with lower down payments as the mortgage rules were relaxed and people borrowing against the equity of their home for other purchases. People with higher incomes may be better positioned to take advantage of either of those opportunities. If so, the apparent relationship between equity and income could turn negative. The negative relationship is stronger for immigrants than natives. The lower the income, the less risky householders are willing to be with their equity investment. This attitude may explain the lack of an income effect on equity at all for ineligible non-immigrants. They instead, have the earlier mentioned direct effect of a significant equity. They have lower income than others, they have been in the United States for only a few years, their status in the United States is uncertain, and increasing income may not make them feel more secure.

Gateway city residents have more equity (conditioning on value) than either other MSA residents or rural/small town residents. Their equity is 29.5 percent higher than the equity held by other MSA residents. Non-MSA residents have 7.7 percent more equity than MSA residents. Equity is higher with the length of time of homeownership (1.1 percent for every year the house is owned) and lower by 42.3 percent if the house was purchased with an FHA loan. Since FHA loans allow applicants to make a smaller down payment than conventional loans this is not surprising. Married householders have less equity than non-married householders. It is possible that married householders (especially in a two income-earner family) can be less risk averse and take equity out of the house for other purposes. There is only a 7.5 percent equity premium associated with having a college degree. Education appears to have a relatively small impact on equity once other variables have been considered.

The combination of these effects shows up in predicted equity in Figs. 4A and 4B. Home equity rises with age for all householders but the gap between all immigrants' predicted equities and natives' is large and significant. Natives are predicted to have much lower equity than all immigrants at all ages. Ineligible non-citizens have the highest predicted equity until the very highest ages. The same gap appears by income. Natives at all income levels are predicted to have lower equity than all immigrants. The gap is the largest in the lowest income groups. Natives begin to catch up to immigrants at the highest income levels. In the end, then, lower equity for ineligible non-citizens results from their low ages and income levels. At every age and income (considering also other factors) ineligible non-citizens are predicted to have the highest equity.

Putting it All Together

There does exist a homeownership gap between immigrants and natives but a careful look reveals a number of ways that its portrayal can be more carefully delineated. First, there is no evidence of a homeownership gap between naturalized citizens and natives. Immigrant citizens and natives have almost the exact same homeownership predictions at every income and age. Further, immigrant citizens and natives have almost exactly the same age and income distribution. Finally, immigrant citizens are predicted to have higher home values and home equity than natives but this difference appears to result mostly from the fact that immigrant citizens are likely to live in Gateway cities, where housing prices are high. Thus, using these standard housing criteria, immigrant citizens and natives look remarkably alike with the exception of residential choices. The homeownership gap is essentially a characteristic of the differences in homeownership between natives and non-citizens. At every age and every income level non-citizens, whether they are eligible for citizenship or not, are less likely to own their own homes. A lack of citizenship may not be the only reason for these lower rates, however. Eligible non-citizens have much higher predictions of homeownership at every income level than ineligible non-citizens. Their predictions by age are also higher and do not decline with age as do ineligible non-citizens'. But overall the homeownership gap appears to be one of "getting one's foot in the door" of homeownership. All non-citizens are predicted to have higher home values and higher home equity than natives at every age and income level. Again, part of this results from residential differences but at least some appears to arise from behavioral

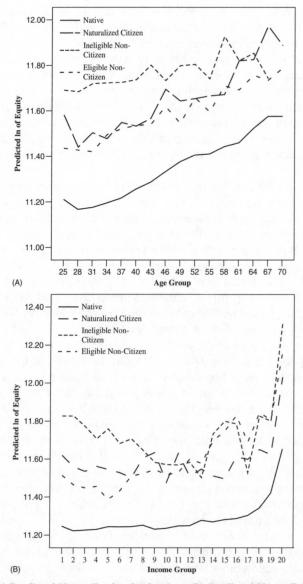

Fig. 4. (A) Predicted Home Equity (ln) by Age. (B) Predicted Home Equity (ln) by Income. *Source:* 1996 SIPP Panel and Author's Calculations. *Note:* There are 20 income groups. Income ranges are set so that 5 percent of natives are in each income group. Sample weights are used in this graph. This graph includes all householders whether or not they are homeowners.

differences. Why these patterns prevail is still an open question. It is possible, but unlikely given the pattern of these results, that people who do not choose to naturalize also choose other investments over housing. One possibility is that non-citizens are more likely to purchase homes in the home country rather than in the United States. If naturalization and homeownership are inextricably tied then the recent trend toward naturalization (after nearly a half a century of declining naturalization rates) will, itself, reduce the homeownership gap. On the other hand, given the patterns in this analysis, mortgage lenders may be erecting credit barriers for non-citizens, making it difficult to purchase housing without high down payments.

Many people ask whether immigrants will keep housing markets viable as the native population ages. Simply examining the probability of home-ownership returns a less than rosy prognosis. Immigrant non-citizens (who are about one-half of all immigrants) are less likely to own homes in the United States than are natives. If non-citizens remain a high proportion of all immigrants, then high rates of immigration will not provide a panacea to housing markets that may suffer as baby boomers age and die. The problems of ownership for non-citizens appear to be twofold. The first is that immigrant non-citizens simply have lower probabilities of homeowner-ship at every age and at every income level. The second is that immigrant non-citizens are significantly younger and earn less money. Young and relatively poor immigrants will not be able to substitute for older and relatively wealthy baby boomers in the housing market in the short run. If non-citizens do not invest in housing because they do not have high enough credit scores, because they may not be able to save enough money for a down payment, or because they may be turned down for mortgage approval then social dilemmas may follow. An inability to stake a claim in housing (and in the United States) could exacerbate problems of incorporation. At the same time, the aging of the non-citizen population can lead to more homeownership in the long run. Ownership predictions increase dramatically with age for eligible non-citizens. They also increase with income, which tends to increase with age and time in the United States.

Housing is wealth for most American families. Wealth differentials represent long-run disadvantages for individuals, an economic disparity that is transferred across generations. Programs that make homeownership more accessible can go a long way toward reducing differences in housing wealth. If high down payments are required of non-citizens and this prevents them from purchasing homes, then, among other efforts, an increasing accessibility to FHA mortgages and other programs that reduce liquidity constraints could provide a significant reduction in existing wealth differentials. In general, programs that push a foot through the door offer the promise of a considerable decrease in wealth inequalities represented by housing.

These results do suggest that once immigrants have a "foot in the door", however, there is no consistent disadvantage to immigrants, whether they be citizens or not. In fact, for both home value and equity, immigrant citizens and non-citizens alike are at an advantage or at no disadvantage to natives. If immigrants choose to buy housing, or are able to buy housing, then they convert their resources into housing value at a higher rate than do natives. If this conversion is also associated with an investment in being part of the community, then important spillover effects could result from promoting immigrant homeownership.

NOTES

1. I did not find any evidence that there is official discrimination by any institutions on the basis of citizenship status.

2. There are certainly many unanswered questions about immigrants' savings and investment decisions. One pertinent question for this chapter is whether there is competition for immigrant funds in the home country. Some immigrants, for example, may not purchase homes in the United States, choosing instead to purchase homes in the home country. Unfortunately the SIPP data do not have information on real estate assets in other places.

3. The systems are estimated using the Heckman procedure in Stata. In each set of estimates, the hypothesis that $\rho = 0$ (or that there was no systematic selection) was rejected at any significance level. Although these sample correction procedures can be unstable as models change, they were robust through many model specifications in this analysis.

4. SIPP survey procedures call for the person in whose name the household is owned or rented to be designated the reference person of the household. But if a married couple jointly owns the house (or jointly signs a lease), either may become the reference person.

5. Householder does not mean homeowner. Householders may own their own homes or rent them.

6. A small number of people living in mobile homes were eliminated from the sample because of the nebulous ownership position of people who own the building but rent the land where it sits. Some people for whom specific important information (like whether or not the house had a mortgage) is missing were eliminated from the sample. Mobile home owners were not asked mortgage questions. Homeownership depends on the house having a value of at least $1000.

7. It is possible that some of the immigrants in the SIPP data set are undocumented in the United States. If undocumented immigrants are less likely to be homeowners because of their status then the housing probabilities reported here

would be underestimates of the housing probabilities of the legal resident immigrant population.

8. People from U.S. territories are citizens, and so may have fewer obstacles to homeownership than those born in foreign countries. However, in many cases, people from Puerto Rico, Guam, and American Samoa are culturally and linguistically more like immigrants. Because of their nebulous position, they are not included in this analysis.

9. An applicant is eligible to file an application for citizenship if he or she has been "lawfully admitted for permanent residence, has resided continuously as a lawful permanent resident in the U.S. for at least 5 years prior to filing with no single absence from the United States of more than one year; has been physically present in the United States for at least 30 months out of the previous five years and has resided within a state or district for at least three months". There are also non-time-related requirements to apply for citizenship (http://uscis.gov/graphics/services/natz/general.htm).

10. The value of earned income and earned income squared is divided by 100 in the regressions to increase the size of the coefficient so that it may be reported more readily.

11. The cities are Atlanta, Boston, Chicago, Dallas, Detroit, Miami, Los Angeles, Houston, New York, Phoenix, Philadelphia, San Francisco, Seattle, and Washington, DC.

12. This variable, while useful for the association with homeownership, does not predict the decision to own a home because the home may have been purchased many years before. The obligation ratio is a figure calculated by mortgage lenders and depends on the number of children in the household.

13. FHA mortgages are insured by the Federal Housing Administration and represent a long-standing program within the U.S. government to promote homeownership for first time homebuyers and traditionally underserved populations by insuring mortgage loans made by private lenders. FHA is not a traditional poverty program because there are no official income limits. To qualify for an FHA mortgage, a potential homebuyer still must have a satisfactory credit history and sufficient steady income to qualify for the loan. "To make sure that its programs serve low- and moderate-income people, FHA sets limits on the dollar value of the mortgage. The current FHA mortgage limit ranges from $172,632 to $312,895" (01.11.2006-http://www.hud.gov/offices/hsg/sfh/ins/203b–df.cfm). FHA mortgages are important to this analysis because FHA mortgages require a lower down payment than commercial mortgages (thus influencing both value and equity).

14. The instrument for value is the predicted value from the value equation, divided by the census poverty income index for the household.

15. For some householders, final wave housing data is not available. For those householders, the latest available housing information is used and the real values and equities are calculated.

16. I have not found any official banking rules or known banking practices that suggest that non-citizenship is grounds for denial of a mortgage.

17. It is often more intuitive to discuss the results in terms of marginals rather than the Heckman coefficients. The average predicted probability is 0.677.

18. These predicted probabilities take into account the influence of all characteristics. They are calculated for everyone in the sample, whether or not the householder is a homeowner.

REFERENCES

Alba, R. D., & Logan, J. R. (1992). Assimilation and stratification in home ownership patterns of racial and ethnic groups. *International Migration Review, 26*(4), 1314–1341.

Borjas, G. (2002). *Home ownership in the immigrant population.* Working Paper no. 8945, National Bureau of Economic Research.

Bostic, R. W., Calem, P. S., & Wachter, S. M. (2004). *Hitting the wall: Credit constraints to home ownership.* Working Paper no. BABC 04-5, Joint Center for Housing Studies, Harvard University.

Chiswick, B., & Miller, P. (2003). Issue paper on the impact of immigration for housing. Issue papers on demographic trends important to housing. U. S. Department of Housing and Urban Development, Office of Policy Development and Research. pp. 1–78.

Coulson, N. E. (1999). Why are Hispanic and Asian homeownership rates so low? Immigration and other factors. *Journal of Urban Economics, 45*, 209–227.

Kossoudji, S. A. (2005). *Rooms of own's own: Gender, race, and home ownership as wealth accumulation in the United States.* Mimeo.

Krivo, L. J. (1995). Immigrant characteristics and Hispanic-Anglo housing inequality. *Demography, 32*(4), 599–615.

Munnell, A. G., Browne, T. L., & McEneaney, J. (1996). Mortgage lending in Boston: Interpreting HMDA data. *American Economic Review, 86*(1), 25–53.

Painter, G., Gabriel, S., & Myers, D. (2001). Race, immigrant status and housing tenure choice. *Journal of Urban Economics, 49*, 150–167.

Quercia, R. G., McCarthy, G. W., & Wachter, S. M. (2003). The impact of affordable home lending efforts on home ownership rates. *Journal of Housing Economics, 12*, 29–59.

Segal, L. M., & Sullivan, D. G. (1998). Trends in home ownership: Race, demographics, and income. *Economic Perspectives. The Federal Reserve Bank of Chicago, 22*(2), 53–72.

FIRST- AND SECOND-GENERATION IMMIGRANT EDUCATIONAL ATTAINMENT AND LABOR MARKET OUTCOMES: A COMPARISON OF THE UNITED STATES AND CANADA

Abdurrahman Aydemir and Arthur Sweetman

ABSTRACT

The educational and labor market outcomes of the first, first-and-a-half (1.5), second, and third generations of immigrants to the United States (US) and Canada are compared. These countries' immigration policies have diverged on important dimensions since the 1960s, resulting in large differences in immigrant source country distributions and a much larger emphasis on skill requirements in Canada, making for interesting comparisons. Of particular note is the educational attainment of US immigrants which is currently lower than that in Canada and is expected to influence future second generations causing an existing education gap to grow. This will likely in turn influence earnings where, controlling only

Immigration: Trends, Consequences and Prospects for the United States
Research in Labor Economics, Volume 27, 215–270
Copyright © 2008 by Elsevier Ltd.
ISSN: 0147-9121/doi:10.1016/S0147-9121(07)00006-4

for age, the current US second generation has earnings comparable to those of the third generation, whereas the Canadian second generation has higher earnings. Importantly, the role of, and returns to, observable characteristics are significantly different between the US and Canada. Observable characteristics explain little of the difference in earnings outcomes across generations in the US but have remarkable explanatory power in Canada. Controlling for a wide array of characteristics, especially education, has little effect on the US second generation's earnings premium, but causes the Canadian premium to become negative relative to the Canadian third generation. The Canadian 1.5 and second generations' educational advantage is of benefit in the labor market, but does not receive the same rate of return as it does for the third generation causing a very sizable gap between the current good observed outcomes, and the even better outcomes that would be expected if the 1.5 and second generation received the same rate of return to their characteristics as the third generation. Why the US differs likely follows from a combination of its lower immigration rate, its different selection mechanism, and its settlement policies and practices.

Immigration-related educational and labor market outcomes depend upon selection, settlement, and related policy and practice over long stretches of time. In this context, comparing across countries can be useful in considering the relationship between policies and outcomes, and can point to factors that are more, or less, strongly affected by alternative choices. This comparison of the United States (US) and Canada looking at immigrants, the second generation, and generation first-and-a-half (1.5) (those who immigrated as children), will lay out the relevant basic empirical regularities for the two countries in a comparable manner. It addresses the fundamental questions: How do the children of immigrants, and immigrants themselves, fare in North America? And, what links can we make between the observed outcomes and a country's policy choices? Of course, it is difficult to separate out the effects of policy in contrast to the effects of, for example, geography (e.g., the US's proximity to Mexico), scale, and international host-country reputation effects, so some conclusions must remain tentative. Nevertheless, a comparison allows some sense of what alternative paths can imply for educational and labor market outcomes.

The country pairing is interesting since the US and Canada pursued broadly similar immigration policies prior to the 1960s using national origin, with an emphasis on northwestern Europe, to allocate immigration visas. In the 1960s, both countries dramatically altered their national immigration policies, and immigration patterns changed very substantially in the subsequent decades. Smith and Edmonston (1997, Ch. 2) provide a brief overview of US immigration history, as do Green and Green (2004) for Canada. See the references in each for other studies. Overall, the two countries, partly by policy design and partly because of geography and other factors, took divergent paths. Four differences are particularly relevant: (1) the immigration rate, (2) the distribution of source countries, (3) the selection mechanism, and (4) settlement policies and practices.

Looking briefly at each of these four areas in turn, it is clear, first, that immigration rates differed markedly across the two countries for much of the last four or five decades, with the US having a much lower one as can be seen in Fig. 1.[1] However, the actual number of immigrants to the US is much larger in absolute terms. The US population is about 9.2 times greater than the Canadian one, whereas in 2004 the US immigration intake was about four, and in 1970 it was only about 2.5, times greater. Thus, while the immigration rates of both countries have increased, and the US rate has increased faster, the US rate is still far below the Canadian one. It is also

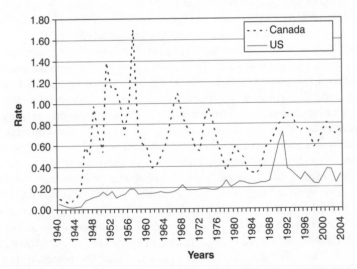

Fig. 1. Immigration Rates, US and Canada (1940–2004). *Source:* US Citizenship and Immigration Services (http://uscis.gov/graphics/shared/statistics/yearbook/2004/table1.xls), and Citizenship and Immigration, Canada (2005).

clear from Fig. 1 that, in contrast to that in the US, Canada pursued a strongly pro-cyclical immigration policy prior to 1990. (Both also have spikes not associated with the cycle; especially, the Hungarian refugee movement for Canada, and the regularization in the late 1980s and early 1990s for the US.)

Second, changes in the distribution of source countries have affected both countries since, in the 1960s, each removed many regulatory and legislative criteria that discriminated against potential immigrants on the basis of race and ethnicity. In the years that followed, the source country mix changed very substantially. In particular, immigration from Europe declined in relative importance for both countries. However, great differences between the two countries also exist because of geography. The US has always had a much greater fraction of its immigrant stream arriving from Central and South America (including Cuba), and Mexico, whereas Canada traditionally received a greater proportion of its immigrants from Europe. After the 1960s, the share of US immigrants from the above-mentioned US source countries, and from Asian countries, grew in importance, while Europe became even less important. For Canada, the increase in the immigration rate from Asia was much more pronounced, and the decline in European immigration was proportionately smaller and regionally more concentrated. While the immigration rate to Canada from North-West Europe dropped very substantially, that from Eastern and Southern Europe, though fluctuating across periods, reduced much more modestly.

Third, as is well-known, the US has largely favored family reunification as the main immigration stream. By contrast, while Canada maintained a family class, in 1967 Canada introduced a "points system" for skilled workers, within a parallel "economic" immigration class and developed an administratively complex immigration policy that sought to maximize domestic national interests while fulfilling the country's humanitarian and other related duties. Although there are subcategories that altered over time, Canadian immigration comprises three main classes that have endured: economic, family, and humanitarian. While this is an important difference, it can also be overstated since, for example, in 2004 the economic class comprised a historical extreme at 54.7% of all immigration, which includes refugees (more typically the economic class has comprised 30–40% of the flow for the past few decades). But, principal applicant skilled workers, most commonly the male of each family, assessed under the points system still only accounted for 20.3% of the entire flow (Citizenship and Immigration Canada, 2005).

Finally, settlement and related policies differ very substantially across the two countries, as do the nations' self-perceptions, and this may have important impacts for the second generation. Tellingly, in 1971, Canada became the first country to adopt an official "multiculturalism policy", and in 1982 the nation's multicultural heritage was recognized in the then new Canadian Charter of Rights and Freedoms, which forms part of the Constitution. This is a symbol of an approach that contrasts with that in the US and may have implications for settlement issues including educational and economic integration both for new immigrants and across the generations. However, the exact nature of the impact is ambiguous. For example, multiculturalism could imply increased retention of ethnic norms, including, for example, maintaining differences in educational attainment. Or, it could imply greater effort at social and economic inclusion leading to faster integration. Of course, alternative elements of the diverse range of settlement policies and services, and national attitudes, could have impacts in different directions. Hence, while we have no strong predictions, settlement patterns and policies are worth bearing in mind since they clearly differ across the two countries and are particularly relevant to the second generation. Of course, the current second generation is partly the children of a previous generation of immigrants who landed as these policies started coming into force, and future second generations will have a different experience.

Together, these four important differences are associated with substantial differences in average immigrant education and earnings, but, perhaps surprisingly, there nevertheless remain many similarities. This paper seeks to identify and explore both the differences and similarities in outcomes, with the goal of learning more from the comparison than would be possible by studying either country in isolation. A broad descriptive overview is provided that examines the data on several dimensions, especially sex, country, and immigration status. The paper proceeds as follows. First, the data is presented and then descriptive statistics are presented to gain a broad understanding of the current state of each jurisdiction. The first set of descriptive statistics combine the two sexes and look at broad generational issues for the entire prime-age population irrespective of labor force attachment, then the analysis explores results by sex and country, and looks at educational and labor market outcomes. Next, regression analysis is used to explore first, educational attainment, and then annual earnings. A conclusion reviews the main findings and attempts to integrate various observations.

1. DATA

For both countries, the sample is restricted to those between the ages of 25 and 65, inclusive, but very few other restrictions are imposed. Country-specific issues are discussed below. Initially, the entire sample is used to generate descriptive statistics without regard to labor force attachment; subsequently, in focusing on wages, all those who are in the labor force and who are not in school are analyzed. We are interested in maintaining as comprehensive a sample as possible to reflect the entire population of immigrants and not a selected sub-sample, such as those who work full-time, full-year. To that end, we include in our earnings analysis all those who are in the labor force, and, for the small group who have zero earnings in the survey year, we set their earnings to one dollar. In looking at educational and labor market outcomes relevant to immigration policy, it is important to address the entire population, and not only those who have earnings. However, we do not go so far as to include those not in the labor force in studying earnings. Selected sensitivity analyses show that this tends to accentuate some of the negative immigrant coefficients, but has no substantive impact on the patterns of the findings. Note that, of particular relevance for women, there is no attempt to adjust for selectivity into the labor force; rather, the sample is based on the observed status in the survey year.

1.1. United States

Seven merged Current Population Survey (CPS) March supplements, from 1998 to 2004, are used to provide insight into outcomes in the US. However, a major reduction in the sample size is made to eliminate all second interviews. As noted by Card, DiNardo, and Estes (2000, footnote 9) in a closely related study, if the entire sample is retained, the standard errors are incorrect, being about 17% too small and thus inference is difficult. Correcting the standard errors is also problematic given the information provided in the CPS. Hence, we only use records reporting that the interview is from one of the first four months (as opposed to the second four), so there are no replicated individuals in our merged sample.

Also excluded from the sample are first or second-generation observations who report that they or their parents were born in American Samoa, Guam, Puerto Rico or the US Virgin Islands. Though relatively small in number, these individuals introduce heterogeneity into the sample, whereas a tighter unit of analysis is desired for this analysis. The classification of race in the March CPS alters in 2003 allowing for mixed race to be reported. To maintain consistency for analysis, we attempt to code all observations in the limited categories used in the first period of the sample: White, Black, American Indian, and the merged group Asian and Pacific Islander.[2] We code those who report mixed race into the minority group of the mixed group, and randomly assign individuals who report two minority groups. This is clearly not ideal, but affects only a tiny fraction of the sample and does not appear to appreciably affect the results. The process is facilitated by our merging the Asian and Pacific Islander groups. Survey weights are used throughout the analysis.

1.2. Canada

The analysis for Canada uses the 2001 Canadian Census individual 20% microdata file, and to reduce computer-processing time a one in four random sample is used. A new question was added to the 2001 Canadian Census referring to the birthplace of the respondent's parents allowing the identification of second-generation immigrants. This marks the first time since 1971 that second-generation immigrants can be identified in Canadian census files. We exclude from the sample individuals who are living in institutions. The 2001 census also allows identification of temporary residents – which refers to people from another country who had an employment or student authorization, or a minister's permit, or who were being processed as refugee claimants at the time of the census – and their family members living in Canada. Although the US data likely contains some temporary residents, we remove them from the Canadian data and restrict the sample to consist of Canadian citizens by birth and immigrants. This latter group consists of naturalized citizens and permanent residents.

The visible minority question in the Canadian Census allows identification of Blacks, Asians, and Aboriginals. For identification of Aboriginals, we also use the separate question of "registered Indian" since not all registered Indians identify themselves as an Aboriginal ethnic minority (Kuhn & Sweetman, 2002). The remaining visible minority categories include Latin American, Arab, multiple visible minorities, and the "other" category which captures non-visible minorities. CPS definitions classify those from the Middle East as White. As a result the non-visible minority ("White") group consists of non-Black, non-Asian, and non-Aboriginals. A separate question on ethnic origin allows identification of Hispanics, and, as with the US data,

Hispanic is classified independently of the other ethnic affiliations. The sampling weights provided for the 2001 Census are used throughout.

2. DESCRIPTIVE STATISTICS

Initially, the paper describes the distribution and demographic character-istics of the populations of the two countries, separately identifying immigrants, and the second and third generations. This is presented for the entire sample, regardless of labor force attachment, and does not distinguish by sex in the results presented, since an examination of these results showed virtually no differences on this dimension. Descriptive statistics looking at educational and labor market outcomes, by sex, follow.

Each of the main groupings – immigrant, second generation (i.e., those born in the country with at least one parent born outside) and third generation (i.e., both parents born in the country) – is also divided into sub-groups as discussed below. However, the treatment of the third generation is worth discussing at this point. One issue in the cross-country analysis is defining a suitably homogeneous comparison group. Normally, the third generation is taken to be this group, but this generation is sufficiently different across the two countries that we divide it into two: first, "third generation type I" a homogeneous majority grouping of those who are non-Hispanic, non-Aboriginal (classified as American Indian in the CPS), non-visible minority (classified as White in the CPS) and who were not born abroad, and, second, "third generation type II", which is the complement of the first. The second group is included in the initial descriptive statistics for completeness, but omitted from the remainder of the paper since this group is not the focus of the analysis.

None of the tables of descriptive statistics present standard errors. This is done primarily to conserve space; the sample sizes are quite large so that the means are estimated very precisely.

2.1. Immigration Status and Demographics for the Entire Population

Table 1 presents each generation's share of the population, and the result of the US and Canada having taken different trajectories with respect to immigration rates is immediately apparent. Immigrants comprise an 8% smaller share of the population in the US than in Canada. The difference in the share of the population that is second generation is similarly large.

Table 1. Population Shares (%).

	Immigrants	Second Generation	Third Generation I	Third Generation II	Total	*N*
US	14.6	6.0	63.7	15.7	100	304,165
Canada	22.6	14.3	60.1	3.0	100	814,054

Source: US: 1998–2004 CPS; Canada: 2001 Census.

Although retention rates (emigration and mortality rates) and, for the second and third generations, fertility rates also play a role, the evidence supports Canada having had a much higher rate of immigration than the US. It is worth noting that, for both countries, the share of the population that is immigrant is much larger than is the share of second generation. This reflects the increase in immigration rates in the last two or three decades. The difference is particularly striking once one considers that the second generation includes the multiple children of families with either one or two immigrant parents. If immigration rates matter for integration, then recent cohorts face a very different environment from earlier ones.

Despite the presence of both more immigrants and second-generation immigrants in Canada, there is only a 3.6% difference in the share that is third generation type I (that is, domestically born non-visible minority individuals). Of course, the converse is true of the third generation type II (those born abroad or members of a visible minority); this group is much larger in the US. Further, the third generation in the US is much more heterogeneous than that in Canada, as will be seen in more detail in Table 4.

The immigrant and second-generation groupings are subdivided in Table 2. Given the literature on age arrival (e.g., Friedberg, 1993; Borjas, 1995; Chiswick & DebBurman, 2003; Schaafsma & Sweetman, 2001), we separate immigrants into those who landed by age 11 and earlier, or age 12 and later. Those who land earlier in their lives appear to have somewhat better outcomes, almost certainly complete their education in the host country, and have outcomes that are more similar to the native-born.[3] Second-generation observations are categorized depending upon whether the father only, or mother only, or both parents were immigrants. The first row for each country reports what percentage of the entire population is comprised by each sub-group, and the second row describes the percentage of the relevant major group (e.g., immigrants) comprised by each sub-group (e.g., immigrants who land by age 11). Interestingly, the relative size of the two immigrant sub-groups is quite similar despite a substantially larger

Table 2. Population Shares: Disaggregating Immigrants and Second
Generation into Subpopulations.

% of		Immigrants		Second Generation		
		Imm > = 12	Imm < = 11	Father only	Mother only	Both parents
US	Population	12.8	1.9	1.8	1.9	2.3
	Generation	87.1	12.9	30.0	31.1	38.9
Canada	Population	19.1	3.4	4.4	3.1	6.8
	Generation	84.9	15.1	30.5	21.8	47.7

Source: US: 1998–2004 CPS; Canada: 2001 Census.

share of the total population falling into each sub-group in Canada. The
second generation, however, display a marked difference. The Canadian
second generation is much less likely to have been born in a household
with only an immigrant mother and more likely to have both parents
immigrants. If intermarriage among the generations is important for social
and economic outcomes, for communities as well as individuals, this may
have implications for integration.

Table 3 explores the regional origins of immigrants and the parents of the
second generation. Given the constraints of both countries' data sources
and our desire for comparability, we employ 13 regional categories, as well
as each host country. Mexico is singled out given its importance in US
immigration, and we construct a non-regional amalgam (non-UK, English,
and developed countries) comprising non-European English-speaking
developed countries (especially, Canada/the US as appropriate, Australia,
New Zealand, and Barbados) since individuals from these countries share
language and cultural traits.

Massive differences in the distribution of each generation across the
source regions are evident in Table 3. Almost 30% of immigrants to the US
are from Mexico, whereas less than 1% of Canadian immigrants derive from
there. Conversely, the rate of immigration from North West Europe is
almost three times higher in Canada than the US, and that from Eastern
Europe is about twice as high. Asian and African immigration is also much
more common in Canada. Among the second generation with only one
immigrant parent, in columns two and three, note that the first row in each
of these columns matches the results in Table 2. The differences between first
column and second and third columns partly reflect changes in source
countries across the decades. Although still very important, the magnitude
of Mexico's contribution to the immigration flow among the US second

Table 3. Geographic Origins of Immigrants and Parents of Second Generation.

	Immigrants (%)	Parents' origins		Second Generation		
		Father (%)	Mother (%)	Probability both parents immigrants Father (%)	Mother (%)	Probability both immigrant parents same region
Panel A: US						
US	–	31.1	30.0	–	–	–
Mexico	27.5	14.4	13.5	64.5	69.0	97.7
Non-UK, English, Dev.	2.4	5.3	6.9	29.2	26.8	76.5
East Europe	4.7	8.0	6.2	51.1	61.1	88.1
NW Europe	5.3	12.1	15.9	46.1	36.5	82.2
S Europe	2.6	9.9	7.3	51.4	66.4	93.1
South America	6.4	1.6	1.7	66.4	67.6	79.7
Central America & Cuba	9.8	3.3	3.5	57.2	56.8	84.0
Caribbean	7.1	1.9	1.9	83.5	80.6	94.7
Asia	20.5	4.6	5.0	79.1	70.5	96.2
Middle East	2.0	1.0	0.7	56.1	79.2	86.4
Africa	2.6	0.5	0.4	48.4	55.4	72.5
Oceania & Japan	6.3	3.0	4.0	63.9	50.1	90.6
Other	2.8	3.1	3.0	73.7	76.5	89.1

Table 3. (*Continued*)

	Immigrants (%)	Parents' origins		Second Generation		
				Probability both parents immigrants		Probability both immigrant parents same region
		Father (%)	Mother (%)	Father (%)	Mother (%)	
Panel B: Canada						
Canada	–	21.8	30.5	–	–	–
Mexico	0.7	0.3	0.3	60.3	65.9	81.6
Non-UK, English, Dev.	4.5	6.6	6.6	24.4	30.5	48.5
East Europe	10.2	15.7	11.5	64.5	81.4	88.3
North-West Europe	18.9	34.8	32.5	52.4	57.9	86.5
South Europe	10.3	14.1	12.4	86.4	96.4	97.1
South America	4.1	0.5	0.5	73.1	75.9	66.5
Central America & Cuba	1.7	0.2	0.2	67.3	82.3	59.6
Caribbean	5.7	1.2	1.0	76.7	86.9	84.1
Asia	29.7	3.1	2.9	86.8	91.9	93.6
Middle East	3.2	0.6	0.5	75.2	86.7	88.6
Africa	5.5	0.7	0.5	72.4	81.8	71.2
Oceania & Japan	5.6	0.6	0.6	77.8	77.8	82.6
Other	0.2	0.1	0.8	25.4	59.5	54.2

Note: Dev. = Developed region.
Source: US: 1998–2004 CPS; Canada: 2001 Census.

generation is about half of what it is among the first. Notice that some regions, especially Asia, show a substantial increase in their share of immigrants to both countries for the more recent, first, generation. Europe, particularly North West Europe, has the opposite trend. Overall, as has been noted before by, especially, Borjas (1993), the distribution of immigrants across source countries is dramatically different in Canada and the US. This, of course, is potentially an important source of differences in outcomes.

Columns 4 and 5 of Table 3 show the probability that both parents are immigrants, given the father's and mother's source region. For both Canada and the US, individuals from the amalgam group of non-UK (or non-European), English-speaking developed countries have a substantially lower chance of marrying an immigrant – around 25 or 30%. Those from North West Europe have the next highest probability, and some groups, especially in Canada, have relatively high probabilities of marrying an immigrant rather than a native. For many groups, the probability of intermarriage (i.e., marrying a native-born individual) is much lower in Canada. If intermarriage is an important measure of ethnic integration, then there are large differences across both regional source country groupings and host countries. The final, sixth, column catalogs the probability that members of each region of origin sub-group with both parents immigrants have both parents from the same region. (Columns 4 and 5 indicate the likelihood that both parents are immigrants among the entire second generation, whereas column six reports the likelihood of both parents being from the *same* region among those who have both parents immigrants.) Clearly, if both parents are immigrants, the probability of them being from the same region is quite high, although, once again, it is lowest for those from the non-UK, English-speaking developed region. Clearly, the regional pairing of parents can affect their children's outcomes and there are substantial differences across both countries and regions.

Basic descriptive statistics of selected demographic variables are presented in Table 4 for each of the seven sub-groups. A few findings are worth highlighting. First, the percentage that are married is higher in the US than in Canada for all groups except those who immigrated later in life, and the second-generation marriage rates appear to be closer to those of the native-born than are those of new immigrants in both countries. Within countries, marital status differs significantly across the groups, with immigrants who arrive at age 12 or older, and the third generation type I in the US, being much more likely to be currently married than the other groups. Also, there are clearly important differences in the ethnic makeup of the two countries.

Table 4. Descriptive Statistics (Mean Values) by Generational Status.

	Immigrants		Second Generation			Third Generation	
	Imm >= 12	Imm < = 11	Father only	Mother only	Both	Native-born non-vismin	Other
Panel A: US							
Age	41.9	36.9	46.2	42.6	40.8	43.5	41.9
Experience	24.0	17.7	26.3	22.7	21.1	23.8	23.1
Male	49.6	51.9	48.6	49.5	49.2	49.2	45.4
Married	72.9	62.6	66.9	63.7	60.1	70.2	48.2
Widow, Sep, Div	12.3	11.6	17.5	17.4	14.0	16.6	23.3
Never Married	14.7	25.9	15.6	18.9	25.9	13.2	28.5
Black	9.8	8.9	3.3	3.4	5.5	–	72.0
Amer. Ind.	0.8	0.8	1.2	0.9	0.7	–	6.9
Asian/P. Islander	26.7	20.4	4.4	6.6	14.7	–	2.8
White	62.6	69.8	91.0	89.0	78.9	100.0	18.2
Hispanic	44.5	42.2	20.1	16.6	34.4	–	17.2
Born Abroad	–	–	7.3	16.8	5.9	–	2.4
Urban	68.4	66.2	51.2	48.5	63.6	32.5	40.0
New York	16.3	15.9	11.2	9.1	17.3	5.1	6.0
Los Angeles	17.2	17.4	8.8	7.9	12.7	3.1	5.4
Miami	4.7	5.7	1.6	1.2	3.5	0.6	1.1
Chicago	4.2	4.2	3.6	2.8	5.1	2.5	4.2

Panel B: Canada

Age	45.6	45.2	44.3	40.2	43.4	40.6
Experience	26.1	25.4	24.4	19.8	24.2	22.7
Male	47.8	48.3	50.1	50.3	49.2	47.2
Married	74.3	60.2	60.1	57.8	56.7	43.5
Widow, Sep, Div	13.2	16.9	16.8	12.1	17.0	18.5
Never Married	12.5	22.9	23.0	30.1	26.3	38.0
Black	7.2	0.9	0.5	2.1	–	6.3
Aboriginal	0.1	2.1	1.5	0.3	–	83.5
Asian/P. Islander	41.2	1.3	1.2	6.6	–	5.1
White	51.5	95.7	96.8	91.1	100.0	5.1
Hispanic	7.0	0.2	0.1	1.4	–	1.3
Born Abroad	–	0.4	1.8	0.6	–	4.2
Urban	90.5	65.2	64.0	78.3	56.5	39.8
Montreal	12.0	6.3	4.7	9.2	13.2	2.3
Toronto	40.1	13.4	14.2	28.4	7.0	4.9
Vancouver	14.3	9.2	9.1	9.6	3.8	5.4

Note: Sep. = Separated; Div. = Divorced; Amer. Ind. = American Indian and P. Islander = Pacific Islander; vismin = Visible minority.
Source: US: 1998–2004 CPS; Canada: 2001 Census.

Recall that while the White, Black, American Indian (commonly called Aboriginal or First Nations in Canada), and Asian and Pacific Islander groups are mutually exclusive and exhaustive, the Hispanic category is independent and may have members in all of the other categories. The US has a far larger Hispanic population in all of the sub-groups, and among the third generation. The third generation type II group also differs dramatically across the countries. North American Indians, or Aboriginals, represent about 7% of the sub-group in the US, but just over 83% in Canada. Conversely, the Black group is 72% of the US sub-group, but only 6.3% of that in Canada.

An interesting observation is that many of the second generation in the US, but far fewer in Canada, and a number of the third, are, in fact, not born in the host country. This is particularly the case where second-generation status is because the mother, and not the father, is an immigrant. Since we have no data on when these individuals moved to the US or Canada, this adds a wrinkle to interpreting what it means to have local information, which is usually assumed for the second and the third generations. For this reason, as mentioned, we have excluded those born abroad from our third generation main comparison group (i.e., they are in the type II group). While we can only speculate as to the reasons for the cross-country difference, it might as well have to do with the proportionately much larger US military presence around the globe.

2.2. Educational Outcomes

Educational outcomes for the sub-groups of interest, as well as for each sex separately, are summarized in Tables 5 and 6. Table 5 presents mean years of schooling, and shows that third generation type 1 Canadians have, on average, about half-a-year less schooling than their US counterparts. The gap is even bigger for the type II third generation (in the column labeled "other"). This lower Canadian base will influence all the comparisons.

Immigrants of both sexes to the US who arrive older than age 12 have fewer years of schooling than immigrants to Canada. One particularly interesting pattern is observable that aligns with cross-country policy differences regarding selection: among immigrants who arrive at an older age in Canada, but not in the US, on average males have appreciably more schooling than females. This aligns with the operation of the Canadian points system. It only looks at the education of the one adult that each

Table 5. Years of Schooling by Generation.

	Immigrants		Second Generation			Third Generation	
	Imm> =12	Imm< =11	Father only	Mother only	Both	Native-born non-vismin	Other
Males							
US	12.0	13.1	14.1	13.9	13.9	13.7	12.7
Canada	14.0	14.4	13.8	13.9	14.4	13.1	11.7
Females							
US	11.8	13.2	13.8	13.8	13.6	13.7	12.9
Canada	13.2	14.1	13.8	13.9	14.5	13.2	12.0

Source: US: 1998–2004 CPS; Canada: 2001 Census.

family designates, most commonly the male. These differences are interesting and quantitatively quite important.

Focusing on the immigrants who land before age 11, in the two countries those who land younger have higher mean education levels than those who land at an older age. In the US, however, this number is in between the mean attainment of the native-born and the mean for those who immigrate older, whereas in Canada those who land younger have substantially greater years of education than both. This suggests that what might be called integration, or at least achievement, is remarkably strong in Canada. Those who land young have remarkably high levels of educational attainment in Canada. This is likely attributable to multiple causes, but multiculturalism/ settlement policy and practice, the distribution of source countries, and the selection system are likely all involved. At a minimum, it speaks to the operation of each country's education system.

For both sexes, second-generation immigrants have greater mean levels of education in the US than do immigrants. This is particularly the case compared to immigrants who arrive after age 12, which is a much larger group. Further, second generation males in the US, and both sexes in Canada, also have greater levels of achievement than do those of the third generation; the numbers are more similar for US females. Perhaps surprisingly, in Canada, for both sexes, second-generation observations where both parents are immigrants have particularly high levels of education, whereas this is not the case in the US. This might be related to the very high levels of attainment of immigrants who land young. It might also be associated with the previously observed greater propensity for the Canadian second-generation parents not to intermarry with the third

Table 6. Educational Attainment by Generation (% at Each Level).

	Immigrants		Second Generation			Third Generation		Total
	Imm >= 12	Imm < = 11	Father only	Mother only	Both	Native born non-vismin	Other	
Panel A: US, Male								
< = 8	21.4	6.5	2.6	2.3	3.3	1.9	3.7	4.9
9–12, incomplete	11.7	12.9	6.2	6.3	7.5	6.7	12.9	8.4
HS/GED	23.2	26.1	25.3	26.8	25.3	32.8	38.3	31.8
Some Col	9.6	17.3	19.5	20.3	19.1	18.1	20.9	17.5
Assoc	4.2	7.8	9.1	8.4	7.1	8.7	7.4	7.9
Bach	16.9	19.0	20.5	22.1	24.4	21.1	12.5	19.3
MA/MSc	7.9	6.2	10.0	8.3	8.2	6.8	3.2	6.5
Prof Sch	2.2	2.7	4.0	3.0	2.6	2.2	0.7	2.1
PhD	2.9	1.5	2.9	2.2	2.2	1.7	0.5	1.7
Total	100	100	100	100	100	100	100	100
Panel B: Canada, Male								
< = 8	9.2	3.0	4.0	3.3	2.3	6.9	13.7	6.8
9–12, incomplete	12.6	13.6	16.7	16.1	13.2	18.4	25.2	16.9
HS/GED	14.4	14.9	16.7	16.0	15.1	20.2	15.4	18.1
Some Col	17.9	22.6	23.5	23.5	23.6	21.2	24.6	21.0
Assoc	16.9	19.7	18.0	18.3	20.7	16.9	13.2	17.3
Bach	15.3	16.8	13.4	14.5	16.9	10.8	5.4	12.3
MA/MSc	7.2	4.4	4.3	4.5	3.9	2.9	1.2	3.9
Prof Sch	4.1	4.0	2.9	3.1	3.5	2.1	0.8	2.7
PhD	2.5	0.9	0.8	0.8	0.7	0.5	0.4	0.9
Total	100	100	100	100	100	100	100	100

Panel C: US, Female

<= 8	21.1	7.4	2.6	1.9	4.3	1.5	2.9	4.4
9–12, incomplete	10.5	9.3	7.2	5.9	7.4	5.7	13.2	7.7
HS/GED	25.5	26.6	27.0	28.7	28.0	34.1	35.6	32.8
Some Col	9.9	16.6	20.2	20.2	18.5	18.9	21.5	18.3
Assoc	6.1	8.1	10.1	10.2	9.1	10.4	8.9	9.5
Bach	18.9	22.4	21.9	22.2	21.2	20.3	12.7	18.9
MA/MSc	5.4	5.8	8.9	7.8	7.9	7.3	4.2	6.6
Prof Sch	1.3	2.6	1.2	1.8	2.6	1.0	0.7	1.1
PhD	1.1	1.3	0.8	1.4	1.1	0.8	0.4	0.8
Total	100	100	100	100	100	100	100	100

Panel D: Canada, Female

<= 8	12.2	3.1	2.5	2.4	1.7	5.8	11.7	6.6
9–12, incomplete	13.8	12.1	16.7	15.4	11.3	16.7	23.1	15.8
HS/GED	15.9	17.8	16.5	17.0	15.6	20.6	12.9	18.7
Some Col	14.6	17.4	17.3	16.4	16.9	15.9	22.1	16.1
Assoc	20.6	24.9	26.2	26.7	26.8	24.3	20.9	23.8
Bach	14.1	16.6	14.5	14.9	19.2	11.8	7.1	12.9
MA/MSc	4.7	4.0	3.4	3.7	3.8	2.5	1.3	3.1
Prof Sch	3.2	3.6	2.7	3.1	4.2	2.1	0.9	2.5
PhD	0.8	0.5	0.4	0.4	0.4	0.2	0.1	0.4
Total	100	100	100	100	100	100	100	100

Source: US: 1998–2004 CPS; Canada: 2001 Census.

generation. The gaps in Canada are more pronounced given the lower level of educational attainment of the third generation. It appears that immigrants, especially those without third generation parents, have extremely good educational attainment in the Canadian school system.

The simple measure of years of schooling is expanded, in Table 6, to explore the highest level of educational attainment. This table is quite revealing. In general, among the second and third generations there is a much greater prevalence of associate (or community college) degrees in Canada, reflecting differences in the two countries' educational investments and institutional structures with Canada's post-secondary non-university system being much larger and its university system being somewhat smaller. Perhaps surprisingly, a similar pattern can also be seen among immigrants who arrive beyond age 12. This might reflect, at least in part, the operation of the Canadian points system, but it could also reflect differences in how source country equivalencies are interpreted. Generally, immigrants are more likely to be in both tails of the education distribution.

Completing high school is much more common in the US for both the second and third generations, but not among immigrants. The low number of years of school in the US for immigrants is largely due to a large number of individuals with very low levels of schooling – less than eight completed years. The finding that the second generation has, relative to the third generation type I comparison group, better educational outcomes in Canada is seen again. Part of this is because Canada has a relatively large proportion of the third generation with incomplete high school, and with an associate's rather than a university, degree. Although not shown here, a preponderance of the third generation type I with low education in Canada is at the upper end of the age distribution.

2.3. Labor Market Outcomes

Labor force attachment in the survey week and related outcomes are addressed in Table 7.[4] In these data, annual earnings capture all employment and positive self-employment earnings in the year. For the US data, the numbers are adjusted to 2000 dollars using the CPI. However, the Canadian earnings data are not adjusted using an exchange rate to make their levels comparable with US earnings; this was not thought necessary since most of our results are from regressions using log wages and we focus on percentage changes. But, since the CPS earnings data are capped, a

Table 7. Labor Force Attachments by Generation.

	Immigrants		Second Generation			Third Generation	
	Imm ≥ 12	Imm ≤ 11	Father only	Mother only	Both	Native-born non-vismin	Other
Panel A: Males							
US							
Employed (%)	85.4	86.2	81.4	84.9	82.5	84.6	74.6
Unemployed (%)	4.6	4.4	3.4	4.1	3.8	3.3	6.2
Out of LF (%)	10.0	9.5	15.1	10.9	13.7	12.0	19.1
Total (%)	100	100	100	100	100	100	100
In Schl FT (%)	2.3	3.3	1.7	1.6	2.9	1.1	1.4
Weeks work in yr	43.7	44.6	42.2	44.2	43.4	44.2	39.2
Annual earnings ($)	32,282	36,978	43,650	44,522	40,840	42,074	27,509
Canada							
Employed (%)	78.0	85.9	80.4	82.4	84.7	80.6	64.8
Unemployed (%)	5.3	4.3	4.4	4.1	3.7	5.5	14.0
Out of LF (%)	16.7	9.7	15.2	13.5	11.5	13.9	21.2
Total (%)	100	100	100	100	100	100	100
In Schl FT (%)	3.6	3.7	2.6	2.8	3.5	2.2	4.4
Weeks work in yr	38.4	43.3	40.2	41.4	42.5	40.5	32.6
Annual earnings ($)	33,167	43,884	40,100	41,801	42,313	37,374	25,180

Table 7. (*Continued*)

	Immigrants		Second Generation			Third Generation	
	Imm > = 12	Imm < = 11	Father only	Mother only	Both	Native-born non-vismin	Other
Panel B: Females							
US							
Employed (%)	58.2	71.4	69.9	74.6	69.9	71.5	68.6
Unemployed (%)	4.3	3.1	2.7	3.0	3.3	2.3	4.8
Out of LF (%)	37.5	25.5	27.4	22.4	26.8	26.2	26.6
Total (%)	100	100	100	100	100	100	100
In Schl FT (%)	2.8	2.6	1.6	2.1	3.4	1.6	2.2
Weeks work in yr	29.3	35.9	35.4	37.4	34.9	36.1	35.2
Annual earnings ($)	14,580	22,255	22,333	23,042	21,548	21,201	18,384
Canada							
Employed (%)	61.4	77.0	69.3	71.0	74.4	69.8	56.8
Unemployed (%)	5.2	3.4	3.2	3.9	3.4	4.1	9.0
Out of LF (%)	33.4	19.5	27.5	25.1	22.2	26.1	34.1
Total (%)	100	100	100	100	100	100	100
In Schl FT (%)	4.0	3.4	2.9	2.8	3.7	2.5	7.3
Weeks work in yr	29.6	37.8	34.0	34.9	36.7	34.0	27.4
Annual earnings ($)	17,606	26,914	22,386	23,457	25,853	21,082	15,084

Source: US: 1998–2004 CPS; Canada: 2001 Census.

similar cap is imposed on the Canadian data using purchasing power parity exchange rates to establish the line.

For males and Canadian females, the most disadvantaged group in both countries appears to be neither immigrants nor the second generation, but the third generation II sub-group.[5] Broadly speaking, similar patterns to those seen for educational attainment can be observed for these labor market outcomes. Just as the US third generation had greater years of schooling than their Canadian counterparts, they have greater weeks of work and related outcomes. However, immigrant males in the US have very high employment rates compared to all other groups despite their educational disadvantages. Further, immigrant women who land older have relatively poorer outcomes compared to their male counterparts (using the third generation type I as a benchmark for both). In particular, they are markedly more likely to be out of the labor force. Perhaps migration is primarily driven by male job-seeking and their partners' job matches are not as successful following the transition.

In Canada, but not to nearly the same degree in the US, immigrants who land young, have extremely good labor market outcomes. The second generation do very well in both countries, with averages that are at or slightly above the third generation ones for the US, and markedly above in Canada. The second generation appears to have relatively better outcomes in general in Canada. One group worth remarking upon is the second-generation subgroup with both parents immigrants. For both sexes in the US, this group fares more poorly on average, whereas in Canada they have very high levels of achievement. The nature of this group and/or its reception into society clearly differs markedly in the two countries.

3. REGRESSION RESULTS

Two sets of regressions are pursued in what follows: first, those where the dependent variable is years of schooling, and, second, those where it is (the logarithm of) annual earnings. Multivariate analysis is particularly useful in this context since there are major differences in age, ethnic and source country compositions across the two host countries, and some differences in urban concentration, marital status, and the like. This will allow us to explore whether the observed differences across countries is primarily the result of composition, or if other factors are at work. In the education regressions the sample is the same as that in the descriptive statistics with two exceptions: those currently attending school full time, and the third generation II group, are omitted. A further restriction is made for the earnings regressions and those not in the labor force are eliminated from the sample. Observations who are in the labor force, but who report zero annual earnings are assigned an income of one dollar to permit the logarithmic transformation. Depending upon the research question being posed, it is sometimes the case that the sample for analysis with respect to earnings is best restricted to those with a high level of labor force attachment. For example, Baker and Benjamin (1994) exclude those who work less than 40 weeks in the survey year. However, in this case, we wish to consider the outcomes of immigrants as a whole and, therefore, we want to cast the net as wide as is feasible in specifying our sample. We think that our broader sample is more appropriate to our empirical questions, and provides a better reflection of the entire immigrant labor force. This difference in approach is not innocuous.[6]

3.1. Education Regressions

Tables 8A, for males, and 8B, for females, present results of estimates from regressions of the form

$$S = b_o + b_g \text{Gen} + b_A \text{Age} + [b_{yr} \text{Year}]$$
$$+ \{b_E \text{Ethnicity} + b_M \text{MartialStatus} + b_C \text{City}\} + \varepsilon \qquad (1)$$

where S is years of schooling, the b's are vectors of coefficients to be estimated and ε is a white noise error term. The term in square brackets is only employed in the US data, and the terms in braces are used optionally in some regressions. The variables are clustered into related sets, the detailed contents of which are mentioned in Table 8, having the following general descriptions: Gen is a vector of generational indicators;[7] Age is a fourth-order polynomial in age where the estimates are not presented to save space; Year, employed only for the US CPS data, is a set of six-year indicators reflecting the underlying merged set of March supplements and is also not presented to save space; Ethnicity; Marital Status and City are sets of indicators, as discussed in Table 4, that are employed in some regressions.

The first and the fourth columns in Tables 8A and 8B, describe differences in years of schooling controlling for age. Patterns similar to those seen in Table 5 are apparent, but they are somewhat clearer with controls added. In the US, immigrants of both sexes have fewer years of schooling than the

Table 8. Educational Attainment by Generation.

	US			Canada		
	1	2	3	4	5	6
(A) Males						
imm <= 11	-0.552***	0.865***	0.550***	1.081***	1.055***	0.570***
	[0.082]	[0.083]	[0.084]	[0.033]	[0.034]	[0.034]
imm >= 12	-1.753***	-0.228***	-0.597***	1.009***	0.897***	0.272***
	[0.045]	[0.056]	[0.058]	[0.020]	[0.025]	[0.026]
Gen2-Mom	0.251***	0.788***	0.644***	0.857***	0.877***	0.576***
	[0.066]	[0.065]	[0.064]	[0.034]	[0.034]	[0.034]
Gen2-Dad	0.407***	1.137***	0.961***	0.799***	0.827***	0.510***
	[0.072]	[0.070]	[0.070]	[0.029]	[0.029]	[0.029]
Gen2-Both	0.239***	1.327***	1.047***	1.145***	1.135***	0.668***
	[0.067]	[0.069]	[0.069]	[0.023]	[0.023]	[0.024]
Black		-0.398***	-0.508***		0.199***	0.160**
		[0.102]	[0.103]		[0.065]	[0.065]
Amer. Ind./Aboriginal		-0.431	-0.374		-1.798***	-1.572***
		[0.273]	[0.271]		[0.131]	[0.130]
Asian/P. Islander		0.910***	0.902***		0.358***	0.124***
		[0.072]	[0.074]		[0.034]	[0.035]
Hispanic		-3.643***	-3.651***		-0.696***	-0.735***
		[0.064]	[0.065]		[0.069]	[0.069]
Married			0.349***			0.490***
			[0.030]			[0.017]
Widow, Div. or Sep.			-0.352***			-0.034
			[0.039]			[0.024]
Urban			0.651***			1.145***
			[0.033]			[0.016]
NY/ Montreal			0.186***			0.118***
			[0.066]			[0.030]

Table 8. (*Continued*)

	US			Canada		
	1	2	3	4	5	6
LA/Toronto			-0.317***			0.161***
			[0.073]			[0.024]
Miami/Vancouver			0.639***			-0.202***
			[0.115]			[0.038]
Chicago			0.099			–
			[0.085]			
State/Prov Indicators	No	No	Yes	No	No	Yes
Observations	108,521	108,521	108,521	362,799	362,799	362,799
R^2	0.0493	0.1434	0.1691	0.051	0.0524	0.0837
(B) Females						
imm <= 11	-0.556***	0.678***	0.369***	0.668***	0.688***	0.307***
	[0.081]	[0.081]	[0.082]	[0.031]	[0.032]	[0.032]
imm > = 12	-1.914***	-0.611***	-0.923***	0.103***	0.152***	-0.260***
	[0.041]	[0.050]	[0.051]	[0.019]	[0.024]	[0.025]
Gen2-Mom	0.155***	0.692***	0.571***	0.717***	0.735***	0.484***
	[0.059]	[0.060]	[0.059]	[0.030]	[0.030]	[0.030]
Gen2-Dad	0.213***	0.869***	0.704***	0.721***	0.747***	0.488***
	[0.061]	[0.059]	[0.059]	[0.025]	[0.025]	[0.025]
Gen2-Both	-0.031	1.052***	0.765***	0.985***	0.994***	0.613***
	[0.063]	[0.063]	[0.064]	[0.021]	[0.021]	[0.022]
Black		-0.287***	-0.529***		0.177***	0.071
		[0.089]	[0.092]		[0.063]	[0.063]
Amer. Ind./Aboriginal		-0.343	-0.285		-1.194***	-1.035***
		[0.273]	[0.273]		[0.109]	[0.110]
Asian/P. Islander		0.435***	0.468***		-0.076**	-0.260***
		[0.069]	[0.071]		[0.032]	[0.033]

	(1)	(2)	(3)	(4)	(5)	(6)
Hispanic	-3.262*** [0.060]	-3.208*** [0.061]		-0.386*** [0.065]	-0.407*** [0.065]	
Married		-0.135*** [0.033]			-0.329*** [0.018]	
Widow, Div. or Sep.		-0.613*** [0.038]			-0.614*** [0.022]	
Urban		0.525*** [0.030]			0.801*** [0.014]	
NY/Montreal		0.239*** [0.059]			0.092*** [0.028]	
LA/Toronto		-0.335*** [0.069]			0.117*** [0.022]	
Miami/Vancouver		0.687*** [0.108]			-0.041 [0.034]	
Chicago		0.245*** [0.080]			–	
State/Prov Indicators	No	No	Yes	No	No	Yes
Observations	114,697	114,697	114,697	377,934	377,934	377,934
R^2	0.0694	0.1459	0.1685	0.0859	0.0863	0.1072

Notes: Robust standard errors in brackets.
Each regression also includes a fourth order polynomial in age. Regressions for the US also include six year indicators reflecting the underlying merged set of CPS samples.
Source: US: 1998–2004 CPS; Canada: 2001 Census.
*significant at 10%.
**significant at 5%.
***significant at 1%.

native-born White population, with those who arrive young having at least a full year more schooling than those who arrive later in life. In stark contrast, immigrants to Canada have more years of education than the third generation, especially among the males. Clearly, the immigrant population of the two countries is quite different.

Individuals in the second generation, in contrast, have at least as many years of schooling as the third generation in the US, with males having somewhat larger gaps than females – up to about 40% of a year. A similar pattern is observed for Canada, but the magnitudes differ, with the second generation having a relatively greater gap relative to the third generation, and that for males and females being more similar. Immigrants and the second generation in Canada appear to be much more successful in the education system.

Controls for ethnicity are added in the second and fifth columns. Note that the comparison group (third generation type I) comprises only those who report being non-Hispanic and "White" in the CPS (and the equivalent in the Canadian data), and, therefore, has all of the ethnicity regression indicators set to zero. Hence, the ethnic indicators are only set to one for a subset of those who are first-or second-generation immigrants. The change in the generational indicators' coefficients between specifications 1 and 2 is pronounced for the US, but, in dramatic contrast, has little impact for Canada. For example, US males who immigrate at age 11 or younger go from having half-a-year less schooling to having 85% of a year more than the third generation. The second generation has even larger positive gaps relative to the comparison group. The coefficients on the ethnic indicators, of course, explain why this is happening. Most importantly, the Hispanic indicator is massively negative, suggesting that Hispanics have, on average, three to three-and-a-half fewer years of schooling, which is a very substantial gap. Since the Hispanic category is dominated by individuals from Mexico, among immigrants and the second generation much of this educational effect is attributable to the low levels of education of immigrants from that source country. In contrast, the American Indian coefficient is effectively zero, indicating that they have the same average level of schooling as the third generation; the Asian/Pacific Islander group has a positive coefficient; and the Black one is somewhat negative. Note also the differences in the increases in the R^2 values across countries; ethnicity is clearly a more important determinant of wages in the US.

The Canadian coefficients tell a very different story. The generational coefficients change relatively little for the most part, while the ethnic variables have two important differences compared to the US case. First, the coefficient on the Hispanic indicator is much smaller (and affects a much smaller fraction of the population, as seen in Table 4), and second, the Aboriginal indicator is large and negative suggesting that this group is much more educationally disadvantaged in Canada than in the US. Moreover, the Black as well as the Asian/Pacific Islander coefficients are positive in Canada. Clearly, ethnic group educational outcomes do not have the same patterns in the two countries.

Finally, in columns three and six, controls for marital status (never married being the omitted group) and urban status are added. Blau and Kahn (2005), Fry and Lowell (2005), and Fry and Lindsay (2006), point to substantial differences in marriage rates among the Mexican and Latino communities, and it is well known that, as seen in Table 3, immigrants are much more highly urbanized than the third generation. Clearly, these variables are endogenous so interpretation needs to be approached accordingly, but it is interesting to see the relationship in this context. Looking at the coefficients, there is a positive association between being married and having greater years of school in both countries for males, but a negative one for females. The relationship is similar for those who are widowed, separated or divorced for females and US males, but is not different from zero for Canadian males. Perhaps, more importantly, there is a difference in the average schooling level between rural and urban areas with those residing in urban areas having higher schooling levels on average, especially in Canada where the gap is over one full year for the males and 0.8 part of a year for females. A few individual city indicators are included in the regressions, and these provide some sense of the variety of outcomes across cities. In terms of interpretation, someone living in, for example, New York would receive the schooling gap associated with the city coefficient as well as that for New York. Additional cities could be added to the regression, but this small number is sufficient to illustrate the heterogeneity that exists. These geographic indicators reflect sorting by educational attainment across geographic areas, differential access to education and likely other factors. They should be interpreted solely as conditional correlations in this context.

Average educational achievement by source region, again controlling only for age using a fourth order polynomial, is presented in Table 9.[8] The sample for each of the regressions is restricted to the group in the column header and the comparison third generation, so all of the coefficients are relative to that group. Note that the categorization is the same as that in Table 3. Also, notice that the immigrant group comprises all immigrants, regardless of age at arrival. Clearly, there are substantial differences in

Table 9. Educational Attainment by Region of Origin.

| | US | | | | Canada | | | |
| | Second Generation | | | | Second Generation | | | |
	Immigrants	Father only	Mother only	Two parents same rgn	Immigrants	Father only	Mother only	Two parents same rgn
Panel A: Male								
Mexico	-4.925***	-1.538***	-1.857***	-1.544***	-2.146***	-1.327**	-0.147	-3.384***
	[0.069]	[0.197]	[0.218]	[0.132]	[0.246]	[0.558]	[0.557]	[0.410]
Non-UK, English, Dev.	0.856***	0.546***	0.627***	0.263	2.534***	0.642***	0.777***	0.466***
	[0.156]	[0.159]	[0.132]	[0.242]	[0.069]	[0.075]	[0.076]	[0.176]
Eastern Europe	0.558***	1.500***	1.135***	1.109***	1.770***	0.925***	1.291***	1.697***
	[0.125]	[0.165]	[0.213]	[0.208]	[0.042]	[0.067]	[0.106]	[0.056]
North Western Europe	1.266***	1.006***	0.502***	1.158***	1.833***	0.783***	0.765***	0.857***
	[0.115]	[0.133]	[0.108]	[0.138]	[0.030]	[0.038]	[0.042]	[0.037]
South Europe	-1.345***	0.418**	0.363*	0.345**	-2.327***	0.742***	1.018***	0.847***
	[0.192]	[0.159]	[0.210]	[0.144]	[0.052]	[0.108]	[0.183]	[0.041]
South America	-0.621***	0.51	0.975**	0.470	0.875***	1.203***	0.736**	0.529**
	[0.109]	[0.463]	[0.421]	[0.364]	[0.074]	[0.446]	[0.364]	[0.251]
Central America & Cuba	-2.929***	-0.407	0.164	0.493**	-0.124	1.464***	2.198***	1.324***
	[0.112]	[0.315]	[0.246]	[0.243]	[0.122]	[0.461]	[0.606]	[0.324]
Caribbean	-1.513***	0.413	1.072**	0.102	0.507***	1.046***	1.785***	1.251***
	[0.118]	[0.582]	[0.515]	[0.445]	[0.064]	[0.291]	[0.396]	[0.186]
Asia	0.983***	1.781***	0.549*	1.853***	1.111***	1.564***	2.028***	2.481***
	[0.070]	[0.366]	[0.287]	[0.208]	[0.034]	[0.216]	[0.320]	[0.102]
Middle East	0.033	1.469**	0.505	0.330	0.994***	1.578***	2.255***	1.628***
	[0.205]	[0.637]	[0.809]	[0.445]	[0.096]	[0.388]	[0.438]	[0.243]
Africa	1.157***	0.640	1.687***	1.225	2.673***	1.702***	1.666***	2.492***
	[0.144]	[0.554]	[0.524]	[0.972]	[0.063]	[0.335]	[0.572]	[0.322]
Oceania & Japan	0.983***	0.342	0.402**	1.309***	1.607***	2.445***	1.916***	1.722***
	[0.111]	[0.343]	[0.188]	[0.220]	[0.062]	[0.459]	[0.344]	[0.258]
Other	-1.114***	0.789*	0.443	-0.983***	-1.094***	-2.303***	-2.317	0.654***
	[0.201]	[0.457]	[0.351]	[0.331]	[0.012]	[0.854]	[1.260]	[0.012]
Observations	101,264	88,070	88,217	88,159	308,958	244,279	239,959	250,551

Panel B: Female

Mexico	-5.105***	-1.532***	-1.466***	-1.867***	-1.446***	-0.758*	-1.469***	-2.404***
	[0.072]	[0.176]	[0.200]	[0.134]	[0.225]	[0.417]	[0.410]	[0.328]
Non-UK, English, Dev.	0.714***	0.594***	0.431***	-0.142	2.028***	0.519***	0.700***	0.806***
	[0.128]	[0.159]	[0.140]	[0.196]	[0.053]	[0.062]	[0.066]	[0.171]
Eastern Europe	0.664***	1.037***	0.851***	1.031***	1.286***	0.906***	0.996***	1.423***
	[0.105]	[0.137]	[0.195]	[0.156]	[0.040]	[0.054]	[0.094]	[0.048]
North Western Europe	0.530***	0.602***	0.348***	0.955***	1.336***	0.633***	0.636***	0.657***
	[0.091]	[0.104]	[0.088]	[0.128]	[0.026]	[0.033]	[0.037]	[0.033]
South Europe	-2.006***	0.061	0.295*	0.324**	-3.301***	0.838***	0.843***	0.783***
	[0.201]	[0.126]	[0.176]	[0.136]	[0.050]	[0.099]	[0.250]	[0.039]
South America	-0.709***	1.126***	0.813**	0.671	0.157**	1.336***	1.084***	0.973***
	[0.101]	[0.404]	[0.327]	[0.415]	[0.068]	[0.347]	[0.400]	[0.313]
Central America & Cuba	-2.881***	0.138	-0.384	-0.033	-0.615***	0.532	1.533*	1.365***
	[0.112]	[0.223]	[0.236]	[0.296]	[0.133]	[0.481]	[0.834]	[0.359]
Caribbean	-1.721***	0.495	1.043**	0.413	0.219***	1.414***	1.050***	1.151***
	[0.101]	[0.536]	[0.494]	[0.286]	[0.054]	[0.289]	[0.385]	[0.170]
Asia	-0.201***	1.632***	0.655**	1.088***	-0.325***	1.913***	2.066***	1.959***
	[0.075]	[0.300]	[0.259]	[0.234]	[0.032]	[0.261]	[0.347]	[0.092]
Middle East	-0.491**	1.436***	0.591	0.389	-0.449***	1.666***	1.809***	0.783***
	[0.225]	[0.403]	[0.739]	[0.402]	[0.101]	[0.451]	[0.655]	[0.247]
Africa	0.025	1.028	1.958**	2.088***	1.016***	2.099***	1.954***	1.856***
	[0.161]	[0.694]	[0.915]	[0.395]	[0.069]	[0.384]	[0.495]	[0.340]
Oceania & Japan	0.743***	0.317	0.163	0.913***	1.428***	1.825***	1.758***	1.500***
	[0.088]	[0.264]	[0.198]	[0.201]	[0.048]	[0.480]	[0.302]	[0.249]
Other	-1.546***	0.174	0.797**	-1.555***	0.965	0.213	-0.621	2.155***
	[0.204]	[0.318]	[0.361]	[0.343]	[2.506]	[1.018]	[0.588]	[0.408]
Observations	106,922	93,046	93,091	93,038	322,845	253,357	247,716	258,260
R^2	0.1723	0.0241	0.0227	0.0285	0.1204	0.0834	0.0824	0.0939

Notes: Robust standard errors in brackets. Each regression also includes a fourth-order polynomial in age. Regressions for the US also include six year indicators reflecting the underlying merged set of CPS samples.
Source: US: 1998–2004 CPS; Canada: 2001 Census.
*significant at 10%.
**significant at 5%.
***significant at 1%.

average years of schooling across source regions, although there is often a broad similarity in source-region coefficient patterns between the US and Canada as noticed by Borjas (1993). The similarity should not, however, be pushed too far. While it is not universally the case, in many of the comparisons the negative coefficients, e.g., for Mexican immigrants, is not as negative in Canada, and the positive coefficients, e.g. for North Western Europe, is more positive for Canada. The magnitudes tell an interesting story, especially when the US third generation having 0.5 years of additional schooling is taken into account. Within source countries, but interestingly not for Asia, the Canadian system seems to select immigrants with higher levels of education. It seems likely that the Canadian points system is having some effect.

Perhaps, the most striking aspect of Table 9 is the shift in educational outcomes between the first and second generations. Almost all of the immigrant groups with less education than the third generation type I comparison group have the same or more education in the second generation. The exception to this in both countries is the Mexican subgroup, but even it has the gap reduced substantially (and the actual increase in average educational attainment is quite large for the Mexican group). In contrast, many of the immigrant groups with greater education than the third generation type I group have gaps that increase in the second generation so that they have even more education. The non-UK, English-speaking developed country group, and for Canada that from North Western Europe, are notable exceptions; for them the gap narrows, although the means stay above the third generation ones. It is worth noting that these groups are the most culturally similar to the third generation. Overall, as seen before, the second generation does very well and accumulates very high levels of schooling on average.

3.2. Counterfactual Education Predictions

The substantial differences in educational attainment across source regions for both the first and the second generation, seen in Table 9, suggest that the changing country-of-origin mix of immigrants has implications not only for the first generation, but also for the second since the outcomes between generations are correlated (see e.g., Dicks & Sweetman, 1999; Aydemir, Chen, & Corak, 2005; Chiswick, 1988). Differences among first generation immigrants will be, although attenuated, transferred to subsequent generations. As mentioned, during the early 1960s both Canada and the

US moved away from immigration policies that favored immigrants from Europe and restricted the entry of certain groups. These policy changes resulted in important differences in the country of origin mix as shown in Table 3. The differences became more apparent in the last few decades as the share of immigrants from Mexico rose substantially in the US, while for Canada the share of immigrants from Mexico remained at less than 1%.

Given the age restriction of 25–65 in this analysis, the second-generation observations in our data are the offspring of immigrants who arrived three to seven decades ago, and hence they mostly reflect a country of origin mix that is not representative of current migration flows. Therefore, the second-generation outcomes we observe today are bound to change in the next few decades as the children of immigrants age and start to reflect country-of-origin distributions more similar to today's migrants. An interesting question is if, and how much, the outcomes for the second generation will change given these shifts in country of origin. The low level of educational attainment among both the first- and second-generation Mexican immigrants and their increasing share makes the question especially interesting in the US context.

The complex and not well-understood nature of intergenerational educational integration, changing economic incentives and government policies make the answer non-trivial; however, we may still gain some insight if we can make some simplifying assumptions. In order to address this question, we first estimate the following regression for a sample of current second-generation immigrants

$$S = b_o + b_A(\text{Age})^{2ndGen} + b_V(\text{VisMinGround})^{2ndGen}$$
$$+ b_c(\text{RegionofOrigin})^{2ndGen} + \varepsilon \qquad (2)$$

where S is years of schooling and we control for a fourth-order term in age along with a set of indicator variables for visible minority status and region of origin. The superscripts indicate the sample employed and are relevant in conjunction with Eq. (3). Given the parameter estimates b_A, b_V, and & b_C, we can predict the schooling level using the visible minority and region of origin characteristics of the current first generation

$$\hat{S} = \hat{b}_o + \hat{b}_A(\text{Age})^{2ndGen} + \hat{b}_V(\text{VisMinGroup})^{1stGen}$$
$$+ \hat{b}_C(\text{RegionofOrigin})^{1stGen} + \varepsilon \qquad (3)$$

These predicted values provide estimates of schooling level that would be observed among second generation if they had the same visible minority and region of origin characteristics as the immigrants in our sample. This exercise assumes that the underlying factors determining the intergenerational transmission mechanism and visible minority differences of today remain the same in the future. It similarly assumes that any trends in educational attainment affect the second and third generations, recognizing that, depending upon intergenerational marriage, the children of many of the current second generation will become a future third generation.

We carry out the above estimation and prediction by gender for the entire second-generation sample and also by second-generation sub-groups[9] and report the counterfactual schooling outcomes in Table 10. The top panel shows the average years of schooling for the second and third generation we observe in the data, similar to Table 5. The difference in years of schooling between the second generation and the third generation non-visible minority group is presented in the last four columns. Panel B reports the counterfactual schooling levels for the second generation obtained from the above exercise.

For Canada, the positive differences observed in Panel A between the second generation and the third generation (i.e., second generation has greater years of schooling) increases dramatically in Panel B. Among males, the difference goes up from 0.98 of a year higher schooling among second generation to 1.66 years. For females the corresponding figures are 0.88 and 1.47. Hence, in Canada the second generation further improves its educational advantage relative to the third generation as the children of immigrants from regions such as Asia increase their share among the second generation. For the US, on the other hand, the opposite result is observed. The slightly higher schooling level among the second-generation males, 26.5% of a full year of schooling, almost disappears dropping to 9% of a full year, whereas for females 7% of a year of schooling advantage in the first generation disappears and turns into 16% of a year lower schooling. Thus, lower schooling attainment observed among the first generation translates into lower schooling levels among the second generation as the share of source regions such as Mexico increases. One needs to be cautious in interpreting these numbers as they depend on important assumptions; however, these results show that a large inflow of low-skilled workers over many decades may substantially alter the second-generation's outcomes. These results are reminiscent of inferior second-generation immigrant outcomes reported in some European countries (e.g., van Ours & Veenman, 2003) that experienced similar low-skill immigrant flows in the past.

Table 10. Counterfactual Years of Schooling for Second Generation.

	Second Generation				Third Generation	Yrs Schl(2nd)-Yrs Schl(3rd)			
	Father only	Mother only	Both	Total	Native born non-vismin	Father only	Mother only	Both	Total
Panel A: Current schooling differential									
Males									
US	14.09	13.93	13.86	13.96	13.70	0.39	0.23	0.16	0.26
Canada	13.77	13.93	14.40	14.11	13.13	0.64	0.80	1.27	0.98
Females									
US	13.75	13.83	13.60	13.72	13.65	0.10	0.18	-0.05	0.07
Canada	13.75	13.86	14.45	14.11	13.23	0.52	0.63	1.22	0.88
Panel B: Counterfactual schooling differential									
Males									
US	13.77	13.56	13.91	13.79	13.70	0.07	-0.14	0.21	0.09
Canada	14.27	14.69	14.99	14.79	13.13	1.14	1.56	1.86	1.66
Females									
US	13.31	13.65	13.55	13.49	13.65	-0.34	0.00	-0.10	-0.16
Canada	14.01	14.57	14.88	14.70	13.23	0.78	1.34	1.65	1.47

Source: US: 1998–2004 CPS; Canada: 2001 Census.

3.3. Basic Earnings Regressions

Turning next to earnings regressions, Tables 11A for males, and 11B for females, perform the same exercise (with the same format) as Tables 8A and 8B did for schooling although there is an extra specification since schooling itself is now a regressor and the sample is, as discussed above, the labor force. These regressions control for age, not potential years of labor market experience as is common. Moreover, they do not control for years since migration as does much of the literature. This is because the regressions answer a simple question: how do people of the same age, both controlling and not controlling for other observable characteristics, fare in terms of earnings? If we are interested in poverty and standards of living, then this approach complements the more common use of controls for experience and years since migration; these latter issues are addressed later. As with education, the findings in the descriptive statistics are reinforced and made stronger once we control for the differences in the age distributions of the different groups.

As seen in columns one and five, immigrants who arrive after age 12 have lower earnings, on average, than members of the third generation of the same age with the gaps being bigger in the US. In contrast, immigrants who arrive young have outcomes that exceed those of the native group in Canada, but are lower for males, or not different for females, in the US. A broadly similar pattern whereby the second generation does relatively better in Canada is also clear. In the US almost all of the second-generation variables have coefficients that are not different from zero, the one exception being those with both parents immigrants who have a marginally positive coefficient. In contrast, every single Canadian second-generation coefficient is positive and the point estimates are mostly quite large in magnitude. As seen before, those with two immigrant parents do particularly well Compared to the third, the 1.5 and the second generations do much better in Canada.

In columns two and six, we add the years of school measure to the regression. Note that the return to schooling coefficient is higher for females than for males in both host countries, and higher in the US than in Canada for each sex. Controlling for education serves to reduce, in absolute value, the statistically significant coefficients in the US regressions (shifting them toward zero), but for Canada it makes all the coefficients more negative. In terms of magnitude, adding this variable has little effect on the US second-generation coefficients, and serves to explain some of the negative immigrant effects. In Canada, it more appreciably reduces the value of all

Table 11. Earnings Differences Across Generations and Visible Minorities.

	US				Canada			
	1	2	3	4	5	6	7	8
(A) Males								
imm <= 11	-0.231*** [0.050]	-0.157*** [0.049]	-0.071 [0.054]	-0.142*** [0.053]	0.184*** [0.022]	0.088*** [0.021]	0.027 [0.022]	-0.018 [0.022]
imm > 12	-0.446*** [0.020]	-0.219*** [0.020]	-0.307*** [0.036]	-0.242*** [0.035]	-0.356*** [0.014]	-0.449*** [0.014]	-0.491*** [0.017]	-0.517*** [0.017]
Gen2-Mom	0.014 [0.041]	-0.015 [0.040]	0.081** [0.041]	0.004 [0.040]	0.133*** [0.024]	0.059** [0.024]	0.001 [0.024]	-0.045* [0.024]
Gen2-Dad	-0.026 [0.048]	-0.068 [0.047]	0.045 [0.048]	-0.068 [0.047]	0.077*** [0.022]	0.009 [0.022]	-0.042* [0.022]	-0.082*** [0.022]
Gen2_Both	0.021 [0.039]	-0.009 [0.038]	0.132*** [0.043]	0.001 [0.042]	0.189*** [0.017]	0.087*** [0.016]	-0.001 [0.017]	-0.055*** [0.017]
Yrs_schl		0.127*** [0.002]	—	0.121*** [0.002]		0.096*** [0.001]	—	0.086*** [0.001]
Married			0.535*** [0.020]	0.518*** [0.020]			0.626*** [0.012]	0.605*** [0.012]
Widow, Divorced or Sep.			0.147*** [0.027]	0.205*** [0.027]			0.240*** [0.018]	0.257*** [0.018]
Black			-0.386*** [0.062]	-0.320*** [0.061]			-0.362*** [0.051]	-0.373*** [0.051]
Amer. Ind./Aboriginal			-0.29 [0.198]	-0.238 [0.206]			-0.827*** [0.137]	-0.701*** [0.138]
Asian/P. Islander			-0.018 [0.045]	-0.123*** [0.043]			-0.449*** [0.023]	-0.460*** [0.023]
Hispanic			-0.470*** [0.037]	-0.021 [0.037]			-0.099** [0.049]	-0.032 [0.049]
Urban			0.291*** [0.021]	0.216*** [0.020]			0.316*** [0.011]	0.216*** [0.011]

Table 11. (*Continued*)

	US				Canada			
	1	2	3	4	5	6	7	8
NY/Montreal			0.058	0.033			-0.025	-0.033
			[0.039]	[0.038]			[0.021]	[0.021]
LA/Toronto			-0.153***	-0.121***			0.125***	0.113***
			[0.045]	[0.044]			[0.015]	[0.015]
Miami/Vancouver			-0.044	-0.116*			0.063**	0.078***
			[0.063]	[0.063]			[0.028]	[0.027]
Chicago			-0.008	-0.022			–	–
			[0.055]	[0.054]				
State/Prov Indicators	No	No	Yes	Yes	No	No	Yes	Yes
Observations	99,251	99,251	99,251	99,251	326,995	326,995	326,995	326,995
R^2	0.0213	0.0699	0.0493	0.0879	0.0148	0.0348	0.0389	0.0545
(B) Females								
imm < = 11	-0.029	0.031	-0.009	-0.071	0.231***	0.156***	0.037	0.001
	[0.062]	[0.061]	[0.069]	[0.068]	[0.025]	[0.024]	[0.025]	[0.025]
imm > = 12	-0.518***	-0.273***	-0.502***	-0.387***	-0.325***	-0.359***	-0.506***	-0.505***
	[0.030]	[0.029]	[0.044]	[0.043]	[0.015]	[0.015]	[0.019]	[0.019]
Gen2-Mom	0.077	0.055	0.083*	0.006	0.095***	0.021	-0.021	-0.073***
	[0.048]	[0.047]	[0.048]	[0.047]	[0.027]	[0.026]	[0.027]	[0.026]
Gen2-Dad	0.023	-0.019	0.032	-0.072	0.110***	0.039*	-0.006	-0.055**
	[0.054]	[0.053]	[0.056]	[0.055]	[0.022]	[0.022]	[0.022]	[0.022]
Gen2_Both	0.088*	0.077	0.095*	-0.026	0.299***	0.186***	0.085***	0.016
	[0.049]	[0.048]	[0.053]	[0.052]	[0.018]	[0.018]	[0.018]	[0.018]
Yrs_schl		0.157***		0.151***		0.134***		0.124***
		[0.003]		[0.003]		[0.002]		[0.002]
Married			-0.382***	-0.335***			-0.068***	-0.012
			[0.023]	[0.022]			[0.014]	[0.013]

	(1)	(2)	(3)	(4)	(5)	(6)	(7)	(8)
Widow, Divorced or Sep.			-0.188***	-0.074***			-0.215***	-0.130***
			[0.027]	[0.026]			[0.018]	[0.018]
Black			-0.098	-0.006			-0.306***	-0.300***
			[0.075]	[0.073]			[0.056]	[0.055]
Amer. Ind./Aboriginal			-0.495	-0.42			-0.566***	-0.471***
			[0.309]	[0.313]			[0.122]	[0.120]
Asian/P. Islander			0.212***	0.139**			-0.217***	-0.190***
			[0.057]	[0.056]			[0.024]	[0.024]
Hispanic			-0.462***	-0.021			-0.149***	-0.071
			[0.049]	[0.049]			[0.056]	[0.056]
Urban			0.309***	0.238***			0.434***	0.336***
			[0.026]	[0.026]			[0.013]	[0.012]
NY/Montreal			0.006	-0.046			0.079***	0.072***
			[0.049]	[0.048]			[0.022]	[0.022]
LA/Toronto			-0.181***	-0.137**			0.202***	0.180***
			[0.060]	[0.060]			[0.017]	[0.017]
Miami/Vancouver			-0.157*	-0.244***			0.095***	0.091***
			[0.088]	[0.086]			[0.030]	[0.030]
Chicago			-0.129*	-0.169**			–	–
			[0.069]	[0.068]				
State/Prov Indicators	No	No	Yes	Yes	No	No	Yes	Yes
Observations	90,052	90,052	90,052	90,052	298,241	298,241	298,241	298,241
R^2	0.0121	0.0524	0.028	0.0613	0.011	0.0406	0.0253	0.0499

Notes: Robust standard errors in brackets.
Each regression also includes a fourth order polynomial in age. Regressions for the US also include six year indicators reflecting the underlying merged set of CPS samples.
Source: US: 1998–2004 CPS; Canada: 2001 Census.
*significant at 10%.
**significant at 5%.
***significant at 1%.

the immigrant and generational coefficients. Some of the "good" immigrant earnings outcomes are explained by each group's higher educational attainment in Canada.

In columns three and seven, controls for marital status, ethnicity and urbanization are introduced, but education is removed to isolate the other effects and any partial correlation between schooling and the other controls, and the dependent variable. In the US, some of the second-generation coefficients become positive and statistically significant, while the coefficient for immigrants becomes slightly more negative. In Canada, as in the previous regression, the generational indicators become more negative suggesting that immigrants and the second generation are, on net, receiving positive premia associated with their set of characteristics. The new regressors' coefficients are unsurprising, but it is worth noting the large marriage (positive for males, negative for females), and urban premiums, given that immigrants are more likely to be married, and they along with the second generation, are more likely to reside in an urban area.

Finally, the specifications in columns four and eight include schooling and the full set of demographic regressors. Overall, for the US the generational coefficients look very much like those in column one, although most of the magnitudes are reduced for immigrants. The second generations' coefficients are neither statistically nor, given the standard errors, even potentially substantively different from the third generation, whereas immigrants who arrive after age 12 have negative coefficients, and the younger arriving group less negative and more mixed results.

For the Canadians, the story is more complicated and poses an interesting contrast. Including controls has a substantial influence. For both sexes the generational coefficients are statistically significantly more negative. The second-generation coefficients, which are positive and statistically significant in the fifth column, are negative and statistically significant in the eighth. The immigrant coefficients show a similar reduction in their point estimates. This is partly caused by the introduction of the measure of schooling, as discussed, but is equally attributable to the other regressors and does not appear to be driven by the ethnic measures, which induce the opposite effect on their own. (But, note the differences that can be seen in the ethnic coefficients across countries.) It appears that the Canadian immigrant and second-generation characteristics, education, marital status, and geographic distribution, are such that they more than explain the earnings premia of the 1.5 and second generations, and they make the older adult immigrant outcomes look even poorer. This is explored further in the subsequent tables.

Overall, some interesting and substantial differences will be seen between the two countries. In Canada, conditional only on age, the results show immigrants who land at a young age and the second generation to have excellent earnings outcomes. However, this earnings advantage is reduced to zero or becomes negative once one controls for observable characteristics, especially education and urban residence. In the US, unconditionally, immigrants who arrive young have lower, not higher, earnings than the third generation (type I), and the second generation shows no differences. When controls are added there is little change except for a small reduction for the 1.5 generation, which becomes somewhat less negative. This is a remarkable difference. In the US, the second generation looks a lot like the US third generation, whereas in Canada the second generation has better earnings. This difference is more than explained by observable characteristics, in particular, education. This suggests that acculturation/settlement, especially navigating the educational system, occurs quite differently in the two countries to the earnings advantage of Canadian immigrants – even if they have a low return to those characteristics.

Put another way, the experience of the 1.5 and second generation in Canada seems to be one where they collect a premium relative to workers of the same age in the third generation. But once additional controls are added, the premium not only disappears but becomes negative. Overall, the 1.5 and second generations have observed characteristics, especially education, that are associated with high earnings. These characteristics are valued in the market, enough to garner earnings that are higher than those of the third generation, but they are not valued at as high a price as that received by the third generation, so conditional on their observable characteristics the 1.5 and second generations receive lower earnings than expected.

3.4. Earnings Regressions that Allow for Generation-Specific Earnings Effects

The literature provides evidence of smaller returns to foreign experience and schooling for immigrants than the domestically born population in both the US (e.g., Chiswick & Miller, 1985), and Canada (e.g., Aydemir & Skuterud, 2005). Differences in the return to schooling and potential labor market experience are explored in Table 12A, for males, and 12B, for females. Given the large number of interactions that need to be undertaken, we only present results for the major groups – immigrants and second generation. However, in work that is not presented, we find that there are no substantive

Table 12. Earnings Outcomes, Returns to Human Capital Characteristics.

	US			Canada		
	1	2	3	4	5	6
(A) Males						
Immigrant	-0.271***	0.263**	-0.03	-0.533***	-0.022	-0.114
	[0.021]	[0.115]	[0.108]	[0.013]	[0.080]	[0.073]
Second Generation	-0.075***	0.104	0.036	-0.087***	-0.126	-0.204**
	[0.025]	[0.164]	[0.164]	[0.013]	[0.089]	[0.089]
Experience (Exp)	0.046***	0.051***	0.041***	0.051***	0.050***	0.036***
	[0.002]	[0.003]	[0.003]	[0.002]	[0.002]	[0.002]
Experience^2 (Exp^2)	-0.001***	-0.001***	-0.001***	-0.001***	-0.001***	-0.001***
	[0.000]	[0.000]	[0.000]	[0.000]	[0.000]	[0.000]
Yrs of School	0.123***	0.140***	0.141***	0.092***	0.112***	0.115***
	[0.002]	[0.003]	[0.003]	[0.002]	[0.002]	[0.002]
Urban	0.199***	0.197***	0.202***	0.190***	0.165***	0.168***
	[0.020]	[0.020]	[0.020]	[0.011]	[0.012]	[0.011]
NY/Montreal	0.012	0.005	0.001	-0.028	-0.041**	-0.03
	[0.038]	[0.038]	[0.038]	[0.021]	[0.021]	[0.021]
LA/Toronto	-0.104**	-0.108**	-0.131***	0.031**	0.035**	0.091***
	[0.044]	[0.044]	[0.044]	[0.015]	[0.015]	[0.015]
Miami/Vancouver	-0.117*	-0.132**	-0.132**	-0.008	0.008	0.070**
	[0.063]	[0.063]	[0.062]	[0.028]	[0.028]	[0.028]
Chicago	-0.017	-0.031	-0.04	—	—	—
	[0.055]	[0.055]	[0.055]			

	(1)	(2)	(3)	(4)	(5)	(6)
exp*immig		-0.019***	—		-0.001	—
		[0.007]			[0.004]	
exp2*immig		0.001***	—		0.000***	—
		[0.000]			[0.000]	
exp*gen2		0.002	0.012		0.030***	0.045***
		[0.009]	[0.009]		[0.004]	[0.004]
exp2*gen2		0.000	0.000		-0.001***	-0.001***
		[0.000]	[0.000]		[0.000]	[0.000]
yrs_schl*immig		-0.036***	—		-0.051***	—
		[0.005]			[0.004]	
yrs_schl*gen2		-0.014	-0.015*		-0.013***	-0.017***
		[0.009]	[0.009]		[0.005]	[0.005]
exp_foreign*immig			-0.013**			-0.046***
			[0.006]			[0.004]
exp_foreign2*immig			0.000			0.001***
			[0.000]			[0.000]
exp_host_country*immig			0.048***			0.112***
			[0.007]			[0.004]
exp_host_country2*immig			-0.001***			-0.002***
			[0.000]			[0.000]
yrs_schl_foreign*immig			-0.046***			-0.075***
			[0.005]			[0.004]
yrs_schl_host_country*immig			-0.037***			-0.067***
			[0.007]			[0.004]
State/Prov Indicators	Yes	Yes	Yes	Yes	Yes	Yes
Observations	99,251	99,251	99,251	326,995	326,995	326,995
R^2	0.0708	0.073	0.0752	0.0359	0.0395	0.052
(B) Females						
Immigrant	-0.321***	0.198	-0.104	-0.506***	0.072	0.114
	[0.029]	[0.168]	[0.161]	[0.014]	[0.091]	[0.085]
Second Generation	-0.03	0.237	0.179	-0.053***	0.603***	0.550***
	[0.030]	[0.221]	[0.221]	[0.014]	[0.107]	[0.107]
Experience (Exp)	0.018***	0.024***	0.016***	0.043***	0.047***	0.035***
	[0.003]	[0.003]	[0.003]	[0.002]	[0.002]	[0.002]

Table 12. (Continued)

	US			Canada		
	1	2	3	4	5	6
Experience² (Exp²)	-0.000***	-0.000***	-0.000***	-0.001***	-0.001***	-0.001***
	[0.000]	[0.000]	[0.000]	[0.000]	[0.000]	[0.000]
Yrs of School	0.158***	0.174***	0.174***	0.136***	0.165***	0.167***
	[0.003]	[0.004]	[0.004]	[0.002]	[0.002]	[0.002]
Urban	0.250***	0.250***	0.253***	0.331***	0.309***	0.314***
	[0.026]	[0.026]	[0.026]	[0.012]	[0.012]	[0.012]
NY/Montreal	-0.048	-0.053	-0.057	0.061***	0.051**	0.054**
	[0.047]	[0.047]	[0.047]	[0.022]	[0.022]	[0.022]
LA/Toronto	-0.151**	-0.157***	-0.174***	0.146***	0.149***	0.196***
	[0.060]	[0.060]	[0.060]	[0.016]	[0.016]	[0.016]
Miami/Vancouver	-0.255***	-0.261***	-0.259***	0.061**	0.073**	0.130***
	[0.086]	[0.086]	[0.085]	[0.030]	[0.030]	[0.029]
Chicago	-0.160**	-0.171**	-0.175**	—	—	—
	[0.068]	[0.068]	[0.068]			
exp*immig		-0.020**			0.010**	
		[0.009]			[0.005]	
exp2*immig		0.001***			0.000	
		[0.000]			[0.000]	
exp*gen2		-0.009	-0.001		0.000	0.012***
		[0.010]	[0.010]		[0.004]	[0.004]
exp2*gen2		0.000	0.000		-0.000**	-0.001***
		[0.000]	[0.000]		[0.000]	[0.000]
yrs_schl*immig		-0.035***			-0.064***	
		[0.008]			[0.004]	
yrs_schl*gen2		-0.012	-0.013		-0.038***	-0.041***
		[0.013]	[0.013]		[0.006]	[0.006]
exp_foreign*immig			-0.029***			-0.048***
			[0.008]			[0.004]
exp_foreign2*immig			0.001***			0.001***
			[0.000]			[0.000]

exp_host_country*immig			0.060***			0.111***
			[0.009]			[0.004]
exp_host_country2*immig			-0.001***			-0.002***
			[0.000]			[0.000]
yrs_schl_foreign*immig			-0.049***			-0.093***
			[0.008]			[0.004]
yrs_schl_host_country*immig			-0.044***			-0.075***
			[0.010]			[0.005]
State/Prov Indicators	Yes	Yes	Yes	Yes	Yes	Yes
Observations	90,052	90,052	90,052	298,241	298,241	298,241
R^2	0.0538	0.0552	0.057	0.0429	0.0468	0.0573

Notes: Robust standard errors in brackets. Regressions for the US also include six year indicators reflecting the underlying merged set of CPS samples.

Source: US: 1998–2004 CPS; Canada: 2001 Census.

*significant at 10%.
**significant at 5%.
***significant at 1%.

differences among the sub-groups, so this restriction is not onerous. Unlike Table 11, Table 12 reports on regressions that control for labor market experience instead of age. As is well-known, if all the other regressors are constant, replacing age by potential (Mincer) experience (given that their relationship is an identity) causes the coefficient on schooling to increase, though the increase need not be large if much of the sample is on the flat portion of the age–earnings profile as is the case in this instance. Rather than including a years-since-migration measure, as is common, we split it into two: years of host-country schooling, and years of host-country potential labor market experience. We believe that differentiating between in-school and post-school years in the host country is potentially important. Also, note that the ethnic variables are not included in these regressions.

In each of Tables 12A and 12B base case regressions are presented in column 1 for the US, and in column 4 for Canada. The geographic variables are the focus of Table 13, not this table, and are included here simply as controls. Columns two and five in each table introduce experience and years of school interacted with generational status in such a manner that the coefficients on the interaction terms measure differences from the base case, which now represents the return to each variable for the third generation. For both sexes, US immigrants have a lower return to the linear component of experience, but a higher coefficient on the quadratic term. Since there is no control for years since migration in these regressions (as is common in research studying economic integration effects following from Chiswick's (1978) work), the combination of coefficients reflects a lower starting value and the "catching up" that is a focus of interest for immigrants. The Canadian coefficients have one statistically significant positive value for each sex, and one that is not different from zero, but the significant one varies by sex. For the second generation, for males in both countries, there is little difference in the return to experience. However, Canadian females have a higher rate of return, and males a more sharply curving experience profile. The rate of return to schooling is much lower for immigrants than the third generation, especially in Canada. For the second generation, the results are mixed across the countries. In the US, there is no statistically significant difference, whereas in Canada the second generation has a lower rate of return than that of the third generation. (Note that this difference in statistical significance for the males may be an artifact of the greater precision of the Canadian estimates given the larger Canadian sample size, since the two countries' point estimates are quite similar.) When the interactions are introduced in columns two and five, the generational

Table 13. Location Premia.

	Males				Females			
	US		Canada		US		Canada	
	1	2	3	4	5	6	7	8
Immigrant	-0.193***	0.007	-0.213***	0.007	-0.293***	-0.079	-0.213***	0.216**
	[0.034]	[0.109]	[0.033]	[0.077]	[0.048]	[0.164]	[0.035]	[0.089]
Second generation	-0.070*	0.052	-0.091***	-0.189**	-0.088**	0.145	-0.089***	0.528***
	[0.037]	[0.164]	[0.024]	[0.090]	[0.044]	[0.223]	[0.027]	[0.108]
Experience (Exp)	0.046***	0.041***	0.051***	0.036***	0.018***	0.016***	0.043***	0.035***
	[0.002]	[0.003]	[0.002]	[0.002]	[0.003]	[0.003]	[0.002]	[0.002]
Experience² (Exp²)	-0.001***	-0.001***	-0.001***	-0.001***	-0.000***	-0.000***	-0.001***	-0.001***
	[0.000]	[0.000]	[0.000]	[0.000]	[0.000]	[0.000]	[0.000]	[0.000]
exp*gen2		0.012		0.045***		0.000		0.013***
		[0.009]		[0.004]		[0.010]		[0.004]
exp2*gen2		0.000		-0.001***		0.000		-0.001***
		[0.000]		[0.000]		[0.000]		[0.000]
exp_foreign*immig		-0.013**		-0.046***		-0.029***		-0.047***
		[0.006]		[0.004]		[0.008]		[0.004]
exp_foreign2*immig		0.000		0.001***		0.001***		0.001***
		[0.000]		[0.000]		[0.000]		[0.000]
exp_host_country*immig		0.049***		0.112***		0.061***		0.111***
		[0.007]		[0.004]		[0.009]		[0.004]
exp_host_country2*immig		-0.001***		-0.002***		-0.001***		-0.002***
		[0.000]		[0.000]		[0.000]		[0.000]

Table 13. (Continued)

	Males				Females			
	US		Canada		US		Canada	
	1	2	3	4	5	6	7	8
Yrs of school	0.123*** [0.002]	0.141*** [0.003]	0.091*** [0.002]	0.115*** [0.002]	0.158*** [0.003]	0.175*** [0.004]	0.135*** [0.002]	0.167*** [0.002]
yrs_schl*gen2		-0.016* [0.009]		-0.017*** [0.005]		-0.015 [0.013]		-0.042*** [0.006]
yrs_schl_foreign*immig		-0.044*** [0.005]		-0.075*** [0.004]		-0.050*** [0.008]		-0.093*** [0.004]
yrs_schl_host_country*immig		-0.035*** [0.007]		-0.068*** [0.004]		-0.045*** [0.010]		-0.076*** [0.005]
Urban	0.217*** [0.021]	0.212*** [0.021]	0.194*** [0.013]	0.165*** [0.013]	0.228*** [0.027]	0.224*** [0.027]	0.333*** [0.014]	0.306*** [0.014]
NY/Montreal	0.048 [0.041]	0.036 [0.041]	0.052** [0.022]	0.046** [0.022]	-0.04 [0.051]	-0.05 [0.051]	0.118*** [0.023]	0.110*** [0.023]
LA/Toronto	-0.099* [0.058]	-0.083 [0.058]	0.123*** [0.020]	0.114*** [0.020]	-0.073 [0.075]	-0.059 [0.075]	0.197*** [0.022]	0.188*** [0.022]
Miami/Vancouver	-0.086 [0.082]	-0.093 [0.082]	0.058* [0.034]	0.064* [0.034]	0.136* [0.083]	0.129 [0.083]	0.160*** [0.036]	0.161*** [0.036]
Chicago	-0.03 [0.058]	-0.04 [0.058]			-0.123* [0.070]	-0.135* [0.070]		—
Urban*immig	-0.149*** [0.051]	-0.102** [0.052]	-0.188*** [0.039]	-0.024 [0.039]	0.029 [0.072]	0.075 [0.072]	-0.177*** [0.042]	-0.015 [0.042]
Urban*gen2	0.067 [0.055]	0.074 [0.055]	-0.007 [0.031]	-0.019 [0.032]	0.187*** [0.069]	0.191*** [0.069]	0.022 [0.034]	0.023 [0.034]
(NY/Montreal)*immig	-0.021 [0.060]	-0.038 [0.060]	-0.434*** [0.047]	-0.357*** [0.046]	-0.026 [0.082]	-0.044 [0.082]	-0.363*** [0.050]	-0.299*** [0.050]
(NY/Montreal)*gen2	-0.175** [0.082]	-0.171** [0.082]	-0.093* [0.054]	-0.111** [0.054]	-0.137 [0.095]	-0.131 [0.096]	-0.028 [0.053]	-0.059 [0.053]
(LA/Toronto)*immig	0.088 [0.074]	-0.015 [0.074]	-0.247*** [0.032]	-0.094*** [0.032]	-0.142 [0.109]	-0.241** [0.109]	-0.186*** [0.035]	-0.049 [0.035]

(LA/Toronto)*gen2	-0.243**	-0.249**	0.003	-0.003	-0.224	-0.233*	0.062*	0.047
	[0.117]	[0.117]	[0.034]	[0.034]	[0.139]	[0.138]	[0.036]	[0.036]
(Miami/Vancouver)*immig	-0.038	-0.074	-0.246***	-0.079*	-0.650***	-0.668***	-0.292***	-0.136***
	[0.115]	[0.115]	[0.046]	[0.045]	[0.147]	[0.146]	[0.050]	[0.049]
(Miami/Vancouver)*gen2	0.144	0.133	0.118**	0.118**	-0.426**	-0.436**	0.066	0.063
	[0.108]	[0.108]	[0.047]	[0.047]	[0.187]	[0.187]	[0.051]	[0.051]
Chicago*immig	0.081	0.033			-0.169	-0.184		—
	[0.082]	[0.081]			[0.135]	[0.136]		
Chicago*gen2	-0.14	-0.145			-0.077	-0.078		—
	[0.119]	[0.119]			[0.141]	[0.140]		
State/Prov Indicators	Yes	Yes	Yes	Yes	Yes	Yes	Yes	Yes
Observations	99,251	99,251	326,995	326,995	90,052	90,052	298,241	298,241
R^2	0.0712	0.0755	0.0369	0.0524	0.0542	0.0574	0.0437	0.0576

Notes: Robust standard errors in brackets.

Regressions for the US also include six year indicators reflecting the underlying merged set of CPS samples.

Source: US: 1998–2004 CPS; Canada: 2001 Census.

*significant at 10%.

**significant at 5%.

***significant at 1%.

coefficients increase markedly in value, except for the second-generation Canadian males.

The final column for each country in both Tables 12A and 12B, splits experience and schooling into that obtained in the source country, and that in the host country. This split is inferred from age-at-the-survey date, age at immigration, and years of schooling assuming that there are no gaps in schooling. Clearly, this assumption is only a rough approximation and introduces measurement error that probably biases the coefficient estimates towards zero.[10] Note that host-country experience is similar to what is commonly called an economic integration (economic assimilation) or "years-since-migration" effect in more conventional specifications in the economics of immigration research literature, but it differs in that it sets all years up to the completion of the highest level of education attained to zero, whereas most use the year of landing for this purpose.

Clearly, pre-immigration labor market experience is worth a lot less for immigrants than labor market experience is for the third generation, especially in Canada and for US females where the interaction term is larger. In addition to reflecting the value of labor market experience, this can also be interpreted as a substantial negative age-at-immigration effect. As age at immigration increases, so does pre-immigration experience and the earnings gap with the third generation of the same age also grows. In contrast, host-country experience has a large and positive coefficient for immigrants, especially in Canada, implying marked wage growth with domestic experience.

The economic return to schooling is everywhere less for immigrants, and the return to pre-immigration schooling is always less than that for post-immigration schooling. The difference in rates of return to schooling is quite substantial, especially in Canada. Note that in this third specification the return to schooling for the second generation becomes more negative in all four sex–country specifications, and the coefficient for males in the US is marginally statistically significant representing a 10% gap with the third generation.[11] Neither immigrants nor the second generation appears to have as high a rate of return to education as the third generation, although the gap is much larger for immigrants.

Overall, immigrants appear to have a low rate of return to pre-immigration experience, and a high return to post-immigration experience. Further, immigrants, and to a lesser extent the second generation, appear to receive a lower rate of return to education, even that obtained in the host country. All of these effects are magnified in the Canadian data.

Table 13 extends Tables 12A and 12B by introducing generation-specific location premia. The key story in these regressions is that immigrants, and to a lesser extent the second generation in the US, receive a much smaller urban earnings premium. The effect is especially large for immigrant males in Canada. Moreover, it is complicated by there being city-specific premia that sometimes differ markedly from the overall urban premium and are very heterogeneous. This difference in urban premia is especially important since a very large fraction of immigrants live in cities and, therefore, the aggregate impact is substantial.

4. DISCUSSION AND CONCLUSION

Clearly, there are appreciable differences with respect to both immigrant and second-generation characteristics and outcomes between the US and Canada. Both immigrants and the second-generation form a markedly smaller share of the US population following from the lower (combined legal and illegal) US immigration rate. The distribution of source countries is also quite different across the two countries with Mexico, and Central and South America, being much more important source countries for the US.

In contrast to the US, where family reunification is the major source of immigration, Canada has employed a "points system" in the context of a sizeable "economic class" and this has had implications for the educational attainment of immigrants, and it has implications for the second generation. As a result of both the source country distribution and the selection mechanism, immigrants to Canada have, on average, more years of schooling than the third Canadian generation (all references to the third generation refer to the domestic born, non-visible minority population), whereas in the US the third generation has greater years of schooling on average. Interestingly, this effect is particularly important for males, who are more likely to be assessed under the points system than females. In both countries, but more markedly in Canada, the second generation accumulates, on average, more years of schooling than the third generation; however the difference increases for the US when controls for ethnicity and geography are added, but the reverse happens in Canada.

Despite the current second generation having educational outcomes that exceed those of the third generation, these contemporary outcomes may not be a good predictor of educational success for the future second generations since the composition of the immigrant flow has changed in both host countries. We, therefore, perform a counterfactual experiment to predict if future educational outcomes will continue to exceed those of the third generation assuming that the structure of the educational attainment process remains constant, but that the composition of the second generation in the future looks like the current immigrant composition. On this dimension, the two countries continue to diverge. In the future, the second generation in Canada is predicted to have an even larger educational advantage compared to the third generation, but in the US the gap decreases or is eliminated. While the assumptions underlying this counterfactual are unlikely to be realized exactly, it does point out that recent immigrants to the US have characteristics associated with lower levels of educational attainment, while the reverse is the case in Canada.

Turning to annual earnings, in regressions controlling for age-at-the-survey date immigrants who arrive younger (age 11 or before – the so-called 1.5 generation) are observed to have an earnings premium relative to the third generation in Canada, but no difference, or a deficit, in the US. Immigrants who arrive older have a substantial earnings deficit relative to the third generation in both countries for both sexes, but it is somewhat larger in the US. The second generation in the US has earnings that are remarkably similar to the third generation there, but in Canada, on average, it has higher earnings, particularly when both parents are immigrants. However, once again the two countries diverge in the manner in which characteristics are treated. The introduction of controls for years of schooling, ethnicity, and geography has little (and positive if any) or no effect on the second generation's return in the labor market in the US, but reverses the positive second-generation effect in Canada, making it negative. In short, the US second-generation population's characteristics, and the rate of return to those characteristics, do not, on net, affect its earnings relative to the third generation. However, the Canadian second generation has characteristics associated with greater earnings potential than the third generation, and while some of that potential is realized, in that the former earn more on average, once those characteristics are taken into account the second generation does not earn as much as would the third generation if it had those characteristics. That is, instead of the large premium expected because of their characteristics, the second generation only receives a small one.

Some combination of Canadian selection and settlement policies and practices cause immigrants and the second generation to have superior observed characteristics and these characteristics do have a payoff. That is, the quantity of positive observables is large; Canada's education system seems to retain immigrants and the second generation, especially if both parents are immigrants, and this is of substantial benefit in the labor market although not as much benefit as would be a similar quantity of education for the third generation. In net, the payoff to these characteristics is lower than that for the third generation, sufficiently so that the observed premium conditional only on age for the 1.5 and second generations becomes a deficit conditional on a broader range of observable characteristics. No such reversal is observed in the US and the reasons behind this remarkable difference are not fully understood.

However, part of the reason for the first, and the second, generational earnings differences is that they appear, on average, to have lower rates of return to education, with the magnitude of the difference being larger in Canada. (Future work will see if it is possible to isolate the source of the gaps in rates of return to education to see if it is associated with a particular educational background.) Economic rates of return to potential labor market experience is more complicated, but it appears that the second generation has an equivalent (in the US), or greater (in Canada) return to experience. For immigrants, in both countries the return to pre-immigration experience is smaller than the return for the third generation, and in Canada the net return is actually negative for both sexes. (That is, given the specifications employed, the negative difference between return to labor market experience for immigrants and the second generation is larger than the baseline return to experience shared by both; see Tables 12A and 12B, column 6.)

Similarly, looking at location premia, neither immigrants nor the second generation appear to receive the earnings premium that the third generation do for living in major urban areas. This is particularly important since in both host countries, immigrants and the second generation are much more likely to reside in an urban area than the third generation. This effect is particularly important in Canada.

Overall, the second generation in both countries has very good educational and labor market outcomes, similar to, and in some cases better than, the third generation, and clearly much better than the first generation. However, the characteristics of current immigrants differ from those of the parents of the current second generation. In the US, current immigrant characteristics, holding the structure of educational attainment and earnings constant, are associated with lower outcomes in the future than is the case for the current second generation, whereas in Canada the reverse can be expected. Looking at annual earnings, the second generation, especially in Canada, does not appear to receive as high a rate of return to its characteristics as does the third generation. Of course, many of those characteristics, such as education and geographic location, are endogenous, and we do not fully understand the process by which they are attained. Most immigrants have, on average, poorer outcomes than the third generation, although the 1.5 generation has quite good outcomes in Canada, comparable to the third generation.

NOTES

1. Note that illegal immigration is a much more important issue in the US than in Canada. The broad trends mentioned here are generally appropriate whether or not illegal immigration is taken into account, although including or excluding the illegal flows clearly affects the magnitude of the effects. Importantly, most observers believe that a high fraction of illegal immigrants are captured in the current population survey data used in this analysis.

2. We use the terminology and classification system of the pre-2003 CPS files in much of the remainder of the paper.

3. Fry and Lowell (2005), and Fry and Lindsay (2006), however, do not find that US Latinos who arrive young have wage outcomes that are comparable to their US counterparts.

4. Note that Canada and the US employ different definitions of the unemployment rate, with the US definition producing a slightly lower rate when applied to the same population as the Canadian one.

5. Note that the tax regime faced by many American Indians/Aboriginals differs from the rest of the population, making many earnings related comparisons difficult.

6. Some researchers might prefer a two-step approach, first looking at the probability of participation beyond some specified threshold such as 40 weeks of work/year, and then looking at the labor market outcomes of those beyond the threshold. Although there is great merit in this approach, we prefer to look at the sample of those who are in the labor force, regardless of earnings or weeks worked, since we think that this is an important group. A preliminary analysis suggests that the results presented in this paper are broadly similar to one with a sample with greater attachment, but that the findings are more extreme since groups with low earnings also appear to have a higher likelihood of being unemployed.

7. Recall that the third generation type II group is always omitted from the regressions and, therefore, to simplify the exposition, we will simply refer to the comparison group or the third generation in discussing the regressions.

8. For the US a set of six survey year indicators were also included in the regressions.

9. We use the characteristics of all immigrants regardless of gender for the prediction. The results are very similar if we use the characteristics of the same gender group (e.g., using only the female first generation immigrant characteristics for predictions of the second generation females).

10. Note, however, that this is not white noise measurement error. An underestimate of pre-immigration schooling (and hence experience) implies the converse for the post-immigration measure. Moreover, gaps in education attendance will cause host-country education to be underestimated, whereas it is difficult to think of a systematic source of overestimates for source-country education.

11. Recall that although the sample size is quite large overall, the interaction coefficient's statistical significance depends in large part upon the size of the second-generation sample, which as seen in table 1 is only a fraction of the total. At least this size of a sample appears to be required to see a 10% reduction in the rate of return to schooling.

REFERENCES

Aydemir, A., & Skuterud, M. (2005). Explaining the deteriorating entry earnings of Canada's immigrant cohorts. *Canadian Journal of Economics, 38*(2), 641–671.

Aydemir, A., Chen, W. H., & Corak, M. (2005). *Intergenerational earnings mobility among the children of Canadian immigrants.* Research Paper Series no. 267. Statistics Canada.

Baker, M., & Benjamin, D. (1994). The performance of immigrants in the Canadian labor market. *Journal of Labor Economics, 12*(3), 369–405.

Blau, F. D., & Kahn, L. M. (2007). Gender and assimilation among Mexican Americans. In: G. Borjas (Ed.), *Mexican immigration*. Chicago: NBER and University of Chicago Press.

Borjas, G. J. (1993). Immigration policy, national origin and immigrant skills: A comparison of Canada and the United States. In: D. Card & R. Freeman (Eds), *Small differences that matter: Labor markets and income maintenance in Canada and the United States.* Chicago: University of Chicago Press.

Borjas, G. J. (1995). Assimilation and changes in cohort quality revisited: What happened to immigrant earnings in the 1980s? *Journal of Labor Economics, 13*(2), 201–245.

Card, D., DiNardo, J., & Estes, E. (2000). The more things change: Immigrants and the children of immigrants in the 1940s, the 1970s, and the 1990s. In: G. J. Borjas (Ed.), *Issues in the economics of immigration* (pp. 227–269). Chicago University Press: Chicago.

Chiswick, B. R. (1978). The effect of Americanization on the earnings of foreign-born men. *Journal of Political Economy, 86*(5), 897–921.

Chiswick, B. R. (1988). Differences in education and earnings across racial and ethnic groups: Tastes, discrimination and investments in child quality. *Quarterly Journal of Economics, 103*(3), 571–597.

Chiswick, B. R., & DebBurman, N. (2003). Educational attainment: Analysis by immigrant generation. *Economics of Education Review, 23*, 361–379.

Chiswick, B. R., & Miller, P. W. (1985). Immigrant generation and income in Australia. *Economic Record, 61*(173), 540–553.

Citizenship and Immigration Canada. (2005). *Facts and figures: Immigration overview permanent and temporary residents.* Cat. No. Ci1-8/2004E-PDF.

Dicks, G., & Sweetman, A. (1999). Education and ethnicity in Canada: An intergenerational perspective. *Journal of Human Resources, 34*(4), 668–696.

Friedberg, R. (1993). *The labor market assimilation of immigrants in the United States: The role of age at arrival.* Mimeo: Brown University.

Fry, R., & Lowell, L. (2005). *The wage structure of Latino origin groups across generations.* Mimeo: Institute for the Study of International Migration, Georgetown University.

Fry, R. B., & Lindsay, L. (2006). The wage structure of Latino-Origin groups across generations. *Industrial Relations, 45*(2), 147–168.

Green, A. G., & Green, D. (2004). The economic goals of Canada's immigration policy, past and present. *Canadian Journal of Urban Research, 13*, 102–139.

Kuhn, P. J., & Sweetman, A. (2002). Aboriginals as unwilling immigrants: Contact, assimilation and economic labor market outcomes. *Journal of Population Economics, 15*(2), 331–355.

van Ours, J. C., & Veenman, J. (2003). The educational attainment of second-generation immigrants in the Netherlands. *Journal of Population Economics, 16*(3).

Schaafsma, J., & Sweetman, A. (2001). Immigrant earnings: Age at immigration matters. *Canadian Journal of Economics, 34*(4), 1066–1099.

Smith, J. P., & Edmonston, B. (Eds). (1997). *The new Americans: Economic, demographic, and fiscal effects of immigration.* Washington: National Academy Press.

SECTION III:
IMMIGRATION POLICY

IMMIGRATION AMNESTY AND IMMIGRANT'S EARNINGS [☆]

Ira N. Gang and Myeong-Su Yun

ABSTRACT

We review the role immigration amnesties have played in US immigration policy, placing them in the context of similar programs embarked upon by other nations. The theory of amnesties suggests rent-seeking, bargaining, and costs as reasons for a country offering an amnesty, often in conjunction with increased border controls, internal enforcement and employer penalties. We model an immigration amnesty in which the destination country has a formal sector employing only legal immigrants, an informal sector employing both legal and illegal immigrants, and open unemployment. The model focuses on the productivity enhancing effects of legalization, and establishes specific conditions under which unemployment, the informal sector and the formal sectors increase/decrease in size. Building on these insights, our empirical work examines Mexican migration to the US. We study who are migrants; among migrants, who are legalized via Immigration Reform and Control Act (IRCA), and who

[☆] Presented at "Conference on Immigration: Trends, Consequences and Prospects for the United States" held at the University of Illinois at Chicago, September 9–10, 2005. We thank conference participants, in particular Barry Chiswick and David Ribar, for their comments and criticisms.

Immigration: Trends, Consequences and Prospects for the United States
Research in Labor Economics, Volume 27, 273–309
ISSN: 0147-9121/doi:10.1016/S0147-9121(07)00007-6

are legalized via sponsorship of family or employer. Furthermore, to measure the impact of amnesty on welfare of migrants, we estimate earnings equations of various migrants groups.

1. INTRODUCTION

With the discussion, passage and implementation of the amnesty provisions of the Immigration Reform and Control Act (IRCA) of 1986 (Public Law 99603), the United States (US) altered its immigration landscape and made immigration amnesties a regular consideration in US policy discussions.

The US has at times invited migrants in, while at other times severely restricted immigration. Indeed, in this type of vacillation and policy ambiguity the US is not much different from other countries. Germany, perceiving itself as having a labor shortage through the 1960s and into the early 1970s, opened its borders to immigrants through its guest worker policies. When this perception changed, the guest worker program was stopped. Similar stories with idiosyncratic variations have occurred in France, the Netherlands, Great Britain, and many other countries. These policies, both the liberalizations and the restrictions, have not been universally favored in the enacting countries, leading often to ambiguous policy directions. Thus, it is not unusual to find otherwise law-abiding citizens and businesses hiring immigrants who lack legal status in the host country.

Amnesties arise out of this ambiguous attitude toward immigration. A fundamental feature of an amnesty is that it only applies to people who have already illegally immigrated. If the recipient country were united behind the policy of limiting immigration and backed the set of laws enacted to enforce this limit (e.g., border and internal controls and enforcement), there would be no illegal immigrants and no potential amnesty issue. Recipient country employers would refuse to hire those without proper documentation – illegal immigrants' probability of obtaining a job would be zero – and eventually they would stop immigrating. There may be other reasons migrants might come without proper documents – certain refugees, for example – but these we do not consider here.

The US and other countries spend significant resources attempting to limit the number/types of immigrants they admit. Yet, more immigrants enter many of the recipient countries than at least the law admits to wanting.

From the migrants point-of-view the potential benefits of migrating, even illegally, must outweigh both the direct and indirect costs. From the recipient country's point-of-view the broadly defined gains from allowing this to happen must outweigh the costs – again both direct and indirect. As the stock of illegal migrants grows they may become a higher cost to the economy than legal migrants. The societal cost may well cross the host's tolerance level. Moreover, the cost of locating, capturing and expelling illegal migrants may be prohibitive. When these occur the scene is ripe for an amnesty, which converts some or all of the illegal migrants into legal migrants.

Under an amnesty, illegal immigrants who can demonstrate that they meet certain requirements, such as continuous employment, length of stay in the country, no criminal record, and so on, are made legal. The exact legal status they obtain varies from country-to-country and program-to-program, from short-term permits with requirements to leave when the permits expire, to citizenship. In Table 1, we see a list of some of the largest amnesty programs over the last 20 years in several OECD countries – in OECD terminology the "regularization" of immigrants in an "irregular" situation. The largest single amnesty by far was the IRCA in the US. Most of the recipient countries on this table offered multiple amnesty programs, each separated by only a few years.

By introducing discussion of the possibility of granting of immigration amnesties, the recipient country is essentially changing the rules of the game after the game has started. Prior to the enactment and implementation of an amnesty (and certainly prior to its discussion), those who migrated illegally did so expecting to remain illegal or, possibly, to obtain legal status through conventional means. An amnesty increases the number of legal immigrants in a "single" stroke. This paper asks two fundamental questions that are present in amnesty debates: Will granting amnesty induce further migrations, especially illegal migrations? How much does amnesty affect migrants' welfare? In both theoretical and empirical studies, we address these two questions by studying the migrants themselves – both illegal and legal – as well as non-migrants, asking who migrates and the impact of an amnesty on their behavior and earnings.

After providing some background discussion on immigration amnesties, especially on the IRCA in Section 2, we review the tiny literature on immigration amnesties in Section 3. In Section 3, we also develop very simple model that addresses the impact of an amnesty on the size and allocation of illegal migrants in the recipient country's labor market. In Section 4, we examine Mexican migrants to the US in light of the lessons

Table 1. Main Regularization Programs of Immigrants in an Irregular
               Situation in Selected OECD Countries.

Country	Year	Numbers Regularized (Thousands)
Belgium	2000	52.0
France	1981–1982	121.1
	1997	77.8
Greece	1997–1998	371.0
	2001	351.0
Italy	1987–1988	118.7
	1990	217.7
	1996	244.5
	1998	217.1
	2002	634.7
Portugal	1992–1993	39.2
	1996	21.8
	2001	179.2
Spain	1985–1986	43.8
	1991	110.1
	1996	21.3
	2000	163.9
	2001	234.6
Switzerland	2000	15.2
US	1986	2,684.9
	1997–1998	405.0
	2000	400.0

Source: Trends in International Migration: SOPEMI 2004 edition – ISBN 92-64-00792-X-OECD 2005.

learned from our theoretical model. In absolute numbers, the US is the world's largest country of immigration; Mexico is the world's major country of emigration. Migration from Mexico to the US is the largest sustained flow of migration in the world. Here we examine some of the labor market impacts of the amnesty provisions of the IRCA on the migrants themselves. We do this using data from the Mexican Migration Project (MMP). We study who are migrants; among migrants, who are legalized via IRCA, and who are legalized via sponsorship of family or employer. Furthermore, to measure the impact of amnesty on welfare of migrants, we estimate earnings equations of various migrants groups. Section 5 concludes.

2. LEGAL AND POLITICAL BACKGROUND IN THE US

Here we summarize some of the background discussions of the IRCA, its major features, and the number of people involved. Our discussion is drawn largely from the papers by Chiswick (1988), Hoefer (1991), and Rivera-Batiz (1991).

The formal introduction of an amnesty provision into the discussion of immigration legislation came in 1975 when Congressman Peter Rodino (Democrat, New Jersey) added a proposal for the legalization of illegal aliens to existing proposals for sanctions against employers who hired undocumented workers. This new proposal stalled in the House Judiciary Committee. However, with the substantial growth in the stock of undocumented migrants during the late 1970s and early 1980s, what emerged from the Congress and signed into law by President Reagan on November 6, 1986, contained two major legalization programs.

In contrast to previous immigration policy reforms, the IRCA of 1986 (Public Law 99603) was targeted to deal with the growing illegal alien population and curtail further undocumented migration. It pursued these goals by providing amnesty to large categories of illegal immigrants and introducing sanctions for employers who knowingly hired undocumented workers (Rivera-Batiz, 1991). There were four major provisions of IRCA (see Chiswick, 1988; Hoefer, 1991; Rivera-Batiz, 1991):

1. Employers were prohibited from knowingly hiring, recruiting or referring for a fee undocumented aliens. Penalties for violating the law ran from civil fines of a maximum of $1,000 per alien for a first offense to criminal penalties of $10,000 per alien and/or imprisonment for further offenses.
2. Increased Immigration and Naturalization Service (INS)[1] funding for enforcement of immigration laws and mandatory state participation in the INS Systematic Alien Verification Entitlement System, an automated on-line system allowing instant verification of an alien's immigration status.
3. Eligibility for temporary resident status for undocumented aliens who had continuously resided in the US illegally since January 1, 1982. Chiswick (1988) suggests that the reasoning for the entrance date is the feeling that more recent migrants were not so firmly established that they could not leave. Applications needed to be filed on or before May 4,

1988. Once a person applied for temporary resident status, he or she was also eligible for permanent resident status, if they filed for it on or before November 6, 1990, and the applicant satisfied the English language requirements. After five years as permanent resident, he or she could apply for citizenship.[2]

4. Eligibility for temporary – and later permanent – resident status for up to 350,000 undocumented field laborers who worked in perishable agricultural commodities for at least 90 days during the year ending May 1, 1986. Under the special agricultural worker (SAW) program, these workers were classified as Group I workers and were eligible for permanent residence on December 1, 1989. Those who also qualified but applied after the 350,000 limit was reached were Group II residential status and permanent residence on December 1, 1990. The SAW program was supplemented by the replenishment agricultural worker (RAW) program which, from 1990 and lasting for three years, allowed US farmers to import foreign laborers to harvest perishable crops if the Departments of Labor and Agriculture agreed there was a labor shortage. These foreign workers are given temporary resident status and, aside from the 90 days of work a year each must spend in US agriculture, they could seek employment elsewhere during the rest of the year. Once a foreign worker is employed under the RAW program for at least three consecutive years, he/she becomes eligible for permanent residency. No shortages were ever found so the RAW never came to pass. According to Chiswick (1988) and Rivera-Batiz (1991), the SAW and RAW programs were added as compromise items to attract the support of producers of perishable agricultural products. These farmers were particularly vulnerable to a sudden drop in the availability of seasonal agricultural workers. However, while there may have been 3–5 million illegals in the US just prior to IRCA, a not insignificant number of the SAW applicants may not have been among them, given the substantial fraud in the SAW program.

Tables 2 and 3 (Rytina, 2002) summarize the impact of the IRCA on changes in immigrants' legal status. The three million persons who applied for legalization under IRCA represent most of the legalization eligible aliens given an estimated illegal immigrant population of 3–5 million in 1986 (Hoefer, 1991). Of those applying, 85–91% were legalized, and of those legalized, 33% became citizens by 2001. The citizenship rate for the regular IRCA legalizations was 40%; for SAW applicants, 23%. Visa overstayers had a much higher rate of naturalization than illegal entrants.

Table 2. IRCA Legalization: Temporary and Permanent Residence, and Naturalization Through 2001.

Category of Admission	Applicants for Temporary Residence (1)	Applicants Granted Permanent Residence (2)	Percent of Applicants Granted Permanent Residence (3) = (1)/(2)	Applicants Who Naturalized (4)	Naturalized as a Percent of Applicants Granted Permanent Residence (5) = (2)/(4)
Total	3,040,475	2,688,730	88	889,033	33
Legalization applicants					
Total	1,763,434	1,595,766	90	634,456	40
Entered illegally prior to 1/1/1982	1,444,925	1,312,058	91	480,871	37
Overstayed non-immigrant visa prior to 1/1/1982	311,071	277,337	89	149,676	54
Blanket enforced voluntary departure/ unknown	7,438	6,371	86	3,909	61
SAW applicants					
Total	1,277,041	1,092,964	86	254,577	23
Group I seasonal agricultural workers 1984–1986	67,308	59,975	89	12,124	23
Group II seasonal agricultural workers in 1986	1,209,733	1,032,989	85	242,453	23
Unknown	473				

Source: From Nancy Rytina, IRCA Legalization Effects: Lawful Permanent Residence and Naturalization through 2001. Column (1) – Legalization Application Processing System (LAPS) and Statistics Division, USINS, as of August 1992. Columns (2) and (4) – Statistics Division, US Immigration and Naturalization Service.

Of those granted permanent residence, those legalized under IRCA made up 44% in 1989, 57% in 1990, 62% in 1991, 17% in 1992, and 0–2% in later years.

Table 4 highlights the major features of IRCA and amnesty laws that followed IRCA. Post-IRCA amnesties were largely extensions of the original act, generally cleaning up and more carefully defining who were to be covered under IRCA. Thus, the story of immigration amnesties in the US is at least until June 1, 2006, properly the story of IRCA.

Table 3. Persons Granted Permanent Residence by Fiscal Year, IRCA Legalization.

Fiscal year	IRCA Totals		Regular IRCA (Pre-1982 Immigrants)				SAWS		
	Number	As % of all immigrants	Total	Illegal entrants	Non-immigrant overstays	Enforced voluntary departures (EVD)/ unknown	Total	I 1984–1986	II 1986
1989	478,883	44	478,882	383,852	95,905	125	1		1
1990	880,940	57	824,272	683,240	137,551	3,481	56,668	56,668	
1991	1,134,509	62	215,399	180,575	32,962	1,862	919,110	1,293	917,817
1992	165,089	17	47,915	39,863	7,328	724	117,174	2,008	115,166
1993	16,702	2	16,702	14,049	2,545	108			
1994	4,083	1	4,083	3,456	607	20			
1995	2,898	0	2,898	2,335	546	17			
1996	3,037	0	3,037	2,534	488	15			
1997	1,300	0	1,300	1,055	232	13			
1998	820	0	818	693	121	4	2		2
1999	6	0	4	4			2	2	
2000	271	0	267	232	33	2	4	2	2
2001	192	0	189	170	19		3	2	1
Total	2,688,730	21	1,595,766	1,312,058	277,337	6,371	1,092,964	59,975	1,032,989

Note: Owing to the elimination of duplicate records, immigrant totals in this table will slightly from those shown in the INS Statistical Yearbook.

Source: From Nancy Rytina, IRCA Legalization Effects: Lawful Permanent Residence and Naturalization through 2001. Originally compiled by Statistics Division, US Immigration and Naturalization Service.

Table 4. Highlights of IRCA and other US Immigration
Amnesty Laws.

IRCA Amnesty, 1986 Immigration and Reform Control Act
http://iscos/gpv/graphics/aboutus/history/eligibility.htm, Accessed 5/29/2005.
Imposed employer sanctions, increased border controls, etc., and allowed for amnesties with the
  creation of two programs for obtaining temporary resident status:

a. Those who could show continuous illegal residence in the US since January 1, 1982 (except for
   "brief, casual and innocent absences"), and not subject to grounds of excludability added to the
   Immigration and Nationality Act in 1965 – e.g., if they had received any public cash assistance
   since 1982. Application period for temporary residency began May 5, 1987, and ended May 4, 1988
   (Section 245A of IRCA). Application for permanent residency began November 7, 1988, and has
   no fixed ending date.
b. Special Agricultural Workers (SAWs) Program – those who worked as agricultural workers for at
   least 90 days between May 1, 1985 and 1986. Must file between June 1, 1987 and November 30,
   1998. Residence did not need to be continuous or unlawful. Public charge excludability applied
   only if had relied on public case assistance. Permanent residency for SAWs virtually automatic if
   granted temporary residency. SAWs aliens who worked on perishable crops for 3 years eligible on
   December 1, 1990.

Immigration Act of 1990
Amnesty extended to family members of those who had taken advantage of amnesty provision of
  IRCA and had taken steps to become US citizens.

Section 245(I) 1994
Passed as part of FY 1995 Commerce Justice State Appropriations bill. In effect FY 1995, sunset
  September 30, 1997. Under special circumstances allows adjustment of immigration status without
  leaving the US.

Section 245(I) Extension 1997
Til January 14, 1998.

Nicaraguan Adjustment and Central American Relief Act (NACARA) 1997   •
Nicaraguans and Cubans who lived in US illegally since 1995, and spouses and children granted legal
  resident status if applied by April 1, 2000. Also included certain Salvadoreans, Guatemalans and
  Eastern Europeans.

Haitian Relief Immigration Fairness Act (HRIFA) 1998
http://iscos/gpv/graphics/publicaffairs/factsheets/hrifafac.htm, Accessed 5/29/2005.
Permanent resident status to Haitians who have continuously (no more than 180 days outside the US
  from December 31, 1995 til HRIFA adjustment granted, unless special circumstances) been in US
  since December 31, 1995, and spouses and children, if apply by September 1, 2000.

Legal Immigration and Family Equity (LIFE) Act 2000 (reinstatement of rolling Section 245(I))
http://iscos/gpv/graphics/publicaffairs/questsans/lifelegal.htm, Accessed 5/29/2005.
Those who were denied and were here before 1982 and were part of lawsuits claiming, they should
  have received amnesty. Must have entered US before January 1, 1982 and resided continuously till
  May 4, 1988, with continuous presence from Nov 6, 1986 to May 4, 1988. Reinstated Section 245(I)
  for the first 4 months of 2001 (January–April). Expires June 4, 2003 (Scheduled). Has family unity
  clause. Spouses and minor children (under 21) of those amnestied under IRCA granted amnesty.

Sources: Various.

3. ECONOMIC THEORY OF IMMIGRATION AMNESTY

In this section, we review the limited theoretical literature on immigration amnesties and offer a simple model, which captures elements of the amnesty decision and its effects. Formal theoretical models are very scarce. The literature includes papers by Epstein and Weiss (2001), Chau (2001, 2003), and Karlson and Katz (2003).

3.1. Aspects of the Economic Theory of Immigration Amnesty

The theory of immigration amnesties asks where do amnesties come from and why do they take the forms they take. There are several considerations behind the theory of immigration amnesties – some entering into the formal modeling, some outside of the modeling but setting its context.

(1) As discussed above, there must be a reason that illegal migrants are present in the first place – that they are tolerated. Someone must be giving them jobs. At some level law enforcement tolerates their presence. Most likely their existence and toleration reflect competing interests in the recipient country.

(2) The coexistence of legal and illegal migrants is puzzling. Epstein and Weiss (2001) discuss this in some detail, offering several explanations, including: (a) immediate legalization of successful entrants will affect the flow of migrants; (b) legalized migrants cannot be deported, so the recipient country may prefer illegal immigrants to allow for a deportation; (c) there may be benefits from having workers confined to certain sectors, which can be guaranteed in a democratic society only if they are illegal (Hillman & Weiss, 1999), or from having them largely unemployed for efficiency wage purposes (Epstein & Hillman, 2000); and (d) it is easier to deny illegal entrants income transfers of various sorts, and to discourage dependent family members from joining them.

(3) If legal and illegal immigrants coexist, the desire to legalize the illegal immigrants must represent some increased benefit to having them legal, or an increased cost to their remaining illegal. The coexistence of legal and illegal immigrants tells us that for the recipient country these two groups have different costs and benefits. The desire to enact an amnesty may arise due to increased border and internal control expenses. Among the explanations they offer, Epstein and Weiss (2001) point out that the

social costs from migrants may increase at a faster rate if the migrants are illegal than if they are legal. At a critical number of illegal immigrants it becomes cheaper to legalize them than to continue bearing this additional cost. Also, the existence of a very large illegal base may signal the natives that illegality is acceptable.[3]

These are political economy questions and indeed the four papers on the theory of immigration amnesties capture these issues in their modeling.[4] Epstein and Weiss (2001) derive an optimal amnesty policy where the decision to migrate depends on relative wages and the probability of being caught and deported. They assume illegal immigration is unwanted with border and internal control expenses incurred to prevent their entry and deport them if they manage to enter, but prevention is not complete. At some point an amnesty will be preferable to having a large number of immigrants outside of the rule of law. An amnesty will also reduce the cost of internal controls, allowing resources to be diverted to border controls. Moreover, they discuss circumstances for the optimality of a delayed amnesty, under which only those in the country for a certain minimum number of years are eligible for the amnesty, as well as for a limited amnesty, in which illegal workers who come forward are granted a work permit for a fixed period, after which they are forced to return to their home country.

Chau (2001) asks why we frequently find employer sanctions and amnesties jointly enacted. She argues that an amnesty credibly commits the host country to continue efforts that it would otherwise choose to discontinue apprehending and deporting illegal immigrants once they have entered the labor force. In a similar vein, Chau (2003) shows that while amnesty may appear to run contrary to the original intent of the immigration reform, it may nevertheless facilitate rent-capture by the politician by "wiping the slate clean" and reducing the deadweight loss of employer sanction measures.

The trade-offs between amnesties, border/internal controls, and enforcement are also approached in Karlson and Katz (2003), who start from the assumption that some illegal immigration is desirable as the recipient country may wish to attract workers to its low productivity sector, which can be made profitable only by hiring low-wage illegal workers. In Karlson and Katz (2003), the wage offer is not enough on its own to induce illegal migration, so it must be supplemented with a probabilistic amnesty which would allow these immigrants to eventually/possibly work in the high-wage sector.

3.2. Amnesty, Size and Allocation of Illegal Migrants:
An Illustrative Model

One major topic not thoroughly discussed in the amnesty literature is whether the amnesty policy is effective in reducing the size of illegal immigrants in the host country. To answer this question, we model an immigration amnesty in which the destination country has a formal sector which employs only legal immigrants, an informal sector employing both legal and illegal immigrants, and open unemployment. The model focuses on the productivity enhancing effects of legalization, and establishes specific conditions under which unemployment, the informal sector and the formal sectors increase/decrease in size.

The elements of this model are:

(1) Immigrants come from a pool of potential migrants in their home country. Labor is homogenous. The only heterogeneity among laborers is that some enter the recipient country legally and some illegally. Note that the heterogeneity of labor is of interest in the empirical modeling.

(2) In their home country potential migrants can earn some sort of a living, possibly on family farms. We will assume full employment in the home country, with the wage inversely related to labor supply, and equal to the marginal product of labor. Variations on this theme can have some interesting implications, but do not change the story's essentials (Gang & Gangopadhyay, 1987a, 1987b).

(3) In the recipient country immigrants can find employment in the formal sector or informal sector, or end up unemployed. In these three sectors workers are paid fixed wages. This greatly simplifies the modeling without grossly deviating from having more relaxed assumptions. The unemployed receive a wage that is indexed at zero. Informal workers receive a wage that is fixed at the subsistence level or near it. Formal workers receive a wage that is substantially above the subsistence level. It is not outside the bounds of the modeling to have the informal wage above the formal wage, although we do not expound on this situation. Also, the informal wage could be above or below the wage in the home country.

(4) Unemployment exists only in the recipient country and the unemployed are actively involved in job search. The unemployed may have entered the recipient country either legally or illegally. We do not distinguish the two, though if all of one type of labor became employed it would have implications for the other type. In the internal equilibrium that we discuss this cannot happen. It would however be relevant in the end

stages where wages in the home country have risen to the level of wages in the recipient country.

(5) While we label the productive sectors in the recipient country formal and informal, they are not necessarily completely populated with only legal or only illegal workers, respectively. Legality here involves possessing a piece of paper giving you certain rights and obligations in the recipient country – e.g., a "green card." Even though an immigrant may possess such a piece of paper, he may choose to work in the informal sector. In fact, he may be one of the entrepreneurs in the informal sector, or hire illegal immigrants to work for his family, or he may employ illegal immigrants in order to hire them out to local employers (see Epstein, 2003 for a full exposition of this relationship). Though legal, he is clearly working in the informal sector. On the other hand, we assume that illegal entrants cannot work in the formal sector.

(6) To close the model, we will assume an expanded Harris–Todaro (Harris & Todaro, 1970) type equilibrium with risk-neutral labor. Essentially, this means that ex ante migrants and potential migrants compare their expected gains (wages) from migrating to what they get if not moving, and equilibrium occurs when these are equal.

(7) An amnesty creates new pieces of paper legalizing people. The new legal immigrants do not necessarily work in the formal sector, as in (5) above.

(8) We only look at immigrants and potential immigrants from the home country. By inference can talk about consequences for recipient country native labor, or past immigrants from the same or different origins. While there are clearly income distribution effects of migration, there is evidence on both positive and negative aggregate implications for wages and unemployment of natives and previous immigrants. While simple theory tells us increasing the supply of a factor will lower the returns to the existing stock of the factor, this ignores international capital mobility (which we ignore here too). If firms cannot get the cheaper labor in the recipient country, they may set up shop in the home country or some other country with cheap labor. This would deny the recipient country the complementary gains from immigration, though it would also reduce costs. Who wins or loses when all issues are properly accounted for is difficult to say. (All we can say is that the world is better off under free everything. And each individual is potentially better off.)

(9) The modeling is heavily drawn from Dutta, Gang, and Gangopadhyay (1989), Gang and Gangopadhyay (1985, 1987b), and, in particular,

Gang and Gangopadhyay (1990). The idea of legalized immigrants functioning in both the formal sector and the informal sector is taken from Epstein (2003).

Consider only migrants and potential migrants; later we will discuss recipient/host country labor. All originate from their home country, all labor is homogeneous, and each laborer is currently in one of the four possible states, three in the recipient country and one in their home country. In the recipient country migrants can either work in the formal sector, F, informal sector, I, or may be unemployed and engaged in job search, L^U. In their home country they work in a "traditional"-type economy, H. We consider labor, L^i, as homogeneous and an input in each productive sector i, $i=F$, I and H.

Legal documentation (the allowed number of legal immigrants, permits, green cards, etc.), K, complements labor in production and is used in the production of both F and I. The total availability of legal documentation is set by the government, here exogenously. As just discussed, legal documentation can move back and forth between both F and I, and does so until its marginal product is the same in both sectors. The increased availability of legal documentation is what we use to capture an amnesty.

The production equations are

$$F = F(L^F, K^F); \quad F_L, F_K, F_{LK} > 0; \quad F_{KK}, F_{LL} < 0 \tag{1}$$

$$I = I(L^I, K^I); \quad I_L, I_K, I_{LK} > 0; \quad I_{KK}, I_{LL} < 0 \tag{2}$$

and,

$$H = H(L^H); \quad H_L = H' > 0; \quad H_{LL} = H'' < 0 \tag{3}$$

Firms are price-takers and final goods prices are fixed and normalized to unity in order to concentrate on the supply-side relationship.

To establish a model with four labor market states we need four specifications for the wage–labor market relationship. In the recipient country both working sectors face effective wage floors. In the formal sector this is $w^F \geq \bar{w}^F$ and is substantially above the subsistence wage; while in the informal sector w^I is limited on its downward side by the subsistence wage, i.e., $w^I \geq \bar{w}^I$. Wages in the home country are flexible. The unemployed receive no wage, $w^U = 0$; i.e., their wages are indexed at zero. In the initial equilibrium we assume,

$$\bar{w}^F \geq \bar{w}^I \quad and \quad \bar{w}^I \geq \bar{w}^H \tag{4}$$

The relationship, $\bar{w}^I \geq w^H$, allows migrants to be attracted directly to the informal sector because of opportunities in that sector itself, not just as a stepping stone for formal jobs and legalization of their statuses.

Firms in the three sectors are to maximize profits so that the employment of labor in each sector is determined by

$$H' = w^H \tag{5}$$

$$I_L = \bar{w}^I \tag{6}$$

and

$$F_L = \bar{w}^I \tag{7}$$

The total amount of labor (migrants and potential migrants) is fixed at L, i.e.,

$$L^F + L^I + L^H + L^U = L \tag{8}$$

The basic story holds if labor supply is variable, though extra conditions are needed and there are some useful additional insights (Gang & Tower, 1990).

Legal documentation, a type of capital, is fixed at total quantity K and can be used by either the formal or informal sectors, so that

$$K^F + K^I = K \tag{9}$$

Furthermore, the market for legal documentation and the people who hold it is such that its marginal products in these two sectors are equated,

$$F^K = I^K \tag{10}$$

To close the model we need to determine how labor allocates itself among its four possible states. Assuming that workers are risk-neutral income maximizers, we invoke an expanded version of Harris–Todaro (1970) labor market equilibrium condition,

$$(\bar{w}^F L^F + \bar{w}^I L^I)/(L^F + L^I + L^U) = H' \tag{11}$$

Eqs. (6)–(11) comprise the system of equations in L^F, K^F, L^I, K^I, L^H and L^U we need to analyze for our model. Workers migrate to the recipient country in search of informal as well as formal jobs, but may end up unemployed. Legal workers can be found in both the formal and informal sectors. Using these equations we derive the following comparative static results, which are useful in studying the effect of amnesty on the reallocation of migrants in the host country.

Comparative Static Results

$dK^F/dK = (-F_{LL})\Delta^I/|D| \geq 0;$

$dK^I/dK = (-I_{LL})\Delta^F/|D| \geq 0;$

$dL^F/dK = F_{LK}\Delta^I[(H_L/(L - L^H)) - H_{LL}]/|D| \geq 0;$

$dL^I/dK = I_{LK}\Delta^F[(H_L/(L - L^H)) - H_{LL}]/|D| \geq 0;$

$dL^H/dK = (-\bar{w}^I I_{LK}\Delta^F - \bar{w}^F F_{LK}D^I)/|D| < 0;$

$dL^u/dK = \{F_{LK}\Delta^I[H_{LL} + (w^F - H_L)/(L - L^H)]$
$\qquad\qquad +I_{LK}\Delta^F[H_{LL} + (w^I - H_L)/(L - L^H)]\}/|D| \gtrless 0;$

where

$\Delta^i = i_{LL}i_{KK} - (i_{LK})^2 \gtrless 0, \quad i = I, F; \text{ and } |D| = -(H_{LL}\Delta^F + F_{LL}\Delta^H) > 0.$

The main question we are interested in is what happens when there is an immigration amnesty – an increase in the number of "legality coupons" which allow illegal workers to become legal. What happens depends crucially on whether there are increasing (IRS), constant (CRS) or diminishing (DRS) returns to scale in the formal and informal sectors. In our model these correspond to the cases where $\Delta^i < 0$, $\Delta^i = 0$ and $\Delta^i > 0$, respectively. However, we cannot entertain the assumption of IRS because it is not consistent with profit maximization by competitive firms, which we assumed in making firms in our model price-takers. Moreover, for a solution to exist, i.e., $|D| \neq 0$, or, in our case, $|D| > 0$ – there cannot be CRS in both the formal and informal sectors. Generally we assume DRS in both sectors, pointing out what happens if CRS exists in I or F.

If there is CRS in the formal sector (F) and DRS in the informal sector (I), then all new legal documentation will end up in the informal sector, and all growth (output increase) will occur there – the formal sector will stagnate. Labor will migrate from the home country and will obtain a job in the informal sector or become unemployed. Unemployment may, on net, rise or fall, depending on the production technology in the home country, the size of the formal and informal sectors in the recipient country and on relative wages (the exact conditions are discussed below). If, instead, there is CRS in I and DRS in F, it is the informal sector which is stagnating and the formal sector which is growing. Of course, with DRS in both sectors, they are growing and the relative growth rates of each sector depend on the production technologies. Below we discuss the specific technologies.

The basis premise of our model is that migrants are looking for some sort of job in the recipient country. They would prefer formal jobs but not all migrants get a relatively high-pay formal job, so some migrate illegally and look for jobs in the informal sector. Some get these jobs and some become unemployed. An amnesty increases the number of legality documents. Generally, both the formal and informal sectors will expand. The informal sector expands for as the formal sector grows more people may be pulled out of the home country by the draw of high-paying jobs than the formal sector can absorb – the higher expected wage (and/or the expectation of future amnesties, which we do not model). These people enter the informal sector or become unemployed. Some legal immigrants may also enter (or stay if they just became legalized) the informal sector, and if one amnesty follows another, for a time the number of illegal workers and unemployment increases. This process has been described in some detail in Gang and Gangopadhyay (1990), though for a simpler economy than we have outlined here.

We now look at the consequences of these forces for the *relative size of the sectors*. Basically, we are concerned with what happens when an amnesty makes more legality documents available to the economy. When the number of legality documents available in the economy increases, some will go into the formal and some into the informal sector, as our allocation rule (10), $F^K = I^K$, tells us they will be allocated in such a way that marginal products are equated.[5] This raises the question of what determines the relative growth rates of legality documents between the formal and informal sectors. The condition is given in the following proposition.

Proposition 1. Let g_K^F be the growth rate of legality documents in the formal sector and g_K^I be the growth rate of legality documents in the informal sector (i.e., $g_K^i = (1/K^i)(dK^i/dK), i = F, I)$, then $g_K^F \gtreqless g_K^I \Leftrightarrow (-e_L^{F_L})[e_L^{I_L}e_K^{I_K} - e_K^{I_L}e_L^{I_K}]$ $\gtreqless (-e_L^{I_L})[e_K^{F_K}e_L^{F_L} - e_K^{F_L}e_L^{F_K}]$, where, $e_j^i = (\partial i/\partial j)(j/i)$, i.e., e is $(1/\eta)$ and η the elasticity of the marginal product curve with respect to the different factors of production.

Proof of Proposition 1. To see this, from the comparative statics results box,

$$(1/K^F)(-F_{LL})\Delta^I/|D| \gtreqless (-I_{LL})\Delta^F(1/K^I)/|D| \Leftrightarrow (1/K^F)(-F_{LL})\Delta^I$$
$$\gtreqless (-I_{LL})\Delta^F(1/K^I) \Leftrightarrow (1/K^F)(-F_{LL})\Delta^I$$
$$\gtreqless -(\partial I_L/\partial L^I)(L^I/I_L)(I_L/L^I)(1/K^I)$$
$$\times[(\partial F_L/\partial L^F)(L^F/F_L)(F_L/L^F)(\partial F_K/\partial K^F)(K^F/F_K)(F_K/K^F)$$
$$-(\partial F_L/\partial K^F)(K^F/F_L)(F_L/K^F)(\partial F_K/\partial L^F)(L^F/F_K)(F_K/L^F)]$$
$$= -(e_L^{I_L}L)(I_L/L^I K^I)[e_K^{F_K}e_L^{F_L}(F_L F_K/L^F K^F) - e_K^{F_L}e_L^{F_K}(F_L F_K/K^F L^F)]$$

i.e.,

$$(-e_L^F L)(F_L/K^F L^F)[e_L^{I_L} e_K^{I_K} - e_K^{I_L} e_L^{I_K}](I_L I_K/L^I K^I)$$
$$\gtrless (-e_L^I L)(I_L/L^I K^I)[e_K^{F_K} e_L^{F_L} - e_K^{F_L} e_L^{F_K}](F_L F_K/K^F L^F)$$

i.e., since $I_K = F_K$

$$(-e_L^{F_L})[e_L^{I_L} e_K^{I_K} - e_K^{I_L} e_L^{I_K}] \gtrless (-e_L^{I_L})[e_K^{F_K} e_L^{F_L} - e_K^{F_L} e_L^{F_K}]$$

We can see that the relative sizes of the elasticities are crucial in determining the growth of one sector versus the other. That is, given the fixed wage differential, $\bar{w}^F - \bar{w}^I$, the relative production technologies provide a snapshot of the effect of an amnesty on the relative size of the sectors. Generally, we should expect to witness switching back and forth – the formal sector growing faster for a while, and then the informal growing faster. Note, however, in a Cobb–Douglas technology of the form $F = \lambda K^\alpha L^\beta$ and $I = K^\alpha L^\beta$, $\alpha + \beta < 1$, $\lambda > 1$, we have the left side of Proposition 1 equaling the right-hand side. That is, as long as the number of unemployed is positive, $L^U > 0$, the rates of growth of the sectors are the same.

Next we ask, as a result of the amnesty, what are the concomitant changes in the labor market? Clearly, as the absolute amount of legality documents increases, employment increases in both the formal and informal sector.

Proposition 2. Let g_L^F be the growth rate of labor in the formal sector and let g_L^I be the growth rate of labor in the informal sector (i.e., $g_L^i = (1/L^i)(dL^i/dL)$, $i = F, I$), then $g_L^F \gtrless g_L^I \Leftrightarrow (e_K^{F_L})[e_L^{I_L} e_K^{I_K} - e_K^{I_L} e_L^{I_K}] \gtrless (e_K^{I_L}) [e_K^{F_K} e_L^{F_L} - e_K^{F_L} e_L^{F_K}]$, where $e_j^i = (\partial i/\partial j)(j/i)$, i.e., e is $(1/\eta)$ and η the elasticity of the marginal product curve with respect to the different factors of production.

Proof of Proposition 2. To see this, from the comparative statics results box, $(1/L^F)(dL^F/dK) \gtrless (1/L^I)(dL^I/dK) \Leftrightarrow (L^I/L^F) \gtrless (I_{LK}/F_{LK})(\Delta^F/\Delta^I)$. Substituting and rearranging, the proof follows as in Proposition 1.

Thus, as with changes in the relative growth of the legality coupons between the formal and informal sectors, there will be employment shifts among the sectors. As we saw above, labor leaves the home country to search for informal and formal jobs. However, total employment may increase or decrease, as we have not yet taken into account what happens to unemployment as people leave the home country seeking the new jobs in the formal and informal sectors. This leads to our next proposition, where E is employment, i.e., $E = L^H + L^I + L^F$.

Proposition 3. Employment falls, or unemployment rises, i.e., $dE/dK < 0$, if and only if $1 + (I_K/F_K)(L^F/L^I)(e_K^{F_L}/e_K^{I_L})\{[H_{LL} + (W^F - H_L)/(L - L^H)]/ [H_{LL} + (W^I - H_L)/(L - L^H)]\} > 0$.

Proof of Proposition 3. To see this, from the comparative statics results box, $dL^u/dK = \{F_{LK}\Delta^I[H_{LL} + (w^F - H_L)/(L - L^H)] + I_{LK}\Delta^F[H_{LL} + (w^I - H_L)/(L - L^H)]\}/|D| \gtrless 0$. Substituting and rearranging, the proof follows as in Proposition 1.

This condition is more complicated than that found in Gang and Gangopadhyay (1990). Here, depending on the relative elasticities, relative wage differentials and the relative size of sectors of the economy, immigration amnesties will have different effects. In particular, we have established conditions under which the informal sector expands more rapidly than the formal, both in its use of legality documents and in employment.

There are two important caveats to our modeling. First, our work concentrates on supply-side relationships, ignoring the demand side. Clearly, changing employment patterns and incomes in the three sectors have implications with regard to effective demand and the extent to which different sectoral output levels can actually be consumed given the intersectoral income distribution and consumption parameters. In a more general and much more complicated model, we would have to account for these. The second caveat is that, in reality, not all labor is homogeneous and skill requirements may differ from one sector to another. Our model could be made more flexible, for example, by allowing different degrees of substitutability between labor skills so that an unskilled worker moving from the home country or informal sector to the formal sector would be only imperfectly substitutable for a skilled worker. While this certainly would help generalize the model, the additional conditions vis-à-vis growth of the informal and formal sectors would yield few additional insights.

Our very simple model shows that the effects of an immigration amnesty are not straightforward, though it is quite clear that an amnesty will impact on the number of illegal migrants and their allocation into sectors of the economy. While our conditions in the theoretical model are in terms of elasticities, which is not our main interest in modeling. The model provides insights into how the labor market adjusts to an amnesty. In our empirical work that follows, we build on these insights and study who the migrants were; among migrants, who were legalized via IRCA, and who were legalized via sponsorship of family or employer. Furthermore, to measure the impact of amnesty on welfare of migrants, we estimate earnings equations of various migrants groups.

4. DATA AND ANALYSIS

So far we have discussed the major US amnesty initiative, the IRCA, setting it in the foreground of similar amnesties in other OECD countries. Using a theoretical model we highlighted the reallocation of the labor force as a result of an immigration amnesty. Together they provide a context for our empirical work. In order to provide greater focus we did not discuss in our theory the wage effects of an amnesty. Generally, these are theoretically ambiguous and need to be determined empirically. Our empirical work examines the Mexican migration to the US, first looking at who migrates and who does not, who became legalized under IRCA, who under other programs and who never became legalized. Against this background we also estimate the wage effects of IRCA on Mexican immigrants to the US.

Unfortunately, even now, almost 20 years after the legislation was signed into law, we still have relatively few studies on the economic consequences of immigration amnesties (Chiswick, 1988; Barreto, Ramirez, & Woods, 2005; Gonzalez-Baker, 1997; Kossoudji & Cobb-Clark, 2000, 2002; Massey, 1987; Phillips & Massey, 1999; Orrenius & Zavodny, 2003; Rivera-Batiz, 1999; Bucci & Tenorio, 1997; Chiquiar & Hanson, 2002; Chiswick & Miller, 1999; Nelson & Xu, 2001). This is not for lack of interest; rather there are a limited number of data sets available for proper study of these issues. The data available either does not ask the right questions, was sloppy in its collection, did not include "control" groups, or simply does not have enough observations. While the US and Mexican Censuses have been used, they and most other data sets fail to identify illegal immigrants and/or IRCA recipients. A notable exception is the 1989–1992 Legalized Population Survey (LPS), collected in conjunction with the implementation of the IRCA. The LPS provides a random sample of illegal immigrants seeking legalization under the regular program. This part of the IRCA amnesties was designed to regularize immigrants with an ongoing long-term commitment to the US labor market. The LPS does not include illegal immigrants legalized under the SAW program, nor does immigrants who did not come forward under any of the IRCA provisions. Unfortunately, the

LPS does not contain information on groups comparable to the IRCA legalized population.

By constructing a synthetic control group using an external data set, Kossoudji and Cobb-Clark (2002) use the LPS to examine the effects of IRCA on wages. They find that the wage penalty for being unauthorized ranges from 14% to 24%, while the wage benefit of legalization under IRCA was approximately 6%. This study complements previous studies, e.g., Kossoudji and Cobb-Clark (2002), by studying the allocation of Mexicans into different sectors, and then estimating their wage equations.

4.1. Descriptive Analysis – Mexican Migration Project Data

We use individual- and village-level data on Mexican–US migration available through the Mexican Migration Project (MMP93). The data comprise almost 16,000 households with over 100,000 people in 93 communities spread out over Mexico (see Fig. 1), selected for their diversity

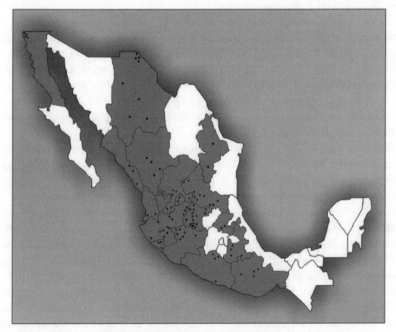

Fig. 1. Mexican Migration Project Communities (MMP93).

in size, ethnic composition and economic development without regard to their degree of involvement with migration to the US. Each year since 1982, 200 households in each of two to five communities are interviewed, though in smaller communities fewer households are chosen. These are retrospective data with each community surveyed only once, which also means that villages that were surveyed in the early years of the project have no information on IRCA. An ethno-survey approach, combining techniques of ethnographic fieldwork and representative survey sampling, is used for data collection.

Interviews are generally conducted in December–January when sojourner US migrants often return to Mexico. If initial fieldwork indicates that US migrants return home in large numbers during months other than December or January, interviewers return to the community during those months to gather a portion of the 200 interviews. These representative community surveys yield information on where migrants go in the US, and during the months of July and August interviewers travel to those US destinations to gather non-random samples of 10–20 out-migrant households from each community. The US-based samples thus contain migrants who have established their households in the US.

Massey and Zeteno (2000) show that the MMP data are a good source of reasonably representative retrospective data on documented and undocumented migration to the US. We use the MMP93 version of the data. Massey, Alarcón, Durand, and Gonzáles (1987), Massey, Goldring, and Durand (1994), and Massey and Zeteno (2000) provide details and some data analysis. Massey and Zeteno (2000) show the data are a source of reasonably representative retrospective data on documented and undocumented migration to the US.

There are a few serious problems with the data. The interviews were free ranging, with the questioners following a semi-structured format. While the questioners tried to cover core questions, this process left many missing observations. Moreover, while the sample may be representative in a particular survey year, it will not be representative across time since it is retrospective and people are surveyed only once. To be included a migrant must have a link to a household in Mexico. Individuals who might have died or migrated permanently would not be in the sample in the survey year but may or may not have been legalized under the IRCA. There are people in the data who were interviewed before IRCA, and there are people in our data that were not legalized under IRCA at the time they were surveyed, but may have later become legalized. It is impossible to know how important the "missing" information is for the analysis, but it may potentially severely bias the results. Also, as the data have been collected over a 20-year period, there are issues with deflating wages, relative price changes and the like.

What is of particular interest to us is the information the MMP contains on the migrant's legal status. We know if individuals ever migrated to the US, whether they were legal or not, and if legal who sponsored them – if they were legalized was it via the regular amnesty of the IRCA, under the SAW, or by other means. Moreover, we have information on, for example, how many times people worked in the US, the aggregate time spent in the US, when they made their first trip and when they made their last trip, how long was each of these trips, whether they were currently working in the US, their wages and occupations in the US, as well as information on the socioeconomic characteristics of the household members such as age, education and marital status. The MMP also contains more detailed migration information on household heads that have migrated.

In the sample we look at here, we restrict age to between 20 and 60 and survey years to 1986 or later since the IRCA was introduced in 1986. We focus on observations with US wage information, which is obtained for the last migration they have taken or is currently under way. For comparison purposes, we select non-migrants with Mexican domestic wage information, assuming that they can potentially migrate to and work in the US. For this reason, we choose those who reported wages from the last formal job in Mexico.[6]

Table 5 shows the mean characteristics of six groups: two groups legalized through IRCA (regular IRCA and SAW/IRCA), two groups legalized through programs or procedures other than IRCA (i.e., sponsored by a family member or employer), those never legalized and non-migrants. As shown in the Table 5.1, migrants legalized by IRCA have the highest hourly wages, followed by those legalized by employer sponsorship. Those legalized via SAW, family member sponsorship and non-legalized migrants have similar wage rates.[7] The age distribution is quite similar, except that non-migrants are a few years older than other groups. Age when migrants last migrated is calculated using year of birth and the year of last migration, adjusted by the duration of migration. There is not much difference between the age at the survey year and age of last migration among legalized migrants whether through IRCA or other sponsorship. However, there are substantial differences between the two ages among immigrants who were not legalized. This indicates that obtaining legal paperwork is important for migration behavior. Those who legalized via regular IRCA and employer sponsorship have more experience than other migrant groups. But non-migrants have the greatest experience.

Table 5.1. Mean Characteristics (Both Sexes).

	Migrants	IRCA	Regular IRCA	SAW	Non-IRCA Legalized	Family Sponsored	Employer Sponsored	Not Legalized	Non-Migrants
US hourly wage[a]	4.687	4.786	4.942	4.613	4.677	4.600	4.882	4.618	–
	(4.586)	(2.756)	(2.825)	(2.670)	(3.302)	(3.192)	(3.604)	(5.693)	
Age†	35.561	35.460	36.929	33.830	36.356	36.064	37.132	35.500	39.486
	(9.624)	(8.727)	(8.379)	(8.825)	(9.999)	(10.441)	(8.757)	(10.162)	(10.491)
Age	32.114	35.038	36.521	33.395	34.655	34.298	35.604	29.583	–
	(9.015)	(8.640)	(8.242)	(8.783)	(9.877)	(9.953)	(9.702)	(8.354)	
Potential experience†	22.886	23.085	24.365	21.666	22.273	21.901	23.264	22.844	25.818
	(11.311)	(10.506)	(10.070)	(10.806)	(11.645)	(12.189)	(10.098)	(11.807)	(12.382)
Potential experience	19.451	22.672	23.973	21.230	20.572	20.135	21.736	16.943	–
	(10.446)	(10.397)	(9.896)	(10.756)	(11.195)	(11.435)	(10.545)	(9.661)	
Education†	6.675	6.375	6.564	6.165	8.082	8.163	7.868	6.656	7.668
	(3.553)	(3.543)	(3.697)	(3.356)	(3.571)	(3.525)	(3.716)	(3.504)	(4.492)
Education	6.663	6.366	6.548	6.165	8.082	8.163	7.868	6.640	–
	(3.526)	(3.500)	(3.619)	(3.356)	(3.571)	(3.525)	(3.716)	(3.484)	
Male	0.856	0.887	0.865	0.911	0.727	0.667	0.887	0.856	0.513
	(0.351)	(0.317)	(0.342)	(0.285)	(0.447)	(0.473)	(0.320)	(0.352)	(0.500)
Surveyed in US	0.211	0.318	0.409	0.218	0.309	0.326	0.264	0.117	–
	(0.408)	(0.466)	(0.492)	(0.413)	(0.463)	(0.471)	(0.445)	(0.321)	
Total months in US	84.384	124.187	153.837	91.309	138.995	132.837	155.377	46.570	–
	(79.095)	(79.522)	(82.088)	(61.798)	(102.581)	(104.781)	(95.503)	(49.319)	
Number of migration in Mexico†	0.636	0.887	0.548	1.263	0.371	0.333	0.472	0.500	0.611
	(1.648)	(2.393)	(1.182)	(3.205)	(0.703)	(0.673)	(0.775)	(0.921)	(1.023)
US northeast region	0.065	0.047	0.039	0.056	0.098	0.128	0.019	0.072	–
	(0.246)	(0.211)	(0.193)	(0.230)	(0.298)	(0.335)	(0.137)	(0.258)	
US western region	0.594	0.690	0.671	0.711	0.593	0.567	0.660	0.525	–
	(0.491)	(0.463)	(0.470)	(0.454)	(0.493)	(0.497)	(0.478)	(0.500)	
US mid-west region	0.088	0.062	0.112	0.008	0.077	0.057	0.132	0.108	–
	(0.283)	(0.242)	(0.316)	(0.087)	(0.268)	(0.232)	(0.342)	(0.311)	
US southern region	0.253	0.200	0.178	0.225	0.232	0.248	0.189	0.295	–
	(0.435)	(0.401)	(0.383)	(0.418)	(0.423)	(0.434)	(0.395)	(0.456)	
Observations	2,184	833	438	395	194	141	53	1,157	3,561

Note: Variables with † are measured when the survey was done and without † are measured when the last migration occurred.
Source: Authors' calculations using MMP93.
[a]US hourly wage when last migrated is deflated using Consumer Price Index (CPI) (1982–1984 = 100). Standard deviations are reported in parentheses.

Education levels are higher among legalized migrants sponsored by family members or employers, and non-migrants. Those who legalized via IRCA, both regular and SAW, have lower education levels. The difference between education levels at the survey year and last migration is minuscule. The proportion of males in each group shows that males dominate among migrants. Only those who legalized through family sponsorship show a lower proportion of migrating males than females, though it is still greater than 50%. Employment-related migration to the US is male dominated. The number of migrations within Mexico is highest among SAW recipients. This may show the nature of temporary agricultural work. The distribution of US migration destinations is concentrated in the West, followed by the South.

These patterns for the mean characteristics are also found in the male sample shown in Table 5.2. This is not surprising, given that most of the people in the sample are men. Generally, the female sample also shows similar patterns for mean characteristics (Table 5.3). However, the hourly wages in the last migration is somewhat different; those legalized via the regular IRCA have lower wages than do those legalized via SAW, and those legalized through employer's sponsorship have lowest wages. It is not clear whether this is due to the smaller female sample size.

4.2. Legalization Categories and Earnings

We present an empirical multinomial logit model of the "choice" of Mexicans into the six groups. This will allow us to discuss who became legalized and who not. This analysis forms the background, and the selection equation that allow us to estimate a wage equation.

Lee (1983) describes a sample selection model when selection is based on the multinomial logit.[8] Let us suppose that s is the selection variable which takes values of $0, 1, ..., J$ for $J + 1$ outcomes. The model for determination of s is

$$P_j = Pr[s_i = j] = \exp(Z_i\gamma_j) / \left[1 + \sum_{j=1}^{J} \exp(Z_i\gamma_j)\right]$$

where i indexes the individual and j the choice or outcome. Selection is based on $s_i = j$. For convenience purposes, we drop the individual subscript for the earning equation below. When the earnings equation is $y_j = X\beta_j + e_j$, the implied regression equation with the selection bias correction term is

$$y_j = X\beta_j + (\rho_j\sigma_j)\lambda_j + \eta_j$$

Table 5.2. Mean Characteristics (Male).

	Migrants	IRCA	Regular IRCA	SAW	Non-IRCA Legalized	Family Sponsored	Employer Sponsored	Not Legalized	Non-Migrants
US hourly wage[a]	4.817	4.912	5.129	4.684	4.873	4.773	5.071	4.738	–
	(4.791)	(2.849)	(2.916)	(2.762)	(2.889)	(2.345)	(3.771)	(6.010)	
Age†	35.557	35.579	37.087	33.992	35.674	34.723	37.574	35.524	40.590
	(9.676)	(8.801)	(8.479)	(8.865)	(9.922)	(10.210)	(9.129)	(10.256)	(10.578)
Age	32.132	35.122	36.628	33.536	34.000	32.968	36.064	29.634	–
	(9.003)	(8.717)	(8.338)	(8.837)	(9.942)	(9.760)	(10.085)	(8.310)	
Potential experience†	22.987	23.275	24.620	21.858	21.660	20.745	23.489	22.962	26.801
	(11.358)	(10.617)	(10.180)	(10.893)	(11.385)	(11.743)	(10.517)	(11.876)	(12.593)
Potential experience	19.574	22.827	24.179	21.403	19.986	18.989	21.979	17.087	–
	(10.462)	(10.513)	(9.995)	(10.864)	(11.128)	(11.133)	(10.965)	(9.630)	
Education†	6.570	6.304	6.467	6.133	8.014	7.979	8.085	6.563	7.789
	(3.524)	(3.543)	(3.699)	(3.367)	(3.523)	(3.398)	(3.798)	(3.464)	(4.667)
Education	6.558	6.295	6.449	6.133	8.014	7.979	8.085	6.547	–
	(3.496)	(3.494)	(3.608)	(3.367)	(3.523)	(3.398)	(3.798)	(3.446)	
Surveyed in US	0.193	0.286	0.377	0.189	0.305	0.309	0.298	0.107	–
	(0.394)	(0.452)	(0.485)	(0.392)	(0.462)	(0.464)	(0.462)	(0.309)	
Total months in US	84.098	123.426	153.116	92.169	147.411	140.851	160.532	45.723	–
	(79.535)	(80.139)	(83.446)	(62.930)	(103.842)	(106.124)	(98.922)	(49.338)	
Number of migration in Mexico†	0.656	0.938	0.573	1.322	0.355	0.298	0.468	0.489	0.672
	(1.739)	(2.507)	(1.235)	(3.321)	(0.718)	(0.685)	(0.776)	(0.922)	(1.143)
US northeast region	0.067	0.053	0.045	0.061	0.085	0.117	0.021	0.076	–
	(0.251)	(0.224)	(0.207)	(0.240)	(0.280)	(0.323)	(0.146)	(0.265)	
US western region	0.583	0.686	0.662	0.711	0.567	0.543	0.617	0.508	–
	(0.493)	(0.464)	(0.474)	(0.454)	(0.497)	(0.501)	(0.491)	(0.500)	
US mid-west region	0.093	0.064	0.116	0.008	0.099	0.074	0.149	0.114	–
	(0.291)	(0.244)	(0.321)	(0.091)	(0.300)	(0.264)	(0.360)	(0.318)	
US southern region	0.257	0.198	0.177	0.219	0.248	0.266	0.213	0.302	–
	(0.437)	(0.398)	(0.382)	(0.414)	(0.434)	(0.444)	(0.414)	(0.459)	
Number of observation	1,870	739	379	360	141	94	47	990	1,827

Note: Variables with † are measured when the survey was done and without † are measured when the last migration occurred.
Source: Authors' calculations using MMP93.
[a]US hourly wage when last migrated is deflated using CPI (1982–1984 = 100). Standard deviations are reported in parentheses.

Table 5.3. Mean Characteristics (Female).

	Migrants	IRCA	Regular IRCA	SAW	Non-IRCA Legalized	Family Sponsored	Employer Sponsored	Not Legalized	Non-Migrants
US hourly wage[a]	3.914	3.792	3.736	3.887	4.158	4.255	3.398	3.905	–
	(2.985)	(1.553)	(1.734)	(1.206)	(4.198)	(4.438)	(1.128)	(3.147)	
Age†	35.583	34.521	35.915	32.171	38.170	38.745	33.667	35.359	38.323
	(9.323)	(8.105)	(7.695)	(8.344)	(10.068)	(10.489)	(3.830)	(9.618)	(10.275)
Age	32.006	34.383	35.831	31.943	36.396	36.957	32.000	29.275	–
	(9.098)	(8.023)	(7.632)	(8.182)	(9.576)	(9.902)	(5.060)	(8.628)	
Potential experience†	22.280	21.596	22.729	19.686	23.906	24.213	21.500	22.150	24.783
	(11.021)	(9.513)	(9.242)	(9.791)	(12.271)	(12.852)	(6.221)	(11.403)	(12.074)
Potential experience	18.717	21.457	22.644	19.457	22.132	22.426	19.833	16.090	–
	(10.333)	(9.402)	(9.199)	(9.534)	(11.327)	(11.804)	(6.735)	(9.833)	
Education†	7.303	6.926	7.186	6.486	8.264	8.532	6.167	7.210	7.540
	(3.664)	(3.517)	(3.655)	(3.275)	(3.722)	(3.775)	(2.639)	(3.696)	(4.297)
Education	7.290	6.926	7.186	6.486	8.264	8.532	6.167	7.186	–
	(3.645)	(3.517)	(3.655)	(3.275)	(3.722)	(3.775)	(2.639)	(3.660)	
Surveyed in US	0.318	0.574	0.610	0.514	0.321	0.362	0	0.174	–
	(0.467)	(0.497)	(0.492)	(0.507)	(0.471)	(0.486)	(0.000)	(0.380)	
Total months in US	86.088	130.165	158.466	82.457	116.604	116.809	115.000	51.593	–
	(76.523)	(74.630)	(73.240)	(48.490)	(96.545)	(101.249)	(51.217)	(49.058)	
Number of migration in Mexico†	0.519	0.489	0.390	0.657	0.415	0.404	0.500	0.569	0.547
	(0.929)	(1.075)	(0.743)	(1.474)	(0.663)	(0.648)	(0.837)	(0.915)	(0.874)
US northeast region	0.048	0	0	0	0.132	0.149	0	0.048	–
	(0.214)	(0.000)	(0.000)	(0.000)	(0.342)	(0.360)	(0.000)	(0.214)	
US western region	0.662	0.723	0.729	0.714	0.660	0.617	1	0.629	–
	(0.474)	(0.450)	(0.448)	(0.458)	(0.478)	(0.491)	(0.000)	(0.485)	
US mid-west region	0.057	0.052	0.085	0	0.019	0.021	0	0.072	–
	(0.233)	(0.226)	(0.281)	(0.000)	(0.137)	(0.146)	(0.000)	(0.259)	
US southern region	0.232	0.223	0.186	0.286	0.189	0.213	0	0.251	–
	(0.423)	(0.419)	(0.393)	(0.458)	(0.395)	(0.414)	(0.000)	(0.435)	
Number of observation	314	94	59	35	53	47	6	167	1,734

Note: Variables with † are measured when the survey was done and without † are measured when the last migration occurred.

Source: Author's calculations using MMP93.

[a] US hourly wage when last migrated is deflated using CPI (1982–1984 = 100). Standard deviations are reported in parentheses.

where $\lambda_j = \phi[\Phi^{-1}(P_j)]/P_j$, ϕ and Φ the standard normal probability density function and cumulative distribution function, respectively; ρ_j the correlation coefficient between e_j and $\Phi^{-1}(P_j)$ and σ_j the standard deviation of e_j.

4.2.1. Multinomial Logit Results

The sample is divided into six groups: two groups legalized through IRCA (regular IRCA and SAW/IRCA), two groups legalized through procedures other than IRCA (i.e., sponsored by a family member or employer), those never legalized and non-migrants.[9] We choose a parsimonious specification: the right-hand side includes age and its square in hundreds, years of education, a dummy variable for male and the total number of migrations within Mexico.[10]

Table 6 shows our estimation of the marginal effects of the multinomial logit model. The reference group is non-migrants whose coefficients are restricted to zero for identification purposes. The chi-squared statistics for

Table 6. Marginal Effects from Multinomial Logit (Both Sexes).

	Regular IRCA	SAW	Family Sponsored	Employer Sponsored	Not Legalized	Non-Migrants
Constant	−0.404***	−0.044	−0.021	−0.066***	0.235***	0.300***
	(0.050)	(0.034)	(0.028)	(0.018)	(0.724)	(0.095)
Age†	0.017***	0.000	−0.002	0.002*	−0.015***	−0.001
	(0.003)	(0.002)	(0.001)	(0.001)	(0.004)	(0.005)
Age squared in hundreds†	−0.024***	−0.004*	0.003	−0.002*	0.011**	0.017***
	(0.003)	(0.002)	(0.002)	(0.001)	(0.005)	(0.006)
Education†	−0.005***	−0.006***	0.001**	0.000	−0.013***	0.022***
	(0.001)	(0.001)	(0.001)	(0.001)	(0.001)	(0.002)
Number of migration in Mexico†	−0.002	0.011***	−0.009***	−0.001	−0.011*	0.012*
	(0.003)	(0.002)	(0.003)	(0.001)	(0.006)	(0.007)
Male	0.086***	0.079***	0.003	0.012***	0.226***	−0.406***
	(0.008)	(0.006)	(0.004)	(0.003)	(0.012)	(0.015)
Actual number	438	395	141	53	1,157	3,561
Predicted number	0	30	0	0	622	5,093

Note: Chi-squared statistics is 1,407.864***. The chi-squared statistic is $2(\log L - \log L_0)$, where $\log L$ and $\log L_0$ are unconstrained log-likelihood and the log-likelihood when all coefficients are restricted to zero except for constant; the values of $\log L$ and $\log L_0$ are −5,809.272 and −6,513.204. Variables with † are measured when the survey was done, without † are measured when the last migration occurred.
Source: Authors' calculations using MMP93.
* Indicate significance at 10%.
** Indicate significance at 5%
*** Indicate significance at 1%.

testing goodness of fit is 1,407.864, which is significant at 1% level.[11] Using the estimated coefficients of the multinomial logit model, marginal effects are calculated. As the mean characteristics in Table 5 suggested, education increases the probability of staying in Mexico (non-migrants) and migration through family sponsorship, while decreasing the probability of having been legalized through IRCA (both regular and SAW) and never being legalized.

Gender also plays a role in the outcome of migration status: Males are more likely to migrate as shown by positive significant marginal effects for all migrant groups except for family-sponsored migrants, and it has a negative significant marginal effect for non-migrants. Agricultural workers may migrate both inside and across the Mexican border as shown by its positive and significant marginal effect. On the other hand, those who legalized through family sponsorship have negative significant marginal effects, hence the more one migrated inside Mexico, and the less likely they become legalized via family sponsorship.

4.2.2. Earnings Estimations

Using the selection bias correction model described above, we estimate US earnings equations for Mexican migrants during their last migration. Again, the specification for the earnings equation is parsimonious as was the specification of multinomial logit model discussed above: The independent variables are potential experience, when last migrated and its square in hundreds, education when last migrated, a dummy variable for male, dummy variables capturing the US destination of migrants (West, Mid-West and South) and the total number of months of experience in the US, in addition to a control variable on whether the survey was conducted in the US or Mexico.[12]

Tables 7 and 8 report estimates of earnings equations using Ordinary Least Squares (OLS) and a selection bias correction method. Table 7 shows that the usual human capital related variables (education and variables of potential experience) do not have a significant impact on earnings except for the education variable for the regular IRCA.[13] Considering that Mexican migrants may take low-skilled jobs in the US where their human capital may not be valued much, this may not be surprising. Even the duration of migration does not substantially affect wage determination, as the variable "total months in the US" is marginally significant in the earnings equation of those legalized via SAW and the non-legalized. Mexican migrants may be slow in assimilating into US labor market. The other finding is that there is a male earnings premium for all migration groups except for those who legalized via employer sponsorship, though its coefficient is virtually the

Table 7.   Earnings Equations for Categories of Mexican Immigrants to
US (OLS, Both Sexes).

	Regular IRCA	SAW	Family Sponsored	Employer Sponsored	Not Legalized
Constant	1.210***	1.384***	1.507***	1.411	1.177***
	(0.220)	(0.186)	(0.311)	(0.901)	(0.115)
Potential experience	0.008	0.002	−0.005	0.028	−0.003
	(0.011)	(0.009)	(0.017)	(0.040)	(0.006)
Potential experience squared in	−0.019	−0.017	0.002	−0.063	−0.009
hundreds	(0.018)	(0.016)	(0.031)	(0.078)	(0.014)
Education	0.014*	0.006	−0.006	−0.027	−0.006
	(0.009)	(0.009)	(0.018)	(0.030)	(0.006)
Male	0.321***	0.160**	0.202*	0.402	0.207***
	(0.071)	(0.072)	(0.103)	(0.313)	(0.047)
US western region	−0.252**	−0.193**	−0.166	−0.125	0.045
	(0.125)	(0.095)	(0.142)	(0.698)	(0.066)
US mid-west region	−0.314**	−0.090	−0.368	0.022	0.181**
	(0.141)	(0.244)	(0.225)	(0.714)	(0.080)
US southern region	−0.275**	−0.090	0.036	0.054	0.160**
	(0.134)	(0.101)	(0.163)	(0.730)	(0.069)
Surveyed in US	0.107**	0.086	−0.074	−0.072	−0.089
	(0.052)	(0.053)	(0.101)	(0.282)	(0.055)
Total months in US	0.000	0.001*	0.000	−0.002	0.001**
	(0.000)	(0.000)	(0.001)	(0.002)	(0.000)
F-statistics	4.01***	3.93***	1.56	1.29	5.56***
Adjusted R^2	0.058	0.063	0.035	0.047	0.034
Number of observations	438	395	141	53	1,157

Source: Authors' calculations using MMP93.
* Indicate significance at 10%.
** Indicate significance at 5%
*** Indicate significance at 1%.

same magnitude as other groups. This may be due to the small sample size
of the employer-sponsored migrant group.

Table 8 includes the selection bias correction term constructed following
Lee (1983). Only two groups have significant estimates for the selection bias
correction term: SAW and not legalized migrants. Note that the second-step
coefficient of the selection bias term is ($\rho_j\sigma_j$), hence the sign is determined by
the correlation coefficient between e_j (error term in earnings equation) and
$\Phi^{-1}(P_j)$ related to the error term in choice equation. Both groups show
positive selection, which means that the unobserved characteristics which
determine the choice of migration status increase their earnings. The human
capital related variables (education and potential experience) do not show

Table 8. Earnings Equations for Categories of Mexican Immigrants to US (Multinomial Logit Selection Bias Correction Model, Both Sexes).

	Regular IRCA	SAW	Family Sponsored	Employer Sponsored	Not Legalized
Constant	1.911***	1.159***	2.290**	−5.434	0.355*
	(0.668)	(0.225)	(1.070)	(6.412)	(0.196)
Potential experience	−0.004	0.001	−0.000	0.069	−0.011*
	(0.015)	(0.009)	(0.018)	(0.078)	(0.006)
Potential experience squared	0.008	−0.021	−0.002	−0.162	−0.007
in hundreds	(0.030)	(0.016)	(0.030)	(0.163)	(0.013)
Education	0.023**	−0.003	−0.009	−0.010	−0.027***
	(0.011)	(0.010)	(0.018)	(0.054)	(0.007)
Male	0.163	0.259***	0.182*	1.421	0.601***
	(0.159)	(0.091)	(0.102)	(1.079)	(0.090)
US western region	−0.247**	−0.182*	−0.152	−0.334	0.009
	(0.124)	(0.094)	(0.137)	(1.221)	(0.065)
US mid-west region	−0.305**	−0.073	−0.354	−0.221	0.153*
	(0.139)	(0.240)	(0.217)	(1.253)	(0.078)
US southern region	−0.272**	−0.080	0.044	−0.201	0.138**
	(0.132)	(0.099)	(0.157)	(1.282)	(0.068)
Surveyed in US	0.106**	0.094*	−0.082	−0.117	−0.028
	(0.051)	(0.052)	(0.097)	(0.490)	(0.055)
Total months in US	0.000	0.001	−0.000	−0.002	0.001***
	(0.000)	(0.000)	(0.001)	(0.003)	(0.000)
Selection bias correction term	−0.288	0.126*	−0.353	2.192	0.605***
	(0.260)	(0.073)	(0.462)	(1.990)	(0.118)
F-statistics	3.73***	3.85***	1.45	1.63	7.73***
Adjusted R^2	0.059	0.067	0.031	0.108	0.055
Number of observations	438	395	141	53	1,157

Source: Authors' calculations using MMP93.
* Indicate significance at 10%.
** Indicate significance at 5%
*** Indicate significance at 1%.

the typical impact on earnings except for the education variable for regular IRCA. For the non-legalized group, education is negatively contributing to earnings. The total months in the US increases wages of not legalized workers; their coefficient is positive and significant. There is still a male earnings premium for SAW and non-legalized migrants.

4.2.3. Earnings Premium of Legalization
We studied the determination of migration legalization categories and the earnings equations of each category using a multinomial logit selection

Table 9. Earnings Equations (OLS and Probit Selection Bias Correction Model).

	OLS			Selection Bias Correction Model		
	Both sexes	Male	Female	Both sexes	Male	Female
Constant	1.227***	1.383***	1.676***	0.786***	1.340***	0.331
	(0.081)	(0.079)	(0.228)	(0.120)	(0.078)	(0.640)
Potential experience	−0.000	0.002	−0.011	−0.004	−0.001	−0.014
	(0.004)	(0.005)	(0.013)	(0.004)	(0.005)	(0.012)
Potential experience	−0.013	−0.017*	0.001	−0.022**	−0.024***	−0.020
squared in hundreds	(0.008)	(0.009)	(0.026)	(0.009)	(0.009)	(0.026)
Education	−0.002	−0.001	−0.010	−0.023***	−0.021***	−0.030**
	(0.004)	(0.004)	(0.011)	(0.006)	(0.006)	(0.013)
Male	0.219***			0.565***		
	(0.033)			(0.075)		
US western region	−0.057	−0.033	−0.315*	−0.071	−0.045	−0.357**
	(0.047)	(0.049)	(0.160)	(0.047)	(0.048)	(0.156)
US mid-west region	0.023	0.057	−0.337	0.011	0.047	−0.374*
	(0.058)	(0.060)	(0.213)	(0.058)	(0.060)	(0.207)
US southern region	0.040	0.072	−0.286*	0.027	0.059	−0.304*
	(0.049)	(0.052)	(0.170)	(0.049)	(0.051)	(0.165)
Surveyed in US	0.012	0.040	−0.119	0.036	0.060*	−0.071
	(0.030)	(0.033)	(0.079)	(0.030)	(0.033)	(0.080)
Total months in US	0.345×10^{-3}*	0.000	0.001*	0.411×10^{-3}**	0.000	0.001**
	(0.194×10^{-3})	(0.000)	(0.0006)	(0.191×10^{-3})	(0.000)	(0.0005)
Regular IRCA	0.130***	0.137***	0.088	0.158***	0.164***	0.120
	(0.035)	(0.037)	(0.107)	(0.035)	(0.037)	(0.104)
SAW	0.094***	0.088***	0.204*	0.140***	0.131***	0.259**
	(0.032)	(0.033)	(0.113)	(0.033)	(0.034)	(0.113)
Family sponsored	0.070	0.060	0.077	0.080	0.077	0.080
	(0.050)	(0.058)	(0.107)	(0.049)	(0.058)	(0.103)
Employer sponsored	0.019	0.017	−0.040	0.039	0.031	0.031
	(0.076)	(0.080)	(0.246)	(0.075)	(0.078)	(0.243)
Selection bias correction				0.451***	0.380***	1.067**
term				(0.087)	(0.078)	(0.418)
F-statistics	8.44***	4.77***	1.28	9.91***	6.15***	1.66*
Adjusted R^2	0.042	0.024	0.011	0.054	0.035	0.027
Number of observations	2,184	1,870	314	2,184	1,870	314

Source: Authors' calculations using MMP93.
* Indicate significance at 10%.
** Indicate significance at 5%
*** Indicate significance at 1%.

model. One question not immediately answered using this procedure is what earnings' benefit can be obtained via legalization. In this section, as a summary, we estimate earnings equations using a pooled sample with dummy variables capturing legalization categories. The reference group is those not legalized. We also estimate the earnings equation using the standard Heckman's two-step method for correcting the migration decision. The estimation is done for the whole sample, and men and women separately. The estimation results are in Table 9.[14]

Table 9 shows that coefficients of selection bias correction terms in all three samples (whole, men and women) are all positive and significant, meaning positive selection is occurring in the migration decision and wage determination. The variables related to human capital do not positively contribute to wage determination. Contrary to human capital theory, the highly educated and the more experienced would have lower wages as the negative coefficients of education and of potential experience square indicate. The US experience measured in terms of total months in the US increases wages.

The benefit of legalization, particularly via IRCA, is demonstrated by the wage premium of those legalized over the wages of non-legalized workers. The coefficients of category variables of regular IRCA and SAW are positive and significant at the 1% level. Overall, those legalized via regular IRCA have enjoyed a higher wage premium over non-legalized than those legalized via SAW. However, in the case of women, only the premium of SAW is significant, and its magnitude is larger than that of the regular IRCA. It is interesting to note that other two legalized migrant categories, family sponsored and employer sponsored do not provide significant wage premiums. In short, those legalized via IRCA, whether it is regular or SAW, have enjoyed wage premium over the non-legalized.

5. CONCLUSION

Unlike capital mobility across borders, there are multifaceted dimensions to labor mobility. Migration is causing challenges to both source and recipient countries. There is great inequality in the world and as barriers to mobility come down, it is very likely that we have begun another period of great international migration as people from low-income countries migrate to richer countries. However, developed countries face big social and economic problems when they perceive there are "too" many migrants. Hence, many countries have imposed various rules and regulations related to migration. These government-imposed barriers create the problem of illegal/undocumented/unregulated migrants in recipient countries. Within the recipient countries there is great debate – the recognition in part of the lack of agreement on whether immigration is good or bad – on how to deal with illegal migrants, from deportation to amnesty. This paper deals with the effect of amnesty on the size and allocation of illegal migrants in the recipient country.

The debate over immigration amnesties has many dimensions. We focus on two questions often addressed in these debates: Will granting amnesty induce further migrations, especially illegal migrations? How much does amnesty affect migrants' welfare? Both in our theoretical and empirical work a clear unambiguous answer is difficult to find. An amnesty will generally increase the flow of both illegal and legal migrants into the recipient country, increasing labor supply to all sectors of the economy, and our model tells us how the labor market adjusts to the amnesty and changes in size and allocation of illegal migrants. The model provides some insight on allocation of different migrant groups in labor market.

For the migration ties between the US and Mexico the great amnesty "experiment" to the present day was the IRCA of 1986. We show which groups moved, and who did better and who did worse, among the Mexican migrants. Those migrants regularized under the IRCA – the regular IRCA – gained the most, followed by the participants in the SAW program. Those sponsored by family or employers, ceteris paribus, did not gain, relative to those who did not migrate.

NOTES

1. On March 1, 2003, the service/benefit functions of the US Immigration and Naturalization Service (INS) transitioned into the Department of Homeland Security as the US Citizenship and Immigration Services (USCIS).
2. The date of eligibility for citizenship and the method of data collection for our sample provide for only a few cases of those legalized under IRCA obtaining citizenship.
3. Epstein and Weiss (2001): "What matters in some sense is not whether these effects actually exist, but since immigration is limited and countries set up controls to keep illegals out, at the very least government officials believe there is some potential harm from allowing free migration."
4. These models, and indeed all of the discussion of illegal migration and amnesties, start from the presumption of a second best world and look not at how to get to the first best, but at alternative second best policies. The related international trade literature frequently starts its discussions with what the first best world would look like. In the standard models with international goods mobility but not international factor mobility the first best policy is free trade; when there is international factor mobility but not international goods mobility the first best policy is unrestricted factor mobility (Mundell, 1957). When there is some distortion that puts us in a second best world, such as an economy-wide or sector-specific minimum wage, the initial question in this literature is what policies can be implemented to

achieve a first best solution (Basu, 1998). The first best solution becomes a reference point from which to measure the costs and success of other policies.

5. In the extreme case of a completely inelastic demand for documents/green cards in the formal (informal) sector, where $F_{LL} = 0$ ($I_{LL} = 0$), all of the document increase goes into the informal (formal) sector.

6. Unfortunately, the year of this last job in Mexico is not reported, hence we do not study wages of non-migrants. Obviously, migrants – except for those legalized through family sponsorship – should have wage information in the US. However, a substantial portion of migrants have not reported their wage information. Since we cannot treat those who did not report the wage information as non-participants in the labor market, we simply ignore them and focus on those who reported wage information.

7. In this sense, it seems not to be desirable to aggregate regular IRCA and SAW. Also those legalized through non-IRCA procedures show different wage rates.

8. The treatment of the multinomial logit is based on Greene (2002). The estimation is done using Limdep, Version 8.

9. Owing to sample size considerations, the model is estimated using the whole sample; we do not separately consider the male and female samples.

10. The total number of migrations in Mexico might be endogenous. Owing to data limitations, we cannot fully model this potential endogeneity. For a robustness check, we estimated the same model without this variable; the results are not changed substantially.

11. The chi-squared statistic is $2(\log L - \log L_0)$, where $\log L$ and $\log L_0$ are unconstrained log-likelihood and the log-likelihood when all coefficients are restricted to zero except for the constant. The values of $\log L$ and $\log L_0$ are -5809.272 and -6513.204.

12. The information on wage of the last migration is assumed to be the wage at the end of the migration. Hence, age and education are adjusted using the duration of the migration. If they are still in the US, then age and education are equal to current age and education level. The wages are adjusted using CPI (1982–1984 = 100). The reference region is the northeast.

13. When the variable "age" is used instead of "potential experience," still those variables related to human capital do not affect the wage determination substantially as human capital theory predicts.

14. The specification of the probit model used for the choice of migration is the same as the multinominal logit model in Table 6. Roughly speaking (averaging the results for the various categories of migrants) the results are basically confirm what we have found in the multinominal logit model. The results of the probit model for the migration decision as the first step of Heckman's two-step model are available from the authors.

REFERENCES

Barreto, M., Ramírez, R., & Woods, N. (2005). Are naturalized voters driving the California Latino electorate? Measuring the impact of IRCA citizens on Latino voting. *Social Science Quarterly, 86,* 792–811.

Basu, K. (1998). *Analytical development economics: The less developed economy revisited*. Delhi: OUP.

Bucci, G. A., & Tenorio, R. (1997). Immigrant-native wage differentials and immigration reform. *Review of Development Economics, 1*(3), 305.

Chau, N. H. (2001). Strategic amnesty and credible immigration reform. *Journal of Labor Economics, 19*(3), 604–634.

Chau, N. H. (2003). Concessional amnesty and the politics of immigration reforms. *Economics & Politics, 15*(2), 193–224.

Chiquiar, D., & Hanson, G. H. (2002). *International migration, self-selection, and the distribution of wages: Evidence from Mexico and the United States*. NBER Working Paper no. 9242. National Bureau of Economic Research, Inc.

Chiswick, B. R. (1988). Illegal immigration and immigration control. *Journal of Economic Perspectives, 2*(3), 101–115. In: F. L. Rivera-Batiz, S. L. Sechzer & I. N. Gang (Eds), *U.S. immigration policy reform in the 1980s*. New York: Praeger.

Chiswick, B. R., & Miller, P. W. (1999). Language skills and earnings among legalized aliens. *Journal of Population Economics, 12*(1), 63–89.

Dutta, B., Gang, I. N., & Gangopadhyay, S. (1989). Subsidy policies with capital accumulation: Maintaining employment levels. *Journal of Population Economics, 2*(4), 301–318.

Epstein, G. S. (2003). Labor market interactions between legal and illegal immigrants. *Review of Development Economics, 7*(1), 30–43.

Epstein, G. S., & Hillman, A. L. (2000). *Social harmony at the boundaries of the welfare state: Immigration and social transfers*. IZA Discussion Paper no. 168.

Epstein, G. S., & Weiss, A. (2001). *A theory of immigration amnesties*. IZA Discussion Paper no. 302.

Gang, I. N., & Gangapadhyay, S. (1985). A note on optimal policies in dual economies. *Quarterly Journal of Economics, 100*(5), 1067–1071.

Gang, I. N., & Gangapadhyay, S. (1987a). Employment, output and the choice of techniques: Trade-offs revisited. *Journal of Development Economics, 25*, 321–327.

Gang, I. N., & Gangapadhyay, S. (1987b). Optimal policies in a dual economy with open unemployment and surplus labour. *Oxford Economic Papers, 39*, 378–387.

Gang, I. N., & Gangapadhyay, S. (1990). A model of the informal sector in development (with S. Gangopadhyay). *Journal of Economic Studies, 17*, 19–31.

Gang, I. N., & Tower, E. (1990). Allocating jobs under a minimum wage: Queues vs. lotteries. *The Economic Record, 66*(194), 186–194.

Gonzalez-Baker, S. (1997). The 'amnesty' aftermath: Current policy issues stemming from the legalization programs of the 1986 Immigration Reform and Control Act. *International Migration Review, 31*(1), 5–27.

Greene, W. H. (2002). *Econometric analysis* (5th ed.). Upper Saddle River, NJ: Prentice-Hall.

Harris, J. R., & Todaro, M. P. (1970). Migration, unemployment & development: A two-sector analysis. *American Economic Review, 60*(1), 126–142.

Hillman, A. L., & Weiss, A. (1999). A theory of permissible illegal immigration. *European Journal of Political Economy, 15*(4), 585–604.

Hoefer, M. D. (1991). Background of U.S. immigration policy reform. In: F. L. Rivera-Batiz, S. L. Sechzer & I. N. Gang (Eds), *U.S. immigration policy reform in the 1980s: A preliminary assessment*. New York: Praeger.

Karlson, S. H., & Katz, E. (2003). A positive theory of immigration amnesties. *Economics Letters, 78*(2), 231–239.

Kossoudji, S. A., & Cobb-Clark, D. A. (2000). IRCA's impact on the occupational concentration and mobility of newly-legalized Mexican men. *Journal of Population Economics, 13*(1), 81–98.

Kossoudji, S. A., & Cobb-Clark, D. A. (2002). Coming out of the shadows: Learning about legal status and wages from the legalized population. *Journal of Labor Economics, 20*(3), 598–628.

Lee, L. F. (1983). Generalized econometric models with selectivity. *Econometrica, 51*(2), 507–512.

Massey, D. S. (1987). Do undocumented migrants earn lower wages than legal immigrants? New evidence from Mexico. *International Migration Review, 21*(2), 236–274.

Massey, D. S., Alarcón, R., Durand, J., & Gonzáles, H. (1987). *Return to Azlan: The social process of international migration from Western Mexico.* Berkley: University of California Press.

Massey, D. S., Goldring, L., & Durand, J. (1994). Continuities in transnational migration: An analysis of nineteen Mexican communities. *American Journal of Sociology, 99*, 1492–1533.

Massey, D. S., & Zeteno, R. (2000). A validation of the ethnosurvey: The case of Mexico–U.S. migration. *International Migration Review, 34*, 766–793.

Mundell, R. A. (1957). International trade and factor mobility. *American Economic Review, 47*, 321–335.

Nelson, D. R., & Xu, Y. (2001). An approach to the positive political economy of illegal migration. http://www.tulane.edu/~dnelson/PAPERS/pemig.pdf. Accessed November 30, 2005.

Orrenius, P. M., & Zavodny, M. (2003). Do amnesty programs reduce undocumented immigration? Evidence from IRCA. *Demography, 40*(3), 437–450.

Phillips, J. A., & Massey, D. S. (1999). The new labor market: Immigrants and wages after IRCA. *Demography, 36*(2), 233–246.

Rivera-Batiz, F. L. (1991). Introduction. In: F. L. Rivera-Batiz, S. L. Sechzer & I. N. Gang (Eds), *U.S. immigration policy reform in the 1980s: A preliminary assessment.* New York: Praeger.

Rivera-Batiz, F. L. (1999). Undocumented workers in the labor market: An analysis of the earnings of legal and illegal Mexican immigrants in the United States. *Journal of Population Economics, 12*(1), 91–116.

Rytina, N. (2002). IRCA legalization effects: Lawful permanent residence and naturalization through 2001. Office of Policy and Planning Statistics Division U.S. Immigration and Naturalization Service. Paper presented at The Effects of Immigrant Legalization Programs on the United States: Scientific evidence on immigrant adaptation and impacts on U.S. economy and society, The Cloister, Mary Woodward Lasker Center, NIH Main Campus, October 25.

WELFARE REFORM AND IMMIGRANTS: DOES THE FIVE-YEAR BAN MATTER?

Robert Kaestner and Neeraj Kaushal

ABSTRACT

Welfare reform banned newly arrived immigrants who came to the US after 1996 from receiving federally funded benefits for five years. One assessment of the success of the five-year ban is the effect it has on behaviors that determine economic success and the likelihood of becoming a public charge. In this chapter, we investigate the effect of the five-year ban on the employment, hours of work, and wages of low-income women. Our results indicate that welfare reform in general caused a significant increase in the employment of low-educated, unmarried mothers regardless of citizenship. Among non-citizens, welfare reform was associated with a 10 percentage point (26%) increase in employment, a two-hour (15%) increase in hours worked per week, and a 10 percent decrease in wages. Surprisingly, we find little evidence that the five-year ban had any additional effect on the employment, hours of work, and wages of low-educated and unmarried, non-citizen mothers.

Immigration: Trends, Consequences and Prospects for the United States
Research in Labor Economics, Volume 27, 311–347
Copyright © 2008 by Elsevier Ltd.
ISSN: 0147-9121/doi:10.1016/S0147-9121(07)00008-8

Paper prepared for the conference on "Immigration: Trends, Consequences and Prospects for the United States," held at the University of Illinois at Chicago, September 9 and 10, 2005.

> The bosom of America is open to receive not only the opulent and respectable stranger, but the oppressed and persecuted of all nations and religion; whom we shall welcome to participate in all of our rights and privileges, if by *decency and propriety of conduct* (emphasis added) they appear to merit the enjoyment.[1]
>
> George Washington

From the very beginning, acceptance of immigrants in the US has been conditional – in George Washington's words – on the decency and propriety of their conduct. There has long been an expectation that immigrants will pull their own weight and contribute to the growth and prosperity of the country. Since the late 1800s, this belief has been enshrined in immigration law that restricts entry of individuals who are likely to become a public charge, and allows subsequent deportation of those who become a state liability (Edwards, 2001). In practice, most of the selection has been done at the time of admission, as there have been relatively few deportations, particularly in recent periods (Edwards, 2001).

The Personal Responsibility and Work Opportunity Reconciliation Act (PRWORA) of 1996 changed the scope of government policy vis-à-vis the immigrant public charge issue. No longer would the federal government rely on deportation to weed out immigrants that made it to the US, but who had become public charges; instead, all new immigrants would simply be barred from receiving federally funded cash assistance and in-kind benefits for five years. The logic underlying the law is straightforward – after surviving for five years without government benefits, and upon becoming eligible for citizenship, foreign-born persons will have established the "decency and propriety of conduct" that George Washington states makes them worthy of attaining the rights and privileges of all Americans.[2]

The special immigrant provisions in PRWORA made eligibility for federally funded benefits contingent on citizenship status, year of arrival and years lived in the US. Citizenship instead of legal permanent residence became the key to receiving benefits. PRWORA barred future legal immigrants (those arriving after passage of the law) from receiving cash assistance under the Temporary Assistance to Needy Families (TANF) program, as well as most other federal means-tested benefits (e.g., Food stamps, Medicaid), for five years, and left it up to states' discretion whether current legal (resident) immigrants should be eligible for such assistance.

Policy experts feared that PRWORA would trigger among states a "race to the bottom" in which immigrant eligibility for benefits would be restricted or eliminated in order to discourage in-migration among low-skilled immigrants (Huber & Espenshade, 1997; Borjas, 2001). However, states' responses to PRWORA proved these fears to be unwarranted. Virtually all states provided TANF and Medicaid benefits to pre-PRWORA immigrants, several provided Food Stamps and Supplemental Security Income (SSI) to them, and a number of states created substitute programs, using own funds, to provide benefits to post-PRWORA immigrants.[3] In addition, political backlash against the initial federal policy led to restoration of Food Stamps and SSI benefits to the elderly and children, and in 2002 Congress restored Food Stamps to all legal immigrants who have been in the country for at least five years. As Borjas (2001, p. 385) elegantly puts it, "the American people do not wish to bear the political, social and economic costs of removing immigrants already in the United States from the welfare rolls."

Two factors are likely explanations of the inclusion of the immigrant provisions in PRWORA.[4] First, there was a huge influx of immigrants prior to PRWORA. According to the Immigration and Naturalization Service (INS), approximately 13.5 million legal immigrants came to the US between 1981 and 1996, and perhaps as many as 5 million undocumented immigrants also entered the country during this period.[5] The only other period that witnessed such large influx of immigrants into the country was between 1900 and 1920. High immigration, and its potential adverse effects may have created some anti-immigrant sentiment that became manifest in the federal welfare–reform law. Second, recent waves of immigrants, especially those that arrived since the seventies, were less educated (relative to natives and more likely to use Aid to Families with Dependent Children (AFDC) and other welfare programs than were earlier immigrants (Borjas, 1995; Borjas & Hilton, 1996).[6] The increasingly greater use of public funds by a growing portion of the population naturally heightened long-standing concerns about immigrants becoming a public charge.

As with most aspects of immigrant policy, PRWORA received mixed support. Supporters of the law hoped that it would reduce inflows of low-skilled immigrants and curtail their dependence on the state. Opponents of the law viewed it as mean-spirited and inconsistent with the fact that non-citizens pay taxes, are eligible to be drafted, and are deserving of the full rights of other residents (Fix & Haskins, 2002). Thus, one measure of success of the law is the extent to which it increased economic independence of newly arrived immigrants – those specifically barred from receiving social welfare benefits. If the law caused a significant improvement in this outcome, it might be viewed as a win–win situation; supporters of the law would be happy with the growing independence of immigrants, and opponents of the law would have less to worry about because fewer newly arrived immigrants would need the benefits that they are seeking to reinstate. Moreover, a large behavioral response that significantly changes the extent of newly arrived immigrants' economic independence would provide evidence that a considerable portion of them did not exhibit the "decency and propriety of conduct" necessary to merit government assistance. It would demonstrate that personal action was a cause of their need for assistance. On the other hand, a small behavioral response to the law would be consistent with the cause of the public charge problem being factors external to the individual, and therefore, not incongruous with a level of "decency and propriety of conduct" that would merit government assistance.[7]

This chapter examines whether the five-year ban on receipt of federally funded, cash assistance caused changes in behaviors that determine economic independence. Specifically, we investigate the effect of the five-year ban on receipt of cash assistance (TANF) on employment and wages of newly arrived, low-skilled mothers. We also identify whether any effect of the law is long lasting – continues even after the ban on welfare receipt expires – or whether the effect is limited to the five-year period during which benefits are denied. We focus on low-skilled, immigrant mothers because it is a group with high rates of benefit use (e.g., cash assistance, food stamps, Medicaid), and as we describe below, allows for the implementation of a more compelling research design. Notably, only one previous study, Kaestner and Kaushal (2005) has examined the effect of the five-year ban separately from welfare reform in general even though it is the five-year ban that is unique to immigrants, as both citizens and non-citizens (legal residents) were affected by the more general provisions of welfare reform.[8] The five-year ban is also the most salient aspect of PRWORA in terms of the debate over who is worthy of entering and staying in the US. As noted above, the ban was a legal affirmation of the longstanding belief that immigrants should not come to the US expecting a handout.

IMMIGRANT USE OF MEANS-TESTED BENEFITS PRE- AND POST-WELFARE REFORM

Researchers reported sharp declines in the use of social welfare programs after the enactment of state and federal (PRWORA) welfare reform, with the decline being more pronounced in the case of immigrants than natives (Borjas, 2001; Fix & Passel, 1999, 2002; Lofstrom & Bean, 2002; Haider, Schoeni, Bao, & Danielson, 2004).[9] Surprisingly, most of these analyses were based on the entire population of immigrant and native households even though only a fraction of households are likely to use means-tested benefits.[10] For example, cash assistance and Medicaid are mainly used by low-income women and their children. Therefore, it would be logical to restrict the sample to low-income women and their children when investigating the prevalence of use of these benefits (Fix & Passel, 2002).

We return to this issue later in the chapter. We begin by providing descriptive statistics on trends in benefit use by populations most likely to be dependent on state welfare programs. We do not intend this to be a definitive assessment of the consequences of welfare reform on immigrant benefit use, but simply a way of showing some general trends that may or may not be consistent with a welfare–reform effect. Data are from the March Supplement of the Current Population Surveys (CPS).

Fig. 1 shows use of cash assistance (TANF) receipt by low-educated (education ≤ 12 years) women by nativity and marital status.[11] The sample

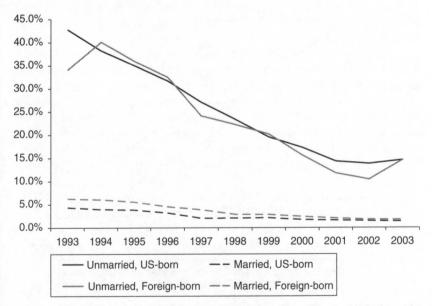

Fig. 1. Receipt of Cash Benefits (TANF) among Low-Educated Mothers, by Nativity and Marital Status.

is restricted to women who are the family reference person or spouse of reference person and live in families with children. These sample selection criteria reflect the fact that information on cash assistance is at the household level. So to avoid double counting households, we use only the reference person or spouse of reference person. As can be seen, cash assistance is used mostly by families of unmarried women, and rates of use are relatively similar for foreign- and native-born women's families. There is a steady decline in use beginning in 1994, which predates federal welfare reform. In 1997, there appears to be a slight increase in the rate of decrease of benefit use among unmarried women, with a somewhat sharper change for foreign-born women. This is consistent with a welfare–reform effect. However, as we noted above, other factors may also explain this pattern, for example, different effects of a growing economy on native- and foreign-born women. By 2003, rates of use of cash assistance are virtually identical for foreign- and native-born women.

Fig. 2 shows the use of cash assistance among low-educated, foreign-born women's families by marital status and years since arrival in the US. The decline in immigrant women's use of cash assistance occurred for both

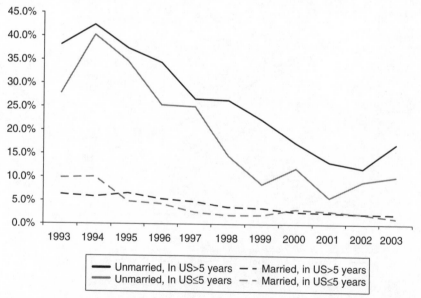

Fig. 2. Receipt of Cash Benefits (TANF) among Low-Educated Non-Citizen Mothers, by Marital Status and Length of Stay in the US.

new arrivals (in the US for ≤5years) and those who arrived earlier (in the US >5years) began prior to federal reform; and the rate of decline is roughly similar for the two groups. However, there does appear to be a significant difference in the rate of decrease of benefit use for new arrivals following welfare reform, which suggests that the five-year ban had some impact.

Fig. 3 shows use of Medicaid by low-educated women by nativity and marital status. Here, the sample includes all low-educated women who live in families with children since information about Medicaid is at the individual level. Unmarried women have higher rates of Medicaid coverage and there has been a decline in coverage between 1993 and 2003 for all groups. However, the decline in Medicaid coverage is noticeably greater for unmarried, foreign-born women than unmarried, native-born women. And again, there appears to be a sharper decline in coverage subsequent to welfare reform. These figures confirm the findings of Kaushal and Kaestner (2005), and others, that welfare reform significantly reduced Medicaid coverage among low-educated, foreign-born women, and that this decline was larger than for native-born women.[12] Fig. 4 shows Medicaid coverage

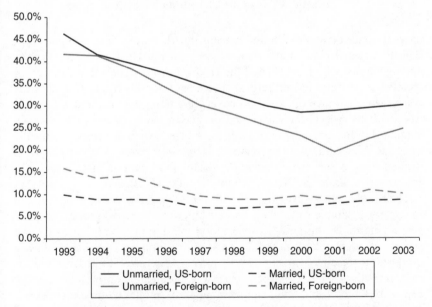

Fig. 3.   Medicaid Participation among Low-Educated Mothers, by Nativity and Marital Status.

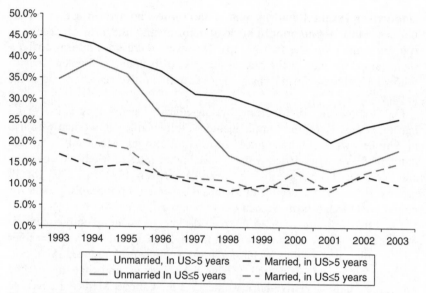

Fig. 4. Medicaid Participation among Low-Educated, Non-Citizen Mothers, by
Length of Stay in the US and Marital Status.

by years since arrival in US and marital status. Again, there seems to be a
slightly larger decline among new arrivals (in the US for ≤5 years) than
among women who have been in the US for longer periods, but the start of
the decline predates federal reform. The most notable aspect of Fig. 4 is the
convergence of rates of Medicaid coverage among married and unmarried
women. This reflects the substantial decline in coverage among unmarried
women due to reduced use of cash assistance, which is programmatically
linked to Medicaid, and the (relative) increase in coverage among married
women due to the expansion of Medicaid (and State Children's Health
Insurance Program (SCHIP)) income eligibility thresholds.

The next benefit we examine is Food stamps, and Fig. 5 shows the trend in
its use for a sample of families headed by a low-educated (education ≤12
years) person. In this case, it is clear that immigrant families' use of Food
stamps has declined more rapidly than native families' use. The decline in
food stamp receipt also appears to have begun prior to federal welfare
reform, with a slightly sharper decrease subsequent to the policy change.
Fig. 6 shows food stamp use among immigrant families by time since arrival
in the US, and there do not appear to be significant differences in food
stamp receipt by length of stay in the US.

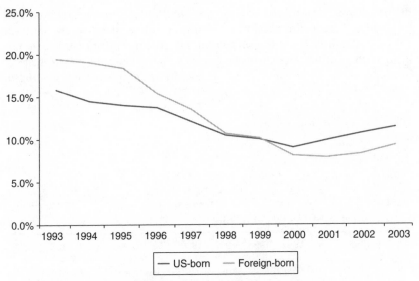

Fig. 5. Participation in Food Stamps Program, by Nativity (Samples Restricted to Families Headed by Low-Educated Persons).

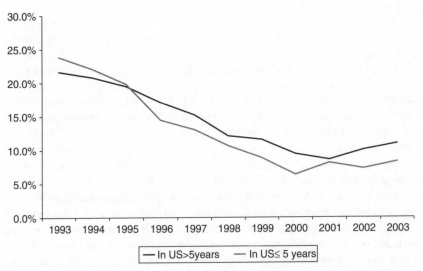

Fig. 6. Participation in Food Stamps Program among Non-Citizens, by Length of Stay in the US (Samples Restricted to Families Headed by Low-Educated Persons).

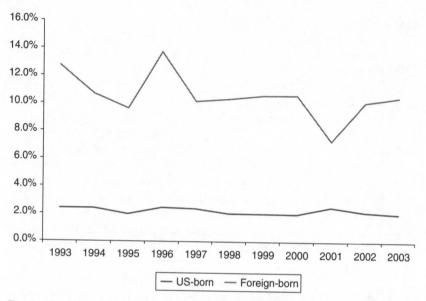

Fig. 7. Receipt of Supplemental Security Income among Low-Educated Elderly, by Nativity.

The last benefit we examine is SSI. In this case we restrict the sample to households headed by low-educated (education ≤ 12 years) persons aged 65 and over since this is the group for which receipt of benefits is primarily based on income and not disability. Fig. 7 shows SSI use by nativity, and the difference is marked. Foreign-born families headed by an elderly person have much higher rates of SSI receipt than native-born families; the difference is approximately 500 percent. There is no obvious trend in the data for either native- or foreign-born persons. We do not present analogous estimates to Fig. 7 by time since arrival because there are too few recent, elderly immigrants in the CPS to obtain reasonable precise estimates.

Figs. 1–7 suggest that immigrants' use of social welfare benefits was quite similar to natives' use of such benefits. Only in the case of SSI was there a marked difference in rates of use by nativity. These figures also indicate a general decline in use of most means-tested benefits for both US-born and foreign-born groups with the decline beginning before federal welfare reform, and accelerating slightly subsequent to federal reform. The pre- and post-welfare reform decline in benefit use tends to be somewhat larger for immigrants than natives. Among immigrants, there was some evidence that new arrivals were more affected by welfare reform.

The implications of Figs. 1–7 are interesting. First, the relatively similar effect of welfare reform on native- and foreign-born persons challenges the "chilling" hypothesis. If welfare reform increased the stigma or fears of deportation associated with use of means-tested benefits more among immigrants than natives, it would likely result in larger changes in benefit use among immigrants than natives. This is not consistently observed, nor is any observed difference very large.[13] Second, the absence of significantly larger changes in benefit use among newly arrived immigrants suggests that the five-year ban on federal benefits was not particularly effective, perhaps because state substitute programs may have effectively muted the effect of the ban. Finally, Fig. 7 illustrates the inherent limitation of relying solely on initial screening to prevent entry of likely public charges. Immigrant use of SSI is nearly five times that of native families. However, since recent arrivals make up a small percentage of SSI recipients (less than five percent of the total foreign-born SSI recipients), it is unlikely that the PRWORA ban will significantly reduce immigrant SSI use. It is long-time, foreign-born residents that account for most SSI use among immigrants. This either suggests that screening to prevent entry of likely public charges has not been effective, or opportunities in the US do not enable a substantial share of immigrants to become independent in old age even after having lived in the US for several years. While PRWORA may discourage some low-skilled persons to immigrate, which would reduce future SSI receipt, this incentive is not likely to be significant in terms of the disparities observed in Fig. 7.

Did Welfare Reform Cause the Change in Means-Tested Benefit Use?

The descriptive evidence presented in Figs. 1–7 shows a decline in the use of means-tested benefits pre- and post-welfare reform. The question is whether this was caused by welfare reform or other factors such as strong economic growth. In addition, there appears to be a slightly larger decline among immigrants than natives. This leads to the question of whether this was a larger immigrant response to welfare reform, say because of a "chilling" effect or the more severe changes in policy for newly arrived immigrants.

There is a relatively large literature examining whether welfare reform caused the decline in receipt of cash assistance, and it is generally agreed that part of the decline was due to welfare reform and part due to other factors (see Blank, 2002 for a review). The question of whether there was differential effect for immigrants is less well studied. Lofstrom and Bean (2002) and Haider et al. (2004) investigate whether changes in receipt of cash assistance pre- and post-welfare reform were larger for immigrants than for natives. Both studies find that macroeconomic conditions (e.g., unemployment rate) can explain almost all of the relative differences in benefit receipt. However, when Haider et al. (2004) limit the sample to non-citizen households, there is a larger pre- to post-welfare reform decline in use of cash assistance among immigrants than natives. These two analyses were based on samples consisting of all immigrant and native households even though only a small proportion of these populations, mostly low-income women and children, were affected by the policy changes of PRWORA. So it is likely that these analyses provided misleading inferences. To see why, consider the following example applied to receipt of cash assistance (TANF):

$$\left(\frac{\text{TANF}}{I}\right)^{I}_{jt} = \alpha^{I}_{jt}\left(\frac{\text{TANF}^{\text{P}}}{I^{\text{P}}}\right)_{jt} \tag{1}$$

Eq. (1) is the proportion of the total immigrant population that receives TANF benefits in state j and year t. It is equal to the proportion of TANF recipients among poor (P) immigrants in state j and year t times the proportion of immigrants who are poor in state j and year t (α^{I}_{jt}). Multiplying by the proportion of poor immigrants is appropriate because only poor are eligible for TANF. TANF use among poor immigrants depends on state-specific effects and welfare reform, which is shown in Eq. (2):

$$\left(\frac{\text{TANF}^{\text{P}}}{I^{\text{P}}}\right)_{jt} = \rho^{I}_{j} + \gamma_{I}\text{REFORM}_{t} + v_{jt} \tag{2}$$

The proportion of the total native population that receives TANF is

$$\left(\frac{\text{TANF}}{N}\right)^{N}_{jt} = \alpha^{N}_{jt}\left(\frac{\text{TANF}^{\text{P}}}{N^{\text{P}}}\right)_{jt} \tag{3}$$

Eq. (3) is analogous to Eq. (1), but it refers to natives, and Eq. (4) is analogous to Eq. (2), but for natives.

$$\left(\frac{\text{TANF}^{\text{P}}}{N^{\text{P}}}\right)_{jt} = \rho^{N}_{j} + \gamma_{N}\text{REFORM}_{t} + \mu_{jt} \tag{4}$$

Substituting Eq. (2) into (1) and Eq. (4) into (3) yields

$$\left(\frac{\text{TANF}}{I}\right)^I_{jt} = \alpha^I_{jt}\rho^I_j + \alpha^I_{jt}\gamma_I \text{REFORM}_t + \alpha^I_{jt}v_{jt} \tag{5}$$

$$\left(\frac{\text{TANF}}{N}\right)^N_{jt} = \alpha^N_{jt}\rho^N_j + \alpha^N_{jt}\gamma_N \text{REFORM}_t + \alpha^N_{jt}\mu_{jt} \tag{6}$$

Note that Eqs. (5) and (6) allow state effects to differ for poor and non-poor persons, and include an interaction between (proportion) poor and the policy variable (REFORM). Combining Eqs. (5) and (6) results in

$$\begin{aligned}
(\text{PrTANF})_{jt} = {} & \alpha^N_{jt}\rho^N_j + I(\alpha^N_{jt}\rho^N_j - \alpha^I_{jt}\rho^I_j) + \alpha^N_{jt}\gamma_N \text{REFORM}_t \\
& + (\alpha^N_{jt}\gamma_N - \alpha^I_{jt}\gamma_I)(I*\text{REFORM}_t) \\
& + \alpha^N_{jt}\mu_{jt} + I(\alpha^N_{jt}\mu_{jt} - \alpha^I_{jt}v_{jt})
\end{aligned} \tag{7}$$

In Eq. (7) PrTANF is the proportion of persons on TANF and the variable "I" is an indicator that the observation refers to immigrants. Neither Lofstrom and Bean (2002) or Haider et al. (2004) used the specification of Eq. (7). Instead they used something similar to the following:

$$\begin{aligned}
(\text{PrTANF})_{jt} = {} & \rho_j + I\pi + \gamma_N \text{REFORM}_t \\
& + (\gamma_N - \gamma_I)(I*\text{REFORM}_t) + \varepsilon_{jt}
\end{aligned} \tag{8}$$

Clearly, Eq. (8) differs from Eq. (7). The proportion of poor among natives and immigrants is not included in Eq. (8), and Eq. (8) restricts state effects to be the same for immigrants and natives and poor and non-poor. If other covariates were included in the model, it would also be necessary to allow the effect of these variables to differ by immigrant and poor status. Finally, the policy variable (REFORM) should be interacted with immigrant status, and the proportion of poor immigrants and the proportion of poor natives. This apparent mis-specification of the model may lead to significantly biased estimates and potentially incorrect inferences.

In contrast to these studies, Kaestner and Kaushal (2005) study the effect of welfare reform on employment of native- and foreign-born, low-educated women – a group that has a large fraction of persons affected by welfare reform. While changes in employment are not the converse of changes in caseload, the two outcomes are linked: a large proportion of changes in the caseload are explained by changes in employment (Kaushal & Kaestner 2001). Kaestner and Kaushal (2005) reported that welfare reform caused a significant increase in employment for native-born, low-educated women. In contrast, welfare reform was not associated with an increase in employment among foreign-born, low-educated women except for those who arrived within the last five years. Kaestner and Kaushal (2005) also found little evidence of a "chilling" effect. They showed that it was the actual eligibility for benefits that matters; employment among newly arrived immigrants in states that created substitute programs did not change pre- and post-welfare reform. One limitation of this analysis is that the data extend only through 1999, which prevented a more complete analysis of the five-year ban. Only immigrants who arrived in the last two years were really affected by the ban, since most states did not implement TANF until 1997. In addition, Kaestner and Kaushal (2005) did not study the effect of the ban on wages and earned income. Wages may be affected because women will take more low-wage jobs due to lack of cash assistance.

Borjas (2003) also studies the effect of welfare reform on the labor supply of immigrants and finds an increase in employment. However, his analysis is also based on all immigrant households, and therefore suffers from the same problems that plague the Lofstrom and Bean (2002) or Haider et al. (2004) papers. This may explain why Borjas (2003) finds larger effects for men than women even though many fewer men were affected by welfare reform.

The effect of welfare reform on Medicaid and health insurance coverage has also been an area that has received considerable research attention. Several studies document a decline in Medicaid enrollment among low-income women and children after the implementation of welfare reform (Families USA Foundation, 1999; Kronebusch, 2001; Ku & Garrett, 2000). Past research also indicates that a substantial number of welfare "leavers" were uninsured in the year after leaving welfare (Moffitt & Slade, 1997; Guyer, 2000; Garrett & Holahan, 2000; Garrett & Hudman, 2002). However, a more comprehensive analysis of the issue, which includes the experiences of both welfare "leavers" as well as those deterred from entering welfare, and which examines private insurance and uninsured, found much smaller changes in health insurance coverage. Evidence in Kaestner and Kaushal (2003) suggests that the approximately fifty percent decline in caseload since 1996 raised the proportion of uninsured low-educated mothers by only two to nine percent.

The effect of welfare reform on the health insurance status of immigrants is less widely researched. In fact, the only papers we are aware of that examine the issue is Borjas (2003) and Kaushal and Kaestner (2005). Kaushal and Kaestner (2005) find that PRWORA is associated with a decline Medicaid coverage that results in between a 17–27 percent increase in the proportion of low-educated, foreign-born unmarried women who are without health insurance. They also find that PRWORA is associated with a 150 percent increase in the proportion of foreign-born children living with low-educated, single mothers who are without health insurance. Finally, Kaushal and Kaestner (2005) find some evidence to support the "chilling" hypothesis; the effect of PRWORA on the health insurance of immigrants was the same irrespective of whether new immigrants lived in states where they had access to both TANF and Medicaid, either TANF or Medicaid or neither. In contrast, Borjas (2003) found that welfare reform was associated with a relative decrease in Medicaid coverage, but this decline was completely offset by an increase in private insurance coverage. Thus there was no change in the proportion uninsured. The difference between the Borjas (2003) and Kaushal and Kaestner (2005) papers is undoubtedly due to the different samples used. Borjas (2003) uses all immigrant households. As discussed above, this assumes that the determinants of health insurance are the same for all sub-populations within this group, and it is possible that there may be significant heterogeneity in the determinants of health insurance coverage within the immigrant sample. For example, the determinants of employer-sponsored health insurance may be quite different for young, unmarried, single mothers than for older, married men. Thus, it is likely that the estimates obtained by Borjas (2003) are biased.[14]

Two studies examined whether welfare reform was associated with differential changes in Medicaid use among native- and foreign-born persons (Lofstrom & Bean 2002; Haider et al., 2004). Both studies found that there were no differences in Medicaid use between immigrants and natives pre- and post-welfare reform. But these studies also use the entire population of immigrant households and therefore the validity of the estimates obtained in these analyses is questionable. These two studies also examine the relative (immigrant versus native) effect of welfare reform on food stamp use and SSI receipt. Lofstrom and Bean (2002) find no relative differences, but Haider et al. (2004) find a difference for foreign-born, non-citizens versus natives. Again, results from these studies should be interpreted cautiously given the potentially serious empirical problems described earlier.

There are only two studies that examine in a multivariate context the effect of welfare reform on immigrants' use of SSI and Food Stamps.[15] Borjas (2004) studies the effect of welfare reform on receipt of either Food stamps or cash assistance. He finds that welfare reform resulted in a decrease in immigrants' use of food stamps. Two potential problems with the Borjas

(2004) analysis are that it does not restrict the analysis to households likely affected by welfare reform, and it assumes that trends in benefit use are the same for immigrants and natives, and poor and non-poor. As described above, the assumption of common trends across income groups and by nativity are a potentially serious problem that can lead to significantly biased estimates. Davies and Greenwood (2004) use administrative data from Social Security Administration to study the effects of welfare reform on SSI receipt. When analyses were restricted to foreign-born persons, Davies and Greenwood (2004) reported that welfare reform was associated with a significant decrease in SSI participation. Interestingly, when the authors pooled the sample of foreign- and native-born, welfare reform was associated with an increase in SSI participation among immigrants. This counterintuitive result illustrates the problem of using native-born persons as a comparison group for foreign-born persons.

Implications for Current Research

This brief review of previous literature on the effects of welfare reform on immigrants reveals the relative dearth of research on the effects of welfare reform on immigrants, which belies the magnitude of the public debate over this issue. It has also identified some potentially important empirical problems with most of the previous studies. Thus, there is still much to learn about the effects of welfare reform on immigrant behavior. Here, we tackle one issue in detail: the effect of the five-year ban on receipt of cash assistance benefits on the employment, hours of work, and wages of newly arrived, low-educated women. The five-year ban was the most draconian aspect of welfare reform and a feature most unique to immigrants. Therefore, examining the consequences of this ban on the determinants of immigrant economic status is of particular public policy importance. We extend the earlier analysis of Kaestner and Kaushal (2005) in several ways. First, we examine more outcomes – employment, hours, and wages. Second, we identify in a more precise manner the group most affected by the five-year federal ban, i.e., those who have lived in the US for five or fewer years instead of just those who have been here for two years. Finally, we investigate whether the effects of the five-year ban extended beyond the initial period. This may be important because changes in employment and wages (human capital) during the five-year period for which the ban is in effect may have affected employment and wages in the period after the ban is no longer binding.

RESEARCH DESIGN

The primary purpose of our empirical analysis is to obtain estimates of the effect of the five-year ban on receipt of cash assistance on employment and wages of newly arrived, low-educated mothers. The analytical motivation of this research is straightforward. Welfare reform denied cash assistance to immigrants who arrived after passage of the law and have been in the country for less than five years. So in response, immigrants affected by this change may work more and accept jobs with lower wages. A simple, textbook model of labor supply is sufficient to establish these predictions. These predictions are not much different from the likely effects of welfare reform more generally; welfare reform placed a time limit on benefit receipt and made it more onerous to receive benefits by imposing work requirements. However, the effect of the ban should be greater since it is a more extreme policy change. It also affects immigrants at a crucial stage – on arrival – and therefore may have impacts that extend beyond the five-year period that the ban is in effect.[16]

Consider a sample of low-educated, foreign-born, unmarried mothers. To identify the effect of the five-year ban for this sample, we will use multivariate regression models based on the following empirical specification:

$$E_{ijt} = \alpha_i + \beta_j + \delta_t + \gamma_1 \text{REFORM}_t + \gamma_2 (\text{REFORM}_t * \text{NEW}_i * \text{BEFORE}_{it})$$
$$+ \gamma_3 (\text{REFORM}_t * \text{NEW}_i * \text{AFTER}_{it}) + X_{it}\Lambda + Z_{jt}\Pi + \varepsilon_{ijt}$$

$i = 1, 2, 3, 4$ (year since arrival cohort, e.g., 1–5, 6–8, 9–13, 14+)

$j = 1, ..., 51$ (state)

$t = 1994, ... 1996, 1998, ..., 2004$ (year)   (9)

Eq. (9) specifies that employment (E) of a foreign-born woman in year t, who has been in the country i years, and who lives in state j, depends on years since arrival (α_i), state effects (β_j), time (quadratic) trends (δ_t), welfare reform (REFORM_t), personal characteristics (X_{it}) such as age, education and race, and state characteristics (Z_{jt}) such as the unemployment rate and real per capita income. Note that the policy variable (REFORM_t) has no state subscript – its value varies only by year reflecting the pre- ($\text{REFORM} = 0$) and post-welfare reform ($\text{REFORM} = 1$) period. We do not use data from 1996 and 1997 when welfare reform was being implemented across the states. Thus, we can control for the effect of time only by using a time trend, and not with year dummy variables since the latter will be perfectly correlated with REFORM. The advantage of our approach is that it avoids any (state) policy endogeneity that may arise because of differences in the timing of implementation. This may be particularly important in an analysis of foreign-born persons who are geographically concentrated in a few states. The disadvantage of this approach is that we do not make use of the temporal variation in the timing of the policy that may help identify the effect of the policy from more general time effects. However, the short window of welfare–reform implementation does not provide for much traction in this regard; for example, a regression of a policy variable on state and year effects yields an R^2 of 0.89, which leaves little independent variation to identify the effect of policy.

The variable NEW_i in Eq. (9) is an indicator (0/1) of whether the immigrant has been in the country less than five years, and the variables $BEFORE_{it}$ and $AFTER_{it}$ are variables indicating (0/1) whether immigrant arrived before or after 1996. Those who arrived during or before 1996 are not affected by the five-year ban and those who arrived after are affected by the ban. The key parameters are γ_1, γ_2, and γ_3:γ_1 measures the effect of welfare reform on employment of low-educated, foreign-born, unmarried mothers, γ_2 measures whether the effect of reform differs for those mothers who are new arrivals and unaffected by the five-year federal ban on receipt of benefits; and γ_3 measures whether the effect of reform differs for mothers who are new arrivals and affected by the five-year federal ban. Similar equations can be estimated for hours worked last week and real wage, although in later case the sample is limited to those who are employed.

The primary limitation of Eq. (9), in terms of identifying a causal effect of welfare reform, is that there may be omitted variables correlated with welfare reform and employment. While we control for the state-specific unemployment rate and per capita income, there may be other time-varying state policies and characteristics that are correlated with welfare reform and employment that we do not measure. One potential solution to this problem is to use a comparison group to control for such factors. Ideally, the comparison group should be similar (identical) to the group affected by welfare reform, but not affected by the policy. In non-experimental contexts such as ours, this is a difficult standard to meet, and therefore, estimates obtained using a comparison group should be interpreted with this limitation in mind. However, at a minimum, the comparison group approach allows researchers to investigate whether the effect of welfare reform was different, for example, more pronounced, for the group affected by the law than for a group unaffected by the policy change.

The comparison group approach is implemented by estimating an equation analogous to (9) using a sample of comparison group members:

$$E_{ijt} = \tilde{\alpha}_i + \tilde{\beta}_j + \tilde{\delta}_t + \tilde{\gamma}_1 \text{REFORM}_t + \tilde{\gamma}_2(\text{REFORM}_t * \text{NEW}_i * \text{BEFORE}_{it})$$
$$+ \tilde{\gamma}_3(\text{REFORM}_t * \text{NEW}_i * \text{AFTER}_{it}) + X_{it}\tilde{\Lambda} + Z_{jt}\tilde{\Pi} + v_{ijt} \qquad (10)$$

The key thing to note about Eq. (10) is that $\tilde{\gamma}_1$, $\tilde{\gamma}_2$, and $\tilde{\gamma}_3$ are expected to be zero since welfare reform did not affect members of the comparison group. Non-zero coefficients would suggest a missing variable problem. If we assume that the effects of these missing variables are the same for the group affected by welfare reform and the comparison group, the true effect of welfare reform on the affected group can be obtained by subtracting $\tilde{\gamma}_1$, $\tilde{\gamma}_2$, and $\tilde{\gamma}_3$ from γ_1, γ_2, and γ_3, respectively. Eqs. (9) and (10) can be combined, and a model estimated using the pooled sample of persons from the affected group and the comparison group. The benefit of pooling the sample is that we can impose restrictions on the parameters to improve the efficiency of the estimates. For example, it may be possible to restrict $\beta_j = \tilde{\beta}j$; $\delta_t = \tilde{\delta}_t$; and $\Pi = \tilde{\Pi}$. The latter two restrictions, if valid, bolster the case for the validity of the comparison-group approach, which assumes that the effect of unmeasured time-varying state characteristics is the same for the affected and comparison groups. Finding that effects of time and the effects of measured state characteristics are the same for these groups would be consistent with the identifying assumption of the comparison group approach. However, rejecting these restrictions does not invalidate the comparison-group approach. It simply suggests that for the outcome of interest (e.g., employment), the target and comparison group have some-what different time trends. In this case, the underlying identification assumption is that after controlling for these different trends, the influence of any remaining time-varying factors is the same for the target and comparison groups.

As noted above, many states created substitute programs that use state funds to provide benefits to immigrants who are barred by federal law from receiving benefits. We can incorporate this information into the analysis as follows:

$$E_{ijt} = \alpha_i + \beta_j + \delta_t + \gamma_{1k}(\text{REFORM}_t * S_k)$$
$$+ \gamma_{2k}(\text{REFORM}_t * \text{NEW}_{it} * S_k)$$
$$+ X_{it}\Lambda + Z_{jt}\Pi + \varepsilon_{ijt}$$
$$k = 1, 2 \qquad (11)$$

Eq. (11) differs from Eq. (9) since it allows the effect of welfare reform to differ by whether the state created a substitute program. The variable S_k indicates whether the state had a substitute TANF program: $k = 1$ indicates a substitute program, and $k = 2$ indicates no program. Note also that the coefficients on the welfare reform variables are subscripted by k. Here, we do not make use of information as to whether the person arrived before or after 1996 because of sample size restrictions.

Eq. (11) allows us to investigate the "chilling" hypothesis. Several authors, most notably Fix and Passel (1999), have suggested that welfare reform caused even eligible immigrants to reduce their use of benefits because of greater stigma. We can investigate this by testing whether $\gamma_{21} = \gamma_{22}$ versus the alternative $\gamma_{21} < \gamma_{22}$, which is the predicted effect since the effect of the five-year ban should be zero in states that created substitute programs ($k = 1$). Allowing the effect of γ_1 to differ by whether or not the state had a substitute program provides a way for us to differentiate between a state effect versus a policy effect. If there is state heterogeneity in the effect of welfare reform corresponding to states with and without substitute programs, we will be able to measure this using Eq. (11). The interpretation of the estimates of Eq. (11) is the same in the comparison-group context.

Another issue that we are interested in is whether the five-year ban had long-term effects. For example, are the employment rates of women who have been in the US for six to eight years different depending on whether they were initially affected by the five-year ban upon arrival? To investigate this question, we use the following specification:

$$
\begin{aligned}
E_{ijt} = {} & \alpha_i + \beta_j + \delta_t + \gamma_1 REFORM_t \\
& + \gamma_2(REFORM_t * NEW_i * BEFORE_{it}) \\
& + \gamma_3(REFORM_t * NEW_i * AFTER_{it}) \\
& + \gamma_4(REFORM_t * ARR6\text{-}8_i * BEFORE_{it}) \\
& + \gamma_5(REFORM_t * ARR6\text{-}8_i * AFTER_{it}) \\
& + X_{it}\Lambda + Z_{jt}\Pi + \varepsilon_{ijt}
\end{aligned}
\tag{12}
$$

Eq. (12) is identical to Eq. (9), but it contains one new variable, $ARR6\text{-}8_i$, which is an indicator that identifies women who have been in the country for six to eight years. Since our data extend to 2004, only women who arrived during 1997–1999 will be in the group identified by this variable.

DATA

In the empirical analysis, we use the monthly Outgoing Rotation Files of the Current Population Surveys (MORG-CPS) for 1994–June 1996 and 1998–2004. The first period (1994–June 1996) captures labor market outcomes before the implementation of PRWORA and the later period (1998–2004), captures the post-PRWORA outcomes. All states implemented PRWORA during July 1996–January 1998 and therefore we drop observations for this period. Dropping these observations eliminates any bias due to policy endogeneity relating to the timing of state implementation. This may be particularly important in an analysis of foreign-born persons who are geographically concentrated.

A key aspect of this data for our analysis is information on respondent's citizenship status, country of birth and year of arrival in the US, which are available in the CPS since 1994. We use family and household identifiers and variables on family relationships to identify women with own children. The sample in our analysis consists of low-educated (i.e., twelve or fewer years of schooling) mothers aged 18–54, and is stratified according to respondent's nativity status. Mother's marital status is used to define the treatment and comparison groups. Specifically, the treatment group is unmarried, low-educated mothers, a group that has a high risk of being on welfare, and the comparison group is married low-educated mothers of corresponding nativity (or citizenship status).[17]

We study three labor market outcomes: whether a woman was employed in the week prior to the survey; number of hours worked in the last week (including zeros for non-workers); and real wage of those employed. The CPS provides data on hourly earnings of workers who are paid on an hourly basis. For others, it provides data on usual weekly earnings (before deductions), which is divided by usual hours worked per week to compute hourly earnings. Hourly earnings are expressed in 2004 prices using the consumer price index. The earnings sample is restricted to observations with real wages between $2 and $250. All regression analyses include controls for age (seven dummy variables indicating the following age categories: 18–22, 23–27, 28–32, 33–37, 38–42, 43–48, 49–54); education (a dummy variable indicating whether the respondent has a high school degree); and race (four categories representing Hispanic, non-Hispanic White, non-Hispanic Blacks and others). Analyses of the foreign-born samples include controls for years lived in the US (≤5 years; 6–8 years; 9–14 years and >14 years) and citizenship status.

The data on welfare policies is drawn from Assistant Secretary for Planning and Evaluation of the Department of Health and Human Services, the Urban Institute (www.urban.org/content/Research/NewFederalism/ Data/StateDatabase/StateDatabase.htm), and from information reported in Zimmermann and Tumlin (1999). Our primary policy variable is whether a state implemented TANF in year t, and is equal to one if an observation is from the post-1997 period, otherwise zero. In the regression analyses, we also include indicators for whether a state implemented an AFDC waiver prior to TANF implementation. The variable on AFDC waiver is a dummy variable equal to one if the state implemented an AFDC waiver, otherwise zero; and is set to zero when TANF is one. State unemployment rate is taken from the Bureau of Labor Statistics and per capita income, deflated with the consumer price index, is from the Bureau of Economic Analysis. State unemployment rate and per capita income of year $t-1$ are merged with January–June MORG-CPS files and state unemployment and per capita income of year t are merged with the July–December MORG-CPS files.

RESULTS

Table 1 presents means and sample sizes for low-educated mothers. We divide these women on the basis of nativity and citizenship in three groups: US-born, foreign-born citizens, and foreign-born non-citizens. Foreign-born non-citizens are a group of particular interest since welfare reform affected them the most. There are a few points to note about the figures in Table 1. Among foreign-born women, citizens are more educated, more likely to be married, have been in the US longer, and work and earn more than non-citizens. Foreign-born citizens have characteristics that are closer to US-born women than non-citizens. However, a much larger percentage of US-born mothers are unmarried (approximately half) as compared to foreign-born mothers (about a quarter).

Table 2 presents an analysis of the effects of reform that is based on simple mean differences between the target and comparison groups. Here we have calculated mean employment, hours worked last week and real wage in the period before and after welfare reform for unmarried and married mothers, by nativity (or citizenship). We show the pre- and post-reform difference (first difference) in these outcomes for unmarried and married mothers, and the difference-in-differences (DD) (first difference in outcomes for unmarried mothers minus first difference in outcomes for married mothers). Among unmarried mothers, employment and hours of work

Table 1. Descriptive Statistics.

	Non-Citizen, Low-Educated Mothers		Foreign-Born Citizen, Low-Educated Mothers		Foreign-Born, Low-Educated Mothers (Non-Citizens + Citizens)		US-Born, Low-Educated Mothers	
	Unmarried	Married	Unmarried	Married	Unmarried	Married	Unmarried	Married
Education								
<12 years	0.70	0.66	0.47	0.40	0.65	0.60	0.33	0.17
= 12 years	0.30	0.34	0.52	0.60	0.35	0.40	0.67	0.83
Age	34	35	38	38	35	35	33	35
Employment	0.51	0.40	0.66	0.60	0.54	0.44	0.58	0.62
Hours worked	18	13.66	23	21	19	15	20	20
Hourly earnings	8.64	8.90	10.40	10.77	9.11	9.49	10.11	11.18
Living in the US								
≤5 years	0.16	0.20	0.05	0.04	0.14	0.16	–	–
= 6–8 years	0.19	0.21	0.07	0.07	0.16	0.18	–	–
= 9–14 years	0.21	0.20	0.12	0.13	0.19	0.19	–	–
>14 years	0.44	0.38	0.77	0.75	0.51	0.47	–	–
Number of observations	15771	56324	4420	17463	20191	73789	132826	267105
Number of observations – wage	7414	20218	2667	9263	10081	29481	73130	144739

Note: Samples are restricted to mothers aged 18–54 years.
Source: CPS MORG, 1994–1996; 1998–2004.

Table 2. Mean Employment, Hours and Real Wage of Low-Educated Mothers by Nativity (Citizenship Status).

	Unmarried			Married			Difference-In-Differences
	1994–1996	1998–2004	Difference	1994–1996	1998–2004	Difference	
Non-citizens							
Employment	0.381	0.569	0.188***	0.378	0.404	0.026***	0.162***
Hours	13.171	19.78	6.609***	13.06	13.87	0.81***	5.799***
Wage	8.818	8.701	−0.117***	8.756	9.005	0.249***	−0.366**
Ln(wage)	2.067	2.100	0.033***	2.075	2.133	0.057***	−0.025**
Number of observations	4046	9715	–	12971	36105	–	–
Foreign-born							
Employment	0.406	0.6	0.194***	0.413	0.456	0.043***	0.151***
Hours	14.186	21.025	6.839***	14.308	15.842	1.534***	5.305***
Wage	9.087	9.229	0.142***	9.266	9.615	0.349***	−0.207
Ln(wage)	2.096	2.145	0.049***	2.128	2.187	0.060***	−0.011
Number of observations	4678	12929	–	15803	48670	–	–
US-born							
Employment	0.484	0.626	0.142***	0.614	0.629	0.015***	0.127***
Hours	16.682	21.778	5.096***	19.534	20.571	1.037***	4.059***
Wage	9.827	10.282	0.455***	10.626	11.543	0.917***	−0.462***
Ln(wage)	2.172	2.239	0.067***	2.257	2.349***	0.092	−0.025***
Number of observations	34099	80250	–	739975	154922	–	–

Note: Samples are restricted to mothers aged 18–54 years. Numbers of observations pertain to the employment and weekly hours worked last year.

Source: CPS MORG, 1994–June 1996; 1998–2004.

*0.05<*p* = <0.10.
**0.01<*p* = <0.05.
***p* = <0.01.

increased significantly pre- and post-welfare reform; employment rates increased by 18.8 percentage points for non-citizens, 19.4 percentage points for all foreign-born, and 14.2 percentage points for US-born. For these same groups, hours of work per week increased by between five and seven pre- and post-welfare reform. The pre- and post-welfare reform differences in real wages among unmarried women are −\$0.12 (3%) for non-citizens, \$0.14 (5%) for foreign-born, and \$0.46 (7%) for US-born. Among married mothers, pre- and post-welfare reform differences in employment and hours are positive, but much smaller than similar differences for unmarried mothers. Real wage changes pre- and post-welfare reform are positive for married mothers: \$0.25 (6%) for non-citizens, \$0.35 (6%) for foreign-born, and \$0.92 (9%) for US-born.

The simple DD are shown in the last column of Table 2. These estimates indicate that welfare reform had the following effects on unmarried mothers: it significantly increased employment by 13 (27%)–16 (42%) percentage points; it significantly increased hours of work per week by four (25%)–six (46%) hours; and it significantly decreased wages by \$0.21 (1%)–\$0.46 (2.5%). These effects are consistent with a simple model of labor supply. The employment and hours effects of welfare reform appear to be larger for non-citizens and foreign-born than for US-born. Wage effects of reform are slightly larger for US-born.

The simple DD in Table 2 control for potentially confounding temporal influences solely through the use of a comparison group. This may be inadequate for a number of reasons. First, there may be changes in sample composition that will be correlated with welfare reform. For example, education levels were increasing, the proportion of the population that is Hispanic was increasing, and state populations were changing pre- and post-welfare reform. We can control for this by including these characteristics in the model. Second, changes in aggregate economic activity may confound estimates in Table 2, although ideally the comparison group approach would account for this. However, this is a heavy burden to place on the comparison group approach. Given that information on aggregate economic activity is available, we can include it in the model. Finally, we can include (quadratic) time trends in the model to account for any unobserved changes in outcomes that are correlated with welfare reform. In fact, preliminary analyses suggest that there were separate time trends for the target and comparison groups.[18]

Adjusted DD estimates are presented in Table 3. We also show separate estimates of the effect of welfare reform (pre- and post-reform) for unmarried (target) and married (comparison) mothers. Model specifications

Table 3. Estimates of the Effect of Welfare Reform on Employment, Hours and Real Wage by Nativity (Citizenship Status) and Marital Status.

Nativity/ Citizenship	Employment			Hours			Log Real Wage		
	Unmarried mothers	Married mothers	DD	Unmarried mothers	Married mothers	DD	Unmarried mothers	Married mothers	DD
TANF									
Non-citizen	0.170***	0.064***	0.099**	5.136***	2.770**	1.991	−0.036	0.078**	−0.098**
	(0.032)	(0.022)	(0.047)	(1.313)	(1.271)	(2.106)	(0.026)	(0.038)	(0.046)
Foreign-born	0.096***	0.046*	0.049	2.386*	2.404**	−0.222	−0.022	0.078**	−0.096
	(0.028)	(0.023)	(0.038)	(1.345)	(1.186)	(1.772)	(0.050)	(0.037)	(0.071)
US-born	0.029*	0.006	0.031	0.945	0.377	1.196	0.009	0.060***	−0.059***
	(0.016)	(0.012)	(0.022)	(0.611)	(0.527)	(0.860)	(0.019)	(0.016)	(0.021)

Note: Figures in each cell are from separate regressions. Hetroscedasticity adjusted standard errors clustered around states are in parenthesis. Column headings describe the dependent variable. Each regression controls for age, race, education, years lived in the US (for foreign-born) and citizenship status (for foreign-born), per capita income, whether a state had an AFDC waiver prior to PRWORA, state unemployment rate, yearly time trend and trend-squared and state fixed effects. In the DD analysis, unemployment rate, real per capita income, whether a state had an AFDC waiver prior to PRWORA, yearly time trend and trend squared are allowed to differ for the target and comparison groups, as F-tests reject the restricted models. DD estimates use low-educated unmarried mothers as the treatment group and comparison married mothers (of corresponding nativity or citizenship status) as the comparison group.

Source: CPS MORG, 1994–June 1996; 1998–2004.

*0.05<p= <0.10.

**0.01<p= <0.05.

*** p= <0.01.

are given in the notes to Table 3. All estimates are obtained using ordinary least squares regression.[19] DD estimates in Table 3 suggest that welfare reform increased the employment of foreign-born and US-born unmarried mothers by between three and ten percentage points, but only the estimate of the effect of reform on non-citizens is statistically significant. It indicates that welfare reform was associated with a 9.9 percentage point (26%) increase in the employment of unmarried, non-citizen mothers.[20] Effect sizes for the other two groups are considerably smaller. For hours of work per week, DD estimates suggest that welfare reform did not significantly affect this outcome, although among non-citizens welfare reform was associated with a two-hour (15%) increase in hours worked per week. These changes in hours are somewhat consistent with the employment effects. To see why, note that welfare reform was associated with a 10 percentage point increase in employment among unmarried, non-citizen mothers. Therefore, average hours of work per week among this group should increase approximately 3.5 hours, which is 10 percent of the average hours worked per week (35) among unmarried, non-citizen mothers who worked. For the other two groups the estimates are less consistent, but the standard errors are relatively large given the effect sizes we seek to identify for these groups. In short, we may not have sufficient statistical power to detect reliably the changes in hours that we expect.

DD estimates of the effect of welfare reform on wages show that reform is associated with a decrease in wages of unmarried mothers, and the effect is statistically significant for non-citizens and US-born mothers. Reform is associated with approximately a ten percent decrease in wages among the foreign-born and a six percent decrease in wages among the US-born. A decrease in the wage is consistent with a simple labor supply model; women will work at a lower wage when cash assistance is not available, so average wages among those who work decline pre- and post-welfare reform.

Estimates in Table 3 suggest that welfare reform had a significant impact on employment and wages of low-educated, unmarried mothers with effects being largest for non-citizens. The larger effects for non-citizens merit discussion. On the one hand, the larger estimates are noteworthy because they are undoubtedly downward biased estimates of the effect of welfare reform on non-citizens who are affected by welfare reform because many, perhaps as much as 50 percent, of non-citizens are illegal residents and therefore unaffected by changes in welfare policy (Passel, Capps, & Fix, 2004). However, the proportion of low-educated, foreign-born mothers that live in households that receive cash assistance is approximately the same as the proportion of low-educated, US-born mothers that live in households that receive cash assistance (see Fig. 1). The primary explanation for this fact is the share of foreign-born women with fewer than twelve years of education is greater than the share of US-born women with fewer than twelve years of education. Very low-educated women are more likely to receive cash assistance than those with twelve years of education. The larger share of this group among non-citizens offsets the lower propensity (in fact zero) of illegally residing non-citizens to receive cash assistance. Thus, it is unclear whether welfare reform had a larger effect on non-citizens, after controlling for education, than on the US-born.

We now turn to assessing whether the five-year ban on receipt of benefits for non-citizens had a significant impact. Specifically, we test whether welfare reform had different effects on newly arrived persons depending on whether they arrived before or after 1996. Those who arrived during or before 1996 were not affected by the five-year ban, while those who arrived after 1996 were. All were affected by welfare reform in general. Table 4 presents the results. The analysis is limited to a sample of non-citizen, low-educated mothers. The first two rows show the effects of welfare reform for those who arrived within the last five years. As can be observed, the effect of welfare reform was very similar for newly arrived non-citizens regardless of whether they arrived before or after 1996. For example, DD estimates indicate that welfare reform was associated with a 7 percentage point increase in employment and approximately an 11–12 percent decrease in wages among newly arrived non-citizens, and these effects did not differ by whether the person arrived before or after 1996.

The third and fourth rows show estimates of the effect of welfare reform for those who arrived six to eight years ago. In this case, there appears to be a larger effect of welfare reform on the employment, hours worked and real wage of the group that arrived after 1996, but the differences (e.g., $0.149 - 0.077$) are not statistically significant. Moreover, it is inconsistent that the five-year ban would have an effect on those who arrived after 1996, but are not currently affected by the ban (i.e., in US for > 5 years), and not those currently affected by it. Thus, we believe the correct inference is that there are no differences in the effects of welfare reform by whether the person arrived before or after 1996. This suggests that the five-year ban was not particularly effective at motivating low-educated, non-citizen mothers to work. It had no greater effect on immigrants than welfare reform in general. The last row in Table 4 pertains to mothers who have been in the US nine or more years. The effect of welfare reform is larger for this group than those who have been in the country for a shorter period. For these mothers, welfare reform is associated with a 12.9 percentage point increase in

Table 4. Estimates of the Effect of Welfare Reform on Employment, Hours and Real Wage by Years since Arrival and Marital Status.

	Arrived after 1996	Employment			Hours			Log Real Wage		
		Unmarried mothers	Married mothers	DD	Unmarried mothers	Married mothers	DD	Unmarried mothers	Married mothers	DD
TANF*in US≤5 years	Yes	0.141***	0.092***	0.069	3.491	3.785***	0.410	0.007	0.129**	-0.111**
		(0.048)	(0.027)	(0.062)	(2.173)	(1.393)	(2.617)	(0.032)	(0.052)	(0.050)
TANF*in US≤5 years	No	0.125	0.063*	0.071	1.100	3.004*	-1.469	-0.009	0.130*	-0.120
		(0.088)	(0.034)	(0.116)	(2.799)	(1.702)	(4.121)	(0.038)	(0.065)	(0.075)
TANF*in US 6-8 years	Yes	0.160***	0.007	0.149*	4.944**	0.396	4.320	-0.021	0.070	-0.086
		(0.050)	(0.033)	(0.062)	(2.231)	(1.537)	(2.634)	(0.066)	(0.044)	(0.056)
TANF*in US 6-8 years	No	0.131***	0.055*[a]	0.077	3.678**	2.529[a]	1.002	0.008	0.082	-0.064
		(0.032)	(0.030)	(0.047)	(1.579)	(1.579)	(2.351)	(0.046)	(0.045)	(0.043)
TANF*in US≥9 years	No	0.194***	0.067**	0.129*	6.473***	2.773***	3.573	-0.060	0.060*	-0.103*
		(0.043)	(0.025)	(0.048)	(1.650)	(1.289)	(2.127)	(0.040)	(0.033)	(0.055)

Note: Figures in each column are from separate regressions. Heteroskedasticity adjusted standard errors clustered around states are in parenthesis. Column headings describe the dependent variable. Each regression controls for age, race, education, years lived in the US (for foreign-born) and citizenship status (for foreign-born), per capita income, whether a state had an AFDC waiver prior to PRWORA, state unemployment rate, yearly time trend and trend-squared and state fixed effects. In the DD analysis, unemployment rate, real per capita income, whether a state had an AFDC waiver prior to PRWORA, yearly time trend and trend squared are allowed to differ for the target and comparison groups, as F-tests reject the restricted models. DD estimates use low-educated unmarried mothers as the treatment group and low-educated married mothers (of corresponding nativity or citizenship status) as the comparison group.

Source: CPS MORG, 1994–June 1996; 1998–2004.

*0.05 < p = <0.10.

** 0.01 < p = <0.05.

*** p = <0.01.

[a] The estimated coefficient for those who arrived in or after 1996 differs from that for those who arrived before 1996.

employment, a 3.6-hour increase in hours worked per week, and a 10 percent decrease in the wage. It is important to clarify again that differences in effect sizes do not necessarily reflect true differences in the effects of welfare reform on those actually affected (i.e., at risk of receiving cash assistance) because the proportion of each group that is truly at risk of receiving cash assistance is unknown and may differ, for example, the proportion of the undocumented among newly arrived immigrants is larger than that among those in the country for more than say nine years.

One explanation for the absence of a significant effect of the five-year ban is that states circumvented the ban by creating substitute programs to provide cash assistance to newly arrived immigrants. To investigate this, we compare the effect of welfare reform among newly arrived mothers (non-citizens only) in states that did and did not have substitute programs. These results are shown in Table 5. Estimates appear to bear out the hypothesis that substitute programs may have eroded the effectiveness of the five-year ban. In general, DD estimates suggest that welfare reform increased employment and hours of work, and decreased wages, more in states without a substitute program than in states with a substitute program. For example, DD estimates indicate that welfare reform is associated with a 5.9 percentage point increase in employment among newly arrived (≤ 5 years), unmarried mothers in states that did not create a substitute program; in states with a substitute program, welfare reform had a zero effect on employment of unmarried mothers. However, welfare reform also had different effects by whether the state created a substitute program for unmarried mothers who have been in the US six to eight years and nine or more years. Among women who have been in the US for six to eight years, DD estimates indicate that welfare reform was associated with a 9.8 percentage point increase in employment among mothers in states that did not create a substitute program; analogous estimate for those in US for nine or more years is 10.3 percentage points. In states with substitute programs, DD estimates suggest that welfare reform had no effect on the employment, hours worked, and wages of those in US for six to eight years; for mothers in US for nine or more years and in states with a substitute program, welfare reform was associated with a 6.1 percentage point increase in employment, little change in hours worked, and an 8 percent decrease in wages. The differential effects of welfare reform by whether the state had a substitute program among immigrants largely unaffected by the substitute program raises some question as to whether the state substitute programs truly did erode the effect of the five-year ban. While it is possible that some non-citizen mothers in the US for six to eight years were initially affected by the

Table 5. Estimates of the Effect of Welfare Reform on Employment, Hours and Real Wage by Years since Arrival, Marital Status and State of Residence.

	State has Substitute TANF	Employment			Hours			Log Real Wage		
		Unmarried mothers	Married mothers	DD	Unmarried mothers	Married mothers	DD	Unmarried mothers	Married mothers	DD
TANF*in US ≤5 years	Yes	0.064 (0.039)	0.106*** (0.029)	-0.009 (0.048)	-0.270 (1.821)	3.931*** (1.292)	-2.879 (1.974)	0.077 (0.059)	0.157*** (0.051)	-0.115** (0.052)
TANF*in US ≤5 years	No	0.155***[a] (0.053)	0.084*** (0.029)	0.059[a] (0.061)	3.084[a] (2.289)	3.593** (1.499)	-0.941 (2.762)	-0.010[a] (0.031)	0.108*[a] (0.054)	-0.101** (0.046)
TANF*in US 6-8 years	Yes	0.045 (0.042)	0.064** (0.029)	-0.010 (0.043)	-0.442 (2.021)	2.462** (1.277)	-2.427 (2.119)	0.125** (0.052)	0.082* (0.041)	0.011 (0.046)
TANF*in US 6-8 years	No	0.161***[a] (0.041)	0.034 (0.033)	0.098*[a] (0.050)	4.467[a] (1.727)*	1.697 (1.739)	1.442[a] (2.278)	-0.049[a] (0.054)	0.073 (0.049)	-0.107**[a] (0.045)
TANF*in US ≥9 years	Yes	0.130*** (0.033)	0.081*** (0.020)	0.061 (0.043)	3.048 (1.342)*	3.041*** (0.972)	0.347 (1.946)	-0.001 (0.049)	0.049 (0.030)	-0.077 (0.058)
TANF*in US ≥9 years	No	0.195***[a] (0.038)	0.066** (0.026)	0.103* (0.052)	6.240[a] (1.464)**	2.684** (1.303)	2.397 (2.321)	-0.071*[a] (0.041)	0.062 (0.039)	-0.111**[a] (0.054)

Note: Figures in each column are from separate regressions. Hetroskedasticity adjusted standard errors clustered around states are in parenthesis. Column headings describe the dependent variable. Each regression controls for age, race, education, years lived in the US (for foreign-born) and citizenship status (for foreign-born), per capita income, whether a state had an AFDC waiver prior to PRWORA, state unemployment rate, yearly time trend and trend-squared and state fixed effects. In the DD analysis, unemployment rate, real per capita income, whether a state had an AFDC waiver prior to PRWORA, yearly time trend and trend squared are allowed to differ for the target and comparison groups, as *F*-tests reject the restricted models. DD estimates use low-educated unmarried mothers as the treatment group and low-educated married mothers as the comparison group.

Source: MORG, 1994–June 1996; 1998–2004.

*0.05<*p* = <0.10.
**0.01<*p* = <0.05.
***p* = <0.01.
[a]The estimated coefficient for those who arrived in or after 1996 differs from that for those who arrived before 1996.

five-year ban, most in our sample were not since our data extend only through 2004.[21] Therefore, the similarity of the findings – that state substitute programs matter – for this group and the group of newly arrived immigrants appears to be a state effect and not a policy effect. However, there were much smaller differences of the effect of welfare reform across states among those in the US for nine or more years. Overall, the evidence in Table 5 is not clear enough to conclude one way or the other whether the absence of an effect of the five-year ban was due to state substitute programs.

CONCLUSIONS

Welfare reform singled out non-citizens for special treatment. Specifically, it banned newly arrived immigrants who came to the US after 1996 from receiving federally funded benefits for five years. The sentiment underlying this provision is consistent with the longstanding concern over whether immigrants will become a public charge and the belief that immigrants should pull their own weight after arrival. The logic of the five-year ban is straightforward and mechanical: an immigrant will not be a public charge for five years at least with respect to direct receipt of federally funded benefits. Based on this criterion, the law was undoubtedly successful. But consider the fact that most of the foreign-born, elderly recipients of SSI have been in the US for many years and that a significant portion of them worked while residing here legally. The five-year ban on receipt of benefits will do nothing to prevent this group from becoming a "public charge." So one assessment of the five-year ban is the effect it has on behaviors that determine economic success and the likelihood of becoming a public charge. In this chapter, we address this question in the context of low-educated mothers who are frequent users of cash assistance. We investigate the effect of the five-year ban on their employment, hours of work, and wages.

Our results indicate that welfare reform in general caused a significant increase in the employment of low-educated, unmarried mothers regardless of citizenship. Among non-citizens, welfare reform was associated with a 10 percentage point (26%) increase in employment, a two-hour (15%) increase in hours worked per week, and a 10 percent decrease in wages. Thus, it appears that welfare reform may have caused an increase in labor market attachment that will have long-term benefits in terms of future economic success. Low-educated, unmarried immigrant mothers will accumulate greater amount of human capital and be in a position to better support themselves and their children. The decrease in wages among this group is a negative for economic independence, but this represents the "initial" change in wages, and not the path of future wages, which may not be adversely affected by welfare reform. There is considerable evidence that wages grow with work experience even for low-wage earners (Gladden & Taber, 2000).

Surprisingly, we find little evidence that the five-year ban had any effect on the employment, hours of work, and wages of low-educated and unmarried, non-citizen mothers. Among the newly arrived of this group, there were no differences in the effect of welfare between those who arrived before 1996, who are unaffected by the five-year ban, and those who arrived after 1996, who are affected by the five-year ban. This is surprising because the ban denied benefits to this group, who, prior to reform were significant users of cash assistance. Therefore, we would expect some fraction of this group to offset the loss of transfer income by working more (i.e., more than those who were affected by the general reforms such as time-limited benefits but not the ban). This is not what we find. One explanation of the failure to find an effect of the ban is that many states, and in particular states with large immigrant populations such as California, created substitute state programs that replaced federal funds with state funds so as to provide benefits to newly arrived immigrants. We examined this issue, but the results were not conclusive, although there was some evidence to support this explanation. A second explanation is that welfare reform had sufficiently strong incentives that there was little effective difference between the five-year ban (denying benefits) and the general provisions of reform such as time-limited benefits, financial sanctions, and work requirements. This explanation is supported by the fact that welfare reform had immediate effects on behavior even though no one was immediately pushed off welfare by time-limits. Previous research has found that unmarried mothers responded well before they had exceeded the time limit for benefit receipt.

The finding that the five-year ban was not particularly effective, or has been effectively circumvented by state policy, suggests that the either the five-year ban should be eliminated, at least in the context of cash assistance, or that states not be allowed to circumvent the federal law. Indeed, Borjas (2001) has called for such restrictions on state behavior. The constitutionality of such a restriction, however, is an issue that has not been addressed. Eliminating the five-year ban would hearten opponents of the ban who see it as punitive and inconsistent with the status of legally residing residents in the US. The fact that it has not had much, if any, effect supports this position, particularly if states are going to continue to have the right to create substitute programs.

NOTES

1. Letter from George Washington to the Volunteer Association and other inhabitants of the kingdom of Ireland who have lately arrived in the City of New York, December 2, 1783 (Fitzpatrick, 1938).

2. This provision may even aid in the denial of entry of likely public charges since it reduces the immigrant's incentive to conceal their true propensity to make use of government benefits since these benefits are no longer available.

3. In all states except Alabama legal pre-1996 immigrants (or those in the US for at least five years) have access to cash welfare; in all states except Wyoming they have access to Medicaid, in 17 states they are eligible to use Food stamps and in 10 states they have access to SSI. Nineteen states that have substitute TANF programs for newly arrived immigrants during the five-year federal ban are CA, MA, MD, WA, PA, OR, CT, GA, MN, HI, WI, MO, UT, RI, TN, NE, ME, VT, and WY. Fifteen states where new immigrants are eligible for Medicaid are CA, IL, MA, MD, VA, WA, PA, CT, MN, HI, RI, NE, NY, DE, and ME (for details on these policies see Zimmermann & Tumlin, 1999). New immigrants are eligible for Medicaid in NY since 2001.

4. Huber and Espenshade (1997) mention another factor that may explain several aspects of the law. In the first half of the 1990s, state governments had sued the federal government for millions of dollars for making state government pay for immigrant services. So by banning all benefits to immigrants, and then leaving it up to state to provide benefits to certain groups, the federal government was protecting itself from any future law suites by state governments.

5. Some of this increase was likely caused by the Immigration and Reform Control Act (IRCA) of 1986, which provided legal residency for nearly three million foreign-born persons many of who later became citizens, which made family reunification easier for this group.

6. It remains true, however, that conditional on observable characteristics, immigrants were less likely to use AFDC than non-immigrants (Butcher & Hu, 2001; Borjas & Hilton, 1996). However, immigrant use of all social welfare programs was greater than that of natives even after adjusting for observable characteristics (Borjas & Hilton, 1996).

7. It could also illuminate the need to improve screening immigrant applicants who because of circumstances in the US will be unable to achieve economic independence.

8. We extend that study in a number of ways: most importantly, we focus on women with children since this is the group most likely affected by welfare reform; we also examine an additional outcome – wages; we identify in a more precise manner the group affected by the federal ban; and we use an additional comparison group.

9. There is a controversy as to whether the decline in use of means-tested programs was experienced by immigrants nation-wide or by only those living in California. Using household as the unit of analysis, Borjas (2001) found that outside of California, the decline in immigrant use of Medicaid and SSI was negligible and the decline in cash welfare and Food Stamps was relatively modest. This led him to attribute the decline in immigrant use of public assistance to the "chilling effect" of proposition 187 enacted in California in November 1994, and not PRWORA.

Others who have used nuclear family as the unit of observation, instead of household, have found the decline in immigrant use of means-tested programs in the rest of the nation was as high, if not higher, than in California (Fix & Passel, 1999, 2002).

10. Fix and Passel (2002) is the exception.

11. Information on benefit receipt is at household level, but to facilitate the exposition, we will not continue to note this fact.

12. Interestingly, Fix and Passel (2002) find larger declines for citizens than non-citizens. They use a sample of all low-income households with children. The difference between their study and ours illustrates the importance of the sample composition. We believe it is best to focus on the group most likely to receive benefits and be affected by welfare reform.

13. One possible explanation of this is that not all foreign-born persons were affected by welfare reform. Those residing illegally in the US were never eligible for benefits. So the changes in benefit use in Figs. 1 through 7 are being driven by the fraction of immigrant families affected by welfare reform. More importantly, the presence of undocumented immigrants was increasing over time, which would tend to dampen the effect of welfare reform (Passel, 2005).

14. Borjas (2003) also uses natives as a comparison group for immigrants. This assumes that in the absence of PRWORA, changes in immigrant and native health insurance status pre- and post-PRWORA would have been the same, which is inconsistent with the mean levels of health insurance that differ significantly between non-citizens and natives.

15. Lofstrom and Bean (2002) and Haider et al. (2004) do not study the effect of welfare reform per se, but the relative (immigrant versus native) effect of welfare reform on food stamp use and SSI receipt. Fix and Passel (1999, 2002) and Borjas (2001) provide pre-and post-welfare reform trends in use of these benefits for citizens and non-citizens, but do not provide more comprehensive analyses that account for potentially important confounding factors such as changes in the macro economy.

16. Welfare reform may have affected the composition of immigrants residing in the US and these compositional changes may affect employment and wages. Ideally, we would be able to control for this selection, but in this chapter this is not feasible. Thus, estimates of the effect of welfare reform may be partly due to selection and partly due to behavioral responses.

17. It is possible that welfare reform affected fertility and marriage, so selecting the sample on these characteristics may result in changes in sample composition. Based on existing evidence, however, we believe the bias due to sample selection will be insignificant. See Grogger, Karoly, and Klerman (2002) for evidence on the effect of welfare reform on marriage and fertility.

18. As noted, in this case, the underlying identification assumption is that after controlling for these different trends, the influence of any remaining time-varying factors is the same for the target and comparison group.

19. We also used alternative regression methods. For dichotomous outcomes we used logisitic regression and for discrete outcomes we used Poisson (with sandwich estimator of covariance). The alternative estimation procedures produced virtually identical results.

20. If we restrict the sample of US-born women to those with less than 12 years of education, we find that welfare reform was associated with a significant increase in employment. Given sample sizes, which prevents us from limiting the sample of foreign-born in this way, and our interest in foreign-born, we do not present results for this group.

21. It would require arriving in 1997 and allowing six years to elapse. So it is only observations from 2003 and 2004 that fall into this category. Observations from 1998 to 2002 would not fall in this category. Overall 70% of the sample was unaffected by the five-year ban.

REFERENCES

Blank, R. (2002). Evaluating welfare reform in the United States. *Journal of Economic Literature, 40*(4), 1–43.

Borjas, G. (1995). Immigration and welfare: 1970–1990. *Research in Labor Economics, 14*, 251–280.

Borjas, G. (2001). Welfare reform and immigration. In: R. Blank & R. Haskins (Eds), *The new world of welfare* (pp. 369–390). Washington, DC: Brookings Institution.

Borjas, G. (2003). Welfare reform, labor supply and health insurance in the immigrant population. *Journal of Health Economics, 22*, 933–958.

Borjas, G. (2004). Food insecurity and public assistance. *Journal of Public Economics, 88*, 1421–1443.

Borjas, G. J., & Hilton, L. (1996). Immigration and the welfare state: Immigrant participation in means-tested entitlement programs. *Quarterly Journal of Economics, 111*(2), 575–604.

Butcher, K. F., & Hu, L. (2001). Use of means-tested transfer programs by immigrants, their children, and their children's children. In: C. David & R. M. Blank (Eds), *Finding jobs: Work and welfare reform*. New York, NY: Russell Sage Foundation.

Davies, P., & Greenwood, M. J. (2004). *Welfare reform and immigrant participation in the supplemental security income program*. Working Paper no. 2004–087. Michigan Retirement Research Center.

Edwards J. R. (2001). *Public charge doctrine: A fundamental principle of American immigration policy*. Backgrounder, Center for Immigration Studies.

Families USA Foundation. (1999). *Losing health insurance: The unintended consequences of welfare reform*. The W.K. Kellogg Foundation, George Gund Foundation & Nathan Cummings Foundation, Washington, DC.

Fitzpatrick, J. C. (Ed.) (1938). *The writings of George Washington from the original manuscript sources* (Vol. 27, pp. 1745–1799). Washington, DC: U.S. Government Printing Office.

Fix, M., & Haskins, R. (2002). *Welfare benefits for non-citizens: Welfare reform and beyond policy brief no. 15*. Washington, DC: The Brookings Institution.

Fix, M., & Passel, J. (1999). *Trends in noncitizens' and citizens' use of public benefits following welfare reform: 1994–97*. Washington, DC: Urban Institute.

Fix, M., & Passel, M. (2002). *The scope and effect of welfare reform's immigrant provisions, Assessing the new federalism*. Discussion paper. Urban Institute, Washington, DC.

Garrett, B., & Holahan, J. (2000). Health insurance coverage after welfare. *Health Affairs, 19*(1), 175–184.

Garrett, B., & Hudman, J. (2002). *Women who left welfare: Health care coverage, access and use of health services*. Washington, DC: The Kaiser Commission on Medicaid and the Uninsured.

Gladden, T., & Taber, C. (2000). Wage progression among less skilled workers. In: D. Card & R. M. Blank (Eds), *Finding jobs: Work and welfare reform*. New York: Russell Sage Foundation.

Guyer, B. (2000). Medicaid and prenatal care: Necessary but not sufficient. *Journal of the American Medical Association, 264*, 2264–2265.

Haider, S. J., Schoeni, R., Bao, Y., & Danielson, C. (2004). Immigrants, welfare reform, and the economy. *Journal of Policy Analysis and Management, 23*(4), 745–764.

Huber, G. A., & Espenshade, T. J. (1997). Neo-isolationism, balanced budget conservatism, and the fiscal impacts of immigrants. *International Migration Review, 31*(4), 1031–1054. Special Issue: Immigrant adaptations and native-born responses in the making of Americans.

Kaestner, R., & Kaushal, N. (2003). Welfare reform and health insurance coverage of low-income families. *Journal of Health Economics, 22*, 959–981.

Kaestner, R., & Kaushal, N. (2005). Immigrant and native responses to welfare reform. *Journal of Population Economics, 18*(1), 69–92.

Kaushal, N., & Kaestner, R. (2001). From welfare to work: Has welfare reform worked? *Journal of Policy Analysis and Management, 20*(4), 740–761.

Kaushal, N., & Kaestner, R. (2005). Welfare reform and health insurance of immigrants. *Health Services Research, 40*(3), 697.

Kronebusch, K. (2001). Medicaid for children: Federal mandates, welfare reform, and policy backsliding. *Health Affairs, 20*, 97–111.

Ku, L., & Garrett, B. (2000). *How welfare reform and economic factors affected medicaid participation: 1984–1996* (pp. 1–52). Washington, DC: Urban Institute.

Lofstrom, M., & Bean, F. (2002). Assessing immigrant policy options: Labor market conditions and post-reform declines in welfare receipt among immigrants. *Demography, 39*(4), 617–637.

Moffitt, R., & Slade, E. (1997). Healthcare coverage for children who are on and off welfare. *The Future of Children, 7*(1), 87–98.

Passel, J. (2005). *"Unauthorized migrants numbers and characteristics" background briefing prepared for the task force on immigration and America's future*. Washington, DC: Pew Hispanic Center.

Passel, J., Capps, S., & Fix, M. (2004). *Undocumented immigrants: Facts and figures* (January 12). Washington, DC: Urban Institute.

Zimmermann, W., & Tumlin, K. (1999). *Patchwork policies: State assistance for immigrants under welfare reform*. Occasional Paper no. 24. Urban Institute, Washington, DC.

IMPACTS OF THE POINT SYSTEM AND IMMIGRATION POLICY LEVERS ON SKILL CHARACTERISTICS OF CANADIAN IMMIGRANTS

Charles M. Beach, Alan G. Green and Christopher Worswick

ABSTRACT

This paper examines how changes in immigration policy levers actually affect the skill characteristics of immigrant arrivals using a unique Canadian immigrant landings database. The paper identifies some hypotheses on the possible effects on immigrant skill characteristics of the total immigration rate, the point system weights and immigrant class weights. The "skill" characteristics examined are level of education, age, and fluency in either English or French. Regressions are used to test the hypotheses from Canadian landings data for 1980–2001. It is found that (i) the larger the inflow rate of immigrants the lower the average skill level of the arrivals, (ii) increasing the proportion of skill-evaluated immigrants raises average skill levels, and (iii) increasing point system weights on a

Immigration: Trends Consequences and Prospects for the United States
Research in Labor Economics, Volume 27, 349–401
Copyright © 2008 by Elsevier Ltd.
All rights of reproduction in any form reserved
ISSN: 0147-9121/doi:10.1016/S0147-9121(07)00009-X

specific skill dimension indeed has the intended effect of raising average skill levels in this dimension among arriving principal applicants.

1. INTRODUCTION

The 1990s have seen major changes in immigration policy in Canada, one of the leading immigrant-receiving countries and the one with the highest per capita immigration rate in the world. Total immigration levels, for example, were kept relatively high over the full business cycle rather than following the previous tap-on/tap-off approach when total immigration levels were linked to absorptive capacity over the business cycle; there was a shift away from an emphasis on family-class immigrants and family reunification role towards an emphasis on independent economic-class immigrants (and their dependants) and a skill-development role for immigration; and there was a major change in the point system (under which economic-class immigrants are evaluated for entry) away from specific occupational preferences and toward broader emphasis on educational credentials, language facility, and young families, again with an eye to human capital and skills development of the host country. Indeed, a recent proposal by the federal government would see a rise in the total immigration rate by about 100 thousand per year or by about 35 percent within 5 years (Campion-Smith, 2005) to help offset the aging of the Canadian population and to contribute to social security and health care costs, and to help supply needed skills and enhance productivity for a growing economy.

A number of other countries such as the United Kingdom, Spain, and Germany are also considering or in the process of bringing in a point system as part of a plan to shift their immigration policies more towards a skill-based focus and possibly to provide tighter control on total inflows. The international competition to attract skilled immigrants is evidently increasing and more attention is being devoted to a point-system approach to evaluate the desirable characteristics of prospective immigrants. While the United States has traditionally emphasized more the role of family reunification in its immigration policy, some debate has initiated over possible adoption of a point system. So it is worthwhile to investigate what lessons can be offered from Canadian experience with their point system and broader inflow policy levers. Any guidelines for reform of immigration policy (Chiswick, 1981) or design for an optimal immigration policy (McHale, 2003) would need to take into account how effective immigration policy levers actually are in bringing about their stated policy objectives.

Canada, like other major immigrant-receiving countries such as Australia, is also currently rethinking the criteria and point weights built into their respective point systems. There are a number of concerns arising from Canada's current emphasis on lots of education human capital: there are real problems with labor market recognition of foreign credentials, increased agglomeration of recent immigrants in three large urban areas (Toronto, Vancouver, and Montreal), and a significantly slower rate of assimilation of recent cohorts of immigrants into the Canadian labor market (Alboim, Finnie, & Meng, 2005; Aydemir & Skuterud, 2005; Picot & Sweetman, 2005). Reitz (2005), among others, provides a call for a new immigration strategy for Canada to improve the utilization of immigrants' skills. There are lessons to be learned and insights to be offered to US immigration policy from the Canadian experience over the 1980s and 1990s.

A vast literature has developed on evaluating the economic outcome of immigrants in their adopted country (see, for example, in the case of Canada, Chiswick & Miller, 1988; Baker & Benjamin, 1994; Bloom, Gunderson, & Grenier, 1995; Grant, 1999; Aydemir & Sweetman, 2005). One of the dimensions of this literature has been on how these outcomes differ by arrival class of immigrants (Duleep & Regets, 1992, 1996; Jasso & Rosenzweig, 1995; de Silva, 1997; Miller, 1999; Abbott & Dougherty, 2004; Chiswick, Lee, & Miller, 2005, 2006). For example, does the skill-selected class of immigrants assimilate more rapidly into local labor markets and get ahead more quickly in terms of earnings, local language proficiency, occupational composition, or incidence of unemployment? But one can view the channels of immigrant adjustment to policy levers, such as skill-testing, as having two quite distinct stages. The first is how the policy levers affect the cohort of immigrant arrivals into the host country. The second stage is how these arrivals succeed (or otherwise) in their adopted environment. The great majority of literature has focused on the second stage of this process. The current paper examines the first stage.

This first-stage process involves several sources of decision-making or behavior. One is the obvious set of government policy levers. Another is the pull of relatives and job opportunities in the host country to potential immigrants from abroad – if you wish, the host country's demand for immigrants. But in addition, there is the decision on the part of potential immigrants from abroad of whether they choose to immigrate, and, at least within the skilled immigrant class, where to immigrate – if you wish, the supply of immigrants. Matters such as economic conditions obviously affect both the pull for additional labor and the attractiveness of the country to such immigrant labor (see Borjas, 1999b, pp. 1709–1717 for more technical details). As international competition for such skilled labor increases, the host country's attractiveness has to be viewed increasingly within the context of other possible substitute destinations. Other countries' immigration policies and world events can also affect the supply of applicants to Canada.

The general question we want to look at in this paper is how responsive are the major characteristics of arrival cohorts of immigrants to changes in immigration policy rules. We make use of a fairly unique administrative data source put together by Canada. Citizenship and Immigration Canada (CIC), the federal immigration department, that contains landing data on all arriving immigrants to Canada over the years 1980–2001 – the so-called Canadian Landings Database (CLD). The major features of this data source are discussed in Section 4. It allows us to test and empirically evaluate several hypotheses on how changes in Canadian immigration policy rules over this period result in changed characteristics of the arriving immigrants. In particular, Canada implemented quite major policy changes on total immigration levels (in the mid-1980s) and on shifting emphasis between family-class and economic-class immigrants and on substantially revised point-allocation schemes in their point system (both in the mid-1990s). The skill characteristics and source-country mix of immigrants also changed quite dramatically over this period. We thus want to estimate reduced-form equations to investigate whether these three sets of policy changes have had identifiable effects on the characteristics of arriving immigrants.

To the authors' awareness, there are very few studies of the effects of immigration policy levers – and specifically of a point system – on the resulting skill characteristics of arriving immigrants, and this is the only paper to do so in detailed empirical fashion.[1] Jasso, Rosenzweig, and Smith (2000) examine the question of how the number and skill of immigrants to the US are likely to be influenced by economic and social conditions in source and destination countries, and by immigration laws and selection criteria in the US. The discussion provides a general analytical framework and some regression results on earnings of some specific groups of immigrant males over 1972–1990 for the United States. Green and Green (1995) examine the effects of changes in Canadian immigration policy on the occupational composition of immigrants. Aydemir (2002) looks at the effects of selection criteria and economic opportunities on the characteristics of Canadian immigrants from the perspective of the potential immigrant. He provides a structural analysis of the separate application decisions and the application review outcome. Chiswick and Miller (2005) use a difference-in-difference approach to empirically isolate the impact of English language skills policy changes in Australian panel survey data. They find that an increased English skill requirement among essentially independent class immigrants appears to have indeed raised English language proficiency among such immigrants.

2. A COMPARATIVE PERSPECTIVE ON CANADIAN AND AMERICAN IMMIGRATION POLICY, 1980–2004

Immigration regulations have played a central role in shaping immigration to Canada and other major immigrant-receiving countries for much of the last century. The evolution of immigration policy between Canada and the United States has followed very different paths. In what follows, we briefly sketch the outcomes of these different approaches as they are reflected in current policy prescriptions. Further details can be found in Antecol, Cobb-Clark, and Trejo (2003), Beach, Green, and Reitz (2003), Chiswick (1987), McWhinney (1998), Reiners and Troper (1992), and Wright and Maxim (1993).

2.1. Canada

Canada adopted a non-discriminatory admission policy in 1962, a few years ahead of the United States (in 1965). Both countries had operated a discriminatory policy before these changes focussing on arrivals from traditional source countries. The shift to a universal immigration policy then opened up the possibility of new arrivals coming from any country and from any background.

For Canada, this shift to a universal immigration policy created problems on the skill level of the new arrivals. In the 1960s, Canada was in the process of shifting towards a more urban-industrial economy and the labor force had to be brought into line with the skill levels needed to support this transition. Immigration policy had to be shifted as well. The solution was the creation of the Point System (in 1967), as an objective way to assess the admissibility of prospective immigrants while at the same time upgrading the skill level of new arrivals.

Table 1 sets out the categories under which a prospective Independent candidate for admission is judged along with the maximum number of points in each factor and the pass mark needed to be admitted. The table covers the period from the introduction of the Point System in 1967 until the present. Despite major revisions to the Immigration Act over the last three

Table 1. The Canadian Points System Over Time (Maximum Points).

Factor	1967	1974	1978	1986	1993	1997
Education	20	20	12	12	16	16
Experience	–	–	8	8	8	8
Specific vocational preparation or educational training factor	10	10	15	15	18	18
Occupational demand or occupational factor	15	15	15	10	10	10
Age	10	10	10	10	10	10
Arranged employment or designated occupation	10	10	10	10	10	10
Language	10	10	10	15	15	15
Personal suitability	15	15	10	10	10	10
Levels adjustment factor[1] or demographic factor	–	–	–	5	8	10
Relative or kinship bonus	5	5	5	10/15	5	5
Destination	5	5	5	–	–	–
Total	100	100	100	95–110	105–110	107–112
Pass Mark	50	50	50	70	70	70

Source: Green and Green (1999, p. 433) plus updated information from CIC.
[1]A discretionary allocation that can be used to control the number of persons entering over a period. Pass mark varies by skill level.

decades (i.e., in 1978 and 2002), the Point System has remained at the core of assessing which Independent (or Economic) class immigrants will obtain entry visas. The Independent class also includes business class immigrants – formally added in 1986 – in the entrepreneur, investor, and self-employment categories. Two other major classes under which prospective immigrants can be admitted are the Family class (family reunification), and the Humanitarian class (mainly refugees). The Family class migrants are admitted solely on the basis of kinship. A Nominated or assisted-relatives class was also introduced as part of the Independent class. Admission under this latter class was partly through kinship and partly through the assessment under the Point System. Bonus points were awarded to prospective immigrants seeking entrance through this class as a result of having relatives already resident in Canada who could help with adapting to their new home. There are also a small number of "other immigrants" consisting largely of retired persons, live-in caregivers or foreign household domestics or deferred removal-order immigrants.

Under the Point System, prospective immigrants originally needed to amass at least 50 out of a possible 100 points to obtain an entry visa (nominated relatives received a 15 point bonus to cover a short-fall in points earned in evaluating their case for admission). As Table 1 shows, prospective immigrants were judged on a wide variety of factors, for example, age, education, work experience, occupational demand, etc. Table 1 also shows that the weights assigned to these factors have changed over time. Indeed, some categories actually disappeared while new ones were introduced. Initially, at least, the weighting scheme for the first two decades after the introduction of this scheme in 1967 reflected past immigration policy, in the sense that it focused on occupational needs in the economy at a particular point of time. The total number of points awarded to occupation-directed categories (i.e., occupational skill, experience, occupational demand, and bonus points for designated occupations) totaled 43 out of a possible 100 points in 1986. The prospective migrant needed to get a certain number of points out of 100 to be admitted to Canada. It is not necessary to get points in every category. Hence, a prospective migrant could score high points for education, age, etc., and zero for occupation demand, and still be admitted.

The occupation-based or gap-filling model used to guide admission was changed in the mid-1990s. In its place was substituted an earnings or human capital model perspective. Under this approach, specific occupational needs were reduced in the weighting scheme while additional points were awarded to education, age, and official language fluency (all three of these categories had been present from 1967, but were given lower weights than those categories dealing with occupational demand). The rationale for the change was that the higher the prospective immigrants scored in these three categories the more easily they would adapt to their new home country and hence the more rapid their ascent to parity in earnings to similarly placed native-born workers.

This shift in weights in Canada signaled a move towards a longer-run view of immigration policy. Less emphasis was placed on gap-filling and more on the factors that supposedly influenced the long-run adaptability of the new migrant. Along with this change went a shift away from an absorptive capacity model (i.e., where the annual immigration flow was adjusted to short-run economic conditions, with an increase in the inflow as unemployment fell and a reduction in the number admitted as economic conditions deteriorated). In its place was put a model that set annual immigration levels at a bit less than one percent of the Canadian population. This number would not change with short-run economic conditions. Hence, as the government sought to increase the skilled share of arrivals, it also shifted immigration policy to a long-run approach, and one based on adaptability rather than one designed to meet short-run occupational needs.

Some key features of the Canadian immigration system are worth mentioning. Under the terms of the British North American Act establishing Canada, immigration is designated as a co-jurisdiction between the provinces and the federal government (i.e., the provinces can have a say in setting policy). Since 1978, Quebec has run its own policy (subject to federal override), with its own Point System. Second, while Australia sets a maximum age for admission of independent migrants at 49, Canada reduces points available to migrants less than 21 and over 49 (Richardson & Lester, 2004). Third, while under Australian immigration policy, prospective immigrants must score at least one point in every category, Canada requires only that the prospective migrant scores enough points to meet the passing grade and so can still be admitted with a zero score in any given category. Finally, Canada does not try to assess whether the skills recorded by the prospective immigrant will be recognized in Canada. The only action taken is to inform the migrant of the education/training needed to meet the requirements for employment in their particular occupation (i.e., physician, nurse, engineer, carpenter, etc.). This is in marked contrast with the Australian approach which is to match the migrant's training to the position before admission is granted (i.e., the migrant is acceptable and can move into the job). In Canada, therefore, the problem of credentialization has become, in recent times, an area of media attention and controversy.

2.2. The United States

Since the passage of the Immigration Act of 1924 and the 1965 Amendments to the Act, the United States has followed a dramatically different path in regulating immigration than Canada. (For a summary of US immigration policy, see Chapter 2 of Smith & Edmonston, 1997.) The most outstanding differences are: (i) US immigration policy has in the main followed a family-reunification approach rather than one based on economic factors. (ii) The level of inflow, until the last quarter century, was low relative to the size of the population and the annual inflow of 180,000 was fixed and independent of short-run economic conditions in the US. Throughout the post–World War II period, the number of legal immigrants increased. It is just in the last quarter of the 20th century that the number of legally admitted immigrants has climbed to nearly a million migrants a year. This formed the basis of the

"New Migration". (iii) Unlike Canada, US immigration policy is highly centralized under federal government control; hence, it operates a single policy that applies to all states. (iv) The 1924 Act was, as in the case of Canada, highly discriminatory. It focused on reuniting families already in the US and so minimized the inflow of less-desirable immigrants from southern and eastern Europe, and continued the policy of virtually barring Asian immigrants. Migration to the US, although more widely geographically based than was the case for Canada, nevertheless, favored immigration from traditional source countries like Northwest Europe. The United States ended its racist admission policy in 1965 and at the same time raised the annual level of intake.

As a result of adopting a non-economic-based immigration policy (i.e., one centered on family reunification), US immigration policy cannot effectively control for the level of human capital inflow. It still attracts some of the most skilled immigrants from around the world, but the average level of skill is probably lower than that of either Australia or Canada. Recently, the US government has taken steps to rectify this shortfall in the share of skilled immigrants coming to that country. In 1998, the government increased the cap on long-stay professional visa (H-1B) and it did so again in 2000 under pressure from the high-tech industries. Also, the 1990 Act expanded the number of employment preference permanent immigration visas, though the overall policy approach remained focussed on family reunification.

A skill-based point system was first proposed for the United States by Chiswick (1981). Recently, Borjas (1999a) proposed that immigration levels be dropped to half their present level and that the US government adopt a modified Point System along the lines of that used in Australia and Canada. Borjas proposes that prospective migrants be assessed in three categories (i.e., English language proficiency, years of schooling, and age). No weights were assigned for each of these categories. The United States, however, is still operating a non-economic (family-reunification) policy with a gap-filling or targeted employment model for selecting economic immigrants and with few policy tools available to it to adjust the composition of the inflow to a more economic and skill-based orientation.

3. CANADIAN IMMIGRANT LANDINGS SINCE 1980: GENERAL FEATURES

Before formulating specific hypotheses to be examined, consider some of the main features of Canadian immigration inflows since 1980. The descriptive results in this section are based largely on published data – hard copy or web-based – from CIC (Immigration Statistics and Facts and Figures, various years) from their landings data. Fig. 1 shows the profile of total immigration levels since 1980. In 1985, the total number of immigrants troughed at 84.3 thousand. The number then shot up in 1987 to 152.1 thousand and continued rising to above 250 thousand in 1992 and 1993. It then drifted down to 173.1 thousand in 1998 and then moved up again to above 250 thousand in 2001, from which it has continued in the 220–230 thousand immigrants per year range (out of a population of about 30 million). The main feature of these results is the distinct up-shift in total immigration levels in Canada beginning in the mid-1980s that has generally continued.

Fig. 1 also shows the numbers of immigrants in the major immigrant classes. The two largest classes are the Family class and the Economic (or Independent) class. The latter includes all dependants arriving with the principal applicant (PA). It also includes Assisted or Nominated Relatives since they also pass through the Point System. The things to notice here are, first, the marked cyclical nature of Economic-class inflows which generally increase in periods of economic growth and prosperity in Canada and decrease during periods of recessions (1981–1983 and 1990–1992). This

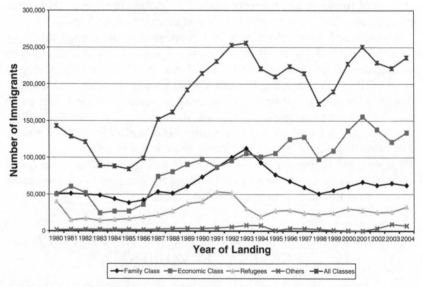

Fig. 1. Total Immigrants to Canada by Class, Annually, from 1980 to 2004. *Source:* Citizenship and Immigration Canada, 1980–2004.

suggests that we will need to be cognizant of arguments related to the attractiveness of Canada to potential immigrants as quite distinct from any immediate immigration policy levers that Canadian authorities may change. And second, note the general decline in Family class numbers since 1993.

Since 1980, there has also been substantial change in the country or region of origin of Canadian immigrants (see Fig. 2). The most noticeable change here has been the increase in the numbers arriving from the Asia and Pacific regions and, to a lesser though still significant degree, from Africa and the Middle East. In the mid-1980s, the numbers of immigrants arriving from Asia and Pacific ran around 30–35 thousand a year, but by 1992 had moved up to over 100 thousand a year and peaked in 2001 at about 133 thousand arrivals. Those from Africa and the Middle East in the early to mid-1980s averaged around 8–9 thousand a year, but by 1991 moved up to over 40 thousand, and since 2000 arrivals have run between 40 and 50 thousand a year. Meanwhile, landings from Europe, United Kingdom, and the United States have been relatively stable over the whole period with 41.8 thousand from Europe and the UK and 7.5 thousand from the US in 2004. In percentages terms, though, they represent a declining share of the total

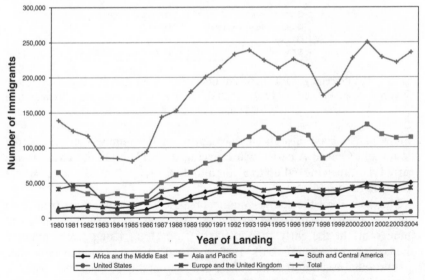

Fig. 2. Immigrants to Canada, by Country of Last Permanent Residence, Annually, from 1980 to 2004. *Source:* Citizenship and Immigration Canada, 1980–2004.

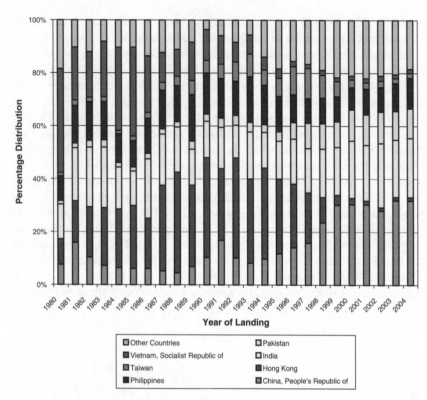

Fig. 3. The Percentage Distribution of Immigrants from Asia and Pacific by Source Country, Annually, from 1980 to 2004. *Source:* Citizenship and Immigration Canada, 1980–2004.

inflow. There have also been fluctuations in the numbers arriving from South and Central America which averaged 14–17 thousand a year in the early 1980s, then moved up to 37 thousand by 1991 and have since eased off to 19–22 thousand a year since 2001.

More detail on the source-country breakdown of immigrants from Asia and the Pacific is provided in Fig. 3. Here, one can see the run up of immigrants in the early to mid-1990s from Hong Kong (from about 6 thousand a year from the early 1980s to a peak of 44 thousand in 1994, then a substantial easing off after 1997 when the hand-over occurred, down to only 1.5 thousand in 2004). The inflows from India and Pakistan pretty steadily increased from the mid-1980s (eg., 4.5 thousand in total in 1985) through to the early 2000s (totalling 43 thousand in 2001 and 38 thousand in

2004). Again, though, the biggest change has been arrivals from mainland China which varied from 2 to 6 thousand in the early to mid-1980s, then over the early 1990s moved up to 20 thousand a year, and in 2001 hit 40 thousand landings and has since eased off slightly.

In contrast, the intended region of destination within Canada has not changed that much since 1980. Most migrants (over 80%) move directly to urban areas on arriving in Canada, so that patterns of settlement are dominated by migration to Toronto for Ontario, to Montreal for Quebec, and to Vancouver for British Columbia. Ontario absorbs over half (52.1% over the period) of all migrants coming to Canada and it has held this position for the last 20 years. The next largest regions of intended destination are Quebec (16.6%) and British Columbia (16.6% as well). Given that the population size of British Columbia is much smaller than that of either Ontario or Quebec, the result is that the rate of migration to the west coast province is quite high. Ontario is indeed the only province that has witnessed a rise in its share of total immigration over the last two decades. The share going to this province grew from about 44 percent in the early–1980s to a high of 60 percent in 2000. The Quebec and British Columbia percentages of arrivals, on the other hand, fluctuate around a trendless share of total arrivals to each province. Both the Prairies (Manitoba and Saskatchewan) and Alberta show declining shares over the covered period with most of the drop occurring in the late 1980s and then holding constant for the reminder of the period. This is a surprising result, at least for Alberta, since this province is one of the most prosperous and high-growth regions in Canada and has attracted a large internal migration to the oil fields and to the rapidly expanding cities of Calgary and Edmonton.

Now consider some of the skill characteristics of landed immigrants since 1980. In Table 2, sample means are presented for education and admission class for immigrants landed in Canada in 1980, 1990, and 2000. The proportion of immigrants with an undergraduate or graduate university degree rose dramatically over the period from 5.8 percent and 1.8 percent, respectively, in 1980 to 25.1 percent and 9.0 percent in 2000. The larger part of each increase occurred in the 1990s and is almost surely due to the reform of the Point System used to select immigrants to Canada under the skilled worker or Economic class category of admission. The changes in 1993 specifically led to a large increase in the weight placed on university education in selecting skilled immigrants.

In contrast, the proportion of new immigrants with post-secondary education below the university level rose from 16.5 percent in 1980 to 20 percent in 1990. However, it declined to below its 1980 level of 15.6 percent

Table 2. Immigrant Characteristics at Landing, Level of Education and Admission Category, 1980, 1990, and 2000 (Proportions).

	Canada		
	1980	1990	2000
Education			
University – post-graduate	0.0177	0.0289	0.0902
University – undergarduate	0.0583	0.1100	0.2506
Post-secondary	0.1645	0.1996	0.1558
Secondary	0.5898	0.5316	0.3526
Elementary or less	0.1676	0.1297	0.1507
Admission category			
Economic	0.3486	0.4419	0.5870
Family class	0.3587	0.3436	0.2663
Humanitarian	0.2819	0.1668	0.1322
Other	0.0108	0.0477	0.0145
Total number of landings	143,136	216,402	227,313

Source: Calculations by the authors from the CLD data.

by 2000. The other large change in the education distribution of newly landed immigrants over the period is the decline at the secondary education level – from 59 percent in 1980 to 35 percent in 2000. The overall result has been a fairly steady increase in the average years of education of arriving immigrants (see Fig. 4).

The distribution of new immigrants across the different admission categories has also varied considerably over the 20-year period. The proportion of new immigrants in the Economic category rose form 34.9 percent in 1980 to 44.2 percent in 1990, then to 58.7 percent in 2000. These increases coincided with decreases in the share of new immigrants arriving under the Family class (35.9 percent in 1980 to 26.6 percent in 2000) and the Humanitarian class (28.2 percent in 1980 to 13.2 percent in 2000). The larger part of the decline in the share of the Humanitarian category occurred between 1980 and 1990, while the larger part of the decline in the Family class (and the increase in the share of the Economic category) occurred between 1990 and 2000. The Humanitarian class intakes are, of course, largely influenced by refugee crises around the world.

In Table 3, the sample proportions for the different education levels are presented for the case of immigrants arriving under the Economic category. The percentage of Economic immigrants with either a post-graduate or an undergraduate degree rose dramatically over the period from 3.3 and

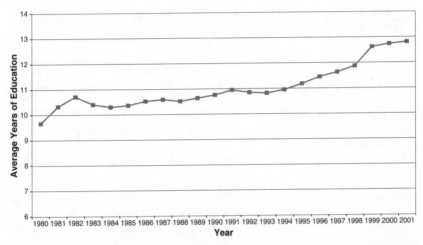

Fig. 4. Average Years of Education of Immigrants to Canada, Annually, from 1980 to 2001. *Source:* Citizenship and Immigration Canada, Landings Data, 1980–2001.

Table 3. Immigrant Characteristics at Landing, Level of Education: Economic Immigrants, 1980, 1990, and 2000 (Proportions).

	Canada		
	1980	1990	2000
University-post-graduate	0.0333	0.0438	0.1337
University-undergraduate	0.0900	0.1365	0.3364
Post-secondary	0.2331	0.2092	0.1389
Secondary	0.4900	0.4797	0.2258
Elementary or less	0.1508	0.1308	0.1652
Total number of landings	49,895	95,627	133,422

Source: Calculations by the authors from the CLD data.

9.0 percent, respectively, in 1980 to 13.4 percent and 33.6 percent, respectively, in 2000 (with most of the increase in each case occurring in the 1990s). The percentage of new Economic immigrants arriving with education at the post-secondary level (below university) and the secondary level fell over the period by just under 10 percentage points in the former case and 26 percentage points in the latter case.

In Table 4, the equivalent sample proportions are presented as those in Table 3, but for the restricted sample of immigrants arriving under the

Table 4. Immigrant Characteristics at Landing, Level of Education: 1990 and 2000, Economic Immigrants Who Were Principal Applicants (Proportions).

	Canada		Quebec		Ontario	
	1990	2000	1990	2000	1990	2000
Education						
University – post-graduate	0.0896	0.2473	0.0838	0.2134	0.0825	0.2579
University – undergraduate	0.2296	0.5363	0.2401	0.3616	0.2255	0.5790
Post-secondary	0.3425	0.1548	0.3217	0.3216	0.3563	0.1134
Secondary	0.3255	0.0555	0.3455	0.0998	0.3231	0.0440
Elementary or less	0.0127	0.0061	0.0089	0.0036	0.0126	0.0057
Total number of landings	37,659	56,292	9,566	8,155	18,195	34,115

Source: Calculations by the authors from the CLD data.

Economic category who were indeed the PAs. These are the immigrants to Canada who are actually selected on their perceived labor market skills since admission under the Point System over the relevant time period was restricted to the characteristics of the PA (and not those of accompanying family members). The results are presented for the years 1990 and 2000 since this is the period over which most of the changes occurred in terms of: (i) the allocation of points for education, and (ii) the distribution of education of new arrivals under the Economic category. From the first two columns, we see that there was a massive increase in the share of immigrants arriving with a university degree between 1990 and 2000 (from 9.0 percent and 23.0 percent for post-graduate and undergraduate, respectively, to 24.7 percent and 53.6 percent, respectively). These increases came at the expense of the share of Economic PAs entering with only some post-secondary and especially secondary levels of education.

Equivalent sample means are presented in the next four columns for the case of immigrants landing in Quebec and immigrants landing in Ontario in Table 4. These are the two most populous provinces in Canada. Also worth noting is that the provincial government in Quebec has an arrangement with the federal government allowing them to choose the points awarded for different characteristics under the Point System allowing them to have a strong say in terms of selecting the immigrants planning to reside in Quebec.

The main motive for doing this is to increase the proportion of immigrants going to Quebec who are likely to live and work using the French language since this is the dominant language in Quebec.

It is interesting to note that the large increases in education over the period appear for both immigrants settling in Quebec and those settling in Ontario. However, the increases at the post-graduate and especially the undergraduate university levels are larger for the case of Ontario than they are for Quebec. Parent and Worswick (2003) argue that the increase in the share of immigrants with high levels of education coming to Quebec in the latter half of the 1990s rose because of the increased emphasis placed on education under the Quebec portion of the selection system, but that it did not rise by as much as what occurred in the rest of Canada because of the emphasis on French language ability in the Quebec selection system.

In Fig. 5, the annual share of new immigrants with a university degree is presented for new Economic PAs landing in Quebec, the "Rest of Canada" (ROC), and Ontario. It is clear for all three groups that the share of new immigrants with a university degree rose over the period with the increase

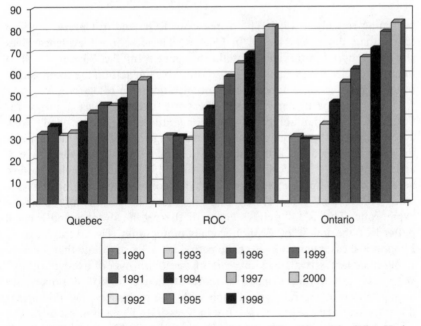

Fig. 5. Percentage of New Economic Immigrants Who Were PAs Who Had a University Degree: 1990–2000.

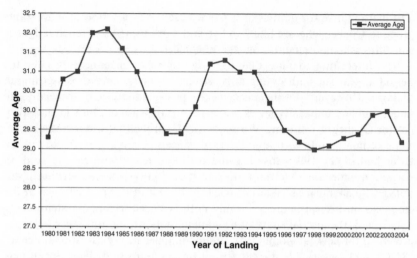

Fig. 6. The Average Age of Immigrants to Canada, Annually, from 1980 to 2004.
Source: Citizenship and Immigration Canada, 1980–2004.

beginning roughly in 1994. The increases in ROC and in Ontario are also larger than those experienced in Quebec. The descriptive evidence gives strong support for the idea that the parameters of the Canadian skilled immigrant selection systems can have noticeable impacts on the composition of immigrants landing under the Economic admission category.

If age and, particularly, youthfulness are interpreted as a proxy for flexibility and adaptability to the Canadian labor market and likely accompaniment by a young family, then average age of immigrant arrivals may also be viewed as a skill characteristic. Fig. 6 shows how average age of arriving migrants has declined slightly since 1980. But the major pattern here is a cyclical one: average age of arriving cohorts increases in recessions (early 1980s and early 1990s) and decreases in periods of economic expansions. This is fully consistent with the previously observed cyclical pattern of the inflow of Economic-class immigrants. The average age of Economic-class immigrants over the period is 26.3 years while that for non-Economic-class arrivals is 31.6 years of age (with overall average of 29.3 years). In expansions, Canada is more attractive to skilled prospective immigrants who are relatively young with young families and this brings down the average age of arrivals. But in recessions, Canada is less attractive to such immigrants and the number of Economic class immigrants attenuates, while the stock of resident immigrants continues to bring in relatives under the Family-class category and these relations are typically parents and grandparents, and hence substantially older.

A further feature to notice in Fig. 6 is that there appears to be a reversal or relaxation of the above cyclical pattern after 1998. That is, the Canadian economy continued to grow well with very little slowdown (particularly relative to the United States) right through from the middle 1990s to the 2000s. So one would expect a continuing decrease in the average age of arrivals. Evidently, this has not happened. In the mid-1990s, however, the Point System was revised to give greater weight to "experience" and "years of schooling", and both these changes would tend to push up the average age at arrival. Also, after 1997, the inflow of immigrants from Hong Kong fell off dramatically and they were typically relatively young.

Finally, also consider the language fluency of arriving immigrants in either English or French. While this skill attribute is self-reported, it is checked or confirmed by the visa-issuing immigration officer. As shown in Fig. 7, there has been a mixed pattern in language proficiency over time. Fluency in English or French has risen slightly from the mid-1980s, but then has slipped a bit since 1996. On average, over the period, 47.4 percent of immigrants are proficient in English, 4.6 percent in French, and a further 3.8 percent as bilingual in English and French. About 44 percent are proficient in neither official language upon arrival (see Table 5). Not surprisingly, fluency in English or French are greater among Economic-class immigrants than in other classes, so less than 36 percent of Economic class arrivals are fluent in neither official language, but almost 51 percent of non-Economic-class immigrants lack such proficiency.

4. TESTING HYPOTHESES ON IMMIGRATION POLICY LEVERS AND LANDINGS CHARACTERISTICS

We now try to pull some of the previous descriptive results and policy discussions together in terms of identifying specific hypotheses and testing them in the framework of regression analysis. A number of papers, including most recently Card (2005), Ottaviano and Peri (2005), and Fougère, Harvey, Mérette, and Poitras (2003), have used quite different approaches to find broad positive effects of total immigration flows on the US and Canadian economies. Fougère, Harvey, Mercenier, and Mérette (2005) find that increasing the proportion of high-skilled

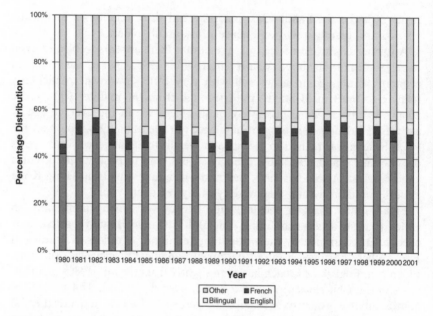

Fig. 7. Percentage Distribution of Immigrants by Language Fluency, Annually from 1980 to 2001. *Source:* Citizenship and Immigration Canada, Landings Data, 1980–2001.

Table 5. Language Fluency of Immigrants by Immigrant Class 1980–2001 (Percent).

	English	French	Bilingual	Other
Economic class	54.1	4.7	5.5	35.7
Non-economic class	42.4	4.2	2.4	50.9
All immigrants	47.4	4.6	3.8	44.1

Source: Calculations by the authors from the CLD data.

(i.e., economic-class) immigrants would, in the long run, raise Canadian labor productivity and living standards and reduce the expected negative impact of population aging on growth of real GDP per capita. And Worswick (2004) provides a call for reweighting the Point System so as to reward applicants for education credentials and relevant work experience which are recognized by Canadian employers. Consequently, the three drivers or policy levers we wish to examine in this study are: (i) the total level of immigrant inflows in a year, (ii) the proportion of the total inflow in the Economic-class category, and (iii) the Point System weights for the general skill levels of educational attainment, (youthful) age, and (English/French) language fluency. In the Canadian Point System, zero points are awarded for a PA having less than a high school diploma, maximum points for a four-year university degree, and partial points for various types of high school and post-secondary training. In the case of age, full points are awarded for PAs aged between 21 and 49, and decreasing partial points for age further away from the 21–49 age interval. In the case of language, zero points are awarded if the PA speaks English and French very haltingly, full points if they are fluent in both official languages, and partial points based on reading, writing, and speaking of English and French.

Administrative data on immigrant landings are employed in the analysis of this paper. Each record in the CLD contains the information available from the immigrant's landing documents at the time of receiving "Landed Immigrant" status in Canada. The microdata set contains landings records for every immigrant who arrived in Canada over the period 1980 through 2001; it is thus very large. The data have detailed information on the immigrant's age, sex, education, official language fluency status, marital status, visa status, country of birth, intended destination, and place of arrival as well as whether the person was the PA (vs an accompanying family member).[2]

The dependent variables or outcome variables for the regression analysis are three sets of skill indicator variables for educational attainment (both number of years of education and the percent of immigrant arrivals with a university degree), years of age, and official language fluency (percentage arriving with English or French language fluency). These three dimensions are generally acknowledged as the major skill indicators for immigrants that the literature focuses on, and these are the three that Borjas (1999a) has suggested that United States immigration policy should also incorporate in a prospective Point System.

4.1. Basic Hypotheses of Interest

Several hypotheses are examined in this paper relevant to the effects on arriving immigrants' skill levels of our three policy drivers. The first refers to total immigration inflow rates: does a larger size of immigrant inflows reduce the overall skill levels of arriving cohorts as the larger numbers of immigrants are likely to be closer to the Point System cut-off line (in the case of Economic-class immigrants) and to bring in more relatives (in the case of Family-class immigrants) who generally adjust more slowly in integrating into the Canadian labor market? The second refers to Economic vs non-Economic-class immigrants: do Economic class immigrants have higher average skill levels, and thus other things being equal, does an increase in the share of Economic-class immigrants in response to shifting government priorities raise the overall skill levels of arriving immigrant cohorts since it is the Economic-class arrivals who are essentially admitted on the basis of their skill? The third hypothesis refers to operation of the Point System: does increasing the Point System weight on some skill dimension – such as educational attainment – indeed have the desired effect of raising overall skill levels of immigrant arrivals in this dimension? And the fourth refers to business cycle effects: does a weaker labor market in Canada result in attracting fewer skilled immigrants so that overall skill levels of arriving cohorts of immigrants are reduced? And, by extension, does a weaker labor market in the United States (a substitute destination), ceteris paribus, lead to an increase in the overall skill levels of immigrants selecting to come to Canada?

We want to estimate the effects of policy driver variables (appearing as independent variables) on the general skill characteristics of landing immigrants (as the dependent variables). Observations are individual arriving immigrants, so the regressions are estimated over microdata points. While we have observations over time, each data point is a landed immigrant in the year of their landing (i.e., their arrival on Canadian soil). So the observations occur in annual cross-sections and do not have a panel or longitudinal dimension. Unfortunately, the database does not record the actual Point System total score or sub-scores awarded to each PA. Since different regions have experienced different degrees of labor market tightness and economic growth, we characterize immigrant arrivals by region of intended residence in their first year in Canada (with six regions: Atlantic, Quebec, Ontario, Manitoba/Saskatchewan, Alberta, and British Columbia).

4.2. Regression Specification and Estimation Groups

The specification estimated, then, includes a time trend to pick up underlying net trend effects, the total inflow of immigrants in a year (in thousands), the Economic class share of total inflow (out of 100), and the maximum points allocated by the Point System to the respective skill measure for that equation as a share of the required pass mark (out of 100). These three "test variables" are used to test Hypotheses 1–3, respectively. The regressions for all immigrants also include admission-class dummy variables (with Economic-class as the default). The regressions also involve six destination region dummies (with Ontario as the default) and seven source region dummies. The default source region is English-speaking countries (consisting of the US, UK, Ireland, South Africa, Australia, and New Zealand). Finally, in order to pick up business cycle effects on immigrant skill outcomes, the regression specification further includes the Canadian annual unemployment rate (for 25–54 year olds from the CANSIM website) as a proxy for labor market tightness and phase of the business cycle. Since potential immigrants may view the United States and Canada as substitute alternative destinations, the specification also includes a US unemployment rate (annual for all persons in the US from the Bureau of Labor Statistics website).[3] These two variables represent a test of the fourth hypothesis.[4]

A further consideration in interpreting the regression results and hypothesis tests is to ask the question: to whom do the hypotheses apply? When Economic-class immigration occurs, one person (the PA – typically the person in the family unit who is expected to score highest on the Point System scale) gets reviewed under the Point System, and if the review is successful the whole family unit arrives and all the family members are classified as Economic-class immigrants. On average over the period covered, there were 2.3 arrivals per PA. But as illustrated in Fig. 8, this ratio of arrivals per PA has not been at all constant over the period and has been generally higher in the 1990s than in the 1980s. Thus, when the share of Economic-class immigrants goes up, there are several changes that can occur: (i) there is a shifting weight towards higher-average-skilled immigrants, and (ii) the average skill levels of arrivals *within* the Economic-class category may change as well. Some simple mathematics can clarify what is going on.

Let S denote skill level in some dimension and w the proportion that Economic class immigrants are in total immigration. Then, the average skill level across all immigrants is the weighted average of average skill levels among Economic-class immigrants (EC) and non-Economic-class immigrants (NEC)

$$E(S) = w \cdot E(S|EC, w) + (1 - w) \cdot E(S|NEC) \qquad (1)$$

where we assume that the average skill level within the Economic class is a function of w. Then, it is simple to calculate that the overall skill effect of

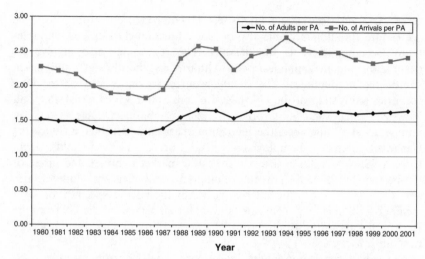

Fig. 8. Number of Economic Class Arrivals per PA, Annually, 1980–2001. *Source:*
Citizenship and Immigration Canada, Landings Data, 1980–2001.

increasing the Economic-class share is given by:

$$\frac{\partial E(S)}{\partial w} = E(S|EC, w) + w \cdot \frac{\partial E(S|EC, w)}{\partial w} - E(S|NEC)$$

$$= [E(S|EC, w) - E(S|NEC)] + w \cdot \frac{\partial E(S|EC, w)}{\partial w} \qquad (2)$$

The first term in square brackets Jasso et al. (2000) label as the
"composition effect" and is unambiguously expected to be positive as we
have seen that average skill levels are higher among Economic-class
immigrants than for non-Economic-class immigrants. The second term of
the expression may be called the "average skill effect" within the Economic-
class of increasing the share of Economic-class immigration. Since total
levels of immigration are being held constant in the regressions, an increase
in w corresponds to an increase in the total number of Economic-class
arrivals – including both PAs and their accompanying family members. It is
also important to note that all terms in the above expression are readily
estimable. The sign of the average skill effect is ambiguous a priori as
arguments could be made for it to go either ways.[5]

There are several outcomes from this derivation. First, the effect of
Economic share on overall average skill levels is a priori ambiguous and

depends on two effects, only one of which can be signed a priori. It becomes an empirical matter what the sign of the second effect is and which of the two effects dominates. Second, in order to estimate and evaluate the average skill effect and to better test Hypotheses 2 and 3, we need to rerun the regressions on the group of Economic-class immigrants.

Third, we can refine the reasoning in Eqs. (1) and (2) further to view principal applicants – the ones who are actually reviewed under the Point System – as the subgroup through which the average skill effect operates. To illustrate, let

$$E(S|EC, w) = p \cdot E(S|PA, w) + (1 - p) \cdot E(S|NPA) \tag{3}$$

where the first expectation on the right-hand side of (3) is the average skill level of principal applicants (possibly a function of w as well), the second expectations term is the average skill level of non-PAs within the Economic-class of immigrants, and p is the proportion of PAs among Economic-class immigrants. Now substitute this result into Eq. (1) and one can derive that

$$\frac{\partial E(S)}{\partial w} = [E(S|EC, w) - E(S|NEC)] + wp \cdot \frac{\partial E(S|PA, w)}{\partial w} \tag{4}$$

Again, the first term is our composition effect and the second term is an alternative expression for the average skill effect. In this case, though, the latter is estimated through running regressions on the subgroup of principal applicants. Note also that principal applicants are the most directly affected and thus the most appropriate group on which to test hypothesis on the effects of changing Point System weights. Indeed, one can refine the statement of Hypothesis 3 now to: does an increase in the Point System weight on some skill dimension (eg., educational attainment) have the desired effect on raising the average skill level in this dimension among PAs?

Fourth, the expressions in Eqs. (2) and (4) provide the basis for *indirect* estimation of overall skill effects on immigrants as a whole. The set of all immigrants includes a great deal of compositional shifts and heterogeneity, and these shifts and heterogeneity may make it difficult to tease out a reliable (direct) estimate of skill effects on immigrants as a whole. Using Eqs. (2) and (4), we can obtain possibly much more reliable indirect estimates of these effects from the regression results estimated on the more homogeneous and more skill-based sub-groups of Economic-class immigrants and of the PAs themselves. These samples are smaller than that for all immigrants, but their results are expected to be much cleaner and provide more clear-cut tests of several of the hypotheses.

The upshot of this discussion is that we will provide regression results for three sets of immigrants: for all immigrants, for Economic-class immigrants, and for PA immigrants. Different immigrant groups are relevant to examining and testing different hypotheses.

5. REGRESSION RESULTS OF POLICY DRIVERS ON IMMIGRANT SKILL DIMENSIONS

This section presents the regression results for our standard specification. The regressions are estimated (by OLS) for each of three groups of immigrants.[6] The all immigrants group consists of all adult immigrants aged 20 or more at the time of landing/arrival. The age restriction is necessary since the CLD does not provide skill attributes for immigrant children. The number of observations in this group is about 2.7 million. The Economic-class group consists of all Economic-class immigrants and their dependants who are aged 20 or more at arrival, and this amounts to about 1.2 million observations. Then, the PAs group consists of those Economic-class immigrants (aged 20 or over) who filed the application for landed immigrant status and hence were evaluated through the Point System. This group accounts for about 750–760 thousand observations (depending on what skill characteristics are reported).

5.1. Effects on Educational Attainment

Regression results for years of education as the dependent variable, estimated across arriving immigrants, are presented in Table 6. Results for all immigrants appear in the first column, results for Economic-class immigrants appear in the middle column, and results for PAs are reported in the third column. For the education regressions in this section, an extra regressor is added – a dummy variable, which takes a value of 1 for the years 1993 onward in order, to capture extra points awarded for a university degree (beyond simply the years of education). Figures in parentheses are OLS standard errors and asterisks indicate coefficient significant at the 1 (**) or 5 (*) percent levels. Given the large numbers of observations, most coefficients are highly statistically significant.

The results for all immigrants include admission class dummies. The three negative coefficients show that, relative to Economic-class immigrants (the default category), Family-class immigrants have lower average

Table 6.   Years of Education Regression Results.

	All Immigrants	Economic Class	Principal Applicants (PA)
Admission class			
Family	−2.639**	n.a.	n.a.
	(0.0052)		
Humanitarian	−2.040**	n.a.	n.a.
	(0.0073)		
Other	−1.719**	n.a.	n.a.
	(0.010)		
Test variables			
Time trend (0–21)	0.1984**	0.1912**	0.1800**
	(0.0014)	(0.0019)	(0.0024)
Total inflow (in '000s)	−0.00310**	−0.00314**	−0.00211**
	(0.000084)	(0.00012)	(0.00015)
Economic share of inflow	−0.00051	0.00656**	0.01338**
(out of 100)	(0.00057)	(0.00080)	(0.00099)
Education points as share	0.01397**	0.02922**	0.03534**
of pass mark (out of 100)	(0.00081)	(0.00114)	(0.00143)
Indicator for 1993 or later	−0.2001**	0.2811**	0.4150**
	(0.0102)	(0.0154)	(0.0197)
Canadian unemployment	−0.0921**	−0.0914**	−0.0967**
rate	(0.0036)	(0.0047)	(0.0059)
US unemployment rate	0.2045**	0.1888**	0.1958**
	(0.0047)	(0.0066)	(0.0082)
Region of residence			
Atlantic provinces	0.580**	0.445**	0.724**
	(0.017)	(0.022)	(0.029)
Quebec	−0.084**	−0.249**	−0.263**
	(0.006)	(0.009)	(0.011)
Manitoba or Saskatchewan	−0.106**	0.130**	0.212**
	(0.012)	(0.019)	(0.024)
Alberta	0.016	0.116**	0.186**
	(0.008)	(0.012)	(0.015)
British Columbia	0.0084	−0.133**	−0.145**
	(0.006)	(0.009)	(0.011)
Territories	−0.0017	−0.323**	−0.295**
	(0.068)	(0.099)	(0.119)
Source region			
Other European	−1.610**	−1.619**	−1.844**
	(0.010)	(0.013)	(0.016)
Africa & Middle East	−0.699**	0.150**	0.070**
	(0.012)	(0.017)	(0.021)
China, Hong Kong, &	−2.125**	−1.355**	−1.293**
Taiwan	(0.010)	(0.012)	(0.016)

Table 6. (*Continued*)

	All Immigrants	Economic Class	Principal Applicants (PA)
India, Sri Lanka, &	−1.582**	−0.708**	−0.759**
Pakistan	(0.010)	(0.015)	(0.018)
Latin America	−2.388**	−1.766**	−2.257**
	(0.011)	(0.016)	(0.020)
Other Pacific	−2.926**	−2.624**	−2.794**
	(0.036)	(0.082)	(0.103)
Other countries	−2.010**	−1.034**	−1.251**
	(0.009)	(0.013)	(0.016)
Intercept	13.159**	11.794**	11.778**
	(0.049)	(0.067)	(0.084)
R^2	0.1760	0.1295	0.1602
p-value for F-test	<0.0001	<0.0001	<0.0001
RMSE	3.642	3.380	3.378
Sample size	2,683,524	1,192,230	753,137

Notes:

1. Standard errors are presented in parentheses.
2. The default categories are: (1) economic class for the admission class controls, (2) resident of Ontario for the region of residence controls, and (3) English-speaking for the source region controls.

* Signficant at 5%.
** Signficant at 1%.

education levels by about 2.6 years and Humanitarian-class arrivals have lower education levels by about 2.0 years.

The coefficient signs and magnitudes, on the whole, are fairly similar across the three immigrant groups. The time trend results indicate that average levels of education have been rising by about 1.8–2.0 years per decade across all three groups. Higher overall immigration levels (holding Economic vs non-Economic-class composition constant) reduce average education levels across all groups. Raising the total immigration by 100 thousand per year is estimated to reduce Economic-class average education level by 0.31 years and overall immigrant education levels by 0.31 years as well, equivalent to about one and a half years of upward trend. These results support the first hypothesis above.

Within the Economic class and PA groups, an increase in the Economic-class share has significant positive effects, with strongest effects on PAs. A rise in the Economic-class share of total immigration (holding constant the total inflow) by 10 percentage points is estimated to yield a 0.13-year increase in the average level of education of PAs. This is not consistent with the argument that bringing in more PAs (for a given total inflow) will attract more "marginal" candidates and hence reduce average education levels among either PAs themselves or among Economic-class immigrants as a whole. Rather, this result is consistent with a view that, in order to bring in more qualified PAs, the immigration officers of CIC put in greater efforts and more administrative resources are applied to the objective, with the outcome that CIC ends up bringing in particularly well-skilled PAs, thus raising average within-class skill levels – what might be called traditional occupational gap-filling applied to skill levels rather than occupations.

One can now use these results to evaluate expressions (2) and (4) of the previous section and obtain an indirect estimate of an increase in the Economic share on average education levels for all immigrants as a whole, based on the more homogeneous and more reliable estimates in columns two and three of the table. On average over the 1980–2001 period, the composition effect for years of education is $(11.77-10.38=)$ 1.39 years. Over the same period, average $(w)=0.4572$ and average $(p)=0.4339$. Hence, the average skill effect is estimated as 0.30 years based on the Economic-class regression or 0.27 years based on the PA regression. The average skill effect is estimated to be positive, but of only secondary size compared to the dominant composition effect. Thus raising the Economic-class share by one percentage point (holding total inflow constant) is indirectly estimated to raise overall average education levels across all immigrants by $(1.39+0.30$ or $0.27)/100=0.0169$ or 0.0166, and thus a 10-point increase in the Economic-class share raises average education levels by 0.17 years – based on either the Economic-class or PA regression results. This result supports the second hypothesis. If one compares this estimate to that of the total inflow effect in the all-immigrants regression, one finds that increasing the total immigrant inflow by 100 thousand arrivals a year would require about an 18 percentage-point rise $(-0.31/0.17)$ in the Economic-class share to counterbalance. This is a pretty substantial effect.

The consequences of increasing the maximum education points (as a share of the total pass mark) in the Point System schedule are very much as expected in all three regressions, with strongest effects for PAs and weakest or most diluted results for all immigrants as a whole. Raising education points by 10 percentage points is estimated to increase PAs' average education level by 0.35 years, Economic-class immigrants' levels by 0.29 years, and overall immigrants by 0.14 years. These results thus support the third hypothesis. While the education 93 dummy came out with "wrong" sign for all immigrants, it showed up with strong positive effects for

Economic-class immigrants and PAs, with again the effect on PAs' education levels being substantially stronger – as one would expect.

Business cycle effects show up with very consistent and robust estimates across all three immigrant groups. Recessions in Canada reduce average education levels of arriving immigrants as fewer Economic-class arrivals occur, but also the average skill levels of those who do arrive decline. Conversely, recessions in the United States have the effect of raising average education levels of immigrants to Canada, both for immigrants as a whole as well as for PAs themselves. These results thus support the fourth hypothesis. Interestingly, the effect of US recessions is about twice as strong as that for Canadian recessions. Immigration of human capital to Canada appears to be very sensitive to the attractiveness of the US economic environment.

Across regions of residence of arriving immigrants, the Atlantic Provinces seem to attract immigrants with the highest average education level, while Quebec and the Territories attract those with the lowest average education level (even controlling for source region). This pattern shows up more strongly among PAs and Economic-class immigrants as a whole. While these differences are much smaller than those across region of origins of immigrants, nonetheless the net difference in average level of education between PAs settling in Atlantic Provinces and in Quebec is about one full year of education.

Across source region of immigrants, the average level of education of PAs is highest among PAs arriving from Africa and the Middle East, and lowest among PAs from Latin America and Other Pacific. In this case, though, the net difference in average level of education between PAs arriving from Africa and the Middle East and from Other Pacific is 2.9 years of education. For immigrants as a whole, the net difference in average level of education between arrivals from Other Pacific and from English-speaking source countries is also 2.9 years of education. The mix of immigrants by country or region of origin clearly has important effects on average skill levels of the landed immigrants.

Further results on educational attainment are found in Table 7 on the proportion of immigrants with a university degree at the time of arrival. These equations are estimated as linear probability models.[7] The set up of the table is the same as the previous one. The results are very much in accord with those on years of education, so a much briefer overview is provided. Again, Economic-class immigrants have a higher proportion of university graduates than other immigrant classes by 23–27 percentage points. Other things being held constant, there has been a net upward trend in the proportion of

Table 7. Proportion with a University Degree Regression Results.

	All Immigrants	Economic Class	PAs
Admission class			
Family	−0.2301**	n.a.	n.a.
	(0.00058)		
Humanitarian	−0.2651**	n.a.	n.a.
	(0.00082)		
Other	−0.2347**	n.a.	n.a.
	(0.0012)		
Test variables			
Time trend (0–21)	0.02335**	0.02963**	0.03171**
	(0.00016)	(0.00026)	(0.00032)
Total inflow (in '000s)	−0.000438**	−0.000487**	−0.000452**
	(0.00000)	(0.000017)	(0.000020)
Economic share of inflow	−0.00137**	−0.00019	0.000627**
(out of 100)	(0.00006)	(0.00011)	(0.00013)
Education points as share	0.00305**	0.00473**	0.00614**
of pass mark (out of 100)	(0.00009)	(0.00015)	(0.00019)
Indicator for 1993 or later	−0.0159**	0.0269**	0.0421**
	(0.0012)	(0.0021)	(0.0026)
Canadian unemployment	−0.0317**	−0.0409**	−0.0471**
rate	(0.00040)	(0.00064)	(0.00079)
US unemployment rate	0.0347**	0.04367**	0.0531**
	(0.00053)	(0.00089)	(0.00109)
Region of residence			
Atlantic provinces	0.0440**	0.0268**	0.0636**
	(0.0019)	(0.0030)	(0.0038)
Quebec	−0.0437**	−0.0886**	−0.0946**
	(0.0007)	(0.0012)	(0.0015)
Manitoba or Saskatchewan	0.0077**	0.0150**	0.0171**
	(0.0014)	(0.0025)	(0.0031)
Alberta	−0.0069**	−0.0172**	−0.0123**
	(0.0009)	(0.0016)	(0.0020)
British Columbia	−0.0188**	−0.0447**	−0.0446**
	(0.0007)	(0.0012)	(0.0015)
Territories	−0.0388**	−0.0986**	−0.0937**
	(0.0076)	(0.0134)	(0.0158)
Source region			
Other European	−0.0256**	−0.0305**	−0.0682**
	(0.0011)	(0.0018)	(0.0022)
Africa & Middle East	0.0050**	0.0857**	0.0672**
	(0.0014)	(0.0023)	(0.0028)
China, Hong Kong, &	−0.0638**	−0.0439**	−0.0254**
Taiwan	(0.0011)	(0.0017)	(0.0021)
India, Sri Lanka, &	0.0294**	0.0868**	0.0645**
Pakistan	(0.0012)	(0.0020)	(0.0024)

Table 7. (*Continued*)

	All Immigrants	Economic Class	PAs
Latin America	−0.1369**	−0.1459**	−0.1936**
	(0.0012)	(0.0022)	(0.0026)
Other Pacific	−0.1852**	−0.2484**	−0.2787**
	(0.0040)	(0.0111)	(0.0136)
Other countries	−0.0094**	0.0369**	0.0214**
	(0.0011)	(0.0017)	(0.0021)
Intercept	0.2923**	0.1071**	0.0578**
	(0.0055)	(0.0091)	(0.0111)
R^2	0.1538	0.1499	0.1974
p-value for F-test	<0.0001	<0.0001	<0.0001
RMSE	0.4092	0.4551	0.4473
Sample size	2,683,524	1,192,230	753,137

Note:
1. Standard errors are presented in parentheses.
2. The default categories are: (1) economic class for the admission class controls, (2) resident of Ontario for the region of residence controls, and (3) English-speaking for the source region controls.
* Significant at 5%.
** Significant at 1%.

immigrants with a university degree of 2–3 percent a year – again strongest for PAs. A higher total inflow is estimated to reduce the proportion with a university degree (PUD).

The Economic-class share effect, however, shows mixed results. It is estimated to be significantly positive for PAs, not significant for Economic-class immigrants and significantly negative for all immigrants. The composition effect in Eqs. (2) and (4) is estimated to be (23.85–10.57=) 13.3 percent or 0.133, so the indirect estimate of the Economic-class share effect on all immigrants is found to be 0.124–0.145. That is, an increase in the proportion of Economic-class immigrants by 10 percentage points (holding total inflow constant) is indirectly estimated to raise the proportion of all immigrants with a university degree by 1.24–1.45 percentage points.

A greater emphasis on education points within the Point System increases PUD, with about twice as strong an effect on PAs as upon all immigrants as a whole. With respect to business cycle effects, again a higher unemployment rate in Canada reduces PUD, while a higher US unemployment rate has the opposite effect. In this case though, the effects are stronger among PAs than for immigrants as a whole, and the strengths of the effects are about the same for the Canadian and US unemployment rates. Evidently, the difference in the Canada–US cyclical effects operates more strongly on the relatively less educated immigrants (i.e., comparing the cyclical results between Tables 6 and 7). Finally, the pattern of regional effects – both region of origin and region of settlement – is pretty much similar to what was found in Table 6 for years of education.

5.2. Effects on Age at Time of Arrival

Regression results for age (at the time of landing) as the dependent variable are presented in Table 8, again in the same format as before. Across the different skill dimensions of regressions, those for age at the time of arrival are the least well fitting in terms of R^2. This may reflect that age is playing several roles as an index of skill and these pull in different directions – adaptability favors youth and younger workers while work experience effects may favor middle- or later-middle age. It may reflect that age points within the Canadian Point System are not one-sided as points are reduced for applicants on either side of the prime 21–49 year age interval. Furthermore, the age distribution of immigrants has changed considerably over the period covered as there has been a considerable shift from Family-class emphasis (whose arrivals are on average relatively older) toward an Economic-class focus (whose arrivals are relatively younger). Nonetheless, virtually all the regression coefficients in all the three equations are highly statistically significant and the overall fits (or regression F-statistics) are highly significant as well.

From the regression estimated on all immigrants, one can see refugees are, on net, the youngest on average across admission classes (about 1.4 years younger than the default group, Economic-class immigrants) and the Family-class arrivals are on average the oldest (6.5 years older than the Economic-class group). The conflicting signs of the trend coefficients attest to several different factors on-going. On the one hand, the shift towards greater focus on Economic-class immigrants and away from an emphasis on family reunification has had the effect of reducing the overall average age of immigrants (by about 0.8 years per decade), while at the same time the average age of PAs has been rising (by about 0.5 years per decade) as greater skill acquisition – through years of education and work experience – takes more time to acquire.

If younger immigrants are more desirable, then increasing the total inflow of immigrants is estimated to result in raising the average age of PAs as

Table 8. Age at Immigration Regression Results.

	All Immigrants	Economic Class	PAs
Admission class			
Family	6.501**	n.a.	n.a.
	(0.018)		
Humanitarian	−1.353**	n.a.	n.a.
	(0.026)		
Other	5.249**	n.a.	n.a.
	(0.037)		
Test variables			
Time trend (0–21)	−0.0815**	0.0238**	0.0487**
	(0.0044)	(0.0043)	(0.0055)
Total inflow (in >000s)	−0.00290**	0.00435**	0.00826**
	(0.00030)	(0.00031)	(0.00038)
Economic share of inflow	0.0377**	−0.00579**	−0.0244**
(out of 100)	(0.0019)	(0.0019)	(0.0023)
Ages points as share of pass	0.03720**	−0.01160**	−0.01707**
mark (out of 100)	(0.0029)	(0.0030)	(0.0037)
Canadian unemployment	0.1690**	0.5717**	0.5144**
rate	(0.0119)	(0.0112)	(0.0143)
US unemployment rate	0.0132	−0.4604**	−0.3926**
	(0.0174)	(0.0175)	(0.0220)
Region of residence			
Atlantic provinces	1.324**	1.975**	2.889**
	(0.061)	(0.0553)	(0.0729)
Quebec	−0.400**	0.155**	0.130**
	(0.023)	(0.0224)	(0.0280)
Manitoba & Saskatchewan	−0.695**	0.061	0.054**
	(0.042)	(0.046)	(0.059)
Alberta	−0.463**	0.259**	0.246**
	(0.030)	(0.030)	(0.039)
British Columbia	0.503**	1.157**	1.305**
	(0.022)	(0.021)	(0.028)
Territories	−1.709**	0.647**	0.631*
	(0.241)	(0.246)	(0.299)
Source region			
Other European	0.747**	−0.977**	−1.137**
	(0.035)	(0.033)	(0.041)
Africa & Middle East	−1.638**	−0.639**	−0.688**
	(0.044)	(0.042)	(0.053)
China, Hong Kong, &	3.400**	0.413**	0.699**
Taiwan	(0.034)	(0.031)	(0.039)
India, Sri Lanka, &	0.219**	−0.383**	−0.054
Pakistan	(0.036)	(0.036)	(0.046)
Latin America	−1.684**	−0.723**	−0.604**
	(0.038)	(0.041)	(0.050)

Table 8. (*Continued*)

	All Immigrants	Economic Class	PAs
Other Pacific	−3.189**	−2.724**	−3.122**
	(0.125)	(0.203)	(0.258)
Other countries	0.364**	0.350**	0.482**
	(0.033)	(0.032)	(0.040)
Intercept	31.140**	32.314**	32.392**
	(0.166)	(0.160)	(0.202)
R^2	0.0728	0.0226	0.0315
p-value for F-test	<0.0001	<0.0001	<0.0001
RMSE	13.126	8.401	8.520
Sample size	2,789,599	1,202,559	757,436

Note:

1. Standard errors are presented in parentheses.
2. The default categories are: (1) economic class for the admission class controls, (2) resident of Ontario for the region of residence controls, and (3) English-speaking for the source region controls.

* Significant at 5%.
** Significant at 1%.

more marginal (i.e., older) candidates are brought in. Increasing the total inflow level by 100 thousand is estimated to raise the average age of PAs by 0.8 years. This effect, however, is attenuated as one moves to broader immigrant groups, so that for immigrants as a whole it actually turns out slightly negative. A reduction in average age for all immigrants would not seem to make sense here. But as PAs get older, they are likely to have more accompanying dependants who make it just above the 20-year old lower-bound age cut-off for inclusion in the database, hence lowering overall average age.

Since Economic-class immigrants are on average (31.55−26.26=) 5.29 years younger than non-Economic-class immigrants, one would expect that increasing the Economic-class share of total immigration would reduce the overall average age of immigrants as a whole. Indeed, the composition effect or first term in expressions (2) and (4) is precisely this mean age differential of −5.29 years. The average skill effect of increasing the Economic-class share is negative for both PAs and the Economic-class group as a whole, consistent with bringing in "more skilled" (i.e., younger) immigrants, analogous to the finding for education in the previous section. The average skill effect in expressions (2) and (4) is thus estimated as between −0.26 (based on the Economic-class regression) and −0.48 (from the PA regression). Again, the average skill effect is far secondary to the basic composition effect. Combining them yields the indirect estimate that increasing the Economic-class share of total immigration by 10 percentage points yields a reduction in the average age of all immigrants of 0.56–0.58 years. The effect on average of all immigrants of increasing the Economic-class share by 10 percentage points is thus almost exactly twice as strong as that of raising the total immigrant inflow rate by 100 thousand arrivals per year. Alternatively stated, the latter effect is equivalent in its effect on overall average age of all immigrants to increasing the Economic-class share by 5.0–5.2 percentage points.

As more weight is allocated to points for age within the Point System schedule with the objective of favoring younger PAs, as expected average age of PAs declines. Increasing the points allocated to age by 10 percentage points is estimated to reduce average age of PAs by 0.17 years. Again, this reduction doesn't show up for all immigrants. But again, this may reflect that younger PAs have younger children who are less likely to be included in the estimation sample for all immigrants because of their age-20 lower bound, hence there would be a reduction in who would otherwise be young accompanying immigrants. Indeed, this lower age bound inclusion criterion for our samples is likely the sources of more anomalous results for the age regressions over all immigrants than for the other skill-dimension regressions over all immigrants. Furthermore, if Economic-class immigrants are getting younger on average while the age weighting effect results in the average age rising among all immigrants, then the average age of non-Economic-class immigrants must be rising. This could occur if a greater emphasis on bringing in younger PAs results in families who might otherwise be admitted as Economic-class immigrants now applying and becoming admitted under the Family-class category, thus raising the average age on non-Economic-class immigrants.

Business cycles also have a quite major effect on average age of immigrants. A higher Canadian unemployment rate brings in older immigrants across all three immigrant groups and a higher US unemployment rate makes Canada relatively more attractive and brings in younger PAs and Economic-class immigrants. Interestingly, here, the Canadian unemployment rate effect turns out stronger than that for the US, which is opposite to what was found for education. Even more interesting is the magnitude of these effects. A one percentage point increase in the Canadian unemployment rate is estimated to reduce PAs' average level of education by 0.10 years (see Table 6), while the same increase is found to raise the average age of PAs by 0.51 years. A one-percentage point increase in the US unemployment rate is estimated to increase PAs' average level of education by 0.20 years, but to reduce PAs' average age by 0.39 years. So, the business cycle effects operate much more strongly on the age of arriving PAs than on their education levels – by about five times with respect to Canadian unemployment rate and by about two times for the US unemployment rate. Again the results are much stronger for PAs than for immigrants as a whole.

With respect to the region-of-settlement controls, the Atlantic Provinces stand out, and to a lesser extent British Columbia, as attracting older immigrants, while Ontario (the most prosperous province over the period covered) attracts the youngest PAs and Economic-class immigrants. Younger non-Economic-class immigrants, however, evidently settle in a number of other regions as well, thus yielding a rather different pattern of coefficient signs for all immigrants as a whole. With respect to region-of-origin controls, the youngest immigrants come from the Other Pacific region, while the oldest come from China, Hong Kong, and Taiwan. Relatively young non-Economic-class immigrants also arrive from Africa and the Middle East and from Latin America.

5.3. Effects on Official Language Fluency

Regression results for English or French language fluency as the dependent variable[8] are presented in Table 9. From the admission class coefficients, one can see that fluency in either official language is highest on net among Economic-class immigrants and markedly lower for Family-class immigrants (by 26 percent) and lower still for refugees (by almost 35 percent).

While the trend is toward greater fluency in an official tongue on net among immigrants as a whole (by about 3 percentage points per decade), among PAs and their dependants interestingly the trend on net has been downwards (by about 5 percentage points per decade) over the period covered. Obviously, non-Economic-class immigrants on net are becoming more fluent in either English or French. Note, however, these trends are net of the positive effect of the increasing weight put on language fluency within the Point System.

Increasing the total inflow of immigrants also has mixed but very small effects on language fluency. An increased inflow of 100 thousand arrivals per year is estimated to reduce the language fluency rate for immigrants as a whole by 1.1 percentage points. The finding of a positive effect on PAs, however, is anomalous and different from results for the other two skill dimensions where an increased inflow had the effect of reducing average skill

Table 9.   English or French Language Fluency Regression Results.

	All Immigrants	Economic Class	PAs
Admission class			
Family	−0.2605**	n.a.	n.a.
	(0.00060)		
Humanitarian	−0.3478**	n.a.	n.a.
	(0.00086)		
Other	−0.0232**	n.a.	n.a.
	(0.0012)		
Test variables			
Time trend (0–21)	0.00309**	−0.00715**	−0.00547**
	(0.00016)	(0.00022)	(0.00025)
Total inflow (in >000s)	−0.00011**	−0.000011	0.000089**
	(0.00000)	(0.00001)	(0.00001)
Economic share of inflow	0.00246**	0.00392**	0.00362**
(out of 100)	(0.000065)	(0.00010)	(0.00011)
Language points as share of	0.00168**	−0.00072**	0.00091**
pass mark (out of 100)	(0.00012)	(0.00018)	(0.00020)
Canadian unemployment	0.02470**	0.04563**	0.04281**
rate	(0.00037)	(0.00049)	(0.00055)
US unemployment rate	−0.00275**	−0.04324**	−0.04317**
	(0.00049)	(0.00069)	(0.00076)
Region of residence			
Atlantic provinces	0.01391**	−0.00973**	−0.00480
	(0.0020)	(0.0026)	(0.0031)
Quebec	0.00315**	−0.00753**	−0.01112**
	(0.00076)	(0.0011)	(0.0012)
Manitoba & Saskatchewan	−0.05480**	−0.02659**	−0.03432**
	(0.0014)	(0.0022)	(0.0025)
Alberta	−0.04932**	−0.00581**	−0.00614**
	(0.00098)	(0.0014)	(0.0016)
British Columbia	−0.05130**	−0.02715**	−0.02280**
	(0.00074)	(0.0010)	(0.0012)
Territories	0.03051**	0.03829**	0.03192**
	(0.00797)	(0.0117)	(0.0126)
Source region			
Other European	−0.4548**	−0.3105**	−0.2462**
	(0.0012)	(0.0015)	(0.0017)
Africa & Middle East	−0.1382**	−0.0636**	−0.0543**
	(0.0014)	(0.0020)	(0.0022)
China, Hong Kong, &	−0.5505**	−0.4102**	−0.3486**
Taiwan	(0.0011)	(0.0015)	(0.0017)
India, Sri Lanka, &	−0.4387**	−0.1256**	−0.0981**
Pakistan	(0.0012)	(0.0017)	(0.0019)
Latin America	−0.2078**	−0.1684**	−0.1287**
	(0.0013)	(0.0019)	(0.0021)

Table 9. (*Continued*)

	All Immigrants	Economic Class	PAs
Other Pacific	−0.0778**	−0.0199*	−0.0219**
	(0.0041)	(0.0097)	(0.0108)
Other countries	−0.3688**	−0.2384**	−0.1852**
	(0.0011)	(0.0015)	(0.0017)
Intercept	0.8129**	0.8473**	0.8124**
	(0.0053)	(0.0074)	(0.0082)
R^2	0.1896	0.1008	0.0935
p-value for F-test	<0.0001	<0.0001	<0.0001
RMSE	0.4339	0.4012	0.3581
Sample size	2,789,626	1,202,569	757,438

Note:

1. Standard errors are presented in parentheses.

2. The default categories are: (1) economic class for the admission class controls, (2) resident of Ontario for the region of residence controls, and (3) English-speaking for the source region controls.

* Significant at 5%.

** Significant at 1%.

levels of PAs. But the magnitude is quite small at less than one percentage point for a 100 thousand increase in overall immigration levels.

An increase in the Economic-class share of the inflow is found to have a fairly strong positive effect on language fluency across all the three immigrant groups. A direct estimate predicts that a 10 percentage point increase in the Economic-class share (holding total inflow constant) will raise fluency rates among all immigrants by 2.5 percentage points. If one calculates an indirect estimate using Eqs. (2) and (4), one finds a composition effect of (64.3−49.1) = 15.2 percent or 0.152 and an average skill effect of 0.0018–0.0007, so an indirect estimate of 0.153–0.154. Again the composition effect clearly dominates. Thus, an indirect estimate of a 10-point increase in the Economic-class share of total immigration is to raise overall fluency rates by 1.5 percentage points. This is comparable to the magnitude of the analogous effect on the proportion arriving with a university degree. Since the total inflow effect on language fluency is so weak, however, the effect of raising the inflow rate by 100 thousand is equivalent in magnitude to raising the Economic-class share by only 2.5 percentage points.

Increasing the maximum language points (as a share of the total pass mark) in the Point System schedule is associated with an increase in official language fluency for both PAs and for immigrants as a whole.

Raising language points by 10 percentage points is estimated to increase PAs' average language fluency rate by 0.9 points, a rather weak effect.

Business cycle effects again turn out to be highly statistically significant, but surprisingly they are exactly opposite in sign to what was found earlier for the other skill dimensions. In this case, recessions in Canada are estimated to increase average level of language fluency, while recessions in the United States have the opposite effect. When separate regressions are run for English fluency and for French fluency, the above pattern of unemployment rate effects is replicated in the English language fluency results, but not in the French language fluency results (see Tables 10 and 11). The current results in Table 9 are thus consistent with the behavior that, when the Canadian unemployment rate is high, immigrants view English proficiency as a greater necessity for finding a job or a greater priority than otherwise, and when the US unemployment rate is high, there is less of a need if they are coming to Canada. Why this should be the case, though, is puzzling. One possible explanation is that those applying with an English language fluency may be more confident in immigrating in recessions because of their language advantage over other immigrants. Another possible explanation is that, in recessions, immigration officers may reduce the numbers admitted – since they do have discretion in awarding points in the case of language fluency – who lack English language fluency, and in expansions they ease up.[9]

With respect to region of settlement, the most fluent go to Ontario, the Territories, and (in the case of all immigrants) the Atlantic Provinces. The provinces receiving immigrants with the lowest degree of official language fluency are Manitoba/ Saskatchewan, British Columbia, and Alberta – all from Western Canada. With respect to region of origin, obviously the source region with the highest degree of official language fluency is the (default) set of English-speaking countries. The regions providing the least fluent immigrants are China, Hong Kong and Taiwan, Other European, and (in the case of all immigrants) India, Sri Lanka, and Pakistan.

Since different patterns may be at work for immigrants fluent in French rather than English, the above regressions were rerun separately for English proficiency and for French proficiency. The results appear in Tables 10 and 11, respectively. The results for English language fluency are virtually the same as already discussed in Table 9. The only differences are the expected ones that immigrants with only English language fluency were less likely to settle in Quebec and more likely to settle in the Atlantic provinces, and they were (obviously) more likely to have come from English-speaking countries and less likely to have come from Latin America, Other European countries, and Africa and the Middle East.

Table 10. English Language Fluency Regression Results.

	All Immigrants	Economic Class	PAs
Admission class			
Family	−0.2558**	n.a.	n.a.
	(0.00062)		
Humanitarian	−0.3247**	n.a.	n.a.
	(0.00088)		
Other	−0.0109**	n.a.	n.a.
	(0.0013)		
Test variables			
Time trend (0–21)	0.00244**	−0.00794**	−0.00585**
	(0.00017)	(0.00023)	(0.00027)
Total inflow (in '000s)	−0.00069**	−0.000015	0.000032
	(0.00000)	(0.000014)	(0.000016)
Economic share of inflow (out of 100)	0.00223**	0.00335**	0.00283**
	(0.000067)	(0.00010)	(0.00011)
Language points as share of pass mark (out of 100)	0.000822**	−0.000997**	0.000702**
	(0.00013)	(0.00019)	(0.00022)
Canadian unemployment rate	0.02639**	0.04873**	0.04607**
	(0.00038)	(0.00052)	(0.00060)
US unemployment rate	−0.00846**	−0.05227**	−0.05341**
	(0.00050)	(0.00073)	(0.00083)
Region of residence			
Atlantic provinces	0.00384	−0.01724**	−0.01376**
	(0.0021)	(0.0028)	(0.0033)
Quebec	−0.2085**	−0.2295**	−0.2517**
	(0.00078)	(0.00011)	(0.0013)
Manitoba or Saskatchewan	−0.05631**	−0.02890**	−0.03753**
	(0.0015)	(0.0023)	(0.0027)
Alberta	−0.05239**	−0.00544**	−0.00631**
	(0.0010)	(0.0015)	(0.0018)
British Columbia	−0.06052**	−0.03690**	−0.03243**
	(0.00076)	(0.0011)	(0.0013)
Territories	0.02096**	0.03705**	0.02940*
	(0.0082)	(0.0123)	(0.0137)
Source region			
Other European	−0.5048**	−0.3772**	−0.3137**
	(0.0012)	(0.0016)	(0.0019)
Africa & Middle East	−0.2858**	−0.2166**	−0.1905**
	(0.0015)	(0.0021)	(0.0024)
China, Hong Kong, & Taiwan	−0.5491**	−0.4044**	−0.3456**
	(0.0012)	(0.0016)	(0.0018)
India, Sri Lanka, & Pakistan	−0.4374**	−0.1271**	−0.1000**
	(0.0012)	(0.0018)	(0.0021)
Latin America	−0.2808**	−0.2412**	−0.2122**
	(0.0013)	(0.0020)	(0.0023)
Other Pacific	−0.0916**	−0.0351**	−0.0381**
	(0.0042)	(0.0102)	(0.0118)

Table 10. (*Continued*)

	All Immigrants	Economic Class	PAs
Other countries	−0.3798**	−0.2433**	−0.1880**
	(.0011)	(0.0016)	(0.0018)
Intercept	0.8778**	0.9354**	0.9225**
	(0.0055)	(0.0078)	(0.0090)
R^2	0.1793	0.1226	0.1330
p-value for F-test	<0.001	<0.001	<0.001
RMSE	0.4459	0.4223	0.3898
Sample size	2,789,626	1,202,569	757,438

Note:

1. Standard errors are presented in parentheses.

2. The default categories are: (1) economic class for the admission class controls, (2) resident of Ontario for the region of residence controls, and (3) English-speaking for the source region controls.

* Significant at 5%.

** Significant at 1%.

The results for French language fluency appearing in Table 11 do show some marked differences from those in the previous two tables. The expected differences indeed show up in regional effects that immigrants with proficiency in French are much more likely to settle in Quebec and much less likely to come from English-speaking countries (and hence more likely to come from everywhere else). There is also a net positive trend in French fluency across all the three immigrant groups including PAs. Also the language points' effect, while positive, is not statistically significant for either PAs or all Economic-class immigrants. But the most dramatic difference is that the coefficient signs for the business cycle effects on French proficiency are opposite to those for English language proficiency. That is, in times of recessions in Canada, French language fluency declines just as other skill dimensions also fall off; and in times of US recessions, French-language fluency of immigrants to Canada increases just as other skill dimensions of Canadian immigrants also improve. So, the apparent anomaly lies in the English language fluency response to business cycle fluctuations.

5.4. Cross-Weight Effects of Skill Points

In each of the above regressions, only the Point System skill weight corresponding to each of the dependent variables was included. But it is

Table 11. French Language Fluency Regression Results.

	All Immigrants	Economic Class	PAs
Admission class			
Family	−0.0445**	n.a.	n.a.
	(0.00034)		
Humanitarian	−0.1085**	n.a.	n.a.
	(0.00048)		
Other	−0.0374**	n.a.	n.a.
	(0.00069)		
Test variables			
Time trend (0–21)	0.00211**	0.00255**	0.00243**
	(0.00091)	(0.00014)	(0.00019)
Total inflow (in '000s)	−0.000049**	0.000072**	0.000174**
	(0.00000)	(0.00000)	(0.000011)
Economic share of inflow	−0.000376**	0.000339**	0.000298**
(out of 100)	(0.000037)	(0.000063)	(0.000080)
Language points as share of	0.000570**	0.0000754	0.0001836
pass mark (out of 100)	(0.000072)	(0.00012)	(0.00015)
Canadian unemployment	−0.00609**	−0.00656**	−0.00759**
rate	(0.00021)	(0.00032)	(0.00042)
US unemployment rate	0.00850**	0.00983**	0.00959**
	(0.00027)	(0.00045)	(0.00058)
Region of residence			
Atlantic provinces	0.02617**	0.01808**	0.02486**
	(0.0011)	(0.0017)	(0.0023)
Quebec	0.3520**	0.4138**	0.4612**
	(0.00042)	(0.00070)	(0.00089)
Manitoba or Saskatchewan	−0.00521**	−0.01139**	−0.01293**
	(0.00079)	(0.0014)	(0.0019)
Alberta	−0.00047	−0.00773**	−0.00862**
	(0.00055)	(0.00095)	(0.0012)
British Columbia	0.01115**	0.00982**	0.00771**
	(0.00041)	(0.00067)	(0.00089)
Territories	0.01698**	0.01648*	0.01304
	(0.0045)	(0.0077)	(0.0096)
Source region			
Other European	0.1178**	0.16219**	0.1752**
	(0.00065)	(0.0010)	(0.0013)
Africa & Middle East	0.2528**	0.2928**	0.2872**
	(0.00081)	(0.0013)	(0.0017)
China, Hong Kong, &	−0.03419**	−0.05218**	−0.05554**
Taiwan	(0.00063)	(0.00097)	(0.0013)
India, Sri Lanka, &	−0.01961**	−0.03728**	−0.04612**
Pakistan	(0.00067)	(0.0011)	(0.0015)
Latin America	0.06428**	0.05630**	0.05519**
	(0.00071)	(0.0013)	(0.0016)

Table 11. (*Continued*)

	All Immigrants	Economic Class	PAs
Other Pacific	0.00795**	0.00109	−0.00032
	(0.0023)	(0.0064)	(0.0082)
Other countries	0.03103**	0.02338**	0.02115**
	(0.00062)	(0.00099)	(0.0013)
Intercept	0.01429**	−0.05189**	−0.05657**
	(0.00299)	(0.00486)	(0.00626)
R^2	0.3067	0.3731	0.4124
p-value for F-test	<0.001	<0.001	<0.001
RMSE	0.2437	0.2636	0.2725
Sample size	2,789,626	1,202,569	757,438

Note:

1. Standard errors are presented in parentheses.

2. The default categories are: (1) economic class for the admission class controls, (2) resident of Ontario for the region of residence controls, and (3) English-speaking for the source region controls.

 * Significant at 5%.
 ** Significant at 1%.

possible that changing the weight on some other Point System skill component could have an effect as well in these reduced-form regressions. For example, since highly educated foreigners are probably more likely to be proficient in English (or French) than their less educated compatriots, raising the Point System weight on higher levels of education could potentially have the side effect of raising the official language fluency of arriving immigrants as well. Such an impact will be referred to as a cross-weight effect, in contrast to the own-weight effects discussed in the previous sets of regressions. Accordingly, all the PA and Economic-class regressions have been rerun so that each includes all three Point System skill weight variables. Thus, each regression will allow for both an own-weight effect as well as two cross-weight effects. This will potentially allow us not only to examine the relative strengths of the own-weight and cross-weight effects, but also to evaluate the degree of complementarity or substitutability among the three skill weight variables and to evaluate possible trade-offs in shifting weights allocated to these alternative skill dimensions within the Canadian Point System.

Results for these own-weight and cross-weight effects are presented in Tables 12 (on the education outcomes of immigrants), 13 (on the age outcomes), and 14 (on language fluency outcomes). Only the own- and cross-weight effects are presented; the rest of the regression results show virtually no differences from what has already been discussed. One should note, as an aside, that the questions being asked here demand a lot from the data. While there are large numbers of cross-sectional observations in the CLD, identification of the own- and cross-weight effects come from a relatively few time-series changes in the Point System weighting scheme and pass mark for admission. Nonetheless, most of the weight coefficients turn out significant at least at the five-percent level.

Inspection of the coefficients in Tables 12–14 reveals, first of all, that the skill weight effects are, in all cases, stronger for PAs than for Economic-class immigrants as a whole, very much as one would expect. Also, own-weight increases have skill-enhancing effects (positive for education and language fluency, and negative for age) in all cases except for French language fluency – which is a change from Table 11 where only the language fluency skill weight was included.

Table 12. Trade-Offs between Skill Weight Effects on.

	(a) Years of Education		(b) Proportion with a University Degree	
	Economic class	PAs	Economic class	PAs
Education points	0.10090** (0.00586)	0.14012** (0.00718)	0.00884** (0.00079)	0.01345** (0.00095)
Language points	−0.05098** (0.00277)	−0.07593** (0.00353)	−0.00498** (0.00037)	−0.00790** (0.00047)
Age points	−0.04483** (0.00616)	−0.06494** (0.00742)	−0.00076 (0.00083)	−0.00235* (0.00098)

Table 13. Trade-Offs between Skill Weight Effects on Age at Arrival.

	Economic Class	PAs
Education points	0.03324* (0.01449)	0.07554** (0.01804)
Language points	−0.08029** (0.00686)	−0.11832** (0.00889)
Age points	−0.00843 (0.0152)	−0.04629* (0.01864)

Table 14.   Trade-Offs between Skill Weight Effects on.

(a) English Language Fluency Proportion			(b) French Language Fluency Proportions		
	Economic class	PAs		Economic class	PAs
Education points	0.01169** (0.00073)	0.01264** (0.00082)	Education points	0.000061 (0.00045)	0.00023 (0.00058)
Language points	0.00106** (0.00034)	0.00266** (0.00041)	Language points	−0.00181** (0.00022)	−0.00230** (0.00028)
Age points	−0.01902** (0.00077)	−0.02007** (0.00085)	Age points	0.00221** (0.00048)	0.00262** (0.00060)

A ten-percentage point increase in maximum points awarded for education is estimated to raise PAs' average years of education by 1.4 years and their proportion with a university degree by about 13.5 percentage points. But it also raises average English language fluency by 12.5 percentage points. It has no statistically significant effect on French fluency rates. And it increases average age of PAs by 0.76 years, as greater education takes longer to get and thus results in older applicants on average. Raising maximum points for age by 10 percentage points results in average age of PAs declining by 0.46 years, but average years of education also declining by 0.65 years (as younger arrivals generally have lower education levels), the proportion with a university degree declining by 2.4 percentage points, the English fluency rate declining by 20 percentage points, and the French fluency rate going up by 2.6 percentage points. Finally, raising maximum points for official language fluency by 10 percentage points is estimated to increase English fluency rates by 2.7 percentage points, reduce the French fluency rate by 2.3 percentage points, reduce PAs' average age by 1.2 years, reduce their average years of education by 0.76 years, and reduce their proportion with a university degree by 7.9 percentage points. All three skill factors have relatively strong effects on the age of PAs and relatively weak effects on their official language fluency rates. Education and language fluency weights have relatively strong effects on the educational attainment of PA arrivals, while the age weight shows up with a relatively weak effect. In general, the strongest skill weight effects are to be had on educational attainment and age, while the weakest effects occur on language fluency outcomes.

The estimates for own- and cross-weight effects show that the education and language fluency outcomes are complements with respect to the education points weight. Education and age outcomes are substitutes with respect to both the age points weight and the language fluency points weight. Among the three skill dimension outcomes, the clearest trade-offs occur for educational attainment where the own-weight effect strongly improves the average education outcomes while the two cross-weight effects turn out to have fairly strong education-reducing impacts. Trade-offs in the other two skill outcome dimensions are not at all clear-cut.

Again, wariness of these cross-weight estimates should be expressed. Three weight coefficients are being estimated from only four sets of policy changes over the period covered. The estimated effects seem unreasonably large. In the age and language fluency outcomes, the own-weight effects are dominated by the cross-weight effects, which does not seem to make much sense. In light of this likely multicollinearity, these results are not highlighted in the summary of main findings in the next section.

6. CONCLUSIONS: LESSONS FOR US IMMIGRATION POLICY

Making predictions or prescriptions for one country based on the experience of another country is always tentative at best. Nonetheless, Canada has had considerable experience over several decades with application of a Point System on skill-evaluated or Economic-class immigrants. The unique Canadian Landings Database used in this paper also provides an unusual opportunity to test empirically a number of hypotheses about the effectiveness of such a system. Relative strength of the different policy levers is set out in Table 15 which expresses the various policy effects all in terms of percent changes in the different skill outcome variables. The total inflow percentages refer to raising the total inflow of immigrants by 100 thousand persons per year. The proportion of immigrants arriving under the Economic class refers to increasing the Economic-class share by 10 percentage points. The Point System own-weights refers to the effect of increasing the maximum skill points for a given skill dimension by 10 percentage points relative to the pass mark on that respective skill.

Five main conclusions arise from the empirical analysis of this paper and that may provide some useful input to the current US debate. First, with respect to total immigration rates, it has been found that increasing overall annual inflows of immigrants lowers the average skill levels of the arriving cohort. This reduction in skill levels occurs most strongly for educational attainment of arriving immigrants, more moderately with respect to age of arriving immigrants, and very weakly (if at all) for official language fluency

Table 15.   Relative Strength of Policy Drivers (Absolute Value of
Percentage Changes in Dependent Variables).

Policy Drivers	Skill Outcomes		
	ED (%)	AGE (%)	FL (E or F) (%)
Total inflow			
Ec. class	2.6	1.7	0.2
– All Iimmigs.	2.8	1.0*	0
Prop. Ec. class			
– All Iimmigs.	1.5	2.0	2.7
Point system own weights			
Pr. App.	2.7	0.6	1.2

Note:

1. "Total inflow" refers to raising total inflow of immigrants by 100 thousand persons per year
   "Prop. Ec. Class" refers to increasing the proportion of immigrants arriving under the Economic Class category by 10 percentage points.
   "Point System Own Weights" refers to the effect of increasing the maximum skill points (within the Point System) for a given skill dimension by 10 percentage points relative to the Pass Mark on that respective skill.
   Pr. App. Referes to Principal Applicant.
2. FL (E or F) stands for language fluency in either English or French.
3. *Indicates figure based on regression coefficient with "wrong" sign.

of immigrants. For example, raising total inflow levels by 100 thousand per year (or by about 35 percent from recent levels) is estimated to reduce average years of education of Economic-class immigrants by 2.6 percent, to increase their average age by 1.7 percent, and to reduce the average rate of English or French language fluency by 0.2 percent.

Second, for a given level of total inflow, increasing the proportion of skill-evaluated or Economic-class immigrants – at least in the way they are designated in the Canadian system – is found to raise the average skill levels of PAs and Economic-class immigrants and, by inference, of all immigrants as a whole. In making the latter inference, the so-called "composition effect" set out in Eqs. (2) and (4) is clearly the dominant factor. Increasing the Economic-class share in total immigration has its strongest effect on official language fluency of arriving cohorts, has a significant effect on average education levels, and has a moderate effect on average age of arriving immigrants. For example, raising the Economic-class share of total immigration by 10 percentage points is estimated to increase average levels of education of all immigrants by 1.5 percent, to reduce their average age by 2.0 percent, and to increase their official language fluency rates by about 2.7 percent.

Third, it is found that business-cycle effects on skill level outcomes of immigrant cohorts to Canada are highly statistically significant, and generally operate so that higher Canadian unemployment rates reduce average skill levels of arriving immigrants (with the exception of English language fluency rates), and higher US unemployment rates have the opposite effect (with the same exception). Such business cycle effects appear to operate more strongly through average age and education levels of PAs.

Fourth, with respect to the operation of the Canadian Point System itself, it has been found that increasing the weights on specific skill dimensions within the Point System schedule indeed has the intended effect of raising average skill levels in this dimension among arriving PAs. Basically, the Point System does appear to work as it is intended. The strongest effects occur for education, moderately strong for language fluency of immigrants, and rather weak effects occur on age of arriving immigrants. For example, if there is a 10 percentage point increase in the weight allocated to a specific skill measure within the Point System (with no cross-weight effects), the result is that the average years of education of PAs are estimated to increase by 2.7 percent, their average age declines by 0.6 percent, and their average official language fluency rate goes up by 1.2 percent.

This study has identified three broad sets of policy tools for bringing about improvements in immigrant outcomes. One is a change in the total rate of inflow of immigrants, the second is a change in the Economic-class share of total immigration, and the third is the various changes in the Point System weights allocated to various skill dimensions. Correspondingly, the study has examined three sets of benchmark changes in these policy tools: increasing the total inflow rate by 100 thousand immigrants per year, raising the Economic-class share by 10 percentage points, and increasing each of the three Point System skill weights by 10 percentage points. When all is said and done, then, which of the three major sets of policy tools appears to be most effective in bringing about desired changes in the skill outcomes of arriving immigrants? It turns out there is no simple across-the-board rule. Again referring to Table 15, it can be seen that the proportion of Economic-class immigrants seems to have the strongest across-the-board impact.[10] The rise in the proportion of Economic-class immigrants, though, would be expected to gradually increase the effect of changing Point System weights on average immigrant skills as a whole. The education outcome variable stands out as being the most responsive among the three skill dimensions. In general, the

Point System appears to have strong effects on educational outcomes of arriving immigrants, moderate effects on language fluency outcomes, and rather weak effects on age outcomes of arriving immigrants.[11] Obviously, further analysis of the issues raised in this study will help refine the design of an effective immigration policy for a complex and dynamic economy.

NOTES

1. Ideally, one would like to estimate these effects across several leading immigrant-receiving countries jointly, say as a set of seemingly unrelated regression equations. But unfortunately, comparable data for other countries were not available.

2. Unfortunately, the CLD database does not include the Point System score (either by skill dimension or in total) awarded to each arriving principal applicant. Nor does it include a variable for pre-arrival work experience even though this is a skill dimension rewarded by the Point System. The CLD values for arriving immigrants refer to information at time of landing rather than at time of original application.

3. Since the regressions already include a time trend variable, this effectively transforms the two raw unemployment rate variables into trend-adjusted cyclical indicators.

4. Data limitations prevent us from also including in the reduced-form skill-outcome regressions such additional potential regressors as the federal immigration department's budget constraints and immigration policy changes in alternative recipient countries such as the United States, Australia, and the European community nations. On the other hand, we have chosen not to include a gender dummy regressor as gender differences in skill outcomes are not an objective of immigration policy and are not of interest in this paper.

5. Indeed, if $E(S|NES)$ were also a function of w, then the average skill effect would involve the difference in the derivatives of $E(S|EC, w)$ and $E(S|NEC, w)$ with respect to w, and would be even more ambiguous.

6. Further empirical work could take into account that total immigration flows and possibly the Economic-class share are not completely exogenous, but reflect in part immigrants' choices. Also the regression errors are likely not fully independent and identically distributed (i.i.d.) and may have clustering characteristics in the time-series dimension (associated with introducing macro-economic regressors in cross-sectional regressions) meaning that OLS-reported standard errors are underestimated.

7. Again, estimating the regressions by OLS rather than by probit or logit maximum likelihood methods means that standard errors are not fully correct in the presence of heteroscedasticity due to the 0–1 nature of the dependent variables. But since conditional means are not close to the 0–1 bounds and the numbers of observations are so large, we opted for the simpler linear estimation technique.

8. See note 7.

9. We wish to thank Professor Weili Ding at Queen's for these suggested explanations.

10. If we use the formula that

$$\frac{\partial E(S)}{\partial w_s} = \text{wp} \frac{\partial E(S|PA, w, w_s)}{\partial w_s},$$

where w_s is the maximum Point System weight allocated to skill dimension S, the implied relative effects on all immigrant mean skill levels of the figures in the last row of Table 15 are 0.5 percent, 0.1 percent, and 0.2 percent, respectively.

11. The reason age comes through as the least responsive of the three Point System variables may reflect that age captures the effects of both youth and work experience (see note 2), and hence is being pulled in conflicting directions. If the CLD reported information on work experience as well as age for all principal applications, these two separate effects being picked up by the age variable could be separately identified.

ACKNOWLEDGMENT

The authors would like to thank, without implicating, participants of workshops at University of Illinois at Chicago, Queen's University, University of Western Ontario, and the Policy Research Initiative in Ottawa for their many thoughtful comments, as well as Professors Michael Abbott, David Green, Paul Miller, and Barry Chiswick for extensive feedback and suggestions on this work.

REFERENCES

Abbott, M., & Dougherty, C. (2004). *Earnings by admission category of male and female immigrants in Canada: Evidence for the first five years.* Unpublished CIC, D.P. (December).

Alboim, N., Finnie, R., & Meng, R. (2005). The discounting of immigrants' skills in Canada: Evidence and policy recommendations. *IRPP Choices, 11*(2).

Antecol, H., Cobb-Clark, D. A., & Trejo, S. J. (2003). Immigration policy and the skills of immigrants to Australia, Canada, and the United States. *Journal of Human Resources, XXXVIII*(1), 192–218.

Aydemir, A. (2002). *Effects of selection criteria and economic opportunities on the characteristics of immigrants.* Research Paper No. 182. Family and Labour Studies Division, Statistics Canada Cat. No. 11F0019MIE-No.182.

Aydemir, A., & Skuterud, M. (2005). Explaining the deteriorating entry earnings of Canada's immigrant cohorts, 1966–2000. *Canadian Journal of Economics, 38*(2), 641–672.

Aydemir, A., & Sweetman, A. (2005). Educational attainment and labor market outcomes of the first and second generations: A comparison of the United States and Canada. Presented at Conference on immigration: Trends, consequences and prospects for the United States. University of Illinois at Chicago, September.

Baker, M., & Benjamin, D. (1994). The performance of immigrants in the Canadian labour market. *Journal of Labor Economics, 12*, 369–405.

Beach, C. M., Green, A. G., & Reitz, J. G. (Eds). (2003). *Canadian immigration policy for the 21st century, John Deutsch Institute, Queen's University*. Montreal: McGill-Queen's University Press.

Bloom, D. E., Gunderson, M., & Grenier, G. (1995). The changing labour market position of Canadian immigrants. *Canadian Journal of Economics, 28*(4b), 987–1001.

Borjas, G. J. (1999a). *Heaven's door: Immigration policy and the American economy*. Princeton, NJ: Princeton University Press.

Borjas, G. J. (1999b). The economic analysis of immigration. In: O. C. Ashenfelter & D. Card (Eds), *Handbook of labor economics* (Vol. 3A, pp. 1697–1760). Amsterdam: Elsevier, Chapter 28.

Campion-Smith, B. (2005). Ottawa throws doors open. *The Toronto Star* (September 24), 1.

Canada. Citizenship and Immigration Canada. (CIC). *Immigration statistics*, Cat. No. MP22-1/ Year; electronic version, various issues. Available on-line at: http://www.cic.gc.ca/ english/pub/index-2.html#statistics

Canada. Citizenship and Immigration Canada. (CIC). *Facts and figures*; electronic version, various issues. Available on-line at: http://www.cic.gc.ca/english/pub/facts[1998–2004]/index.html

Card, D. (2005). Is the new immigration really so bad? *The Economic Journal, 115*(507).

Chiswick, B. R. (1981). Guidelines for the reform of immigration policy. In: W. Fellner (Ed.), *Essays in contemporary economic problems: Demand, productivity, and population* (pp. 309–347). Washington, DC: American Enterprise Institute for Public Policy Research.

Chiswick, B. R. (1987). Immigration policy, source countries, and immigrant skills: Australia, Canada, and the United States. In: L. Baker & P. Miller (Eds), *The economics of immigration: Proceedings of a conference at the Australian National University* (pp. 163–206). Canberra: Australian Government Publishing Service.

Chiswick, B. R., & Miller, P. W. (1988). Earnings in Canada: The roles of immigrant generation, French ethnicity, and language. In: T. P. Schultz (Ed.), *Research in population economics* (Vol. 6, pp. 183–228). Greenwich, CT: JAI Press.

Chiswick, B. R., & Miller, P. W. (2005). *Language skills and immigrant adjustment: What immigration policy can do!* IZA Discussion Paper No. 1419. In: D. Cobb-Clark & S. E. Khoo, (Eds), *Public policy and immigration settlement*. Cheltenham, UK: Edward Elgar, (forthcoming).

Chiswick, B. R., Lee, Y. L., & Miller, P. W. (2005). Immigrant earnings: A longitudinal analysis. *Review of Income and Wealth, 51*(4), 485–503.

Chiswick, B. R., Lee, Y. L., & Miller, P. W. (2006). Immigrants' language skills and visa category. *International Migration Review, 40*(2), 419–450.

Duleep, H., & Regets, M. C. (1992). Some evidence on the effect of admission criteria on immigrant assimilation. In: B. R. Chiswick (Ed.), *Immigration, language and ethnic issues: Canada and the United States* (pp. 410–439). Washington, DC: American Enterprise Institute.

Duleep, H., & Regets, M. C. (1996). Admission criteria and immigrant earnings profiles. *International Migration Review, 30*(2), 571–590.

Fougère, M., Harvey, S. Mérette, M., & Poitras, F. (2003). Ageing population and immigration in Canada: Economic, abour market and regional implications. Presented at Canadian economics association meetings in Ottawa, June.

Fougère, M., Harvey, S., Mercenier, J., & Mérette, M. (2005). Population ageing, high-skilled immigrants and productivity. Presented at Canadian economics association meetings in Hamilton, May.

Grant, M. L. (1999). Evidence of new immigrant assimilation in Canada. *Canadian Journal of Economics, 38*(3), 930–955.

Green, A. G., & Green, D. A. (1995). Canadian immigration policy: The effectiveness of the point system and other instruments. *Canadian Journal of Economics, XXVIII*(4b), 1006–1041.

Green, A. G., & Green, D. A. (1999). The economic goals of Canada's immigration policy: Past and present. *Canadian Public Policy, XXV*(4), 425–451.

Jasso, G., & Rosenzweig, M. R. (1995). Do immigrants screened for skills do better than family-reunification immigrants? *International Migration Review, 29*(1), 85–111.

Jasso, G., Rosenzweig, M. R., & Smith, J. P. (2000). The changing skill of new immigrants to the United States: Recent trends and their determinants. In: G. J. Borjas (Ed.), *Issues in the economics of immigration* (pp. 185–225). Chicago: University of Chicago Press, Chapter 5.

McHale, J. (2003). Canadian immigration policy in comparative perspective. In: C. M. Beach, A. G. Green & J. G. Reitz (Eds), *Canadian immigration policy for the 21st century* (pp. 217–253). Montreal: McGill-Queen's University Press.

McWhinney, M. (1998). *A selection criteria chronology, 1967–1997: Critical changes in definitions, the point system and priority processing.* Strategic Research and Review Branch Research Paper, Citizenship and Immigration Canada, April.

Miller, P. W. (1999). Immigration policy and immigrant quality: The Australian Points System. *American Economic Review,* (2), Papers and Proceedings (May), pp. 192–197.

Ottaviano, G. I. P., & Peri, G. (2005). *Rethinking the gains from immigration: Theory and evidence from the U.S.* Working Paper no. 11672 (September). National Bureau of Economic Research.

Parent, D., & Worswick, C. (2003). *Qualifications et immigrations: Réforme de la grille d'admission du Québec et composition de la population d'immigrants s'établessant au Québec.* Research Paper prepared for the Department of Finance, Government of Quebec.

Picot, G., & Sweetman, A. (2005). *The deteriorating economic welfare of immigrants and possible causes: Update 2005.* Statistics Canada, Business and labour market analysis division, Analytical Studies Research Paper no. 262 (June).

Reiners, D. M., & Troper, H. (1992). Canadian and American immigration policy since 1945. In: B. R. Chiswick (Ed.), *Immigration, language and ethnic issues: Canada and the United States* (pp. 15–54). Washington, DC: American Enterprise Institute.

Reitz, J. G. (2005). Tapping immigrants' skills: New directions for Canadian immigration policy and the knowledge economy. *IRPP Choices, 11*(1).

Richardson, S., & Lester, L. (2004). *A comparison of Australian and Canadian immigration policies and labour market outcomes.* The National Institute of Labour Studies: Flinders University, September.

de Silva, A. (1997). Earnings of immigrant classes in the early 1980s in Canada: A reexamination. *Canadian Public Policy, XXIII*(2), 179–202.

Smith, J. P., & Edmonston, B. (Eds). (1997). *The new Americans: Economic, demographic and fiscal effects of immigration, National Research Council.* Washington, DC: National Academy Press.

Worswick, C. (2004). Immigrants' declining earnings: Reasons and remedies. C. D. Howe Institute Backgrounder no. 81 (April).

Wright, R. E., & Maxim, P. S. (1993). Immigration policy and immigrant quality: Empirical evidence from Canada. *Journal of Population Economics, 6*(4), 337–352.

SET UP A CONTINUATION ORDER TODAY!

Did you know that you can set up a continuation order on all Elsevier-JAI series and have each new volume sent directly to you upon publication? For details on how to set up a **continuation order**, contact your nearest regional sales office listed below.

To view related series in Economics & Finance, please visit:

http://www.elsevier.com/economics

The Americas
Customer Service Department
11830 Westline Industrial Drive
St. Louis, MO 63146
USA
US customers:
Tel: +1 800 545 2522 (Toll-free number)
Fax: +1 800 535 9935
For Customers outside US:
Tel: +1 800 460 3110 (Toll-free number).
Fax: +1 314 453 7095
usbkinfo@elsevier.com

Europe, Middle East & Africa
Customer Service Department
Linacre House
Jordan Hill
Oxford OX2 8DP
UK
Tel: +44 (0) 1865 474140
Fax: +44 (0) 1865 474141
eurobkinfo@elsevier.com

Japan
Customer Service Department
2F Higashi Azabu, 1 Chome Bldg
1-9-15 Higashi Azabu, Minato-ku
Tokyo 106-0044
Japan
Tel: +81 3 3589 6370
Fax: +81 3 3589 6371
books@elsevierjapan.com

APAC
Customer Service Department
3 Killiney Road #08-01
Winsland House I
Singapore 239519
Tel: +65 6349 0222
Fax: +65 6733 1510
asiainfo@elsevier.com

Australia & New Zealand
Customer Service Department
30-52 Smidmore Street
Marrickville, New South Wales 2204
Australia
Tel: +61 (02) 9517 8999
Fax: +61 (02) 9517 2249
service@elsevier.com.au

30% Discount for Authors on All Books!

A 30% discount is available to Elsevier book and journal contributors on all books *(except multi-volume reference works)*.

To claim your discount, full payment is required with your order, which must be sent directly to the publisher at the nearest regional sales office above.